BEST RESTAURANTS
OF SAN FRANCISCO

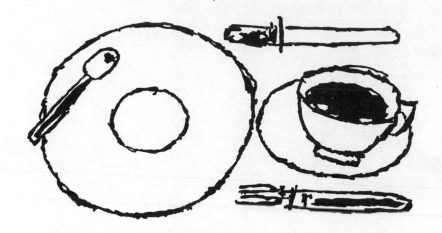

THE SAN FRANCISCO CHRONICLE
GUIDE TO FINE DINING

EDITED BY PATRICIA UNTERMAN

CHRONICLE BOOKS • SAN FRANCISCO

Printed in the United States of America

Library of Congress Cataloging in Publication Data
Unterman, Patricia
   Best restaurants of San Francisco : The San Francisco Chronicle guide to fine dining / edited by Patricia Unterman.
      p.   cm.
   Includes index.
   ISBN 0-8118-0065-2
      1. Restaurants, lunch rooms, etc.—California—San Francisco Bay Area—Guide-books.   I. San Francisco Chronicle.   II. Title.
   TX907.3.C22S367   1991
   647.95794'6—dc20   91-12908
                                                                      CIP

Editing: Paula Tevis
Book design: Words & Deeds
Cover illustration: Ward Schumaker
Composition: Words & Deeds

Distributed in Canada by Raincoast Books,
112 East Third Avenue, Vancouver, B.C. V5T 1C8

10 9 8 7 6 5 4 3 2 1

Chronicle Books
275 Fifth Street
San Francisco, CA 94103

♲ printed on recycled paper

CONTENTS

FOR TIM AND HARRY—
MY CONSTANT, IF SOMETIMES RELUCTANT,
DINING OUT COMPANIONS.

A RECENT HISTORY OF SAN FRANCISCO RESTAURANTS

BY PATRICIA UNTERMAN

San Francisco offers the most dynamic restaurant scene in the United States. The ethnic diversity and originality of the cooking, fueled by a supply of extraordinary produce all year around, and a burgeoning cottage food industry, means that almost anything can emerge from restaurant kitchens—and almost everything does. Each new culinary development is attended by an avid dining out public kept up-to-the-minute by prolific food media. No audience, outside of France, follows the careers of cooks and restaurants more closely, and nowhere have so many individuals expressed themselves with such intensity and popular acclaim through cooking. Furthermore, as a widely traveled observer of restaurants, I believe that every nationwide restaurant trend for the past fifteen years has started in San Francisco. If it happens here, so goes the rest of the nation.

The phenomenon started sixteen years ago when Alice Waters opened Chez Panisse in Berkeley. Completely untrained as a chef, but under the spell of the idealism of the sixties and a year spent in Europe, Waters brought to cooking what the Free Speech Movement brought to a whole generation of American students—a rethinking of accepted values. She started by reproducing the dishes of Provence and ended up changing the nation's ideas about the way food should be grown, gathered, prepared and eaten.

Frustrated early on in her attempts to find raw materials of the quality she found in France, Waters called on local gardeners to raise lettuces and vegetables, and encouraged growers and producers to come to the door of the restaurant with their food. Agri-business dominated the food market in the United States at the time, but she, single handedly, started a trend toward small, organic production by demonstrating to her patrons, and the press, how much more delicious this kind of ecologically raised food could taste.

Waters was speaking, through her restaurant, to the largest and most affluent generation of consumers the United States had ever produced—the Baby Boomers, who were born from 1945 to 1960. University educated, well traveled, turned on to food, cooking, and dining out in restaurants, they formed the audience for a new generation of cooks, many of whom worked in the food community at Chez Panisse and left to open their own restaurants. Chez Panisse continues to be a temple dedicated to the purity and glory of naturally-raised food and the communal pleasures of being at the table. It provides a standard by which other restaurants are judged.

One of the most famous alumni of Chez Panisse is Jeremiah

Tower, an ex-architecture graduate from Harvard, who opened Stars, San Francisco's premier bistro, eight years ago. In his huge open dining room with a completely visible kitchen, Tower puts out everything from grilled fish burgers to lobster ragout, with urbane style. Where Waters rethought and simplified French cooking, adapting it to local ingredients, Tower invented his own cuisine, an eclectic, California mix of ideas and ingredients.

High rollers, star gazers, and everyone in between picked up on Stars, which Tower fashioned to be a cross between Paris' great cafe, La Coupole, and an elegant three star house like Taillevent. Celebrants in black tie can spend a fortune on food and rare wines, while drop-ins, dressed in black Levi's, eye the scene while sipping Bellinis in the bar. Tower himself embodies both camps. He's flamboyant, witty, and dedicated to the most luxurious things in life, a taste, he says, he acquired from royal, Russian emigree relatives, but he's no snob. His restaurant treats everyone well. Whatever mode you prefer, Stars will take care of you.

Taking the concept of the restaurant as community resource a step further, the Zuni Cafe grew eccentrically over the years to become San Francisco's hippest meeting and eating spot. This happened in large part because of the offbeat culinary vision of Judy Rogers, yet another veteran of Chez Panisse. Open from morning until late at night, the Zuni's fully exposed kitchen cranks out everything from luscious chickens and pizzas cooked in a wood burning oven to buckwheat waffles. Rogers uses unexpected techniques to cook humble ingredients. She deep-fries olives and chickpeas as bar snacks, puts up her own duck and rabbit giblet confits, and pairs a single cheese with just the right dried or fresh fruit for dessert. Her cooking somehow tastes traditional and experimental at the same time.

Joyce Goldstein who was the first cook at the cafe upstairs at Chez Panisse, also founded her own place, Square One, five years ago. In a large, airy, modern dining room with a partially open kitchen, she prepares a daily changing menu of rustic, spicy, sensual Mediterranean dishes that encompass Italy, Morocco, Spain and sometimes the Middle East and Brazil. Formerly a cooking school teacher and a cookbook writer, she is a scholar of old Italian and Spanish cookbooks where the inspiration for many of her smartly constructed dishes originate. Her master sommelier son has put together an extensive international wine list to go with the food.

Goldstein herself is a frequent contributor to periodicals, magazines, and food journals. In a monthly column in the *San Francisco Chronicle,* she writes frankly about the problems involved with running a restaurant from the restaurateur's perspective. Though the restaurants of San Francisco collectively pioneered community involvement and fund raising for charitable programs, Goldstein has been one of its most tireless contributors and organizers. The Berkeley experience influenced her in a profound political way.

Cyndi Pawlcyn, the executive chef of the wildly successful group of operations called Real Restaurants, represents the new generation of the city's chefs. She trained at an American culinary academy and opened her first restaurant eight years ago in the Napa Valley called Mustards, famous for barbecued ribs and other American/California classics. The Fog City Diner, followed soon after, the first take off on the old fashioned American diner. Roti, a California/Mediterranean grill, Bix, a chic, art deco, dining room and bar that fills up late at night when a jazz trio plays, and Tra Vigne, a stunningly decorated Post Modern Italian restaurant with outdoor dining, also in the Napa Valley, are other achievements.

Pawlcyn's signature is a whimsical juxtaposition of ingredients that have never shared a plate before. Even her most far flung ideas have so much style that they work. That one organization could create so many original restaurants rather than replicate the same place over and over is due to Pawlcyn's creativity, culinary commonsense, and an enlightened management team. All her restaurants are notable for reasonable prices and handsome decors.

Finally, when it comes to revitalization of American cuisine, no one has been more influential than Bradley Ogden, who opened Campton Place, and now has the charming Lark Creek Inn in Marin County, where he cooks suckling pigs in a wood burning brick oven, smokes fish, corns beef, and generally puts out the most inventive, heartiest, and most luscious American food anyone ever imagined.

Besides the San Francisco love affair with the star chef, several other major food obsessions have gripped the area. One was started by Alice Wong, who imported her family's Hong Kong Flower Lounge to California shores. The Flower Lounge, and a number of other Chinese restaurants from Hong Kong, have introduced a higher level of Cantonese cooking to San Francisco than has ever been seen before in America. The reversion of Hong Kong to mainland China in 1997 has resulted in a huge influx of Hong Kong professionals and entrepreneurs to San Francisco, bringing with them an appetite for high quality Chinese cooking. Alice Wong, who opened three outposts of the Hong Kong Flower Lounge, intended to satisfy them.

The depth and range of these kitchens are dizzying. The Flower Lounge uses the highest quality fish, poultry, and vegetables to turn out subtle dishes at incredibly reasonable prices. The city's huge Asian population alone would keep these large restaurants full, but the Flower Lounge branches have become universally popular. People have become addicted to the succulent, crisp-skinned chickens, elegant, clear soups, impeccable whole steamed fish, and bright-flavored Chinese vegetables.

San Francisco's location on the edge of the Pacific, has spawned many excellent Thai, Cambodian, Laotian, Singaporean, and Burmese restaurants, serving an ever growing Southeast Asian population. Japanese restaurants also abound, especially in centrally located Japantown. Yet, a new species of restaurant has developed along with San Francisco's growing cultural ties to the Orient. Represented by Barbara Tropp's charming China Moon Cafe and Bruce Cost's superb Monsoon, these restaurants offer fascinating menus of pan-Asian dishes accompanied by well-chosen wine lists and lovely, exotic desserts. Though much more expensive than the Hong Kong-style restaurants, they are the fruits of these Western chefs' experimentation with Eastern techniques and ingredients.

The other, current restaurant phenomenon rejuvenates an old San Francisco passion for Italian cooking. Tomato sauce-smothered, southern Italian cooking was the rule until about ten years ago when modern, Milan-influenced Italian restaurants came onto the scene. The current crop are large scale, beautifully designed, reasonably priced operations with huge menus of pasta, pizza, antipasti, and main courses complemented by extensive Italian wine lists. The newest and most highly designed, Il Fornaio, Etrusca, and Palio d'Asti, are like Italian dream restaurants that offer just about anything Italian under the sun. What may elude these urbane trattorias is the rustic simplicity of ingredient-based cooking one actually finds in Italy, but then, Italian cooking will not be the last cuisine to be re-invented in California.

After all the media attention given to star chefs and multi-million dollar restaurants, the fact is that most of the restaurants in San Francisco are small, family owned, ethnic operations that enrich the daily life of every neighborhood in the city. Practically every Asian and Central American country is represented by at least two or three restaurants, and not just a few of the most creative chefs in town get ideas from eating at them. San Francisco's particular demographic of people from different cultures adds immeasurably to the city's culinary vitality.

SOME NOTES ON THIS BOOK

Best Restaurants of San Francisco represents a compendium of restaurant reviews from 1988 through 1991. Every restaurant was visited anonymously, at least twice, with fact checking done by assistant editor, Paula Tevis, within a month of publication. Though every effort has been made to be accurate and up-to-date, things change. Regarding restaurants, in particular, things change from one week to the next. If a dish is written about that is no longer on the menu, realize that most of the best restaurants in the city have menus that change daily, let alone seasonally or yearly. Also, hours fluctuate from season to season, so it is always best to call ahead if you plan to eat at an off hour.

The restaurants included in this book were chosen because they are consistently good. Obviously many fine restaurants did not get in the book, simply because they have not been visited within the last three years. One highly regarded restaurant, Donatello, is currently in a state of flux, so it was not included. The few restaurants that get critical remarks are included because they are some of the most popular restaurants in the city and need to be addressed.

"Wheelchair accessible" means full accessibility. "Partially accessible" means the entrance is accessible but not the restroom. "Not accessible" means the entrance has a step or is less than 32 inches wide. All information regarding wheelchair accessibility was provided solely by the restaurants themselves.

ABOUT THE AUTHORS

Patricia Unterman is co-owner of the Hayes Street Grill, which opened in 1979, and Vicolo Pizzeria, which opened in 1984. She joined the *San Francisco Chronicle* as a restaurant critic twelve years ago. To avoid any conflict of interest, Ms. Unterman never reviews restaurants that specialize in fish and seafood, nor does she review restaurants in close geographic proximity to her own, unless she can review them favorably.

Stan Sesser was restaurant critic at the *San Francisco Chronicle* for seven years before leaving the paper in August 1990 to write for *The New Yorker* magazine where his pieces on Laos, Burma, and the vanishing rain forests of Borneo have appeared. He came to restaurant reviewing as a consumer reporter and avid, international eater. Mr. Sesser was West Coast editor at *Consumer Reports* for 15 years.

Michael Bauer, currently food editor for the *San Francisco Chronicle*, was a restaurant critic and food editor at the *Dallas Times Herald* for four and a half years, and food editor of the *Kansas City Star* for two and a half years. Mr. Bauer contributes regularly to *Food and Wine Magazine*, *Travel and Leisure*, and *The Wine and Food Companion*.

Though every critic has his or her own, personal point of view, ratings are weighted towards food. In the *San Francisco Chronicle*, restaurants get rated separately for food, service, and atmosphere, but food counts double or more in computing one, overall rating, which is the only rating used in this book.

KEY TO RATINGS

★★★★	Extraordinary
★★★	Excellent
★★	Very good
★	Good

Inexpensive	entrees under $7
Moderate	entrees $7 to $14
Expensive	entrees $15 to $20
Very Expensive	entrees over $20

RESTAURANTS

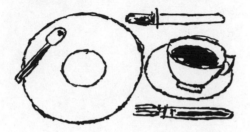

ACE CAFE ★½

1539 FOLSOM STREET, SAN FRANCISCO. 621-4752. OPEN MONDAY THROUGH FRIDAY 11:30 A.M. TO 1 A.M., SATURDAY 6 P.M. TO 2 A.M., SUNDAY 6 P.M. TO 1 A.M. BEER AND WINE. ALL MAJOR CREDIT CARDS. 25% NONSMOKING. PARTIALLY WHEEL-CHAIR ACCESSIBLE. RESERVATIONS FOR PARTIES OVER 10. INEXPENSIVE.

The Ace Cafe is typical of the emerging, artsy, south of Market hangout/coffee house. Instead of old world clutter, the Ace projects a new wave motorcycle theme, not in its purposely primitive, rough-edged decor, but in a core of patrons it attracts. They arrive on BMW and Moto Guzzi bikes, in jeans, black leather lace-up boots, long, brightly dyed hair, and complicated black leather jackets. Motorcycle and car magazines are scattered about the small lounge area at the entrance. Most of the other clientele represent a SOMA melange—lots of black outfits, lots of people coming in late after movies, and at lunch, people who work in the nearby clothing warehouses. At Ace, everyone looks at you when you walk in.

The Ace bears the endearing earmarks of a first effort. The interior is long on ideas and a bit short on execution. There are varnished cement slab floors and walls, banks of windows that look out onto an alley, a small bar area and lots of original furniture. The heavy chairs have thick, curved metal backs, triangular wooden legs, and black vinyl seats. Clever lighting fixtures and lamps abound. Experimentally finished wood, stone, and metal textures make the Ace look like it was designed by clever art students.

Indeed, the service may be performed by distracted art students—it's completely empty headed. But the spry menu of sandwiches and appetizers using all the latest ingredients is fun and cheap. The Ace Cafe does not have a full kitchen so the menu offers only salads and warm sandwiches.

Two of the best sandwiches are a seared ahi tuna with cucumber, tomatoes, and basil accompanied with an excellent salad of assorted greens; and a thick ham and melted cheese sandwich with whole grain mustard and fresh tasting but bland potato salad. Also nice is Ace's version of a BLT, substituting pancetta, frisee, and basil garlic mayonnaise for the usual bacon, head lettuce, and jarred mayo. Gruyere melted on unseasoned hard vegetables reminds me of something from a bad health food restaurant.

Both a blue cheese salad with bacon, and a radicchio and rocket salad with pancetta, pinenuts, and shaved Italian parmesan are competent. Toasts with buttery mushrooms on them turn out to be delicious and a bargain to boot.

The desserts are brought in from Just Desserts but one variation involving toasted slices of poppyseed cake, fresh strawberries and sabayon takes on a life of its own. Cappuccino is good and I particularly enjoyed Spaten and Newcastle Brown Ale both on tap. Wines are pricey.

The Ace fills a coffeehouse niche south of Market and its popularity proves that the ambience of a hangout can be more important than the food or the quality of service. The SOMA crowd likes the open, awkward, slightly wacky room. The Ace provides the right backdrop for making the scene.

PATRICIA UNTERMAN

ACQUERELLO ★★★½

1722 SACRAMENTO STREET (BETWEEN POLK AND VAN NESS), SAN FRANCISCO. 567-5432. OPEN TUESDAY THROUGH SATURDAY FROM 6 TO 10:30 P.M. WINE, BEER. MASTERCARD, VISA AND PERSONAL CHECKS. NONSMOKING DINING ROOM. RESERVATIONS RECOMMENDED. EXPENSIVE.

Acquerello is the work of Giancarlo Paterlini, the former maitre d'/manager/sommelier at Donatello, and Suzette Gresham the former chef there. They were a great pair at their previous location, but I think they may have achieved perfection at Acquerello. The small size and understated tone of the dining room lends itself to the refined Italian cooking and personal service these two specialize in. Their restaurant fills one of the few dining out voids in the city, offering first class, regional Italian food in a relaxed, quiet setting. Though prices are high, the tasteful trattoria ambience of Acquerello is more inviting and less formal than the stiffer three star houses.

The restaurant consists of one high ceilinged dining room with pale, rosy-colored walls studded with wall sconces, and a large and lavish flower arrangement on a table in the middle of the dining room. Tables are small and close together. The new owners have hung the walls with water colors—hence the name. A small anteroom serves as a check in point, a place to hang your coat, and a wine room. This is the only part of the restaurant where smoking is allowed.

The cooking is influenced by different regions of Italy though its overall refinement suggests the elegant restaurants of northern Italy. The small menu is divided into an antipasti section, a first course section of pastas, and a roster of main courses. Portions are small enough to order from each section at one sitting.

Ms. Gresham has a light hand with pastas. Her wild mushroom ravioli, gossamer thin noodle dough filled with whole shiitake mushrooms nestled into a bright green herb sauce, is splendid. Tender squares of yellow and green pasta, flavored with basil and saffron, are interlaced with slices of scallop and moistened with scallop-infused cream. A special one evening brought ravioli stuffed with a loose mixture of salmon and scallops, in a cucumber sauce given body by a salmon and dill-infused broth. The best pasta of all is a rustic penne coated with a thick, savory rabbit and tomato sauce perfumed with rosemary. Ms. Gresham is one of the few chefs around that knows how to use herbs with restraint.

Antipasti bring one-of-a-kind dishes like a warm squab salad of slices of tender squab breast on a mound of cooked chard, seasoned with extra virgin olive oil and surrounded by toasted pinenuts. Tomato slices are spread with a mild paste of anchovies, capers, and cooked egg yolks and served with slices of flavorful goat milk mozzarella.

One of the best main courses on the current menu is a rolled filet of beef, cooked all the way through but butter tender and moist, stuffed with a mixture of prosciutto, parmesan, and rosemary. Another creation focuses on local sole filets rolled around buttery spinach, and sauced with olive oil that has been infused with shrimp. The shrimp themselves and strips of sun-dried tomato are sprinkled on top of the fish. A pair of quail get a moist stuffing and a sharp, appealing sauce made with grappa-soaked golden raisins. All the main courses come with braised baby artichokes, crisp, little green beans, and a whole red potato with a sage leaf in its middle.

For dessert, a warm zabaione made with port turns a North Beach standby into something new. Sauteed strawberries on layers of Italian butter sponge cake with whipped cream, caramelized rice pudding with fresh peaches, light lemon ricotta cheese cake, and sparkling fresh fruit ices and ice creams are all lovely. Espresso is so thick and creamy you can almost chew it and the decaffeinated version is not far behind.

The menu will probably be different by the time you read this, but Ms. Gresham has such good taste, strong technique, and a genius for pastas that I trust the ever changing menu you will experience will be just as enticing. It turns out that she is a scholar of old, regional Italian recipes which she adjusts to fit her kitchen. Mr. Paterlini is an expert on Italian wines and a master at helping people have the most wonderful evening of dining. Acquerello has brought two artists together.

PATRICIA UNTERMAN

ALBONO ★½

545 FRANCISCO STREET, SAN FRANCISCO. 441-1040. OPEN MONDAY THROUGH SATURDAY 5 TO 10 P.M. BEER AND WINE. MASTERCARD, VISA, DISCOVER. 100% NONSMOKING. PARTIALLY WHEELCHAIR ACCESSIBLE. RESERVATIONS RECOMMENDED. MODERATE.

Albono adds a new twist to the city's dining out scene in that it specializes in dishes from Yugoslavia's Istrian peninsula. Istria has been occupied by the Italians, Turks, Spaniards, French, Austrians, and Slavs. You'd never guess it from the photos of the sleepy village of Albono at the entrance to the restaurant, which show a charming cluster of houses with red tiled roofs nestled into tree covered hills, where the chef/owner, Bruno Viscovi, was born. But you can taste the varied cultural lineage in the food.

All the dishes made with cabbage are great. You can start off with a bowl of Yugoslavian cole slaw, finely sliced red cabbage in a snappy vinaigrette, or a bowl of meltingly tender braised sauerkraut infused with the savory flavor of prosciutto. Then you can finish off with juicy broiled pork chops with piquantly seasoned braised cabbage.

The unique pasta dishes should also be ordered. A plate of bready little dumplings, called *crafi albonesi*, are stuffed with a slightly sweet mixture of cheese studded with just a few raisins and pinenuts, and topped with a saucy stew made with tiny cubes of sirloin tip. The same ragout, instead of the usual bolognese style meat sauce, is spooned over penne in an Istrian dish called *pastasuta con sugo de carne*, but this time cumin and other aromatic spices are more pronounced in the sauce.

After cabbage and pasta, try the lovely, light chocolate ricotta cake delicately seasoned with cinnamon, or a delicate, refreshing, orange-scented Spanish flan.

The small, wood trimmed dining room has an uncluttered, slightly formal air about it, with banquettes running along two walls and a few white-linen covered tables in the center of the carpeted room. The kitchen can take awhile getting the food out and sometimes the service is not very professional.

Patricia Unterman

ALFRED'S ★★½

886 BROADWAY (ABOVE THE TUNNEL), SAN FRANCISCO. 781-7058. OPEN 5:30 TO 10 P.M. SUNDAY THROUGH THURSDAY, UNTIL 10:30 P.M. FRIDAY AND SATURDAY; THURSDAY LUNCHEON 11:30 A.M. TO 2:30 P.M. FULL BAR. ALL MAJOR CREDIT CARDS. 25% NONSMOKING. FULLY WHEELCHAIR ACCESSIBLE. RESERVATIONS RECOMMENDED. EXPENSIVE.

Alfred's, one of San Francisco's oldest restaurants, reassures me that the steakhouse, especially a traditional, clubby one with Italian over-tones, is still alive and fun to go to. A couple of recent visits prove how attentively Alfred's is being kept up. The place sparkles. It's booths, banquettes and walls glow in subdued red splendor. Light bounces off the crystal and gold chandeliers and the arched, antiqued mirrors. All surfaces are clean and fresh, well dusted, vacuumed, and polished. Alfred's dining room gives off an aura of care, of being cosseted, and of course, this treatment extends to the customers. The waiters, in black bow ties, have that innate sense of timing and the assurance to guide customers to the best the restaurant has to offer.

Though the menu puts forward a number of Italian dishes, every-one knows to stick to the steaks. The T-bone and the Alfred's steak, a

6

bone-in New York cut, are exemplary, full of flavor and miraculously tender. I have not eaten better beef anywhere. The Chicago rib eye, served with the bone in, is not quite as tasty. The Porterhouse is magnificent. Soft Chateaubriand, served for two and carved at the table, is dressed up with a lovely bearnaise sauce but doesn't bring the ultimate satisfaction of those bone-in New Yorks and T-bones, as far as I'm concerned. With these steaks come baked Idaho potatoes, properly soft, dry, and light textured. Only restaurants that have maintained a long relationship with the best purveyors get this top grade of meat, and Alfred's dry ages it to bring out its flavor. Also, the steaks get expert grilling over mesquite charcoal. No acrid burned grill marks or cold centers mar these slabs of meat. The cooks at Alfred's know how to control the fire.

To start, try a mixed green salad of assorted tender leaves in a slightly sweet, blue cheese dressing. Additional blue cheese is sprinkled over the top. The Caesar for two is constructed at tableside of crisp romaine and a tart, but good dressing. A single order of deep-fried zucchini sticks brings enough for the whole table. One foray into the Italian side of the menu will convince you that Alfred's remains first and foremost a steakhouse.

Though American nutritionists are tolling the death knell of red meat, I personally know that every once in a while an Alfred's meal really hits the spot. That this steakhouse is maintaining its standards on every level makes me think that I'm not the only one who can tuck into a pound and a half of rich beef and survive to tell about it.

PATRICIA UNTERMAN

ALL SEASON'S CAFE ★★½

1400 LINCOLN AVENUE, CALISTOGA. (707) 942-9111. OPEN THURSDAY THROUGH MONDAY, 9 A.M. TO 10 P.M., TUESDAY, 9 A.M. TO 4 P.M. CLOSED WEDNESDAY. BEER AND WINE. VISA, MASTERCARD. 100% NONSMOKING. FULLY WHEELCHAIR ACCESSIBLE. RESERVATIONS SUGGESTED WEEKENDS. MODERATE.

All Season's Cafe is a restaurant and wine shop that offers a dizzying number of French and American wines at close to retail prices, and a multi-faceted menu that allows for snacking or a full scale meal. The menu suggests which kinds of wines to drink with each type of dish. The food I tasted was simply composed, with exceptionally fresh ingredients. This cafe is meant to be an everyday kind of place in the best sense.

A tasty melange of salad greens from a local garden are tossed in a tart balsamic dressing. A warm spinach salad gets extra punch from crumbled feta as well as pancetta, seived egg, and tangy tat soi greens. A terrific presentation of real Italian prosciutto comes with watermelon, cantaloupe, and a drizzle of mustard cream.

7

A puffy-edged, Mexican-style pizza is covered in tomatillo salsa, fresh tomatoes, bits of pork, and dry jack cheese. An even better choice from the Italian section of the menu is a beautiful, tender lasagne layered with mild goat cheese, spinach, and a satiny cream sauce. A filet of halibut arrives under a tantalizing cloud of deep-fried leek and carrot threads and a gingery papaya-mango relish. My favorite dish, a rare filet of beef topped with a sharp, but workable relish of lemon zest, green olives, and sun-dried tomatoes comes with a plateful of squashes, pole beans, and baby carrots.

Desserts continue the fresh and seasonal emphasis with such delights as a mixed summer berry pie with house made vanilla ice cream and a plate of assorted ice creams in a lace cookie cup splashed with raspberry sauce and whipped cream. A cheese plate makes perfect sense with the remains of a bottle of big red wine instead of dessert.

A long, dark wood, wine bar runs along one side of the restaurant with a whole wall of wine racks above it. The dining room has a cafe-like feel with bentwood chairs, butcher paper over white linen, and big windows that look out onto Calistoga's main street. One consideration when ordering a white wine from the massive, supplementary tasting list is that it will take awhile to be chilled.

PATRICIA UNTERMAN

AMERICAN CHOW ★★

340 DIVISION STREET, SAN FRANCISCO. 863-1212. OPEN MONDAY THROUGH FRIDAY FROM 11 A.M. TO 2:45 P.M., SATURDAY 9 A.M. TO 2:45 P.M., SUNDAY 10 A.M. TO 2:45 P.M.; DINNER 5 TO 10 P.M. NIGHTLY. BEER AND WINE. MASTERCARD, VISA. 100% NONSMOKING. FULLY WHEELCHAIR ACCESSIBLE. RESERVATIONS FOR PARTIES OF 6 OR MORE. MODERATE

American Chow is a diner in a redone clapboard shack underneath the freeway. The outside boasts an eyecatching neon sign, but the structure itself is plain white with a cheerful red and blue trim, a motif which is continued inside. Banks of multipaned windows add a surprising degree of architectural distinction, and blue-green shades emphasize them even more.

At one end of the cabin-like dining area, there is an open kitchen and a counter with five stools. The small dining room has sturdy gray carpeting, aluminum-trimmed Formica tables, and wooden chairs with blue vinyl seats. Horizontal pinewood wainscoting and the pine trimming on the windows give American Chow a cozy-cottage feel.

The food is as clean and honest as the decor. A bellwether of any restaurant is its salads and American Chow's are treated with respect. A hearty spinach salad gets a creamy garlic dressing and a generous sprinkling of real bacon bits, hard-boiled egg, and blue cheese. The mixed green salad brings floppy greens in a well-balanced vinaigrette.

The thinnish charcoal-crusted hamburgers on soft sesame buns are totally satisfying; the fries are cooked in clean oil. There's no stinting on the bacon in a classic BLT on white toast, and milkshakes in vanilla, chocolate, and coffee flavors are just about the best around—milk and ice cream blended to a thick but drinkable consistency.

At both breakfast and lunch, American Chow serves the kind of corned beef hash that I adore. Finely ground corned beef with soft, shredded potato seasoned with lots of black pepper and onion, it fries up crisp with a soft interior. Topped with a perfect sunny-side up egg and grilled tomato slices, it's a great dish. Clam chowder is full of tender clams, halves of soft red potato, celery, and onion in creamy clam broth. The thick, red bean and ground beef chili is mildly spicy and sweet from lots of onion.

A soft, soothing beef pot roast comes with whole roasted potatoes, a sea of pleasant brown gravy, and nicely cooked zucchini and carrots. A pair of moist, deliciously charred pork chops comes with cinnamon applesauce and a heap of cornbread pan stuffing. What a great plate! The kitchen also puts out a gently curried pork stew on rice with raisins and onions, accompanied with zucchini and red peppers.

Finally, American Chow makes its own desserts with a special aptitude for pies. The crusts are crisp, the fillings not too sweet, and the portions reasonably small, so don't hold back. The pumpkin pie is spectacular; the coconut cream a model of the coffeeshop genre. Fresh apple cranberry pie is no small achievement, either. The housemade cakes are a little heavy for my taste, with almost as much frosting as cake.

American Chow puts out the whole repertoire of American coffeeshop food, and then some, with integrity, restraint, and real skill. It's a terrific neighborhood restaurant.

PATRICIA UNTERMAN

❙ ANGKOR BOREI RESTAURANT ★★★

3471 MISSION STREET (BETWEEN 30TH AND COURTLAND), SAN FRANCISCO. 550-8417. OPEN FOR LUNCH EVERY DAY FROM 11 A.M. TO 4 P.M.; DINNER 5 TO 10 P.M. BEER AND WINE. MASTERCARD, VISA, AMERICAN EXPRESS. 30% NON-SMOKING. FULLY WHEELCHAIR ACCESSIBLE. RESERVATIONS RECOMMENDED. INEXPENSIVE.

One always approaches the out-of-the-way, ethnic neighborhood restaurant with a little trepidation. In some ways you're facing the same cultural challenge as when you travel to exotic places. You don't know exactly how the food should taste, or whether you'll like it even if it is well-prepared. Ordering from long menus with transliterated ethnic names and convoluted English descriptions can be difficult, especially if your waitperson doesn't speak English. Finally, there's the problem of the ambience. Will there be any and how will it feel to be the only party in the dining room? What one doesn't worry about is the price of the meal and whether you can bring the kids.

At first glance Angkor Borei, tucked away on the outer fringes of the Mission, appears to be the typical, modest, family run Cambodian restaurant, open on a shoe-string. In fact, the basics of the decor, tables covered with pink cloths and woven placemats kept pristine under glass, and pink walls, have remained unchanged through several previous Southeast Asian restaurants, except that the room is now hung with handsome Khmer artifacts instead of Thai travel posters. The extensive menu, however, is completely new and wonderful.

There are crisp, bright yellow pancakes folded over a crunchy filling of finely chopped shrimp and pork, tofu, bean sprouts, and shredded coconut, over which a clear, lemon-garlic sauce studded with minced peanuts, carrots, and red peppers is spooned. The ravishing tapestry of flavors, textures, and colors is indicative of every preparation you order here. Like the art, Cambodian food is composed of many tiny, exquisite elements like a mosaic. Hence, patties of cold white noodles, meticulously julienned cucumbers, bean sprouts, basil, red chiles, and carrots, all separate, come with a small bowl of intriguing coconut milk curry in a Cambodian version of salad and dressing. Delicate Cambodian springrolls have papery skins and moist, vegetable-rich fillings of celery and bean-thread noodles, black mushrooms, water chestnuts, and carrots seasoned with a little ground pork.

The green curry here is delicious and fiery, aromatic with fresh Thai basil and lemongrass. It sauces slender purple Japanese eggplants, big white chunks of fish, and straw mushrooms. Red curry has a smoothing coconut milk base with many deep layers of flavor which enhance tender sauteed shrimp on a bed of bright green spinach.

The charcoal broiling shows equal skill. A dramatic dish of long skewers of thinly sliced beef wrapped around water chestnuts, comes with an arrangement of colorful pickled vegetables and a piquant dipping sauce, as does moist, marinated, charcoal broiled chicken, cut into strips with the bones still in.

The single noodle dish on the menu is opulent, a magnificent bright orange melange of chewy rice noodles with slivers of pork, egg, bean sprouts, and tofu, topped with ground peanuts and threads of raw red cabbage. The aromatic rice served from a covered silver tureen, has a marvelous nutty flavor and chewy texture.

The food at Angkor Borei is so accomplished, artfully presented, and complex, yet so light, well balanced, and delicious, that anyone can appreciate it. This so called neighborhood place is really a world class restaurant, another treasure in this city of exotic, Asian culinary gems.

PATRICIA UNTERMAN

ANGKOR CAFE ★★½

637 LARKIN STREET, SAN FRANCISCO. 775-1318. OPEN EVERY DAY FROM 8:30 A.M. TO 4:30 P.M. NO ALCOHOL. NO CREDIT CARDS. 80% NONSMOKING. FULLY WHEELCHAIR ACCESSIBLE. RESERVATIONS FOR LARGE PARTIES ACCEPTED. FOOD TO GO. VERY INEXPENSIVE.

The Angkor Cafe is a spectacular Cambodian noodle house—and the only one in the city. It was recently opened by Sonny Sok, the chef/owner of the superb Angkor Palace on Lombard Street. Mr. Sok has visited Phnom Penh several times since the holocaust, doing research to reproduce his favorite foods from home. He visited the best noodle vendors all over Phnom Penh to check out their broths. As a veteran noodle eater myself, albeit on the streets of Bangkok, I can only say that Mr. Sok has come up with both a fish and a beef broth that compete with the best of them. This tiny, immaculately clean cafe is putting out some of the most irresistible street food I've tasted anywhere.

The basic unit is a big bowl of broth with either wide or skinny rice noodles and a plate of crunchy raw vegetables, like red leaf lettuce and bean sprouts, on the side. You throw the vegetables right into the broth and squeeze fresh lime over all. That's it. The broths have a homemade flavor. The various chile sauces and pickled fresh chiles at the table seem superfluous to me, but many people seemed to be dipping their noodles into them. These soups have so much character that they stand on their own.

The beef broth with wide rice noodles, gelatinous meat balls, rare, tasty flank steak, and slices of brisket, a house specialty and the first item on the menu, is indeed a classic, though #7, a fish broth with beautiful, juicy shrimp, ground pork, and squid with thin rice noodles, is my all time favorite. You can also order egg noodles in the soups, but the rice noodles have such a lovely texture, especially the thin ones, that I am converted.

If you don't feel like soup, several stir-fried noodle dishes are offered like a crispy, pan-fried egg noodle pancake topped with shrimp and broccoli in a light Cambodian brown sauce. The stir-fried dish not to be missed is #20, *Lott Chhar*, pan-fried short rice noodles with bean sprouts of exactly the same size, tossed with scallions and topped with a gently fried egg. The texture of this dish is something to experience. It dances on your tongue.

Finally, for congee (or rice porridge) lovers, Angkor Cafe makes a great one with seafood, wilted lettuce leaves, and slices of ginger topped with a dab of hot yellow chile sauce. Cambodian congee is thicker than Cantonese, with whole grains of rice, and this preparation has an exhilarating kick to it. For dessert, have a tall glass of sweet, rich Cambodian iced coffee.

PATRICIA UNTERMAN

ANGKOR PALACE ★★★

1769 LOMBARD STREET (BETWEEN OCTAVIA AND LAGUNA), SAN FRANCISCO. 931-2830. OPEN EVERY NIGHT FROM 5 TO 11 P.M. BEER AND WINE. MASTERCARD, VISA, AMERICAN EXPRESS. 65% NONSMOKING. PARTIALLY WHEELCHAIR ACCESSIBLE. RESERVATIONS REQUIRED ON THE WEEKENDS. MODERATE.

The Angkor Palace, an immaculate, attractively appointed Cambodian restaurant, is a place where you can take people who don't normally like ethnic food. The cooking here is always lovely, light, and clean. Some dishes may be hotter than others, some may have more exotic ingredients, but when it comes right down to satisfying its customers, this place crosses cultural barriers. The whole operation, from the cooking to the service to the decor, charms everyone.

Though the outside of the building looks like a pink garage, customers step into a romantic, well-appointed dining room. Seating is at low tables on richly upholstered banquettes scattered with bright silk cushions. Pits under the tables allow the less nimble to hang their feet comfortably. The walls are decorated with authentic Khmer antiques, including an intricate and very beautiful tea service in a glass case. Cosseted by silk, and reclining on low couches, diners can't help but feel intimate and convivial here.

The food has an elegance as well. Many of the appetizers and salads are composed of finely julienned ingredients, all perfectly cut and colorfully interwoven in taste as well as appearance. A Cambodian Crepe, a thin egg pancake, is folded over a mixture of chicken, shrimp, and bean sprouts, all cut to exactly the same width. Cambodian salads are refreshing, especially shredded green papaya tossed with shrimp and mint leaves in a lemony dressing, or finely chopped beef with lemongrass, onions, and bean sprouts.

Children love the tiny, thumb sized spring rolls filled with shredded pork and bean thread noodles, accompanied by a crisp, pickled vegetable salad. The meat of Cambodian-style deep-fried quail is dark and velvety, delicious dipped into a lemon and black pepper dressing.

The magnificent soups at Angkor Palace resemble bright flavored stews. In chicken-fruit soup, big chunks of green banana, green papaya and pumpkin float in a clear, clean chicken broth. Cambodian Fish Chowder combines a light coconut milk broth thickened with rice and seasoned with shredded ginger with an array of shrimp, crab, and rockfish.

Chicken and pork are stir-fried with vegetables, or marinated, skewered, grilled and served with salads. Both methods invariably turn out tender and juicy products. Angkor Palace does wonders with catfish, either whole, deep-fried and crispy, or as unbattered filets sauced with garlic, lemon, chiles, and green onions. A shrimp curry has a rich, deeply flavored green sauce.

For dessert try the delicate coconut ice cream with fried bananas. Otherwise, the waitresses will bring you a plate of cut oranges. On all visits the service staff steered us to the most stunning dishes and recommended others to go with them. Ice cold Thai beer and a Vouvray, a medium dry chenin blanc from France, both go wonderfully with the food.

Whenever I drive past the odd looking, bright pink Lombard Street building, I marvel that it could hold such a gem inside.

PATRICIA UNTERMAN

ASTA ★★½

101 SPEAR STREET, 1 RINCON CENTER, SAN FRANCISCO. 495-2782. OPEN FOR LUNCH MONDAY THROUGH FRIDAY 11:30 A.M. TO 2:30 P.M.; DINNER MONDAY THROUGH SATURDAY 5 TO 11 P.M. FULL BAR. MAJOR CREDIT CARDS. 75% NON-SMOKING. FULLY WHEELCHAIR ACCESSIBLE. RESERVATIONS RECOMMENDED. EXPENSIVE.

The name of this fanciful new restaurant refers to the terrier belonging to the high living Nick and Nora Charles in the *Thin Man* film series. Since it can be reached only through the food court/atrium of the Rincon center, it is a completely created space, inspired by the posh, urbane surroundings of these high society detectives. At lunch, when every table and chair in the roaring atrium/food court is filled, walking into the relatively quiet, luxurious Asta presents a stunning contrast. The carved out, contoured dining room, not much bigger than a Park Avenue living room, with Art Deco bar and lounge on a raised platform, seems like a haven. Banquettes and tables with tall-backed, lacquered chairs are large, comfortable, and generously spaced. The bar pours well-made cocktails in elegant glasses.

A wonderful lunch can be put together from the starters, like light, crisp, goat cheese and pistachio-filled turnovers of flaky puff pastry served with a sun-dried tomato and olive relish, or a salad of tiny, crusty, roasted potatoes, arranged on a bed of big arugula leaves slightly wilted in a bacon and honey-mustard dressing. Asta's blue corn pancakes have more flavor and texture than any I've tasted. A plateful of tiny ones topped with bits of smoked pork and creme fraiche with a black bean and corn relish on the side present an opportunity to eat many of them.

A main course of moist chicken breast cut into thin slices on greens topped with cubed apples and sweet glazed walnuts in a creamy dressing played a catchy variation on the theme of Waldorf salad. An open-face turkey sandwich at Asta goes even further. Juicy slices of roast turkey sit atop delicious blue corn bread, though I'm not sure I prefer the sesame seed-scented mole sauce to good old fashioned gravy. The sweet potato and onion hash browns with it were terrific.

At dinner, when the Rincon Center is completely deserted, Asta becomes a hideaway, a special private club for those who know about it. It's worth gaining admittance for the starter of fresh foie gras, expertly sauteed with poached pear slices, a cranberry port sauce, and a refreshing pile of undressed arugula leaves. A curried fish soup was a dream of clean, bright, spice-infused broth with chunks of salmon and a subtle coconut milk enrichment. Sweetbread and wild mushroom crisp turned out to be a breadcrumb-topped gratin of a mixture that tasted like rich stuffing. Other choices included oregano-scented tuna on a delicious, warm, white bean, leek, and fennel salad, and a crisp, southern fried cornish game hen served with mashed potatoes, addictive, smoky, tasso gravy, and cole slaw.

Some of Mr. Reilly's characteristically multi-faceted dishes had a few ragged edges. The Maryland-style crab cakes lacked texture and tasted of deep-frying oil. Grilled shrimp quesadillas at lunch one day could have used fresher shrimp, and the muddy flavored catfish in a fried catfish po'boy was not helped by a strangely flavored orange mayonnaise seasoned with sesame oil.

Big, hearty, American desserts are freshly made and not too sweet, a meal in themselves. Tall, lovely, olallieberry and strawberry shortcake with softly whipped cream; a warm, custardy, cherry and banana brown betty with a brown sugar crust served in a tea cup; a wedge of pecan-studded, fresh pineapple upside-down cake with a particularly moist battercake base are all an ode to American home cooking.

I have always been entertained by chef Stefen Reilly's cooking. Sometimes the ideas behind the rethought American dishes get to be a little far out, but Reilly is one chef who is able to take a plateful of ingredients and tie them together in a satisfying way.

PATRICIA UNTERMAN

THE AVENUE GRILL ★★

44 EAST BLYTHDALE AVENUE, MILL VALLEY. 388-6003. OPEN SUNDAY THROUGH THURSDAY FROM 5:30 TO 9:30 P.M. AND 5:30 TO 10:30 P.M. ON FRIDAY AND SATURDAY. BEER AND WINE. MASTERCARD, VISA. SMOKING IN BAR ONLY. FULLY WHEELCHAIR ACCESSIBLE. RESERVATIONS RECOMMENDED. MODERATE.

The Avenue Grill is a bustling, enthusiastically run, Marin County restaurant that caters to people who want a good feed. A cross between an American diner and a California grill, the Avenue Grill serves up big plates of meat and potatoes, substantial salads and appetizers, and gigantic desserts. It's all prepared with a sure hand and served in rather posh surroundings for this type of food.

The Grill, in both menu and decor, has borrowed bits and pieces from other restaurants, past and present. Its most striking feature is a white tiled open kitchen with a charcoal broiler and a beautiful vertical rotisserie. If you want a very close look, you can sit at the counter in front of it. A dark green and cream color scheme, a floor of linoleum squares, old-fashioned Venetian blinds, mirrors, handsome hanging light fixtures, and some upholstered benches have all been juggled into the right places. The tables are covered with crisp white linen, which adds a tone of dressiness, but the Avenue Grill is patronized by lots of families. It's noisy enough to muffle even the shouts of young children.

The cooking explores the earthy side of California cuisine. Portions are huge, presentations straightforward, seasoning broad. One unique feature of the menu is that it acknowledges producers, most of them organic.

I'm a fan of Avenue Grill's green salads. Their Caesar, made with small, whole, inner romaine leaves sprinkled with garlicky croutons and freshly grated parmesan cheese, has all the bite and richness of the best versions. A plate of mixed lettuces with a pleasant, creamy vinaigrette stays interesting from first bite to last.

My very favorite dish at Avenue Grill is their Avenue Burger, made of ground, naturally raised beef that stays amazingly juicy and full of flavor when ordered medium rare. It is deliciously charred on the outside. As you bite into the soft, poppyseed bun, piled with grilled onions, the juices run out onto the plate. A pile of french fries accompanies.

I'm also an advocate of the Green Plate Special which changes nightly. One time a pile of sliced, house-cured ham, really a brined leg of pork with a moist texture and slightly sweet and aromatic flavor, came with sweet potatoes, green beans, and authentic coffee-flavored red eye gravy. Another evening the Green Plate brought slices of delicately smoked and roasted turkey with garlic mashed potatoes, fresh cranberry sauce, sagey bread stuffing, and made from scratch gravy.

The All-American Meatloaf serves as a model of its kind. Loosely packed, moist, well-seasoned, it's too bad it gets a winey gravy that detracts from its hominess. A heap of the garlic mashed potatoes and crisp vegetables comes with it. Timing is all important when you order rotisseried half chicken. If you can get it right off the rotisserie, it will be delicate and juicy with a crisp skin. Good coleslaw and fries are heaped on the plate.

Desserts carry on the style of simple abundance. A big bowl of fresh apple crisp could be a meal in itself, and individual lemon meringue pies look mountainous with their caps of fluffy meringue.

The Avenue Grill does an admirable job of turning out American favorites. They capture the heartiness and comfort of the originals while adding their own interesting twists. If you're hungry and want something comforting that you know will be made with high quality ingredients, head for the Avenue.

PATRICIA UNTERMAN

BAHIA ★★½

41 FRANKLIN ST. AT MARKET, SAN FRANCISCO. 626-3306. OPEN 11 A.M. TO 2 P.M. MONDAY THROUGH FRIDAY, AND 5 TO 10 P.M. SUNDAY THROUGH THURSDAY, UNTIL 11 P.M. WEEKENDS. BEER, WINE. VISA, MASTERCARD. 90% NONSMOKING. FULLY WHEELCHAIR ACCESSIBLE. RESERVATIONS RECOMMENDED. MODERATE.

If you leaf through a regional cookbook, the food of Brazil sounds wonderful. But in real life—as translated to restaurants in the U.S—it can be an unmitigated disaster with one dish more leaden than the other. Now however, at long last, San Francisco has a Brazilian restaurant that makes those cookbook pages come alive. The food is relatively light, remarkably interesting, and a real bargain to boot. You can even order salt cod—a dish that normally resembles bleached shoe leather—and get an idea of why people in Brazil and Portugal actually eat the stuff.

The restaurant is called Bahia, a colorful, rollicking place on Franklin Street just in from Market. On a decorating budget that must have been closer to $2,000 than the $2 million that some restaurants spend these days, they've created a place that's so pleasant and so happy that you start smiling before you even taste the food. Bahia is the creation of Valmor Neto, who came to the United States a few years ago and worked in a series of restaurants cooking everything from Jewish food to nouvelle cuisine. He named his restaurant after the coastal state in northern Brazil that his family came from. His cooking, which uses lots of coconut milk, reflects Bahia's tropical climate.

Neto, who is irrepressibly cheerful, is part of the reason Bahia is so much fun. He's constantly running out of the little open kitchen to hug customers he knows and talk with those he doesn't. In the midst of this, he somehow manages to turn out perfectly cooked food for a restaurant that is filled most nights. Neto demonstrates with some of his entrees a lesson lots of restaurants have forgotten: good food isn't necessarily confined to delicate little things artistically arranged on a plate and surrounded by baby vegetables. The cooking at Bahia is hearty peasant-style, heaped on a plate with no particular finesse, but absolutely bursting with wonderful flavors.

Two of the best examples are the roast leg of pork and the chicken marinated in dark beer. The pork has been stuffed with bits of bacon, carrots, black olives, garlic, and cilantro, then baked with white wine. Fresh tomatoes, cilantro, and a reduction of juices from the pork go into the sauce. As for the chicken, the marinade includes oregano, basil, cilantro, onions, and rosemary besides the beer. The whole thing is baked, with the taste of the marinade permeating every bite of chicken. The flavors are so marvelous I even find myself chewing on all the chicken bones.

Two other outstanding entrees evoke the richness of coconut milk. *Muqueca de peixe* is a red snapper filet marinated in lime and simmered in a reduction of fresh tomatoes, coconut milk, fish stock, and spices. Pacific red snapper (which isn't really snapper) is far from my favorite fish, but this one emerges fluffy and not a bit overcooked and filled with nice flavors. Coconut milk is also used in the *bobo de galinha*, a boneless chicken breast sliced into strips and baked in a casserole dish with onions, cashew nuts, and yucca root. Then there's the salt cod, *bacalhoada*, baked in olive oil with fish stock, potatoes, bacon, olives, and onions. Miraculously, it ends up neither salty nor leathery, the only descriptions I could use for any version I've had in the past. But salt cod has a strong, unusual flavor that's definitely an acquired taste; the problem is that few people will like it enough the first time around to want to make the acquisition.

Bahia is one of those restaurants that make you feel it's a pleasure to eat out. For anyone who hasn't been to Brazil, it offers a chance to sample an interesting new cuisine done the way it should be prepared. It's really fun. And the food comes at a remarkably reasonable price.

STAN SESSER

▌ BARRIO FIESTA ★★

909 ANTOINETTE LANE, SOUTH SAN FRANCISCO. (TAKE THE WESTBOROUGH AVE. EXIT EAST FROM I-280, CROSS EL CAMINO, TURN LEFT AT THE FIRST TRAFFIC LIGHT.) 871-8703. OPEN 11 A.M. TO 10 P.M. MONDAY THROUGH THURSDAY, 11 A.M. TO 11 P.M. FRIDAY, SATURDAY, AND SUNDAY. NO ALCOHOL. CASH ONLY. 100% NONSMOKING. PARTIALLY WHEELCHAIR ACCESSIBLE. NO RESERVATIONS. INEXPENSIVE TO MODERATE.

There's no such thing as a one-star Filipino restaurant; more likely, the food is either going to be good or completely awful. That's because so much of Filipino cooking involves deep-frying or else heavy sauces. In the hands of a less-than-skilled chef, you'll wonder whether you've come to feed yourself or to lubricate your car. That's why I don't take lightly the task of running out to review a new Filipino place. Since even a restaurant critic's stomach has its limits, I want a couple of solid recommendations first. And that's exactly what I got with Barrio Fiesta in South San Francisco; the letters I received about it made it sound too good to miss.

They were right. The frying is impeccable, the sauces flavorful, the menu so interesting, and the portions so huge you'll be sorry you didn't come with ten people so you could sample more of the food. Barrio Fiesta is the latest branch of a chain of 24 restaurants in the Philippines and one in Los Angeles. While I'm always a bit suspicious of far-flung chains, our Barrio Fiesta could be as authentic as any, since it's presided over by Rey Ongpauco, whose mother founded the

■ **THE FRYING IS IMPECCABLE, THE SAUCES FLAVORFUL, THE MENU SO INTERESTING, AND THE PORTIONS SO HUGE YOU'LL BE SORRY YOU DIDN'T COME WITH TEN PEOPLE SO YOU COULD SAMPLE MORE OF THE FOOD.**

whole thing three decades ago. Moreover, all the cooks have had years of experience at the Manila Barrio Fiestas.

Rey and his wife Cecilia have created a restaurant that exudes the atmosphere of the tropics. There are rattan chairs, bamboo ceilings, pink walls, and waiters in fancy Filipino shirts. Not only many of the ingredients, but lots of the crockery come directly from the Philippines. For wonderful, bounteous food and very pleasant service, prices are reasonable. But despite the nice atmosphere and good food, Barrio Fiesta has some potentially frustrating problems. First, it's relatively small, takes no reservations, and is already crowded on weekends. Then, once you order—even if it's a dozen dishes, like at my first dinner—every single thing is brought out at the same instant. (I defeated the system my second meal by ordering only a couple of things at a time.)

That's the downside of Barrio Fiesta, but the food will make you forget about any of these annoyances. Let's consider the frying first. Everything deep-fried comes out absolutely impeccable; the oil is always fresh, the frying always crisp and greaseless. If you're a fried-food fan, start with the *lumpia*, the Filipino-style egg rolls. There are big ones (*pritong lumpia*, stuffed with water chestnuts, onions, shrimp, ground pork, and vegetables) and small ones (*lumpia Shanghai*). Then you could move on to the whole-fried catfish in the thick brown adobo sauce (*adobong hito*) and the battered crispy chicken. Cecilia says her husband is embarrassed by the crispy chicken, considering it no better than the Kentucky Fried variety; I say no fried chicken this good has ever crossed Colonel Sanders' portals.

But you could never taste a fried dish and still love Barrio Fiesta. Consider the *lapu-lapu*, a whole grilled rock cod, impeccably fresh, topped with a lemon butter sauce and grilled Pacific oysters, carrots, and potatoes. Or the *kare-kare*, a hearty stew in a clay pot featuring chunks of beef, oxtails, tripe, and eggplant, in a rich orange-colored peanutty sauce.

At its worst, Filipino food can be intimidatingly greasy and heavy. At its best—the way Barrio Fiesta presents it—it's an absolutely delightful venture into what for many people is a new ethnic cuisine. In the Bay Area, with a huge Filipino population and the rest of us always on the prowl for something different, a restaurant like Barrio Fiesta is long overdue.

STAN SESSER

BELLA VOCE ★½

FAIRMONT HOTEL, NOB HILL, SAN FRANCISCO. 772-5199. OPEN EVERY DAY FOR BREAKFAST FROM 6 A.M. TO 11 P.M.; LUNCH FROM 11 A.M. TO 3 P.M.; DINNER FROM 5:30 P.M. TO 11:30 P.M. SINGERS AT DINNER ONLY. FULL BAR. ALL MAJOR CREDIT CARDS. 75% NONSMOKING. FULLY WHEELCHAIR ACCESSIBLE. RESERVATIONS ACCEPTED. MODERATE TO EXPENSIVE.

It finally happened. I nearly lost my long-suffering constant dining out companion to a young opera singer—a mezzo soprano actually—with a lilting, nuance-filled voice and an off-the-shoulder peasant blouse. We were eating pasta, indifferent but nicely served, at the Bella Voce restaurant in the basement of the Fairmont Hotel. Music was exploding all around us—from a grand piano and a troupe of opera singing waiters and waitresses who were holding forth all over the dining room, in chorus, in duets and trios, and arias. One of our servers sang so movingly right into my dining companion's eyes, that he dropped his fork and cried. You never know what will happen in restaurants these days.

This relatively new room in the Fairmont is a hit, not only because pasta and pizza has become so popular, but because the singing is so good. To carry off an operation like this, where singers are constantly performing around the room while the normal activities of a restaurant are taking place, requires a serious commitment. The management of the Fairmont has made it. The troupe has a carefully planned nightly program, punctuated by many happy birthdays sung to the tune of Handel's Hallelujah chorus. Every table has two servers, one a professional waiter, the other a professional opera singer posing as a waiter, who takes drink orders and helps serve the food. Everyone, except the piano player and an occasional wine steward, is in Italian period dress of some unidentifiable sort. Service halts when your singer/server is bringing tears to someone else's eyes instead of bringing you your martini. But for the most part, the meals do get out, albeit a bit fitfully. No one would go to this restaurant just to eat, anyway.

The best dishes to order while you're immersed in the music come from the pasta and pizza sections of the menu. A pizza alla salsiccia brings six generous slices of a yeasty, crisp crust generously topped with good mozzarella, tomato sauce and lean pepperoni. A calzone, or folded over pizza, has the same excellent crust sprinkled with sesame seeds. This unconventional addition actually adds a needed dimension of flavor to a very simple filling of prosciutto and imported fresh buffalo mozzarella.

The pastas come on attractive deep plates that can easily be passed for sharing. Best among them are spaghettini alla carbonara with a smokey, pancetta-infused sauce of egg yolk, cream, and parmesan, and spaghettini with a good, simple sauce of tomatoes, basil, and garlic.

Fettucine Alfredo, a sometimes cloyingly rich preparation of cheese, butter, and cream, was distinctive for its lightness here. The bolognese sauce on angel hair pasta was authentic in texture, but tired in flavor. Leaden gnocchi in a gorgonzola cream sauce and a pallid pesto that tasted more like green cream sauce served over cappellini should be avoided. All of the pastas would have tasted better more al dente.

Main courses are expensive and not successful, but a few antipasti are worth ordering like the *antipasti freddi*, a plate of prosciutto and air-dried beef called bresaola, delicious marinated eggplant, pickled onions, and olives. A plus at Bella Voce is the completely Italian wine list with lots of interesting bottles at reasonable prices.

Bella Voce is not for everyone, but if you are an opera lover or someone who likes to be entertained while they eat, the Bella Voce is exhilarating. The voices are really top notch.

PATRICIA UNTERMAN

BENTLEY'S ★★

185 SUTTER STREET, SAN FRANCISCO. 989-6895. OPEN MONDAY TO SATURDAY 11:30 A.M. TO 10 P.M.; SUNDAY BRUNCH 10 A.M. TO 3 P.M.; DINNER 5 TO 9 P.M. FULL BAR. ALL MAJOR CREDIT CARDS. 50% NONSMOKING. FULLY WHEELCHAIR AC-CESSIBLE. RESERVATIONS RECOMMENDED. EXPENSIVE.

Chef Amey Shaw developed the Southwestern-inspired Fourth Street Grill in Berkeley, but her style was muted a bit when she moved across the Bay to the Maltese Grill and Girapolli. Now, she's back on track at Bentley's at Sutter and Kearny.

This seafood restaurant, one of the duller stars of the Kimpton properties which include Kuleto's, Splendido's, and Postrio, is beginning to shine under Shaw's vibrant touch.

She has a marvelous way of pairing spicy ingredients with seafood, and she's at her best here. Her arrival brings Bentley's into the running as one of the city's best seafood restaurants.

Many combinations are of three-star caliber, but the desserts—on all visits—would need improvement to be considered even mediocre. The service, and to a lesser degree, the atmosphere, combine to lower the overall rating.

One of the best salmon dishes I've ever tasted is a broiled version with a horseradish-citrus glaze. The combination of the sweet acid and the pungent horseradish is electric. It's accompanied by green beans and boiled new potatoes. Another ethereal dish is salmon sausage, a mousse-like mixture flecked with red and green chiles. Taste and texture are first-rate, nicely complemented by a sake sauce and crunchy flying fish roe caviar.

To satisfy meat eaters, there's one beef entree; a grilled New York steak topped with roasted shallot butter with oregano. The meat is tender and has a good flavor, but the real attraction is the slightly lumpy garlic mashed potatoes. Only one entree failed, a pasta with prawns. Of the appetizers I recommend crab, shrimp, and scallop cakes, round patties of seafood with a crispy exterior, accompanied by a mildly spicy mayonnaise. Caesar salad is good, with a dressing well-balanced between acid and garlic. The croutons are crisp and fresh, the whole romaine leaves are cold, and the anchovies are meaty and mild.

The nearly exclusive California wine list has 30 still wines and eight sparkling wines—mostly recognizable names, but the selections are well chosen for the food. Skip the desserts. On my visits, we tried everything. The only one worth ordering was a sundae with rum sauce and toasted pecans.

On all visits, it was evident that the dining room staff needed more training—a problem made worse by under-staffing. The servers seemed frazzled and rather chilly. That's doubly bad, because the decor could use a dash of warmth. There's no problem with the bar area downstairs, which is elaborate and features a piano and small tables. The mezzanine dining room, however, looks commercial and impersonal with its black wrought-iron railing topped with brass, black and white photos lining the staircase, and white-clothed tables. The lighting, all of it coming from the ceiling, also makes the place appear a little dull.

MICHAEL BAUER

THE BIG FOUR AT THE HUNTINGTON HOTEL ★½

1075 CALIFORNIA ST., SAN FRANCISCO. 771-1140. OPEN FOR BREAKFAST MONDAY THROUGH FRIDAY 7 TO 10 A.M., UNTIL 11 A.M. WEEKENDS AND HOLIDAYS; OPEN DAILY FOR LUNCH 11:30 A.M. TO 3 P.M.; DINNER 5:30 TO 10:30 P.M. FULL BAR. MAJOR CREDIT CARDS. 75% NONSMOKING. PARTIALLY WHEELCHAIR ACCESSIBLE. RESERVATIONS RECOMMENDED. VERY EXPENSIVE.

The Big Four restaurant in the Huntington Hotel turns out to be a depressingly somber room with dark wood paneling and green leather banquettes, where many of the tables are so dark you can't read the menu. What sort of food would you expect in such a stuffy place, so formal that the waiter the entire evening adopts a condescending "whatever monsieur desires, I will do" attitude? You're wrong. It's not Continental with heavy food and leaden sauces. In fact, it's quite the opposite. The menu is enticing, the food light, nouvelle, and beautifully presented.

The Big Four, which looks exactly like a men's club, has a young and enthusiastic female chef named Gloria Ciccarone-Nehls. Her menus—one page that changes each season, a second page of nightly specials—are about as appealing as they come; you want to order every dish. I fault several things but, except for the soups, it is never because the ingredients aren't good or the preparation competent. Rather, while some dishes are completely wonderful, I feel that others are too dull and muted, lacking any intensity of flavor.

The portions are generous, but the food at Big Four doesn't come cheap. In choosing an appetizer, consider the pasta of the evening which is served in appetizer portions, or else a seafood salad. The pastas are interesting and a real bargain. One night there was a black pepper linguine with grilled prawns, Japanese eggplant, tomatoes, pine nuts, and pesto; the next dinner we were offered a deliciously spicy egg fettuccine with tasso, grilled eggplant, red onions, and leeks in a creole tomato sauce. Like several of the appetizers and entrees, the pastas are served on a black plate. With their multi-colored ingredients, they look ravishing.

Among the entrees, three are nothing less than sensational. A perfect piece of grilled swordfish comes in a real lobster-cream sauce—you can see chunks of lobster, and the sauce is infused with its flavor. Alongside is a crepe stuffed with corn and cheese souffle, a wonderful idea. A second fish dish does equally well: A perfect salmon steak, coated with spices, seared, then roasted in the oven, is served in a broth of fish stock with julienned vegetables, lemongrass, and shiitake mushrooms. All of this is accompanied with homemade saffron-flavored noodles in a bow-tie shape. The third winner is the breast of Peking duck, boned and pan-roasted, in a raspberry vinegar sauce that tastes heavily of raspberries and is tart rather than sweet.

The Big Four doesn't quite make it to a two-star level. But if you order the right things, you can have a meal that will be among the most competent and most interesting of San Francisco's California cuisine restaurants. That's a lot more than I expected when I first walked into the dining room.

STAN SESSER

BIG NATE'S BARBEQUE ★½

1665 FOLSOM STREET, SAN FRANCISCO. 861-4242. OPEN 11 A.M. TO 10 P.M. MONDAY THROUGH SATURDAY, NOON TO 8 P.M. SUNDAY. BEER, WINE TO GO. CASH ONLY. NO SMOKING AT TABLES. PARTIALLY WHEELCHAIR ACCESSIBLE. FOOD TO GO AND DELIVERED. INEXPENSIVE.

Most San Franciscans remember Nate Thurmond as a great rebounder for the Golden State Warriors, but they may not know that he is also a restauranteur. His latest venture, Big Nate's Barbeque, is a bright yellow cinderblock building at the foot of SoMa's trendy part of Folsom Street. Thurmond, who retired from basketball in 1977, is no amateur to the restaurant business. He operated The Beginning on Fillmore Street for 10 years, a popular, upscale soul food restaurant.

Big Nate's Barbeque is a much simpler operation, focusing on ribs, chicken, and large cuts of meat slowly cooked in a red-brick, wood-burning oven that is visible behind the counter. You can smell the delicious aromas a block away.

The meats emerge from the oven moist, tender, and smoky, glazed with a well-balanced, natural-tasting barbeque sauce that comes in three degrees of hotness, the hottest being quite manageable. The succulent chicken has a velvety texture and a marvelous smoke-licked flavor. Long, meaty pork ribs are tender and tasty. There are no baby back ribs, though I wish Nate's offered them.

My favorite food from Nate's oven is something called Memphis Pork, satiny, fat-marbled pork butt that takes to smoking and barbeque sauce like a seven-foot athlete to basketball. When you order the Memphis Pork at dinner, you get a plate piled with coarsely chopped, barbeque sauce-soaked pork with whole wheat bread on the side.

On all the dinner-size orders, cole slaw and potato salad are included. Unlike most rib places, Nate's makes the cole slaw with freshly cut cabbage in a tart dressing, and the potato salad is made from scratch, bound with a judicious amount of real mayonnaise. Instead of the typical, commercial white bread, Nate's uses a more wholesome wheat bread that is still soft enough to soak up the sauce and juices.

For dessert, a good, fresh sweet potato pie has a firm filling, spicy with ginger. Most of Nate's food is sold to go or ordered over the phone and delivered. However, there are several tables for eating in the smokehouse, next to a wall hung with Thurmond memorabilia. The tables are generally occupied during prime hours, but turn over quickly, perhaps because beer and wine are sold only to go.

A 7-year-old customer was told that Nate might be found at his rib place, with pen in hand, during the days and in the evenings on Fridays and Saturdays. As far as the food and the service are concerned, Big Nate's has every reason to entrust the place to his staff. The barbeque is delicious and the people behind the counter couldn't be nicer.

PATRICIA UNTERMAN

BIRK'S ★★

3955 FREEDOM CIRCLE, SANTA CLARA. (408) 980-6400. OPEN FOR LUNCH MON-DAY TO FRIDAY, 11:30 A.M. TO 2:30 P.M.; DINNER MONDAY TO SATURDAY 5 TO 11 P.M., SUNDAY UNTIL 9 P.M. FULL BAR. ALL MAJOR CREDIT CARDS. 90% NON-SMOKING. FULLY WHEELCHAIR ACCESSIBLE. RESERVATIONS RECOMMENDED ESPECIALLY AT LUNCH. EXPENSIVE.

Birk's in Santa Clara is a great addition to dining on the Peninsula, although it doesn't do much for the landscape. This American grill-style restaurant, which opened about a year and a half ago, looks vaguely like a toy version of San Francisco International Airport, plopped into an anonymous office park off Interstate 101 at Great America Parkway.

Yet the atmosphere inside belies the copper roof and hard-edged stucco structure. Past the mahogany doors, it feels like an upscale brasserie, with overtones of a modern men's club. The rich interior was conceived by Pat Kuleto, designer of such places as Postrio, Kuleto's, and Splendido's.

The food, under the direction of Jim Stump, is simple and well prepared, with grilled chicken, steaks and fish being the specialities. The excellent mixed grill features a small lamb chop with mint jelly, a chunk of beef fillet with bearnaise, a thin crispy crab cake with sherry mustard sauce, and a vibrantly flavored chicken breast. Other grilled meats are just as good, especially the barbequed baby back ribs slathered with a mildly sweet sauce, accompanied by cumin-infused black beans with a taste of masa, and cole slaw. Birk's strip steak is great, with the oak-wood grilled flavor enhancing the juicy, mildly sweet meat. It comes with baked potato, but the staff readily substitutes garlic mashed potatoes, which are a bit gummy, or fries, which are medium-thick and crisp. The meat is further enhanced by a side order of sauteed button mushrooms redolent of parsley and garlic.

At times, however, the chef seems to lose control of the fire. On one visit, the seafood sausage, coarsely ground with a spicy kick, tasted charred, even when doused with honey-mustard sauce. Another time it was fine, but on that visit the swordfish lost the fight with the flames.

The only dish to avoid is the Mexican shrimp saute appetizer. The black pepper-coated seafood is submerged in oil and flecked with nearly raw chunks of garlic, although the menu calls them crisp-fried. And the shrimp are unpeeled, upping the odds for a tie-spattering incident.

Better starts include the Caesar salad with just a hint of anchovy, or the nightly paté.

The diverse, please-everyone menu is enhanced with a well-chosen wine list featuring California wines (with the exception of sparkling wines). Although there are fewer than 60 selections, care has been taken in each category to represent different styles and prices.

Desserts are all good efforts. Try the mile-high cheesecake, berry shortcake or the bananas-Foster brownie, a rich, chewy square topped with intensely flavored banana ice cream and fudge sauce.

Part of the charm of Birk's upscale interior is service that's more homey than sophisticated. In some misguided attempts to be perky, the staff may make a few inane comments ("Try that dessert—it's yummy, yummy"), but generally the servers are helpful and congenial.

A dish may be given to the wrong person and wine may not be poured, but overall most mistakes are corrected before they become annoying. It all adds up to a very good dining experience.

MICHAEL BAUER

▌ BISTRO CLOVIS ★★½

1596 MARKET ST. AT FRANKLIN, SAN FRANCISCO. 864-0231. OPEN 11:30 A.M. TO 11 P.M. MONDAY THROUGH THURSDAY, UNTIL MIDNIGHT FRIDAY, AND 5 P.M. TO MIDNIGHT SATURDAY. BEER AND WINE. VISA, MASTERCARD. 50% NONSMOKING. FULLY WHEELCHAIR ACCESSIBLE. RESERVATIONS SUGGESTED. MODERATE.

I get lots of calls from people about to go to France and asking where to eat. But many of them aren't interested in the great Michelin-starred restaurants, even though these represent some of the best food in the world. They don't want to feel intimidated; they don't want to eat a heavy, four-hour dinner; they don't want to pay all that money. Instead, they ask me for the names of bistros.

A bistro is one of the most difficult kinds of restaurants to transplant to the United States. Bistro Clovis, at the corner of Market and Franklin in San Francisco, succeeds. While the food is quite decent, it hardly can be said to soar over that of its competitors. But Clovis, in every respect, is a true bistro. Prices are very reasonable. That includes the wine list, where little known wines from France, that are good values, are featured. The wood floors, little black tables, lace curtains, and blackboard menu all speak of France. And when you see the proprietor, Max Boureille with his bushy black mustache, you don't have to ask in what country he was born.

Boureille offers some great bargains in both food and wine. The menu has no clear delineation among appetizers, salads, and entrees; it's more "tapas-style," a series of little dishes, except that some of the portions aren't that little. Sweetbreads in red vinegar butter, my single favorite dish, would fill up anyone. This is a plate of wonderfully tender sweetbreads on a bed of green leaf and butter lettuce, with a tangy sauce of red wine vinegar with shallots and butter. If there's one quarrel I have with the food at Clovis, it's that some of the dishes lack assertive spicing; they tend to be too bland. But there are several exceptions. Pieces of boned rabbit are cooked with lots of fresh rosemary in a sauce of creme fraiche, pink peppercorns, and white wine. A boned chicken breast is stuffed with an appealing combination of goat cheese, tarragon, chervil, and Italian parsley, and it's served in a light sauce that includes chicken stock, white wine, shallots, and whipped cream. One of the nicest ideas is the baby vegetable salad with salmon. A strip of salmon is sauteed in butter and served without any sort of sauce. But next to it is a generous heap of al dente pieces of broccoli, carrots, and leeks, tossed with olive oil, sherry vinegar, dijon mustard, tarragon, and lemon.

As a starter, you should try the onion soup Les Halles, a rich beef stock filled with onions and topped with garlic toast spread with melted emmenthaler and parmesan cheeses; it's a delicate version much superior to many you get around Les Halles itself, because there's not a thick layer of stringy, gooey cheese. (Les Halles is the former market district of Paris, and many people used to go to surrounding restaurants after midnight for onion soup.) There are two other excellent starters: rounds of baked, lightly breaded goat cheese on a bed of butter lettuce, and warm potato salad tossed with a mustard vinaigrette with little boneless strips of marinated herring.

Clovis is a real bistro—friendly, inexpensive, and very French—with a good wine list and excellent desserts. While there's nothing particularly innovative about the food, I find the overall experience completely satisfying.

STAN SESSER

BISTRO ROTI ★★

155 STEUART ST., SAN FRANCISCO. 495-6500. OPEN MONDAY THROUGH THURS-DAY 11:30 A.M. TO 10 P.M., FRIDAY UNTIL 11; BRUNCH SERVED SATURDAY AND SUNDAY 10:30 A.M. TO 2:30 P.M.; DINNER FROM 5:30 TO 11 P.M. SATURDAY, UNTIL 10 P.M. SUNDAY. FULL BAR. ALL MAJOR CREDIT CARDS. 60% NONSMOKING. FULLY WHEELCHAIR ACCESSIBLE. RESERVATIONS RECOMMENDED. MODERATE.

There's something going on in every corner of Bistro Roti, the French country restaurant opened by Cindy Pawlcyn and the gang that brought us Bix, Fog City Diner, and Tra Vigne and Mustards (both in the Napa Valley).

The long narrow restaurant, tucked into the side of the newly renovated Griffon Hotel, stretches from Steuart to the Embarcadero. The look is warm and inviting, much like a men's club with etched glass panels separating dining areas, comfortable banquettes, bistro chairs, and lots of wood and brass.

In the front, you're next to the window and nestled next to the bar action. In the center area, you're overlooking the massive fireplace with a slowly revolving spit filled with chicken and ducks. In the back, you have an unexpected view of the Bay Bridge and the open kitchen complete with counter seating.

The food is simply prepared and for the most part delicious, though consistency can be a problem. Pawlcyn's menu always has some interesting twists: chicken roasted with garlic and mint, or a grilled pork chop with baked pears and an exotic-flavored warm slaw. Both are delicious, though the pork on the last visit was a bit dry from overcooking.

One of the best salmon preparations to be found is a fillet that's pounded to cover a platter, and popped under the broiler to cook. It's topped with sun-dried tomatoes and a drizzling of mustard sauce. Another subtle twist on the oysters Rockefeller theme pairs plump mussels with chard, chervil, and a dusting of buttery-tasting crumbs. It's a delicious appetizer.

In a more traditional mode, crispy, creamy sweetbreads are loaded with what seemed like a jar full of capers and a well-balanced lemon sauce. Don't miss the accompaniments; the fries or the lacy-thin fried onion rings. They come piled sky-high on the plate and they're guaranteed to disappear quickly.

The wine list illustrates how a well-thought-out list can enhance and support the overall theme of a restaurant. The 75 item list, printed opposite the menu, concentrates on gutsy but versatile rhones, a few bandols and interesting and hearty California selections.

For dessert, I'd head for creme brulée with the traditional hard caramelized crust topping an unexpected layer of slightly runny chocolate which melds with the silken custard as your spoon goes to work. It's the best example I've found. For even more robust appetites, there's a cherry and apricot brioche bread pudding that's rich, decadent, and delicious.

MICHAEL BAUER

BIX ★★

56 GOLD ST. (BETWEEN JACKSON AND PACIFIC), SAN FRANCISCO. 433-6300. LUNCH SERVED MONDAY THROUGH FRIDAY 11:30 A.M.; DINNER MONDAY THROUGH THURSDAY 5:00 TO 11 P.M., UNTIL MIDNIGHT FRIDAY AND SATURDAY, 6 TO 10:00 P.M. ON SUNDAY. FULL BAR. ALL MAJOR CREDIT CARDS. 20% NONSMOKING. FULLY WHEELCHAIR ACCESSIBLE. RESERVATIONS RECOMMENDED. MODERATE TO EXPENSIVE.

Bix is one of the most stylish restaurants around. It has a 1920s supper club feel with a dramatic grand mezzanine, large columns, and a beautiful bar backed by an impressive mural.

The action is always lively and it doesn't take much imagination to feel as if you've traveled back to another slightly decadent era of ill-gotten alcohol, when dining was a grand, glorious experience. Even the location, tucked into the narrow alley-like Gold Street, in the shadow of the imposing Transamerica Pyramid, adds to the deliciously illicit feel. The live entertainment—a jazz pianist and a torch singer—augments this speak-easy quality, but it also adds another element to the uproarious din of chat and clinking ice-filled glasses.

The light California food propels you to the 1990s. The restaurant recently went to a daily changing menu, but many favorites, such as the chicken hash continue to appear. One of the most whimsical dishes is a lobster chow mein, that's brought to the table in a white Chinese to-go carton, and dumped on a plate of crispy noodles. The flavors and textures are great. The standard apple Waldorf salad gets an update with blue cheese and walnuts. An arugula salad is topped with little squares of fried polenta. Crisp potato and leek pancakes are topped with a good quality smoked salmon. Fried soft-shell crab, in season, is served with herbs, ginger, and garlic. There's also a good blend of straightforward, traditional preparations such as crab cakes, or pork chops with mashed potatoes and peas. At times, the execution isn't up to the ambition, but it's always interesting to sample, and the prices are reasonable for the overall experience.

The wine list features 125 wines from California and Europe with a standard restaurant mark up. One of the added pluses on the list is the strong representation of the small California boutique wineries. The best dessert is the rich mocha pot de creme or the Bananas Foster, a classic that has been appropriately revived.

Service is always exuberant and friendly, which adds to the party atmosphere, though at peak times it can be slow. In that case just kick back, have another drink, watch the crowd, and listen to the singer.

MICHAEL BAUER

BLUE FOX ★★★

659 MERCHANT STREET, SAN FRANCISCO. 981-1177. OPEN MONDAY THROUGH SATURDAY 5:30 TO 11 P.M. FULL BAR. ALL MAJOR CREDIT CARDS. 80% NON-SMOKING. FULLY WHEELCHAIR ACCESSIBLE. RESERVATIONS RECOMMENDED. VERY EXPENSIVE.

Gianni Fassio, son of one of the former owners of the Blue Fox, bought this dinosaur several years ago, refurbished it, and hired chef Patrizio Sacchetto to launch an updated version of the restaurant. The look remains pretty much the same with Louis XVI armchairs, crystal chandeliers, and curtains stretched taut across the walls between columns in the middle of the dining room. The Blue Fox looks like a Mayfair restaurant; white, formal, spacious, conservatively decorated, and well lit. In addition to this main room, there is a labyrinth of dramatic banquet rooms in the wine cellar and in the upstairs Bacchus room with walls covered with lacquered grape leaves. You enter the restaurant itself through a spacious anteroom with a bar.

The kitchen offers a tasting menu as well as a la carte choices. Unlike the old Blue Fox which was famous for continental cuisine, the new kitchen is inspired by what restaurants in northern Italy are doing today. There are no French sauces, Caesar salads or bastardizations of Italian dishes anymore. Everything is authentically Italian.

This is the place to go for risotto. This creamy Italian rice preparation comes out of the kitchen deeply flavored and perfectly cooked. Quail risotto, made with rich stock and topped with a boned, braised, quail breast wrapped around a forcemeat, is stellar. A seafood risotto with tiny clams, crab, and tomatoes may be lighter, but not a whit less tasty. In another version, several cheeses, including *dolcelatte gorgonzola* and teleme, enrich the rice. There isn't a restaurant in town that makes them better.

The pasta dishes bring surprises as well. Venison tortelloni with wild mushroom sauce are tender packets filled with coarsely chopped game, strewn with roughly chopped porcini moistened with reduced stock, and a sprinkling of fresh herbs. The same fine hand with pasta dough produces a gossamer, multi-colored noodle blanket that covers a little pile of lemony lobster.

The chef likes to work with venison. He pounds and marinates it in white truffle oil to make a carpaccio, which is draped over a deliciously dressed salad of endive and arugula. Traditional starters, like a smartly arranged plate of grilled radicchio and smoked Italian ham, or prosciutto and green figs, are also represented.

Local red snapper, wrapped in a crisp pancake made of paper thin rounds of overlapping potato, sauced in a red onion coulis, is one of Sacchetto's best dishes. The fish stays juicy inside its crunchy wrapper and the slightly vinegared red onion sauce tastes fantastic with it. Another wonderful main dish brings a succulent roast, partially boned rabbit, infused with thyme, that comes with golden brown, twice-cooked potatoes formed into croquettes, and greens. The various veal presentations of medallions or loin, feature thick slabs of tender white meat scattered with artichokes, or mixtures of wild and domestic mushrooms. Rack of lamb wrapped in a bread crumbed vegetable mousse is juicy and cooked to exact specifications. One of the more fanciful preparations, a chicken breast stuffed with lobster meat, thinly sliced and sauced with a citrus flavored red onion coulis, works amazingly well.

For dessert there are ripe, grappa-baked butter pears served with hazelnut ice cream under a round of crisp pastry, or a rich, apple tart with a thick layer of mascarpone and caramel sauce.

The wine list is reasonably priced for an expensive restaurant and full of well-chosen Italian bottles. Service is formal but generally excellent. Mr. Fassio is a man who actually seems to be rethinking the role of restaurateur in European terms. His Blue Fox reflects an urbane sensibility about dining out. The combination of enlightened management and creative, elegant northern Italian cooking fills a niche in this city for high end Italian dining. That it arrives under the aegis of the resonant old Blue Fox makes it all the better.

PATRICIA UNTERMAN

THE BLUE LIGHT CAFE ★★

1979 UNION STREET, SAN FRANCISCO. 922-5510. OPEN FOR DINNER SUNDAY THROUGH WEDNESDAY 6 TO 10 P.M., UNTIL 11 P.M. THURSDAY, FRIDAY AND SATURDAY. FULL BAR. MASTERCARD AND VISA. 65% NONSMOKING. PARTIALLY WHEELCHAIR ACCESSIBLE. RESERVATIONS ACCEPTED. MODERATE.

The Blue Light, owned by local rock hero Boz Skaggs, serves Tex-Mex, California, and Louisiana-style dishes that fulfill the requirements of bar fare and complement the tone of the place. If Marsha Ball, Jeff Healey, or Lou Ann Barton dropped in, they would no doubt find something appropriate to eat and be able to listen to themselves on the Blue Light's excellent sound system.

The Blue Light is about equally divided into a bar and a dining room. Decor vestiges from former restaurants, like galvanized sheet metal walls and perforated stainless steel ceilings fight a little with etched glass panels depicting scenes of the Louisiana bayous. Half of a once open kitchen has been blocked off from view. Tall-sided booths and banquettes are situated comfortably away from the smokey bar. The place is intimate and lively.

The Mexican-accented dishes are my favorites. A light chicken tamale made with loosely packed cornmeal filled with green olives, sweet peppers, and seasoned with dried chiles makes for a tasty appetizer. Black bean soup has a chunky, chile-like texture and deep flavor. *Enchiladas Suizas* turn out to be a soothing, rich, Tex-Mex casserole layered with tortillas, sour cream, cheese, chicken, and tomatillo salsa.

One of the nicest parts of dinner is the basket of freshly baked cornbread, moist whole wheat bread, and finely textured white bread that is set down at each table. Though not typically considered bar food, salads are not neglected here. One very good one, a mixture of romaine, carmelized pecans, pears, and blue cheese with sherry vinaigrette, offsets a dull house salad composed of elephantine leaves in a bland vinaigrette.

Main courses are expectedly substantial. A spicy, moist, Cajun-seasoned meatloaf topped with mashed potatoes in a red wine gravy with overtones of BBQ sauce, called Louisiana-Style Shepherd's Pie, is a signature dish along with a gigantic plate of tender, sliced pot roast, served with big chunks of carrot, celery, onion, and parsnip and a pile of mashed potatoes. Barbequed ribs are meaty but could be crustier and smokier. Freshly dressed cole slaw and tame, nicely balanced BBQ sauce give the rib plate a lift. This winning cole slaw is also paired with grilled chicken brochettes, and crisp, battered, deep-fried pieces of breast.

Desserts are terrific. A warm pear tart with caramel sauce could have emerged from the best pastry kitchen in town, and a surprisingly delicate Brownie Tart with a crisp chocolate cookie crust has a lovely, smooth texture. The chunky filling in a pumpkin pie, one night, was irresistible.

Details, like a daily changing menu, wines by the glass, margaritas made with fresh lime juice, good decaf coffee, pleasant and efficient service, and a genial host at the front door, are further indications that the Blue Light has stayed vital and well managed over the six years it has been open. The light shines on.

PATRICIA UNTERMAN

BOHEMIAN CIGAR STORE ★★★

566 COLUMBUS AVENUE, SAN FRANCISCO. 362-0536. OPEN MONDAY 10 A.M. TO 11 P.M., TUESDAY THROUGH SATURDAY 10 A.M. TO MIDNIGHT, SUNDAY 10 A.M. TO 6 P.M. BEER AND WINE. CASH ONLY. PARTIALLY WHEELCHAIR ACCESSIBLE. NO RESERVATIONS. FOOD TO GO. INEXPENSIVE.

The Bohemian Cigar Store is currently one of the best coffee houses in the city. Mario's, as it is fondly called in the neighborhood, has it all; charm, patina, character, the best focaccia sandwiches in town, terrific coffee, and superb Italian cheesecake.

It's a tiny place, right on the corner of Columbus and Union across the street from Washington Square Park, with seating at a well worn bar and at six or so tables along the windows. The bar is cluttered with wine and aperitif bottles, plates of cheesecake, photos of the Bohemian's patrons and owners, glasses and coffee cups. Operated by Mario, Liliana, and son Paul Crismani for the last 15 years, the place exudes lived-in warmth. The Bohemian Cigar Store feels like it's been there forever, and indeed, it has been open for business for 70 years in one guise or another.

The Bohemian puts out expertly made cappuccino and espresso, using Graffeo beans, and Italian sandwiches on fresh focaccia bread from neighboring Danilo or Liguria bakeries, depending on the filling. Both focaccias are very soft and full of olive oil. Most spectacular is the meatball sandwich, a warm, saucy creation of savory housemade meatballs, thinly sliced onions, and buttery tomato sauce heated in a miniature pizza oven until everything warms through and melts together.

Both the chicken and the eggplant sandwiches start off as crisp, breaded cutlets which are slipped into the focaccia with just the right amount of sauce and some mozzarella, then into the oven until all becomes oozy and delectable. If you want something lighter, try the open-faced tuna salad with cheese and onions melted on top of it, the tastiest tuna sandwich in town. On Thursdays, if you haven't eaten all day and don't plan to the next, try the polenta with Italian sausages.

I don't mean to give the impression that the food here is heavy.

■ BOTH THE CHICKEN AND THE EGGPLANT SANDWICHES
START OFF AS CRISP, BREADED CUTLETS WHICH ARE
SLIPPED INTO THE FOCACCIA WITH JUST THE RIGHT
AMOUNT OF SAUCE AND SOME MOZZARELLA, THEN INTO
THE OVEN UNTIL ALL BECOMES OOZY AND DELECTABLE.

Rather, it is incredibly rich, tasty, and homemade. I've never been able
to eat a sandwich and a piece of cheesecake at the same sitting, but a
tumbler of good Chianti does wonders for the digestion. I love the
sandwiches, the cheesecake, and the coffee. You can always get into a
good conversation if you want, or read the paper in peace. This place
is the tops.

PATRICIA UNTERMAN

BOMBAY CUISINE ★★

2006 9TH STREET, BERKELEY. 843-9601. OPEN TUESDAY THROUGH SUNDAY FOR
LUNCH 11:30 A.M. TO 3 P.M., DINNER 5 TO 9 P.M, UNTIL 9:30 P.M. FRIDAY AND SAT-
URDAY. BEER, WINE. ALL MAJOR CREDIT CARDS. 100% NONSMOKING. PAR-
TIALLY WHEELCHAIR ACCESSIBLE. RESERVATIONS RECOMMENDED ESPECIALLY
ON WEEKENDS. INEXPENSIVE.

University Avenue in Berkeley is turning into Little India with sari
shops, Indian gift and import stores, Indian food markets, Indian video
stores, and Indian restaurants filling up both sides of the street. Walking into a spacious food shop like Milan International, an Indian
supermarket stocked with hundreds of whole and ground spices, dahls
in all colors and forms, flours, oils, basmati rice, bottled chutneys,
cooking utensils, frozen foods, hard to find Indian produce, Indian
movie videos, incense, and calendars, practically transports you to
New Delhi.

Next to this great food store is a small restaurant adjunct, called
Bombay Cuisine. Though management of both the restaurant and
store seem to go through cyclical changes for better or worse, depending on the whims of a complicated, extended-family relationship,
the current regime is running the operation with conviction. The little
restaurant produces some of the best Indian vegetarian dishes that I've
tasted outside of an Indian home. They are prepared by three cooks:
two women, Sudha Shastri and Purnima Parmar, and one man,
Chinna Swami. They make south Indian snacks like *wadas*, or balls of
different ground dahl, *dosas*, *idli* and *uttapam*, as well as vegetable curries and wonderful *chapatis*, *poori*, and *parathas*, Indian breads cooked
on a griddle. Unlike most other Indian restaurants, Bombay Cuisine
does not have a tandoori oven, which means their menu is liberated

from the omnipresent Punjabi lamb-centered formula. If you are a vegetarian, or just someone who wants to taste some delicious, authentic Indian dishes, Bombay Cuisine is currently cooking at its best.

I always order the "snacks" because you can't find them anywhere else. *Dahi wada*, small, tender, fried balls of dahl flour are sauced in creamy yogurt and served with pruney tamarind chutney. Balls made with potatoes, called *bataka wada*, are deep-fried and served with a fresh cilantro chutney with mint and chiles. Fried chickpea *wada* flattened into a patty and laced with onion, are particularly crisp and savory, a favorite of mine. A white chutney made from dried coconut and chiles comes with them. *Dhokla*, airy steamed squares of chickpea flour tastes like some nutty, fragrantly risen bread. I particularly like Bombay Cuisine's thick *raita*, yogurt mixed with onion and cucumber.

The restaurant makes two daily changing vegetable curries and they are distinctively different in flavor and texture. They go with fluffy, bright yellow basmati rice, and hot, thin, buttery, whole wheat *chapatis*, pieces of which you tear off to scoop up the curry and rice. Deep-fried *chapatis* called *parathas*, stuffed with potatoes or fenugreek leaves, are richer and eaten on their own. The spectacular puffed up bread called *pooris* are worth ordering just for the warm, wheaty breath they expel when you tear into them. The *papadum*, paper-thin lentil wafers, are so carefully fried they melt on your tongue without leaving the slightest hint of cooking oil.

For dessert, *gulab jamun*, Indian versions of doughnuts, stand out for their fluffy texture beneath a syrup of rosewater and sugar.

The small dining room is clean, pleasantly decorated, and well attended. The food tastes handmade. Textures are refined, spices sensitively layered, the labor intensive dishes carefully executed. You get the feeling that the cooks get true satisfaction from cooking for an expatriate Indian community that longs for tastes of home.

PATRICIA UNTERMAN

BRASSERIE SAVOY ★★½

580 GEARY STREET, SAN FRANCISCO. 474-8686. OPEN FOR LUNCH 11:30 A.M. TO 2:30 P.M. MONDAY THROUGH FRIDAY; DINNER NIGHTLY 5:30 TO 10 P.M., LATE SUPPER MENU 10 P.M. TO MIDNIGHT. FULL BAR. ALL MAJOR CREDIT CARDS. 50% NONSMOKING. FULLY WHEELCHAIR ACCESSIBLE. RESERVATIONS RECOMMENDED. EXPENSIVE.

Step into Brasserie Savoy and you're transported to Paris. The feel and look is authentic, from the traditional black and cream woven leather chairs that look like rattan, to the waiters in long white aprons, black vests, and ties. The central bar covered in rich paneled wood, marble floor, high ceiling, zinc bar, and white-clothed tables lined up against the wall all hark back to France.

It's one of the few places where ambience transcends food, which is in the brasserie style with a California bent. Fortunately, it's very good, which makes the experience even better.

The restaurant and hotel next door are owned by Manou and Vesta Mobedshahi, who also own the Sherman House, a Victorian home built in 1876, that they converted into an elegant hotel. The Mobedshahis went to New York's An American Place to hire chef Marc Meyer, who lived in the Bay Area when he was a student at UC Berkeley. Meyer has cleverly adapted some of the best brasserie dishes to fit the climate. His version of a traditional brandade with salt cod is excellent: the mixture has a creamy mousse-like texture loaded with garlic and sandwiched between crisp potato galettes. It is served in a pool of vinaigrette spiced with lemon, and a confetti of vegetables.

One of the best and simplest appetizers is a selection of warm cheeses, lightly dressed with a charred tomato vinaigrette. It's particularly delicious with the basket of walnut rolls served with the meal. The cheesy bread sticks and the crusty, rough-textured bread also are stellar.

The *choucroute*, which reminded me of the kind found all over France, is made of quail, intensely flavored garlic sausage, and smoky bacon. The kraut is mild, almost sweet. *Steak frite*, a large strip steak with fries, is dressed with artichokes, pearl onions, and mushrooms. It's almost a good dish—the accompaniments and the fries are excellent. Unfortunately, the meat had little flavor despite proper cooking.

The restaurant specializes in seafood and many dishes shine. One side of the menu features oysters and other shellfish, which come from the seafood bar at the back of the restaurant. The Extravaganza is a marvelous sampling of shrimp, mussels, oysters, and lobster, presented on a molded mound of ice. Half a lobster is doused with a tropical melon relish. Chilled mussels are accented with an orange mayonnaise. Oysters are served with a selection of three sauces. The real treats are the salads; both a squid and an impressive rock shrimp concoction with corn, bell peppers, and an interesting spicy note from allspice and chilies. Of the hot appetizers, six plump grilled oysters presented on earthy mushrooms didn't work because the roasted garlic and chive sauce was too subtle, and the earthiness of the other ingredients overpowered the seafood. A scallop and mushroom entree in a red wine sauce failed for the same reason. One of the best dishes is the grilled whole Pacific sole served on a bed of apples and celery root with some of the best french fries I've had.

The wine selection is reasonable. A single-page list offers about 50 wines, with a mix of French and Californian from smaller producers.

Desserts are uneven: Citrus rice custard, white chocolate and walnut charlotte with a bitter coffee caramel sauce, and warm apple and fig tart tatin with a vanilla creme fraiche were all undersweetened.

It would be hard to improve on the thick, rich creme brulée or the assorted cookie plate. With the food, ambiance, and service achieving the rare combination of efficiency and friendliness, you'll want to linger in the lively atmosphere. It might even save you a ticket to France.

MICHAEL BAUER

BRIDGES RESTAURANT AND BAR ★★★

44 CHURCH STREET, DANVILLE. 820-7200. OPEN FOR LUNCH TUESDAY THROUGH SATURDAY 11:30 A.M. TO 2:30 P.M.; DINNER TUESDAY THROUGH SUNDAY 5:30 TO 9 P.M.; SUNDAY BRUNCH 10 A.M. TO 2:30 P.M. FULL BAR. AMERICAN EXPRESS, MASTERCARD, VISA. 90% NONSMOKING. FULLY WHEELCHAIR ACCESSIBLE. RESERVATIONS RECOMMENDED. MODERATE TO EXPENSIVE.

Bridges, a beautiful and serene new restaurant in Danville, was built out of aesthetic conviction. The moderate price of a meal here couldn't begin to cover the expense of designing, building and furnishing a restaurant of such understated elegance. The whole operation is a gift to the public from a Japanese businessman who, for personal reasons, wanted to make a cross cultural statement. The idea was to come up with an East-West blend but the resulting restaurant has taken on a greater and more subtle identity of its own. Stunningly sophisticated and civilized, Bridges projects a warmth and harmony rarely felt in modern restaurants.

The food holds up its end of the aesthetic statement. The dishes on the small regular menu, augmented by a brief daily card, are all made with organic and natural ingredients. Color and texture provide the focus of each dish. Flavor comes from the high quality raw materials, good olive oils, and fresh herbs rather than sauces. The overall approach has the same originality as the design of this restaurant, with the same intelligent emphasis on the completed whole.

One dinner brought a chunky soup of meltingly soft fennel and creamy new potatoes in a clear broth. A smokey, hot, brightly seasoned lamb sausage came with a grilled radicchio salad dressed in a piquant green vinaigrette, a superb dish. Malespina oysters on the half shell were plump, briny, and sweet. A salad of mustard greens and baby lettuces tossed with slices of moist Chinese barbequed pork and glazed walnuts had a delicious walnut oil vinaigrette. A bowl of small, sparkling fresh mussels scattered with julienned leeks in a buttery broth came with toasts and a spicy red mayonnaise called rouille.

Main courses were as interesting and pretty as the appetizers. Marinated, white-fleshed tombo tuna was draped over a pile of grilled asparagus in ginger lime butter and some airy scallion pancakes. A pan-fried filet of salmon topped with a sweet sake butter came on a bed of julienned carrots and fluffy rice with shrimp, flecked with hot and sweet red peppers. Meltingly tender sauteed scallops were tossed into sweet and sour Singapore-style rice noodles, slashed with slant cut snow peas, brown threads of deep-fried shallots, and toasted peanuts. A presentation of barbequed pork loin slices in an orange juice/dried chile marinade, served with a relish of black beans, sweet and hot peppers, with a garnish of a mild goat cheese quesadilla, tasted like it came straight from Santa Fe.

The wine list is long and complete with many excellent and reasonably priced choices.

Dessert brought a delightful nut shortcake, sweetened with burnt sugar, napped with a blood orange compote and softly whipped cream. A dense, rich bread pudding was studded with prunes and apricots, and enriched even further with armagnac creme anglaise. A mile high chocolate coconut cake reminded me of Black Forest cake without the cherries, but with the happy addition of coconut ice cream. Good espresso brought this near perfect and exciting dinner to a close.

The highlights of a subsequent lunch included a bowl of thick, spicy, chili-like black bean soup topped with fresh salsa, and a thick, pureed asparagus soup that really captured the elusive flavor of asparagus. A salad of roasted baby vegetables and slices of raw tuna, grilled around the edges, came with tapenade, an olive relish. A soft crusted pizzetta topped with very smokey chicken, tomatoes, and olives was another agreeable option.

A caramel sundae in a deep-fried noodle cup and a pretty fruit compote served with rose geranium sorbet hit the spot on a hot Danville afternoon.

If there was ever a reason to drive to sleepy, woodsy Danville from San Francisco, Bridges is it. This restaurant easily could be located in the city, Paris, or New York, but it resides peacefully in Contra Costa County. Perhaps having to cross the bridge to get there makes a visit all the more meaningful.

PATRICIA UNTERMAN

BROTHERS DELICATESSEN ★★

1351 HOWARD AVE., BURLINGAME. 343-2311. OPEN SUNDAY THROUGH TUESDAY, 8 A.M. TO 7:45 P.M., WEDNESDAY THROUGH SATURDAY 8 A.M. TO 9 P.M. BEER, WINE. VISA, MASTERCARD, AMERICAN EXPRESS. 40% NONSMOKING. PARTIALLY WHEELCHAIR ACCESSIBLE. RESERVATIONS ACCEPTED. INEXPENSIVE TO MODERATE.

Brothers is the best Jewish deli I've found in the Bay Area. It looks just like a Jewish deli should, with a deli counter, Formica tables, ugly frosted light fixtures, and plastic wood paneling. In fact, all that's missing are Jews. The waitresses look as if they'd be far more at home on a surfing beach than dishing out chopped liver.

The lox at Brothers is brought up from Los Angeles, and it's the best. It's never presliced, as in other so-called delis in these parts, since preslicing allows the oil to congeal on the surface and the salmon to dry out. The corned beef and pastrami sandwiches are remarkable, with the meat cooked on the premises. You get a huge, overstuffed sandwich, the corned beef lean, juicy, and tender, the pastrami containing just the right amount of spice.

The Reuben sandwiches aren't classic (toasted pumpernickel is used instead of rye), but the melted Swiss cheese, decent sauerkraut, and fantastic corned beef make a lovely combination. The matzoh brie (scrambled egg with matzoh) is perfectly cooked, the eggs soft and buttery. The matzoh ball soup is as good as you can get anywhere, the broth rich and flavorful, the matzoh balls light and fluffy.

Much to my surprise, the chicken in the pot (boiled chicken with noodles, matzoh ball and carrots, in its own broth) is delicious. Normally, Jewish boiled chicken is an overcooked disaster, but this chicken is juicy and tender, an indication that it has been simmered, not boiled.

Now listen to this: That marvelous Jewish cook at Brothers turns out to be Sam Hou, and he is very Chinese. He and his wife Cathy bought the deli a decade ago. His background for opening a Jewish deli includes a stint as an air force pilot in Taiwan. I wonder what my mother would think if she knew her son was asking a Taiwanese fighter pilot for his recipe for matzoh ball soup?

How does Sam do it? "I learn from the customers," he says. "They give me recipes, tell me a little bit of this, a little bit of that. I cook the corned beef and pastrami myself." All that remained was to ask Sam whether he eats Chinese or Jewish food at home. "Chinese food," he admits. "But the problem is you can eat it and you're hungry. With one Jewish sandwich, six hours later you still don't want to eat."

STAN SESSER

| BURMA'S HOUSE ★★

720 POST ST. AT JONES, SAN FRANCISCO. 775-1156. OPEN FROM 11:30 A.M. TO 10 P.M. DAILY. BEER, WINE. VISA, MASTERCARD. 65% NONSMOKING. FULLY WHEEL-CHAIR ACCESSIBLE. RESERVATIONS RECOMMENDED. INEXPENSIVE.

It used to be that every Southeast Asian restaurant in San Francisco pretended it was a Chinese restaurant; the Thai dishes, or whatever else the nationality, would be hidden among the Chinese dishes on the menu. Those days, of course, are long gone as far as Thai food is concerned. But it's still the style for most of our Burmese restaurants for two reasons. First, I think there's a general feeling among Asians that western palates will rebel over anything that tastes substantially different from sweet and sour pork. Second, the Bay Area's 20,000 Burmese are mostly Chinese in origin, and they feel comfortable eating Chinese food too. Burma's House, on Post and Jones in downtown San Francisco, offers a mere 112 dishes on its dinner menu. Probably no more than 20 are actually Burmese, and they're not easy to find since they're scattered among the Chinese listings. But it's worth the hunt, because this is first-rate Burmese food, very much as it tastes in Rangoon.

Burma's House is owned by a Burmese of Chinese ancestry named Wei Wong. His wife, Lao, prepares the Burmese dishes, and two other cooks do the Chinese food. It's a pleasant if unpretentious restaurant, with a carpet, tablecloths, and lots of blond wood. The waitresses, all young Burmese women, are very attractive and very friendly, but they pay little attention to what their customers need, and you'll probably find yourself waving your arms to flag them down. Unless you want every entree to appear simultaneously, impress upon them your desire for only a couple of dishes at a time.

The appetizers and soups at Burma's House are an excellent introduction to Burmese food. The cuisine of Burma can best be described as a cross between that of India and Thailand, although not nearly as hot as either. While Burmese entrees are most often aromatic curries, there are some appetizers that are completely distinctive, especially the *lap pat dok*. This is the pickled tea leaf salad that Burmese eat for snacks morning, noon, and night. The tea leaves—which have been suspended in a river for several weeks, then buried for weeks more until they taste like a tender vegetable—are tossed with yellow peas, fried garlic, sesame seeds, ground shrimp, and green chiles. It's a delicious dish tasting like nothing else you've ever eaten, and the Burma's House version is quite good.

Two curried entrees are nothing short of perfection. Beef curry with potatoes, onions, and carrots has the rich, aromatic sauce that's a hallmark of Burmese cooking. Curried, deep-fried fish balls, another typical dish, has a spicy, tomato-based sauce, and the fish balls are served surrounded by a circle of bright green broccoli flowers. A third entree which shouldn't be missed is the *cain mongkyaw*, a leafy sour Burmese vegetable that looks like spinach, in a light but fiery sauce.

Burma's House is the sort of Asian restaurant that gives the San Francisco food scene such depth: Here is an unusual cuisine rarely found in the United States, authentic and delicious, and served at rock-bottom prices. The only problem is that you have to do a little detective work, picking out the Burmese dishes from a mainly Chinese menu.

STAN SESSER

BUTLER'S ★★

625 REDWOOD HIGHWAY (OFF SEMINARY EXIT OF 101), MILL VALLEY. 383-1900.
OPEN FOR LUNCH MONDAY THROUGH FRIDAY 11:30 A.M. TO 2 P.M.; DINNER
TUESDAY THROUGH THURSDAY 6 TO 9:30 P.M., FRIDAY AND SATURDAY UNTIL
10 P.M.; SUNDAY BRUNCH FROM 10 A.M. TO 2:00 P.M., DINNER 5 TO 9 P.M. FULL BAR.
MAJOR CREDIT CARDS. 90% NONSMOKING. NOT WHEELCHAIR ACCESSIBLE.
RESERVATIONS SUGGESTED. MODERATE.

This airy, loft-like restaurant that overlooks Richardson Bay was
started by Perry Butler of Union Street fame. It has changed hands, but
the pristine white dining rooms are as cheerful and immaculate as ever,
and the food just as bountiful, fresh, and creative.

The chefs working in the sparkling open kitchen put out corn and
red pepper fritters that melt in your mouth, and crunchy, deep-fried
calamari. Freshly shucked oysters are topped with spinach, hollandaise,
and a healthy pinch of cayenne and stuck under the broiler to become
Butler's version of oysters Rockefeller. Flaky pastry turnovers called
empanaditas are stuffed with goat cheese and onion confit and drizzled
with an ancho chile sauce.

Main courses bring such comfort food as rabbit pot pie, actually a
cut-up, half rabbit in a delicious, slightly thickened red wine sauce.
Baby turnips, carrots, onions, and potatoes hide under a dramatic top
hat of ethereal puff pastry. A gigantic half of a roasted chicken with
soft, sweet potato fries and roasted white potatoes have the superior
flavor of free-range birds. Tasty, thinly sliced flank steak has a pleasing
Southwest tang nicely set off with roasted onions and grilled pineapple. Scallops in a California-style pasta are very fresh and sweet,
tossed into barely sauced fettucine along with arugula and tomatoes.
You are not quite sure if you are eating a salad or a plate of noodles.

All the breads and pastries are baked on the premises and they're
excellent, especially a Meyer lemon tart filled with a tingling lemon
mousse, and velvety textured, true flavored ice cream and ices accompanied by sandy-textured walnut cookies.

On Sundays the upstairs restaurant offers a prix fixe breakfast
highlighted by a basket of exquisite breakfast pastries which includes
buttery, crisp, pecan caramel rolls, thin sliced brioche bread layered
with raisins and cinnamon, light, airy apple ginger muffins, and
delicate whole wheat raisin snails.

Butler's takes a creative approach to breakfast fare that works well.
Red flannel hash, a corned beef hash made with beets, cabbage, and
potatoes, is topped with two poached eggs, red pepper relish, and
housemade ketchup. Spicy patties of lamb sausage share a plate with
sweet potato and white potato pancakes topped with eggs. Butler's
Benedict used soft, crumbly, cheese-herb scones as a base for Canadian

bacon, poached eggs, and hollandaise. Crusty, onion laced "brunch potatoes" are a little breakfast masterpiece.

The ambience at Sunday brunch is enhanced by the light that pours in off Richardson Bay, where the egrets and water fowl live. The view takes in layer upon layer of the coastal hills and you can imagine how bucolic Marin County was before the spate of development that actually produced the building that Butler's is in. Butler's may be located in Marin County, but I recommend it as one of the best San Francisco options for dining with a view.

PATRICIA UNTERMAN

CAFE FOR ALL SEASONS ★★½

50 EAST THIRD AVENUE, SAN MATEO. 348-4996. OPEN MONDAY THROUGH FRI-DAY FOR BREAKFAST 8 TO 10:30 A.M.; LUNCH 11:30 A.M. TO 2:30 P.M.; DINNER SERVED NIGHTLY 5:30 TO 9:30 P.M., SUNDAY 5 TO 8:30 P.M.; BRUNCH SATURDAY FROM 10 A.M. TO 2:30 P.M., SUNDAY 9 A.M. TO 2:30 P.M. FULL BAR. MASTERCARD, VISA, AMERICAN EXPRESS. 65% NONSMOKING. FULLY WHEELCHAIR ACCESSIBLE. RES-ERVATIONS FOR 6 OR MORE AT LUNCH AND DINNER. RESERVATIONS AC-CEPTED AT BREAKFAST. MODERATE.

The first spin-off of a successful West Portal Avenue operation, Cafe For All Seasons feels right the moment you walk through the door. Located in downtown San Mateo in the old Benjamin Franklin Hotel, it has high, pressed-tin ceilings and a gigantic, shiny, open kitchen. The blonde parquet floor, mauve walls and floor-to-ceiling front windows keep the look bright and casual. The dining room is utilitarian in the best sense of the word. The polished wooden tables may not be covered with table cloths but at the Cafe's prices, you realize that you aren't paying for them either. Cafe For All Seasons has struck a harmonious chord of comfort, quality, and price.

What sets this place apart is the hearty, full-flavored food. At lunch one day, the kitchen put out an ingenious special of a grilled salmon club sandwich, an uncannily workable combination of the moist fish, crisp, Oregon pepper-cured bacon, ripe roma tomatoes, lettuce, and housemade mayonnaise on gently toasted egg bread. With a pile of excellent, skinny, french fries, some American black olives and pickle slices, it made for a very satisfying plate of food, especially preceded by a cup of sorrel and potato soup, a tart broth with chunks of creamy potato, croutons, and chopped sorrel. Hamburgers are thick and juicy, grilled exactly to specification.

At dinner, the menu offers several appealing starters which could act as the center of a relatively low fat meal. Vegetable quesadillas stuffed with peppers, a little shredded cheddar-type cheese, topped with yogurt and fresh tomato salsa were clean and colorful. A Szechuan, minced chicken stir fry served in lettuce leaves was moist, crisp, and savory.

The Cafe sells lots of salads and they tend to lean toward the old fashioned kind with mayonnaise-based dressings. The greens have been impeccable and the vegetables noticeably bright and fresh. Pastas take up a large portion of both lunch and dinner menus and they are consistently well made. Imported cappellini, the noodle of choice here, went well with fresh tomatoes, olive oil, basil, and a lot of garlic, as it did with artichoke hearts, mushrooms, and just the right amount of lemon.

The restaurant does all its own baking which means that there are delicious Gravenstein apple pies with housemade vanilla ice cream, oatmeal-topped Gravenstein crisps, and warm, rich, apple cake with caramel sauce and mounds of whipped cream. The only non-apple dessert I tasted was a good one, a mound of fresh white cheese made firm by a little gelatin, and surrounded by raspberry sauce. At weekend brunch, the meal begins with delightful, tiny, raisin scones with sweet butter and housemade raspberry jam. The fresh orange juice, for once, tastes sweet and just squeezed.

There's something very appealing about a restaurant that serves its neighborhood. The Cafe For All Seasons people found a spacious, centrally located spot to launch their honest, attractive operation. The mid-Peninsula didn't have anything like it and I wonder how they got along all these years without one.

PATRICIA UNTERMAN

CAFE BEAUJOLAIS ★★★

961 UKIAH ST., MENDOCINO. (707) 937-5614. OPEN THURSDAY THROUGH MONDAY 8:30 A.M. TO 2:30 P.M.; DINNER 6:15 TO 9:30 P.M. OPEN EVERYDAY DURING THE SUMMER. BEER, WINE. NO CREDIT CARDS. 100% NONSMOKING. FULLY WHEELCHAIR ACCESSIBLE. RESERVATIONS REQUIRED. EXPENSIVE.

Cafe Beaujolais in Mendocino started out as a great discovery: a cute little house with a talented chef, Margaret Fox, who turned out fabulous lunches, and breakfasts that couldn't be matched for any price in San Francisco. Then Margaret hired an equally talented dinner chef, Chris Kump (and ended up marrying him). Finally came a separate building with wood-fired ovens for pizzas and breads. While all this was happening, the crowds were arriving, and a discovery was becoming an institution.

When a restaurant expands and becomes well-known, the food normally goes straight downhill. But the amazing thing about Beaujolais is that the food, over the years, has gotten better and better. It's no longer simply a good choice if you find yourself on the north

■ BREAKFAST IS STILL THE MEAL HERE THAT BRINGS TEARS TO MY EYES, BECAUSE IT SHOWS WHAT BREAKFAST COULD BE, BUT NEVER IS, ANYWHERE ELSE. THE BUTTER-MILK-CINNAMON COFFEE CAKE IS BEYOND DESCRIPTION.

coast; it's now one of the best restaurants in Northern California, period. I have only one complaint about Beaujolais—that it's a four-hour drive from my home.

Breakfast is still the meal here that brings tears to my eyes, because it shows what breakfast could be, but never is, anywhere else. The waffles and pancakes, often with nuts and other wonderful things in the batter, have so much flavor that you don't need to pour on maple syrup. The omelets are moist and fluffy and filled with a tempting combination of ingredients: one example is Italian sausage, green peppers, roasted red peppers, red onions, smoked mozzarella cheese, and sour cream. The buttermilk-cinnamon coffee cake is beyond description.

With a breakfast like this, it's impossible to eat lunch, but then you'd be missing two Fox classics: the Chinese chicken salad and an astonishing black bean chili. You'd also be passing up sandwiches like thinly-sliced applewood-smoked ham on homemade bread with aioli, red onions, smoked mozzarella cheese, kumquat-rhubarb chutney, lettuce, and tomatoes. And skipping dessert would be a disaster, because poems could be written about Margaret's lemon curd tarts and bread pudding.

Chris approaches dinner with the same innovation and enthusiasm of Margaret's breakfasts and lunches. The fish is always very fresh and always cooked perfectly; there's no better place for local salmon when it's in season. But his real talent is combining local ingredients with French and sometimes Thai cooking techniques. Consider a spicy Thai beef salad made with Niman-Schell steak smoked on the premises, seared scallops with coconut milk, black chanterelles, and chervil, or a giant ravioli of shrimp, scallops, and black truffles in a crayfish consomme.

There are often a couple of fixed-price dinners along with an a la carte menu that offers a half-dozen entrees. Desserts are equally appealing; in the summer some will be made with fresh berries picked that day. And the wine list offers a chance to drink the excellent wines of the Anderson Valley, a region whose wines rival their better-known competitors from Napa.

A meal at Cafe Beaujolais makes a visit to Mendocino, one of the most attractive spots in California, a magical experience.

STAN SESSER

CAFE AT CHEZ PANISSE ★★★★

1517 SHATTUCK AVENUE, BERKELEY. 548-5525. OPEN MONDAY THROUGH SATURDAY 11:30 A.M. TO 4 P.M. AND 5 TO 11:30 P.M. BEER, WINE. MAJOR CREDIT CARDS. 100% NONSMOKING. WHEELCHAIR ACCESSIBLE AT LUNCH. RESERVATIONS ACCEPTED FOR LUNCH. MODERATE.

Under the guidance of chefs Catherine Brandel and David Tanis, the upstairs Cafe at Chez Panisse is cooking some of the most delectable food in its eleven year history. Anchoring the menu are crusty pizzas, aromatic from the wood-fired brick oven, and the definitive salad of the tastiest little greens with garlic croutons and perfect vinaigrette. The now classic warm round of fresh goat cheese dusted with bread crumbs is offered every day, and Acme bread and provencal olives greet diners when they sit down. On top of these, new, simple, beautiful dishes come onto the menu each day, and they are a revelation of how delicious and flavorful dishes prepared with naturally raised ingredients can be.

The international inspiration behind these dishes is unified by the Chez Panisse cooking style, which emphasizes clarity of flavor, refined but unfussy presentation, and superb balance. One day an Indian-style marinated chicken breast was teamed with saffron-streaked basmati rice and a cucumber and yogurt salad, all of which sounds only slightly exotic, but in the hands of Chez Panisse cooks was transformed into something extraordinary. The free-range chicken breast was meltingly tender. Each grain of rice was imbued with character and some magic had been performed on the salad to make it taste as if the cucumber and yogurt had merged into a new food. I know this sounds hyperbolic, but you have to eat one of these honed Chez Panisse dishes to understand.

Other great dishes have been as ingenuous as toasts covered with wild mushrooms, soaked in fragrant olive oil, and baked in the wood fired oven; or a pureed soup of white beans, seasoned with sage, that achieves exactly the right texture. One day the Cafe served a rustic Brunswick stew, a braised rabbit in Cajun spices with okra and andouille sausage; on another, an elegant grilled quail salad with persimmons and toasts spread with duck liver mousse. Sand dabs have a golden crust and are swathed with lemon butter; crispy fried oysters, dredged in bread crumbs, come with a piquant, Italian salsa verde.

Desserts are always a highpoint of a meal at the Cafe, restrained, never too sweet, but always satisfying. Ice creams and sorbets capture the most elusive flavors of seasonal fruits. Dried and fresh fruits are poached in various elixirs and served with buttery, oven-fresh cookies. Tarts, filled with nuts or lemon curd, seem to dissolve on your tongue. Again, balance, clarity, and natural flavor create the sensation.

You really do feel elevated by a meal at Chez Panisse because so much thought, sensitivity, and artistic talent is at work behind each dish. The advantage of the Cafe is that you can experience this kind of cooking for moderate prices in charming, casual surroundings, anytime you want. Since the cafe takes reservations for lunch only, people drop in and sip a glass of Bandol, a drinkable red wine from Provence that has become the signature of the restaurant, while waiting for a table.

Every detail, from the interesting array of wines by the glass to the 15% service charge added onto your check, comes from an all encompassing, very much considered philosophy, that takes in all aspects of the restaurant experience. At Chez Panisse, no stone is left unturned, but then they are all rearranged in an artful way that never lets you know how much they have been shaken up.

PATRICIA UNTERMAN

CAFE CLAUDE BAR ZINC ★★½

7 CLAUDE LANE, SAN FRANCISCO. 392-3505. OPEN 8 A.M. TO 9 P.M. MONDAY THROUGH FRIDAY, 10 A.M. TO 4 P.M. SATURDAY. BEER AND WINE. NO CREDIT CARDS. 30% NONSMOKING. FULLY WHEELCHAIR ACCESSIBLE. NO RESERVATIONS. INEXPENSIVE.

Cafe Claude has the cachet of being hidden away. You just don't happen upon it. When you find the alley (between Bush and Sutter, Kearny and Grant) and see the tiny green metal cafe tables and chairs set outside on the narrow sidewalk, you know you've made a discovery. It only gets better inside. One of the owners was living in Paris and noticed that a building that housed a small bar and tabac in the 13th arrondisement was about to be demolished. He bought all the furnishings from the owner and had them shipped over to Claude Lane. He installed vintage fifties chairs, banquettes and tables, zinc bar and back bar, cinema posters and even condiment trays, in a narrow space with wooden floors, a high ceiling, and big front windows. The only thing that lets you know you're in San Francisco is the crisscrossed metal beams used to earthquake-proof the structure.

The cafe's offerings are handwritten on the traditional French bar menu. A list of the different wine producing regions of France runs down one side with blank lines for the prices of *bouteilles* and *pichets* to be filled in. The actual wine list is on the back and the selection is almost as good with glasses of inexpensive rhone, bourgogne, macon, and California pinot noir among others.

Claude prepares the most delicious *Croque Monsieur*, buttery and crisp, with cheese melted on the outside of a sandwich filled with smoky Black Forest ham. How wonderful this sandwich is with a glass of rhone! It can be preceded by a pretty salade maison of mixed green and red lettuces in a good, strong, vinaigrette. A charcuterie plate brings slices of creamy paté, hams and salamis with toasts spread with olive paste and pimento cheese. A basket of typical French baguettes— airy inside and crisp out—works with them. These very fresh baguettes make for fine prosciutto, Black Forest ham or salami sandwiches spread thickly with sweet butter, layered generously with thin, thin slices of meat and lightened with a few leaves of lettuce. You can add French mustard yourself from the shapely little jar on the table. A tasty red and green cabbage salad, nicoise olives, and cornichons complete the bountiful plates.

Whoever is doing the cooking has a good sense of color as evidenced by a stunning salad of endive, roquefort, walnuts, and red apple in a fine walnut oil vinaigrette. The Caesar of crisp, torn romaine gets a mild, creamy dressing and a lot of parmesan shredded on top of it. It looks and tastes luscious. The salade nicoise also benefits from an excellent dressing and a big portion of high quality Italian canned tuna.

What would a French cafe be without onion soup? Cafe Claude puts out an honest one with a light oniony broth and melted gruyere on a crouton. In a more modern vein, slices of focaccia bread are spread with fresh goat cheese mashed with sun dried tomatoes, walnuts, and herbs and then warmed in the oven. Each day the cafe prepares a special dish. One day brought a savory, warm, open-face prosciutto sandwich with mustard butter, served with a green salad garnished with melon; another, a half avocado stuffed with some pretty awful crab meat, the only disappointing dish I had at the cafe.

The charm of Cafe Claude rests in its unfailing dedication to French style. The food and the wine are exactly right and the people who work there, and in fact, go there, could have stepped out of a neighborhood Parisian cafe.

PATRICIA UNTERMAN

CAFE FANNY ★★★

1603 SAN PABLO, BERKELEY. 524-5447. OPEN MONDAY THROUGH FRIDAY 7 A.M. TO 3 P.M., SATURDAY 8 A.M. TO 4 P.M., SUNDAY 9 A.M. TO 3 P.M. BEER AND WINE. CASH OR CHECK. NO SMOKING. PARTIALLY WHEELCHAIR ACCESSIBLE. NO RESERVATIONS. INEXPENSIVE.

Cafe Fanny is a charming little stand-up cafe in the tradition of tabacs and Italian espresso bars, but the open-faced sandwiches, individual pre-baked pizzas, pastries, and breads are a cut above anything else of their kind. This is because Alice Waters, of Chez Panisse, has put together the menu based on all the Chez Panisse resources for ingredients, and impressed her unfaltering sensibility on it.

This means that you get salads made of the tiniest lettuces topped with baked goat cheese, or a farm egg salad sandwich topped with imported sun-dried tomatoes and salt-packed anchovies. The ready-made sandwiches on fresh Acme bread are always full of juicy ingredients. Little pizzettas have bright, Provencal toppings. For dessert there's wonderful fruit crisps and bowls of fresh fruit with heavy cream.

The cafe au lait served in bowls is strong and fortifying, especially with a couple of poached farm eggs on buttered Acme levain toast. Housemade granola is so popular it has been packaged for customers to take home. Lacy buckwheat crepes served with housemade conserves sell out early. Crunchy millet muffins are some of the best muffins I've ever tasted. Orange juice is always sweet and freshly squeezed, usually a combination of the best citrus around.

Though there is only a stand-up bar and a few benches along the wall, the satisfaction you get from a quick, informal meal here lasts all day. In warm weather people sit outside under a trellis on benches. You can also buy a loaf or two of oven fresh Acme bread and a few bottles of good, inexpensive French wine. Both the Acme bread bakery and Kermit Lynch's wine shop are right next door.

PATRICIA UNTERMAN

CAFE GRECO ★★

423 COLUMBUS AVENUE, SAN FRANCISCO. 397-6261. OPEN MONDAY THROUGH THURSDAY FROM 7 A.M. TO 11:30 P.M., FRIDAY FROM 7 A.M. TO 12:30 A.M., SATURDAY 8 A.M. TO 12:30 A.M., SUNDAY 8 A.M. TO 11:30 P.M. BEER AND WINE. NO CREDIT CARDS. NONSMOKING TABLES AVAILABLE. PARTIALLY WHEELCHAIR ACCESSIBLE. NO RESERVATIONS. INEXPENSIVE.

Cafe Greco distinguishes itself by making consistently excellent coffee. It may seem odd that it's hard to find a great cappuccino in North Beach, but all too often they are unsatisfying. The coffee will be bitter or too weak. The proportion and texture of the steamed milk will be wrong. Whatever fortuitous coming together of espresso machine, coffee grinders, coffee beans (Greco uses Illycaffe), brand of milk and machine operators has occurred at this small cafe, the result has been glorious coffee.

Greco also buys pastries well. Their croissants and raisin rolls are some of the best I've tasted, exceptionally buttery, flaky, and crisp. The rich chocolate cakes are also good. Sandwiches come on crusty toasted focaccia bread, quite different from the softer versions used in other cafes. Filled with different combinations of mozzarella, prosciutto, peppers, hams, basil and tomatoes, they're warm, crunchy, and savory. Pickled Italian vegetables come on the side. Attractive salads are on display in a refrigerated glass counter. The calamari salad stands out for the tenderness and freshness of the squid; its dressing achieves the perfect balance of vinegar and olive oil. Several pasta salads are offered but they don't taste as good as they look. The texture of cold pasta in vinaigrette quickly disintegrates.

This small cafe is perpetually full. With large front windows right on Columbus, Greco draws tourists and regulars alike. The problem is that the chairs and tables are so tightly packed that you can barely squeeze into a chair or get up from one, which you have to do often because there is no table service. Customers wait in a free form line at the counter to order. Coffees are made on the spot, but sandwiches and salads are brought to your table later, usually without enough silverware or napkins. It seems as if you are always navigating the room in circuitous routes for the sugar or a napkin or a fork. And the tables are barely big enough to comfortably read your newspaper. Well, that's life in North Beach. In order to get the best coffee, you suffer the most discomfort.

PATRICIA UNTERMAN

CAFE KATI ★★½

1966 SUTTER STREET, SAN FRANCISCO. 775-7313. OPEN FOR DINNER WEDNESDAY THROUGH SUNDAY FROM 5:30 TO 10 P.M., AND FOR SUNDAY BRUNCH FROM 9 A.M. TO 1 P.M. BEER AND WINE. VISA AND MASTERCARD. 100% NON-SMOKING. FULLY WHEELCHAIR ACCESSIBLE. RESERVATIONS RECOMMENDED. MODERATE.

Cafe Kati is a new bright spot in San Francisco's expanding selection of small chef-owned restaurants. The owners, Tina Kwok and Kirk Webber, took over the space vacated by Borel's Cajun restaurant on Sutter Street, between Fillmore and Webster Streets, and did most of the fixing up themselves.

They've created two pleasant intimate dining rooms bathed in pastel peach with a vivid aqua wood strip painted around the ceiling. The owners have paid attention to details such as black vases with sprigs of rosemary on the white-clothed tables, divided salt and pepper bowls, and black or aqua Fiesta-style pottery dishes that show off the food marvelously.

Unlike the glitzy million-dollar counterparts where the soul of the restaurant is limited to the decor, Cafe Kati makes a strong culinary statement. Most of the food is excellent and even the failures are perfectly executed. The menu, which changes every few weeks, is limited to four appetizers and seven entrees with a nightly special or two. Portions are generous and the most expensive main course is about $13.

One creative combination is a confit duck salad that blends bite-sized portions of poultry with a large julienne of beets and jicama in a light honey-mustard vinaigrette. Arranged on top, pinwheel fashion, are thin slices of ripe pears. A pile of bitter greens cuts the sweetness of this mixture. Another winner is Sonoma greens with phyllo triangles filled with tangy goat cheese.

Webber's creativity shines on ravioli stuffed with dried shiitake mushrooms, salmon, and scallops in thin, almost translucent pasta, and served with fresh tomato coulis. For main courses, grilled pork loin comes with creamy-textured *spatzle* topped with diced tomatoes and scallions. The real masterpieces on the plate, however, are wedges of red tomatoes pickled in a bold blend of red wine vinegar, cumin, turmeric, and other spices and topped with *raita* (a blend of cucumbers and yogurt). These delightful tomatoes show up on several other plates and particularly shine on the vegetarian plate du jour, which consists of half a dozen labor-intensive preparations such as linguine with cream sauce topped with butternut squash, tempura-battered eggplant and squash, a saute of carrots and squash, sauteed bok choy and a ratatouille-like mixture with roasted peppers and mushrooms.

The 15-item wine list is reasonably priced, with most selections below $20. The wines are adequate and cover all the bases, but with such an eclectic menu, it's hard to get the proper variety in such a short list.

The best of the four desserts is the creme brulée. Cafe Kati's version is rich and slightly runny with raspberries on the bottom and a crisp sugar top. The cookie plate also is a good way to end a meal.

Commitment, passion, and vision are clearly evident at Cafe Kati and the service follows the same casually competent track. Within a year, this intimate restaurant should be firmly established as one of the best small chef-owned restaurants in the city.

MICHAEL BAUER

CAFE PESCATORE ★★

2455 MASON STREET, SAN FRANCISCO. 561-1111. OPEN DAILY FOR BREAKFAST, LUNCH AND DINNER FROM 7 A.M. UNTIL 10 P.M., 11 P.M. ON WEEKENDS. FULL BAR. MAJOR CREDIT CARDS. 75% NONSMOKING. FULLY WHEELCHAIR ACCESSIBLE. RESERVATIONS FOR PARTIES OF SIX OR MORE (CALL 30 MINUTES OR SO AHEAD TO BE PUT ON A WAITING LIST). MODERATE.

It's been years since a good fish restaurant has opened at the Wharf, one that would pull in local clientele as well as tourists. Bill Kimpton—the mastermind behind Masa's, Postrio, Kuleto's, and Corona Bar and Grill, to name a few—decided it was time.

On warm days the large windows looking onto Mason Street slide open, so diners indoors sit next to the people at the seven outside tables. It's so refreshing, it doesn't matter that the view is of the Safeway parking lot entrance.

The interior of the 90-seat restaurant includes a large mahogany bar and wainscoting, with an open kitchen backed by multicolor tile, and a dining counter with a canopy of hanging food. The oars and the model ships suspended from the ceiling seem a little much, but the fishing pictures in rich frames that cover every inch of wall space, the rose travertine floors, and the comfortable wicker chairs give a solid, high quality feel.

The bright combinations of food include nightly fish specials such as sauteed halibut on a bed of arugula and leeks with a great spicy mango-currant chutney, or tuna topped with a red pepper rouille nesting on squash blossoms and julienne of carrots and celery.

Cafe Pescatore also makes a perfect rendition of the classic *pasta puttanesca*, a Neapolitan dish with tomato, chiles, anchovy and capers. The seafood stew, with a tomato broth filled with shrimp, squid, mussels, and hunks of white fish, has a gutsy seaside flavor that conjures up images of the early days at the Wharf.

Appetizers also are excellent, including carpaccio with capers, onions, and sun-dried tomatoes; a light and crispy fried calamari; and roasted tomato soup with a spicy kick and a dollop of soft polenta infused with herbs. Pizzas have a tender crust with a crispy outside. The mushroom with roasted garlic pizza is a great combination.

The wine list is small, containing 40 moderately priced selections. Most are easy drinking such as the Righetti Soave, Lungarotti Chardonnay, Fontodi Chianti Classico, or Robert Mondavi Pinot Noir.

The only real disappointment comes with dessert. The selections on my visits were limited and poorly executed and chosen; there was not a single fruit dessert. The best bet is a moist chocolate torte served with whipped mascarpone cheese.

Service is competent, but a subtle attitude prevailed that makes a local feel like a tourist. Waiters don't seem to cultivate the guest; they give superficial answers and bring the check before the first bite of dessert. It's a get-them-in-and-out attitude. Even with the service considered, the good at Cafe Pescatore outweighs the bad. Besides, it's a perfect place to take Aunt Martha when she insists on touring the Wharf.

MICHAEL BAUER

CAFFE ESPRIT ★★

16TH STREET AT ILLINOIS, SAN FRANCISCO. 777-5558. OPEN EVERY DAY FROM 9 A.M. TO 2:30 P.M. BEER AND WINE. MASTERCARD AND VISA. 75% NONSMOKING. PARTIALLY WHEELCHAIR ACCESSIBLE. RESERVATIONS ACCEPTED. INEXPENSIVE.

Caffe Esprit is a restaurant about style. That it happens to be an appealing one is lucky and not surprising. Esprit, the gigantically

■ THE INDUSTRIAL, INDESTRUCTIBLE SIDE OF CAFFE ESPRIT APPEALS TO CHILDREN.

successful clothing manufacturer, has made its mark by designing some of the cleverest garments in the fashion world and reproducing them relatively inexpensively. The colorful Esprit style aspires to an offbeat look, which seems to appeal strongly to the pre-teen and teen set, as evidenced by the demographics in the two-hour line in front of the Esprit factory outlet one summer day.

Located by the bay in a warehouse district, patrons enter Caffe Esprit through a cement courtyard with outdoor tables, benches, and sail-like umbrellas. The industrial, indestructible side of Caffe Esprit appeals to children, who like the climbable fixed benches and elevated round picnic tables downstairs, and the feeling of open space, contributed to by a retractable wall of windows. The elegance of the materials—three inch thick white ash table tops, stone composition floors, a sparkling exhibition kitchen—and the structure's conceptual design make it interesting and dramatic for adults as well.

The food in the Caffe has picked up on the most stylish casual food around today. The small menu offers several salads, pizzas in small and large sizes, sandwiches, hamburgers, a Double Rainbow soda fountain, and an espresso bar. The principles of freshness, lightness, good quality and color are adhered to with a fair amount of rigor. Meats are naturally-raised and vegetables are organic. One of the most popular dishes is Pizza Margherita with a simple topping of cheese, fresh tomatoes, and a sprinkling of fresh basil. A pancetta and garlic pizza has a terrific crisp, sweet white crust topped with a combination of provolone, sun-dried tomatoes, and Italian bacon.

A huge plate of assorted young lettuces strewn with edible blossoms and fresh herbs, ever so lightly dressed with good olive oil and pear vinegar, tastes as pretty as it looks. I love the sandwiches. A grilled chicken breast club constructed on three pieces of airy, toasted brioche bread layered with excellent bacon and flavorful lettuces is amply moistened with chive mayonnaise. The Caffe Hero starts with a fine crusty roll that gets filled with paper thin slices of prosciutto and salami, dry jack and provolone, tissue thin slices of pickle and onion, shredded lettuce, and roasted peppers with vinaigrette and mayonnaise for lubrication. The net effect of all these paper-thin ingredients is juicy, fruity and savory.

The soda fountain puts out a spritzy lemonade in place of soda pop, and a handsome hot fudge sundae with softly whipped cream and roasted pecans. After a session in the ever crowded Esprit factory outlet it's wonderful to have the Caffe next door.

PATRICIA UNTERMAN

CAFFE FREDDY'S ★½

901 COLUMBUS AVENUE, SAN FRANCISCO. 922-0151. OPEN FROM 7:30 A.M. TO 2:30 P.M. MONDAY, WEDNESDAY, THURSDAY, FRIDAY, 8 A.M. TO 4 P.M. SATURDAY, 8:30 A.M. TO 4 P.M. SUNDAY. BEER AND WINE. 75% NONSMOKING. FULLY WHEELCHAIR ACCESSIBLE. NO RESERVATIONS. CASH ONLY. INEXPENSIVE.

Half of this cafe, located just between Fisherman's Wharf and North Beach, is a long blue counter with stools, where you order all the food and drinks. The cooking is done at one end on a miniature pizza oven and a couple of hot plates. An array of pastries, made by the excellent Bette's Ocean View Diner bake shop in Berkeley, look enticing set out in baskets near an old brass espresso machine. The small, daily-changing menu is chalked onto a blackboard over head. You take your food to the other room in the cafe furnished with two rows of large booths that provide great coffeehouse seating. There's space to read the papers, and big picture windows let you look out at clanging cable cars. Paintings of cityscapes by one of the owners, David Bruce, decorate the walls.

The casual food has a logic of its own—mainly because the cooking facilities are so limited. The small pizza oven allows for little pizzas, the delicious crusts prebaked by Bette's bake shop especially for the cafe, the toppings put on at the last minute. One of the best is the Morning Pizzetta topped with pancetta, new potatoes, mozzarella, hard boiled egg slices, and spinach leaves. Another yummy pizza gets a topping of aromatic pesto, melted cheese, and tomato slices. The excellent pesto made at Caffe Freddy's is wonderful on open face sandwiches of polenta with melted cheese.

The green salads are pretty and well dressed. One day the Caffe made a fine walnut, apple, fennel, and shaved parmesan salad. A spinach salad served with croutons smeared with red onion confit makes for a particularly happy combination. A delicious roast chicken sandwich, dressed with garlic mayonnaise and watercress, comes with thick slices of excellent Acme whole grain bread. Eggplant caponata with capers and olives comes on little plates. A garlicky eggplant spread on croutons is served with a parsley leaf salad sprinkled with parmesan. A soup is made each day such as a mildly seasoned lentil.

Unfortunately, coffees can be inconsistent though desserts are not. Bette's fudgey, chewy chocolate cookies, or old fashioned custard filled chocolate eclairs are sent over fresh daily. The housemade apple crisp served with a dollop of creme fraiche is a divine combination of tart apples with crunchy brown sugar and butter topping.

Caffe Freddy's has all the right instincts. The owners are coming at it from a food angle instead of a coffeehouse perspective and this gives customers the best of two worlds. Now North Beach denizens can have something good to eat as well as a congenial place to hang out.

PATRICIA UNTERMAN

CAIRO CAFE ★★

STRAWBERRY VILLAGE SHOPPING CENTER, MILL VALLEY. (FROM SAN FRAN-CISCO, TAKE THE SEMINARY DRIVE EXIT OF 101, TURN LEFT AFTER THE EXIT RAMP). 389-1101. OPEN TUESDAY THROUGH SUNDAY FOR LUNCH AND DINNER. BEER, WINE. VISA, MASTERCARD, AMERICAN EXPRESS. 100% NONSMOKING. FULLY WHEELCHAIR ACCESSIBLE. RESERVATIONS RECOMMENDED ON WEEK-ENDS. INEXPENSIVE.

I take back everything I've ever said about the food in suburban shopping centers. Growing up in Cleveland, my bouts with shopping center cuisine left me deeply traumatized, filled with memories of wilted iceberg lettuce, stale balloon bread, and enough grease to float a ship. I vowed never to do battle with one of these places again.

But now I've found a shopping center restaurant to make me change my mind. Squeezed between a laundromat and a Safeway in Mill Valley's Strawberry Village is the Cairo Cafe, to my knowledge the Bay Area's only Egyptian restaurant. In this eight-table place, where prices are astonishingly reasonable, you can get one of the best meals to be found in Marin County.

Cairo Cafe is the creation of Attif Hassan, the chef, waiter, and—because restaurant help is often hard to get in affluent Marin—sometimes the busboy. No one can accuse Hassan of lacking experi-ence. He first became a restaurant owner, believe it or not, at the age of six. His father had died and his grandfather bought him the restaurant to insure his financial security. It still exists today, the Liberty Restaurant in Cairo, run by his brothers.

Some of the dishes at Cairo Cafe are unique to an Egyptian menu; others can be found in lots of Middle Eastern cuisines. But whatever you order, Hassan's cooking is unusual for the region of the world it represents. He's a fanatic about freshness; whatever possible is prepared to order, and the tomato sauce is made from scratch with fresh tomatoes. Also, he cuts down on salt in his entrees and sugar in his desserts. The result is a real purity of taste—the Middle Eastern spices don't have to compete with excessive salt, grease, or old ingredients.

Start your meal with a *falafel* sandwich to see what I'm talking about. These little balls of garbanzo beans pureed with spices, deep-fried and served in the pocket of a pita bread, can be a greasy disaster if the frying isn't perfect or if they're not made absolutely fresh to order. Hassan not only passes the frying test, but he adds parsley, onions, leeks, and bell peppers to the batter, producing a complex and satisfying blend of flavors. Cairo Cafe proves an oasis for vegetarians, not only for the *falafel,* but also for a simple but delicious dish called *kooshiri.* It starts in the morning when lentils and rice are simmered slowly with sauteed onions. Then, when you order it, Hassan boils macaroni and chops it up; he refuses to do the macaroni in advance because it won't taste fresh. You get a heaping plate of the lentils, rice, and macaroni topped with a tomato sauce made from fresh tomatoes, garlic, vinegar, allspice, and cumin.

You can start your meal with a Cairo combo, a platter that would be plenty as an appetizer for three people. Grape leaves, cabbage, green peppers, and potatoes are all stuffed with an aromatic mixture of ground beef, rice, parsley, onions, fresh tomatoes, dill, garlic, and cumin. The stuffed potatoes are the most interesting; I've never eaten anything like them before. Equally good as starters are the creamy *hummus* (mashed garbanzo beans with sesame seed paste, lemon juice, and spices) and the *baba ghanoug,* the garlicky puree of smoked eggplant and olive oil.

STAN SESSER

CAMBODIANA ★★★

2156 UNIVERSITY AVE. (ABOVE SHATTUCK), BERKELEY. 843-4630. OPEN FOR LUNCH 11:30 A.M TO 3 P.M. MONDAY THROUGH FRIDAY AND FOR DINNER FROM 5 TO 10 P.M. MONDAY THROUGH THURSDAY, TO 10:30 P.M. FRIDAY AND SATURDAY, AND TO 9:30 P.M. SUNDAY. BEER, WINE. VISA, MASTERCARD, AMERICAN EXPRESS. 100% NONSMOKING. FULLY WHEELCHAIR ACCESSIBLE. RESERVATIONS RECOMMENDED ON WEEKENDS. INEXPENSIVE TO MODERATE.

California cuisine, as practiced by some of the better restaurants in the Bay Area, has borrowed a lot from Asia in the past couple of years: new spices, new ingredients, different cooking techniques. But when we think about the virtues of Asian food, we never think much about the sauces. Even when they're not too cornstarchy or too salty, Asian sauces in themselves aren't usually interesting enough or sophisticated enough to be worth much attention. A Cambodian restaurant in Berkeley called Cambodiana, however, represents a dramatic exception. Cambodia was occupied for almost a century by the French; this may have been a disaster politically but it definitely proved a triumph gastronomically. The French adapted their cuisine to the native ingredients that were available; the Cambodians liked what emerged and integrated some of that into their own culinary tradition. One result was sauces for Cambodian dishes as flavorful and refined as French sauces.

When you taste what Cambodiana Restaurant does with sauces, you'll want to push away the beer and order a nice bottle of French wine. The whole menu is grouped around sauces; six different ones ranging from light and delicate to rich and pungent. Under each sauce,

■ THE SPICES AND THE CAMBODIANA SAUCE ALSO DO WONDERS FOR A HEAPING PLATE OF FOUR LAMB CHOPS, ACCOMPANIED BY SAUTEED MUSHROOMS, TOPPED WITH GARLIC AND BUTTER.

there are several entrees you can choose from. But the sauces aren't the only thing good about Cambodiana. The ingredients are splendid; everything is sparkling fresh, including first-rate fish and beautiful al dente vegetables served with each entree. And although you're eating a meal as satisfying as a fine French dinner, you're paying insanely low prices.

The most conventional dishes on the menu are the Cambodian appetizers, but that doesn't make them any less good. The chicken salad is a delectable blend of shredded chicken breast, cabbage, chopped peanuts, carrots, and fresh mint leaves, in a tangy orange dressing of lemon juice, garlic, fish sauce, and other ingredients. It looks pretty, blends both crunchy and soft textures, and the dressing is so appealing you'll be tempted to spoon up every drop. The tiny little spring rolls stuffed with shrimp and ground pork turn out to be both greaseless and tasty. Stuffed, boneless chicken wings are like a delicious spicy sausage, deep-fried and then sliced.

Now you have to choose among the six sauces. My only advice is to have one of each since they're all distinctive and all excellent. But several of the entrees fall into the "can't be missed" category. For people who aren't great fans of steaks—and I'm one of them—the beefsteak angel could change your mind. It's a good piece of New York steak, grilled medium rare, but that's the least of it. The steak is enlivened immensely by chopped lemongrass and red chilis on top, and a remarkable sauce (called Kandal cottage sauce) that includes chili, garlic, shallots, lemongrass, black pepper, and lime juice. The spices and the Cambodiana sauce also do wonders for a heaping plate of four lamb chops, accompanied by sauteed mushrooms, topped with garlic and butter, and served in a sauce of lemongrass, galangal, ginger, lemon leaves, and garlic.

Then comes the Naga princess sauce (the sauces all have real Cambodian names, but on the menu they get fanciful English names.) It's a creamy sauce of tamarind, galangal, ginger, lemongrass, garlic, and coconut milk, and a good way to try it is on juicy boneless chunks of charbroiled chicken. Salmon in Kandal curry sauce is a thick, perfectly poached slice of salmon topped with curried shrimp, in an aromatic brown sauce that can be ordered fiery hot. If this isn't enough evidence of the wonders Cambodiana works with fish, try the delicate catfish filet served in a spicy, orange-colored curry sauce.

STAN SESSER

CAMPTON PLACE ★★★½

340 STOCKTON STREET, SAN FRANCISCO. 781-5155. OPEN 7 A.M. TO 2:30 P.M.,
MONDAY THROUGH FRIDAY, 8 A.M. TO 2:30 P.M. SATURDAY AND SUNDAY; DIN-
NER 5:30 TO 10 P.M. SUNDAY THROUGH THURSDAY, 5:30 TO 10:30 P.M. FRIDAY AND
SATURDAY. FULL BAR. ALL MAJOR CREDIT CARDS. 85% NONSMOKING. FULLY
WHEELCHAIR ACCESSIBLE. RESERVATIONS RECOMMENDED. VERY EXPENSIVE.

Jan Birnbaum has been at the helm of the Campton Place kitchen for a year and a half now, stepping into the shoes of Brad Ogden, who put the restaurant on the map. Birnbaum has established his own solid repertory of dishes on a menu he changes every month. A recent visit confirmed that Campton Place remains one of the top rooms in the city, for service, ambience, and luxurious food, due in large part to the personal energy Birnbaum brings to his position.

Campton Place broke the mold of what people expected in a fancy restaurant when it opened almost seven years ago, and continues to do so. Instead of being French, the food is American. Instead of tuxedoed waiters and a commanding maitre d', the dining room is run by women. The wine list is mostly California; the dining room brighter, more open, simpler than most other expensive rooms. Yet all the trappings of a posh experience are in place, too. The tables are laid with Wedgewood, graceful crystal glasses, and silver. Tables are large, napkins gigantic, chairs soft and substantial. The acoustics of the room and placement of tables allow for comfortable conversation. But what really sets Campton Place apart is service—not only personal service from a well trained staff, but food service, in the range of dishes available at all three meals, and the way food is presented.

Caviar service is offered and an ounce of sturgeon eggs at Campton Place makes a memorable present for someone you want to treat. Diners are given a card that offers three kinds of high quality, Petrossian caviar—beluga, osetra, and sevruga—priced by the gram. The caviar comes in a little glass jar set on a special bowl of crushed ice. Tiny Chinese saucers of capers, creme fraiche, onions, chives, and sieved egg are placed around it. Warm, crustless triangles of toast and sweet butter are set on the table and everyone gets a tiny, silver, demitasse spoon. To complete the experience, you can order a glass of iced vodka or a flute of champagne off the same card.

Part of the pleasure of dining in an expensive restaurant is being able to choose from many lavish dishes. Campton Place fulfills that expectation. On a recent autumn menu, sweet, velvet-textured, seared foie gras came with tiny green beans and toasted hazelnuts. Three briny, small fried oysters were the garnish for a brilliant flavored celery root soup. Each bite of a seemingly odd combination of gossamer ravioli filled with butternut squash in a pancetta flavored sauce studded with leeks and cranberries, tasted like a whole Thanksgiving dinner.

A breast of guinea hen, moist, tender, and gamey, was topped with a crisp sausage dressing and supported by a ragout of acorn squash and wild mushrooms, a luscious fall plate. A thick, moist filet of salmon roasted in a horseradish-breadcrumb crust was served with a gratin of scalloped potatoes infused with lobster. A tender loin of lamb came on a bed of saucy rice and black eyed peas, which New Orleans native Birnbaum calls Hoppin' John risotto. A meaty sauce, tingling with fresh mint, worked smartly. For dessert, a thin, hot apple tart, baked to order, lived up to the rest of the meal.

Service, as always, was informed, anticipatory, and gracious. The basket of warm corn sticks, miniature biscuits, and chewy white bread, always gets the meals at Campton Place off to a good start, though the extensive American wine list is marked up dizzyingly high.

It's a feat to keep any restaurant vital, year after year, and particularly difficult to keep people coming to very expensive ones. Campton Place succeeds by keeping its standards as high as its prices.

PATRICIA UNTERMAN

RISTORANTE CAPELLINI ★★

310 BALDWIN (AT B STREET), SAN MATEO. 348-2296. OPEN MONDAY THROUGH FRIDAY 11:30 A.M. TO 2 P.M. FOR LUNCH; 5 TO 10 P.M. FOR DINNER MONDAY THROUGH SATURDAY, UNTIL 9 P.M. ON SUNDAY. FULL BAR. VISA, MASTERCARD, AMERICAN EXPRESS. 95% NONSMOKING. FULLY WHEELCHAIR ACCESSIBLE. RESERVATIONS RECOMMENDED. MODERATE.

From the time it opened, Ristorante Capellini, a big, brassy Pat Kuleto-designed extravaganza in downtown San Mateo, was an unmitigated hit. Owner Aaron Ferer, who also owns Carpaccio in Menlo Park, spent well more than $1 million on the interior and has been able to achieve an urban feel with surburban prices.

This Cal-Ital restaurant, with a menu similar to Il Fornaio and Kuleto's, blazes no culinary trails. Preparations are simple but the results can be very good. One outstanding dish is roast chicken, permeated with smoke after slowly roasting on an impressive spit in the open kitchen. It's served with grilled vegetables that include incredibly sweet carrots, barely warm and under-seasoned tomatoes, excellent zucchini cooked to tenderness, and somewhat gluey roast potatoes. Calamari steak with lemon butter is another pleasant surprise. It comes lightly coated in an egg batter with just enough sauce to make it glisten.

Three different pasta dishes suffered basic preparation problems. Sauces were fine but the pasta stuck together. The pizzas also were a disappointment. The cornmeal-flecked crust was soggy and didn't support the cheese and sausage, and the topping was bitter with garlic. Instead, try the gutsy square of polenta, moistened with cheese and

56

topped with a zesty marinara sauce and pesto. For a lighter start, eggplant is delicious, dressed with a sweet-sour Champagne vinaigrette with slivers of carmelized garlic and shredded mint.

Desserts on all visits seemed to have the same texture, with fruit in short supply. The best bet is the walnut torte on a sturdy shortbread-style crust and blanketed with gooey chocolate.

The 50-item wine list needs some work. Although it's well-priced, the selections appear to lack unity. Varietals such as pinot noir, zinfandel, and merlot are given cursory nods. And, on our visit, the lone merlot wasn't available. There are six chianti, but it's hard to choose because there are no vintages listed, and the waiters don't know the list. This becomes even more perplexing when you see the sophisticated cellar, which is the focal point for the downstairs dining room.

You can see Pat Kuleto's touch everywhere in the 165-seat restaurant, which consists of a mezzanine, an intimate downstairs room, and the main dining area that's visually partitioned into three sections. It has lofty ceilings, a basket-weave marble floor, an impressive dark wood bar backed by mirrors, and Kuleto's trademark exotic light fixtures.

As with everything Kuleto does, the design alone would pack people in. However, the service needs an overhaul. The staff is friendly, but not well trained. Though the food at Capellini is very good, it has the potential to be much better, with a few adjustments.

MICHAEL BAUER

CAPP'S CORNER ★★

1600 POWELL, SAN FRANCISCO. 989-2589. OPEN FOR LUNCH MONDAY THROUGH FRIDAY 11:30 A.M. TO 2:30 P.M., FOR DINNER MONDAY THROUGH THURSDAY 4:30 TO 10:30 P.M., UNTIL 11 P.M. FRIDAY AND SATURDAY, SUNDAY 4 TO 10:30 P.M. FULL BAR. MASTERCARD, VISA, DINERS CLUB. 20% NONSMOKING. PARTIALLY WHEELCHAIR ACCESSIBLE. RESERVATIONS ACCEPTED. INEXPENSIVE.

An old North Beach standby, Capp's ambience hasn't been changed one bit over the years. The old Victorian bar at the front of the restaurant still stays active all day with a neighborhood clientele. The Celebrity Corner of the dining room has remained intact with photos of the All Time Italian-American Baseball Team, Italian boxers in action poses, and autographed star photos of actors like Jack Lord and Lorne Greene. This gallery is hung above an alcove of red and white checked Formica tables with red vinyl banquettes and matching vinyl seated wooden chairs. Ancient linoleum floors, acoustic ceilings, and plywood veneer walls give Capp's that authentic North Beach look. Modest though it is, Capp's dining room on weekday nights is sprinkled with sportscasters, private eyes, journalists, and big eaters.

■ **WHENEVER WILLY BISHOP'S CALAMARI IS POSTED ON THE BLACKBOARD, ORDER IT. IT'S A SICILIAN SQUID DISH BY WAY OF THAILAND. THE SQUID STAYS UNDISPUTEDLY FRESH AND DELICATELY TENDER BATHED IN THE SPICY VEGETABLE STEW.**

The family style meals, prepared by locally well-known chef/character Willy Bishop, are fresh, lively, and infinitely better tasting than any served before Mr. Bishop hired on.

One night, dinner began with a tureen of fine minestrone soup made with real stock, lots of cabbage, celery, beans, and pasta tubes. The vegetables weren't cooked to death and the broth had a deep natural flavor. A crisp, hand-torn romaine salad was dressed in a basic, tart Italian vinaigrette amplified by garlic. A big slice of lasagne followed, homey, not too rich, but substantial with cheese and a good tomato sauce.

You get to choose your main course from seven or eight items and you will not be let down even after all that preliminary eating. We were served tender, succulent slices of gently garlicked roast pork, a half of a baked chicken with a crisp skin and moist flesh, and spicy, lean Italian sausages in a chunky tomato and green pepper sauce. Rosemary-scented roasted potatoes and the most delicious freshly cooked chard and zucchini accompanied the meats.

At another meal you might get a peppery, mushroom barley soup made with the rich stock; then, al dente penne, tube shaped pasta, bathed in a beautiful light green basil sauce made with butter and lots of parmesan. A large, thin veal T-bone chop is carefully grilled and served with a Provencal-inspired sauce of peppers, mushrooms and tomatoes, all finely minced and incorporated into reduced stock. Whenever Willy Bishop's calamari is posted on the blackboard, order it. He quickly sautees it with fresh tomatoes, red peppers, spicy green chiles, and whole leaves of basil with a sort of bolognese sauce base. It's a Sicilian squid dish by way of Thailand. The squid stays undisputedly fresh and delicately tender bathed in the spicy vegetable stew.

The braised dishes can taste a little tired, like rabbit in tomato sauce which had lost its spunk from spending too much time in the stewing pot. Osso bucco, a thick slice of veal shank simmered with mushrooms, tomatoes, and stock satisfied without thrilling. If you stick to the roasted meats, cooked-to-order chops and sautees, you can't go wrong. These dishes are accompanied by the extraordinary sauteed vegetables, again, freshly and crisply cooked. All meals end with passable coffee and commercial spumoni.

PATRICIA UNTERMAN

CARIBBEAN ZONE ★

55 NATOMA STREET, SAN FRANCISCO. 541-9465. OPEN FOR LUNCH MONDAY THROUGH FRIDAY 11 A.M. TO 2:30 P.M., FOR DINNER MONDAY THROUGH SATURDAY 5 TO 11 P.M., SUNDAY 5 TO 9:30 P.M. FULL BAR. VISA AND MASTERCARD. 65% NONSMOKING. PARTIALLY WHEELCHAIR ACCESSIBLE. RESERVATIONS FOR PARTIES OF EIGHT OR MORE. MODERATE.

Trader Vic may have invented the tropical hideaway where potent drinks and deep fried *pupus* put patrons in a carefree vacation mood, but the Caribbean Zone takes the concept to new, campy heights. Like Trader Vic's, the Caribbean Zone is located in an alley. When you finally find it off Howard Street, between First and Second, you marvel at how inviting a sheet metal beach shack under a freeway can look. When you walk into a jungle of plastic tropical plants complete with a waterfall tumbling over artificial rocks, and a real airplane cabin as a cocktail lounge, you know it's time to forgo the resolves of moderation and get into some tropical drinks.

The tropical drinks here are good and expensive. Unlike the cloyingly sweet concoctions in Cosmo Alley, these use fresh fruits and juices and restraint with sweeteners. They also have ridiculous names like Sex in the Jungle, which is a rum spiked slush of guayabana pulp with quite a bit of nutmeg sprinkled on it, or, my favorite, Goomba Boomba, fresh banana, lime and rum blended with ice.

As you can imagine, the Caribbean Zone is a place where life can be zany and laid back. The signature Caribbean weathered wooden chairs, tables, and walls in pastel shades signal that beach attire is welcome. I like the wacky stuff like the airplane cabin, the outside of which serves as the back of the bar. The inside, a little world unto itself, is outfitted with real airplane seats, and breezes from a large fan by the waterfall. Video monitors of the moving sky serve as windows along one side of the cabin while the other windows look down on the bustling jungle.

Waiting for a table with tropical drink in hand can work up an appetite and here the Caribbean Zone falters a bit trying to put out a theme menu that loosely covers the east coast of Mexico and the multi-cultured Caribbean islands. Inventing a cuisine is difficult and this place doesn't seem to have an experienced kitchen. Some things turn out greasy, sloppy, not tasty at all. Other items are passable, especially after a couple of Goomba Boombas.

In the "Whets" section, the tender conch fritters served with garlic mayonnaise are nicely seasoned if greasy. *Piononos* are bland, heavy, plantain rolls wrapped around an oily, spicy hot, minced beef filling. They are served with a strong onion and pineapple relish, spiked with chiles. The Yucatan Tamales are leaden and taste only of cinnamon. An awful coleslaw with crab and raisins dressed in an assertive ginger mayonnaise is redeemed only by the crunchy, fresh cabbage that is used. Corn chowder has a comforting, creamy broth seasoned only with a hint of chile. The best bet is a jerk chicken salad of redleaf lettuce, chunks of cold grilled marinated chicken, and crisp carrots and cucumber in a hot/sweet dressing.

I can recommend three of the main courses—a *chipotle* chili-rubbed loin of pork, moist and tender, fanned out in slices on a bed of black beans, fried plantains and a strange papaya chutney that tasted like watermelon pickle; a marinated ribeye steak smothered with onions, peppers and sauteed garlic served with absolutely tasteless, mealy, yucca fries; and jerk chicken rubbed in a lively spice mixture and grilled.

For dessert I would choose a fresh tasting mango mousse or Chunkey Monkey Ice Cream studded with banana, chocolate and nuts, drizzled with fudge sauce and served in a buttery lace cookie cup. A strange, dense, gelatinous creation called Banana Ground Nut Pie comes from some part of the Caribbean I hope never to visit. Decent espresso and trademarked Caribbean Zone sparkling water will be necessary at some point in the meal.

Don't get me wrong. This place is fun. I'd slip into the Caribbean Zone with great anticipation on any occasion that called for Sex in the Jungle.

PATRICIA UNTERMAN

CASA MADRONA ★★★

801 BRIDGEWAY, SAUSALITO. 331-5888. OPEN FOR LUNCH MONDAY THROUGH FRIDAY FROM 11:30 A.M TO 2:30 P.M.; DINNER EVERY NIGHT FROM 6 TO 10 P.M.; BRUNCH ON SUNDAY FROM 10 A.M. TO 2:30 P.M. BEER AND WINE. MASTERCARD, VISA, AMERICAN EXPRESS. SMOKING IN THE BAR ONLY. NOT WHEELCHAIR ACCESSIBLE. RESERVATIONS RECOMMENDED ESPECIALLY ON WEEKENDS. MODERATE TO EXPENSIVE.

With its panoramic view of the Marin side of the bay, the Casa Madrona provides one of the most romantic settings in Northern California for dining. That the kitchen also turns out excellent meals is an added advantage and comes as no surprise. The Casa Madrona has a long history of showcasing first-rate chefs, some of whom have moved on to open their own places. The current chef, Kirke Byers, combines a contemporary sensibility with high level professional technique. His colorful dishes draw on the wide range of seasonal produce available in Bay Area markets and he is able to cook meat, fish and poultry to make them taste their best.

The dining room at Casa Madrona is part of a sprawling hotel perched on a hill overlooking the bay. Though customers enter off Bridgeway, Sausalito's main tourist boulevard, they take an elevator to the fifth level and then walk up two flights of stairs. They are rewarded for their climb by being able to sit in a glassed-in aerie—if they call ahead to reserve a table in it—or a more conventional room that still affords a wonderful view of the bay. During the day in particular, the vista and light in the glassed-in room is spectacular.

While you're gazing at the view, nibble on a delicious Asian chicken salad with toasted cashews, napa cabbage, shredded carrots, and moist chicken all tossed in a vivid peanut-sesame-scented vinaigrette. Grilled scallops on greens is also stylishly done, tossed with tasty, small lettuces of great variety, peeled orange segments, and an orange vinaigrette.

A pizzetta comes on a round of focaccia strewn with roasted eggplant, squashes, and red peppers with a nice balance of fontina and pesto melted underneath. One of the most appealing dishes, salmon cakes, are made with fresh, moist salmon mashed with red onion, celery, and a whisper of ginger, sauteed until crusty on the outside but still soft and fragile inside. A creamy, piquant tartar sauce is spooned over them and a lovely slaw of radishes, napa cabbage, carrots, and slivered snow peas accompanies.

Dessert brings a sensational, crumbly, individual nut cake, split and filled with whipped cream, dried cherries, pecans, and caramel sauce, and an exquisite, moist, coconut cake with lemon, lime, and orange curds between the layers.

At dinner, I felt that the kitchen was pushing a little to dress dishes up. For example, a whole leaf Caesar salad had a pleasant dressing, but I'm not sure if it showed off to best advantage prosciutto-thin slices of the excellent, smoky duck breast that came with it. The main courses demonstrate how well the kitchen prepares such varied meats as pheasant, chicken, pork, and lamb. They all retained their juices, natural flavor, and tenderness without being undercooked. Their tastiness also speaks to the high quality of the ingredients used by the restaurant.

Service is professional and cordial. At lunch the waiter helped to arrange the courses so that they would come out of the kitchen in a timely manner. A thoughtfully compiled wine list concentrates on better California bottles. Both coffee and espresso are aromatic and full flavored.

The panoramic view is the main decor attraction of the restaurant, but white tablecloths, candlelight, and live piano music at dinner support the romantic image. The Casa Madrona at night makes for a smart assignation—it's kept so dark, no one could ever spot you. During the day, when the dining room is flooded with light and Sausalito looks like a fishing village down below, you can go there to admire the food and the view.

PATRICIA UNTERMAN

CASA ORINDA RESTAURANT ★★½

20 BRYANT WAY, ORINDA 254-2981. OPEN FOR DINNER FROM 4 TO 10 P.M. SUNDAY THROUGH THURSDAY, UNTIL 11 P.M. FRIDAY AND SATURDAY. FULL BAR. MAJOR CREDIT CARDS. 30% NONSMOKING. PARTIALLY WHEELCHAIR ACCESSIBLE. RESERVATIONS RECOMMENDED. EXPENSIVE.

In the restaurant world, where trends change as quickly as the fog comes in, it's great to find a business such as Casa Orinda, which has been under the same ownership for 25 years. The food is familiar Italian-American, but it's fresh and done very well. It proves that classics such as chicken cacciatore can be as vibrant today as they were in an earlier time.

Casa Orinda has a long history here. It was a popular hangout with workers building the Caldecott Tunnel in the early 1930s. The food acquired the Italian leanings about 25 years ago when the business was taken over by John Goyak and his family.

The interior has been spruced up, with a moose over the fireplace and antlers above the bar bespeaking a cowboy motif. The high-gloss tables are branded. Some chairs have palomino-patterned cushions. Plates sport brown cowboy boots, and cups are decorated with Stetsons. Fortunately, the large bouquets of fresh flowers and the young enthusiastic staff help to lighten the mood.

Casa Orinda does the simple specialties so well, it's like having dinner with a long-forgotten friend. The appetizer of fettuccine sings with garlic, oil, and cheese. Cannelloni, smothered with cheese and a filling of ground veal and spinach, miraculously retains distinctive tastes and textures. Tomatoes Macedonia, tomatoes on a bed of iceberg lettuce and topped with thin slices of red onions, is served with a creamy Italian dressing that has a powerful tang to pull the elements together. It's great with a sprinkling of fresh pepper.

Four pieces of crispy golden-skinned fried chicken are served with a choice of potatoes. French fries are good, but need salt, and the mashed potatoes are creamy with just a few lumps so you know they're homemade. Veal cutlet is breaded in the same manner as the chicken and tastes like the best Texas chicken-fried steak you'll ever find. The cream gravy underneath is splendid; light and fresh tasting with the added zing of ground white pepper. One specialty is a 12-ounce veal T-bone blanketed in sliced mushrooms. It's simple but delicious.

Like the food menu, the wine list lacks innovation, but it's selected to be easy to drink and reasonably priced. You'll find vintners such as Joseph Phelps, Beaulieu, Louis Martini, Sterling, Grgich Hills, Raymond and Wente offering a good mix of varietals and styles. Desserts are worth ordering. Cheesecake has a rich, crumbly texture with a sour cream topping. The pecan pie is excellent, with a flaky crust, a medium caramel-colored filling that's not too sweet and fresh-toasted pecans on top. Also, try the lemon tart which sports an intense tang or the mud pie with a crust of ground Oreo cookies flavored with coffee and topped with housemade mocha ice cream, hot fudge sauce, whipped cream and more ground cookies.

It was the desserts that finally wiped away the initial skepticism I felt upon encountering the Wild West theme decor. Casa Orinda proved that anything prepared well is worth eating.

MICHAEL BAUER

RISTORANTE CASTELLUCCI ★★

561 COLUMBUS AVENUE, SAN FRANCISCO. 362-2774. OPEN MONDAY THROUGH THURSDAY 5 TO 10 P.M., FRIDAY AND SATURDAY 5 TO 11 P.M. BEER AND WINE. ALL MAJOR CREDIT CARDS. 40% NONSMOKING. PARTIALLY WHEELCHAIR ACCES-SIBLE. RESERVATIONS SUGGESTED. MODERATE.

This shiny, white tiled restaurant is bright and welcoming, with open kitchens, wooden tables and a banquette along one wall. Unlike many touristy North Beach eateries, Castellucci's reasonable prices and simple, satisfying food attracts a wide range of patrons, including many North Beach regulars.

The soups are a high point. Colorful minestrone with big chunks of vegetables and rich, prosciutto flavored broth, a superb, lentil soup thick with beans, or a silken leek and potato can be the centerpiece of a meal. The salads are not sophisticated but they radiate freshness. The mixed salad brings romaine, tomatoes, radishes, and cucumber in a tart house vinaigrette. The beautiful, whole-leaf Caesar is a bargain, and the tomato salad with anchovies and onions keeps up its standards despite the season.

Other attractive starters include a slice of grilled polenta napped with fresh tomato sauce and a creamy gorgonzola sauce, a nicely presented veal carpaccio dressed with olive oil, capers, and shaved parmesan, and a colorful plate of very vinegary pickled vegetables for those who like tart things.

The constructed-to-order ravioli are exceptional—tender, light, and irresistible. One day they were stuffed with eggplant puree and topped with fresh tomato sauce; on another, with an aromatic mushroom and dried porcini filling napped in a creamy, tomato sauce. Or, you can choose your pasta shape, like fettucine, linguini or spaghetti, and then select a pesto, fresh tomato or creamy tomato sauce to go on it.

Careful grilling is done here, especially on an Argentinian steak called *Churrasco al Chimichurri*, a marinated New York with a sauce of parsley, garlic and red peppers. Marinated porkchops and a long, skinny, housemade sausage on a bed of spinach are excellent too.

Soft Italian ice cream, with real, burgundy-colored maraschino cherries and their liqueur drizzled over it, makes for a wonderful dessert. The flan is very firm and the tiramisu heavily soaked with coffee syrup. Espresso is excellent.

Castellucci defies classification. Marta and Jose Castelluci come from Argentina and the national penchant for grilled meats shows up on the menu. But the pasta and appetizers are Italian, and the salads American, so the cooking is a home grown expression of three nationalities. What sets this North Beach restaurant apart is the warmth with which this melange is put on the table. Castellucci fulfills my idea of a good neighborhood restaurant. It's not a place you'd drive across town for, but the kind of place you'd drop into when you were hungry. Once you're there, you don't want to leave.

PATRICIA UNTERMAN

CELADON ★★

881 CLAY, SAN FRANCISCO. 982-1168. OPEN MONDAY THROUGH FRIDAY 10 A.M. TO 3 P.M., 5:30 TO 10:30 P.M., SATURDAY AND SUNDAY 9 A.M. TO 3 P.M., 5:30 TO 10:30 P.M. FULL BAR. ALL MAJOR CREDIT CARDS. 50% NONSMOKING. PARTIALLY WHEELCHAIR ACCESSIBLE. RESERVATIONS RECOMMENDED. MODERATE.

Celadon is one of the few, dressy Chinese restaurants in Chinatown. The mysterious gray-green color of celadon pottery, after which the restaurant was named, makes its appearance in the carpeting, the napkins, and on interior columns. The white linen covered tables are set with rice shot porcelain tea cups, silver soup spoons, candles in lamps, and a silver rack upon which to lay chopsticks and other utensils between courses. Upholstered banquettes and solid, tall backed, lacquered chairs provide dignified seating. The front door of Celadon is a huge, stunning piece of cast bronze. Yet for all its flourishes and amenities, Celadon remains a moderately priced restaurant, less expensive than the older Grant Street contingent of fancy Chinese restaurants.

You can get a meal composed of delicacies like Peking duck, steamed lobster, and deep-fried squab for a moderate sum, and this is with formal table service in which dishes are brought out sequentially, presented, and then carefully arranged on individual plates. Warm towels appear after courses that require the use of fingers. The whole experience is carefully orchestrated. Everything is done for you at a leisurely pace that allows for good talk around the table. You feel pampered and civilized at your meals.

The menu is reassuringly small by the standards of most Chinese restaurants. Dishes from a number of different provinces are represented though the kitchen seems most at home with Cantonese-style cooking.

The lobster dishes are unique here, especially Steamed Lobster, Celadon-style, which is served in a small amount of intensely flavored broth infused with garlic and actually thickened with melted scallions and lobster fat. The tender meat, which easily came out of the shell, and the sweet lobster tomalley are tip-offs that the lobster was alive seconds before it was steamed. My only regret was that I didn't have a piece of French bread to soak up the fantastic liquid. A similar dish, Lobster Steamed in Garlic Sauce, was more delicate. Its light, clear, aromatic sauce had the pungent but unintrusive quality of long simmered garlic.

Another signature dish at Celadon, a soup cooked and presented in a coconut called Coconut Nectar, tastes and looks like a chowder except that the milk comes from fresh coconuts and the broth is studded with tiny shrimp, bits of winter melon, and pine nuts. Squab Shatin, a preparation for squab lovers, is for those who like the gamey quality of pigeon. The aged birds are deep-fried with absolutely no spices or aromatics. The skin emerges dark and crisp, the flesh deep brown and creamy. You dip the pieces into finely ground white pepper and salt for seasoning.

There are plenty of familiar dishes on the menu as well. Potstickers are just about perfect here with thin, tender noodle coverings and juicy meat fillings. Minced Squab in a Green Purse is a crunchy dice of squab, fresh water chestnuts, pine nuts, and black mushrooms quickly stir fried and presented in iceberg lettuce cups. One of the most addictively tasty dishes in all of Chinese cuisine is Peking duck and Celadon makes a worthy production of it. Both soft white steamed buns and thin white pancakes serve as receptacles for the burnished ducks, skillfully sliced at tableside by the white gloved maitre d'.

After lobster and duck, it's always nice to eat some simply steamed vegetables. Celadon finishes off both steamed Chinese broccoli and bok choy with a quick turn in the wok in the lightest of sauces. Bowls of rice are served at the end of the meal unless requested sooner. Share Celadon's rich coconut custard for dessert. It has the flavor of real coconuts.

PATRICIA UNTERMAN

CHA CHA CHA ★★

1805 HAIGHT, SAN FRANCISCO. 386-5758. OPEN FOR LUNCH MONDAY THROUGH FRIDAY 11:30 A.M. TO 3 P.M., SATURDAY AND SUNDAY NOON TO 3 P.M.; FOR DINNER SUNDAY THROUGH THURSDAY 5 TO 11 P.M., FRIDAY AND SATURDAY 5:30 P.M. TO MIDNIGHT. BEER AND WINE. NO CREDIT CARDS. 20% NONSMOKING. PARTIALLY WHEELCHAIR ACCESSIBLE. NO RESERVATIONS. INEXPENSIVE.

Cha Cha Cha is a vibrant little place in the Haight. It's a complete original. A tiny storefront, the dining room has one tall brick wall stencilled with palm trees and a high ceiling with green lattice work which sprouts spotlights in different colors. The whole place must have been put together on a shoestring, but the ideas all work. When you walk in, smells of spicy grilled meats whet your appetite, the best effect of all. Most likely every seat will be taken, so you move to the back of the restaurant, past three wooden booths painted red and blue and five or six tables, to a tiled tapas bar with a few stools. A bulbous glass jar of sangria sits at one end, afloat with orange slices. You can wait agreeably there for a table, eating tapas and drinking glasses of sangria.

The tapas include charred, grilled, marinated whole sardines which are absolutely delicious; succulent marinated chicken wings bathed in a dusky garlic sauce; thin strips of beef coated with searing hot, cracked black pepper in a thick, slightly sweet cream sauce; and peeled shrimp in a fantastic, hot, creamy Cajun sauce pink with cayenne. Piquant cold mussels on the half shell topped with a fresh tomato and onion relish have an authentic Caribbean-Creole flavor. Thinly sliced scallops are full of the pungent flavors of garlic, red and yellow peppers, and white wine in which they were sauteed.

The main courses are not as much fun as the little dishes though several are excellent. A Spanish-style pan-fried trout, crisp and succulent, gets a sprightly sherry and brown butter sauce. I also like a blackened hamburger that stays moist and rare, with a side of creamy sauce infused with Cajun spices. All entrees come with mashed potatoes and carrots, and a medley of vegetables. You also get a tiny cup of a cilantro and chile-spiked chicken soup that is hot, lemony, and full of big chunks of chicken.

For dessert, a chocolate mousse cake with raspberry sauce is light, and not too sweet.

The unifying theme behind all the food seems to be a Caribbean-Creole mix of Spanish, Cuban, African, and Latin American flavors. The emphasis is on spices and hot chiles. Most everything has a kick to it, just like the dance rhythm the restaurant was named for.

PATRICIA UNTERMAN

CHAMPA THAI CUISINE ★★

5249 MISSION STREET (NEAR GENEVA), SAN FRANCISCO. 584-3629. OPEN FOR LUNCH MONDAY THROUGH FRIDAY 11:30 A.M. TO 3 P.M.; DINNER FROM 5 TO 10 P.M. BEER AND WINE. MASTERCARD AND VISA. 80% NONSMOKING. PARTIALLY WHEELCHAIR ACCESSIBLE. RESERVATIONS RECOMMENDED FOR PARTIES OF THREE OF MORE. INEXPENSIVE.

At Champa Thai Cuisine the kitchen turns out juicy pork and chicken satays fragrant with lemongrass; crisp and clean Thai spring rolls filled with a particularly delicious mixture of cabbage, minced

pork and bean thread noodles; and dense, deep fried fish cakes paired
with chile-marinated cucumbers and cool lettuce leaves.

Thai salads blast your mouth with hot chiles and cools it down with
crisp vegetables and lime. They are some of my favorite dishes. *Som-
tom*, a shredded green papaya salad topped with succulent whole
shrimp, performs all these acrobatics. With inner white cabbage leaves
to wrap up the juicy papaya sticks dressed with peanuts, chiles, and
lime, this salad is hot, crunchy, and refreshing all at once. Slices of
warm grilled beef, onion, and mint leaves dressed in a mild sweet and
sour sauce leaned more towards savoriness as did *lab*, a salad of cold
iceberg lettuce in a warm dressing of ground chicken infused with
chiles, ginger, peanuts and salty Thai fish sauce.

The clear broths in Thai soups allow the muted pastel colors of
seafood and Asian vegetables to shimmer through. *Po-tak*, a Thai soup
served in a covered metal bowl with a burning chimney in the center,
was a stunning composition of straw mushrooms, squid, shrimp, huge
imported red fleshed mussels, scallions, and cilantro in a hot and sour
broth perfumed with lemongrass and lime. *Mok-din* has the same clean
flavors but is a seafood stew cooked in heavy crockery that blends
together glass noodles, shrimp, squid, and scallops with cabbage and
straw mushrooms in hot pot style.

At Champa Thai, the Chef's Specials section of the menu is a good
place to start ordering. Champa Thai prepares spectacular stuffed and
deep-fried boneless chicken wings. *Pla Naung* offers one of the best
treatments of local rockfish I've tasted by topping steamed filets with
enoki mushrooms and a fragrant, gingery, red bean sauce. Do try the
most voluptuous dish on the menu, a half of a smoky eggplant piled
high with whole shrimp, buttery pork, onions, fresh tomato, peas, and
scallions in a Thai oyster sauce. The combination of ingredients is
wonderful. The green chicken curry with whole basil leaves is multi-
layered, rich, and smouldering, a fine example of the genre.

Jasmine tea and iced Thai coffee bring the meal to a close. I cannot
resist the deep-fried bananas with coconut ice cream for dessert
though *tako*, a cool, firm custard studded with corn kernels and water
chestnuts topped with coconut cream, is light and refreshing.

The small dining room has three semi-enclosed tables under a
thatched roof that are fun and cozy. Tables are covered with red
tablecloths under glass. Lighting is too dim and the ventilation system
in the kitchen didn't seem to be working very well during two of my
visits. However, the delicious cooking makes up for the modest
surroundings and out-of-the-way location.

PATRICIA UNTERMAN

CHEZ PANISSE ★★★★

1517 SHATTUCK AVENUE, BERKELEY. 548-5525. OPEN TUESDAY THROUGH SATURDAY, FOR FOUR SEATINGS AT 6, 6:30, 8:30, AND 9:15 P.M. BEER, WINE. MAJOR CREDIT CARDS. 100% NONSMOKING. FULLY WHEELCHAIR ACCESSIBLE. RESERVATIONS REQUIRED. EXPENSIVE

The famous prix fixe dinner that has been served for nearly 18 years has gone through many changes in tone, wrought by many now famous chefs. However, the unifying sensibility belongs to Alice Waters, whose insistence on pristine, naturally raised ingredients, and a completely integrated approach to serving a meal, transforms dinner into a brush with art. When you sign on for a meal downstairs, you have to give up your preconceptions and put yourself in her hands. For the $75 to $100 or so it will cost you—with service compris added in and wine extra—you get no choice about what you will be served. Suffice it to say that whatever it is, it will add up to something greater than its parts, even though the parts will be wonderful.

The restaurant is not fancy. The hand-crafted wooden interior has clean lines and rustic simplicity. Stunning and unusual arrangements of flowers, and an open kitchen stocked with baskets of bread and vegetables add color and warmth. Meals are served by a small cadre of waiters who will help you with wines and anticipate your needs. The downstairs format, in which practically everything is decided for you, allows diners a certain freedom. The restaurant performs for you and you get to talk with your companions, a rare commodity these days in noisy, demanding restaurants.

Meals always begin with a basket of different Acme breads, olives, glasses of mineral water, and glasses or bottles of wine. Recently, the first course was a plate of hors d'oeuvres assembled from a buffet of Italian-style antipasti set up in the kitchen that included artichoke salad, the biggest, creamiest marinated white beans, juicy calamari salad, and Italian braising greens dressed in olive oil. Then, a confit, breast, and foie gras of goose came with a crisp tian of winter vegetables. The breast, from a goose raised for its foie gras, grilled over charcoal, was like no other meat I've ever tasted. It was pure velvet. A tray of beautiful, ripe cheeses from Androuet in Paris served with a still-life of perfect fruit in a basket came next, and for dessert there was a refreshing crepe stuffed with tangerine sorbet. The whole meal worked like a charm. There were foods I'd never tasted before and dishes I'd had many times, but never quite prepared in a way that revealed their full potential. The balance of rich and clean, of fresh and cured, and the purity and seasonality of everything that arrives at the table makes the meals here unique. They express a very particular vision about food and eating. I happen to think it's the most enlightening one to come along in the past twenty years because it has changed the way I, and many other people, think about and appreciate food.

This kind of fame causes diners here to have such high expectations that no meal could live up to them; especially the subtle, quiet, almost simple cooking done here. In fact, there have been many imitators who have taken away superficial style without understanding the substance. Others who eat here, don't get it at all. Chez Panisse is a far different experience than the classic 3-star houses of Paul Bocuse or Taillevent, but for those who want an experience of dining in one of its purist, most aesthetic, and most delicious forms, you owe yourself a visit to Chez Panisse.

PATRICIA UNTERMAN

CHIANG MAI ★★

5020 GEARY, SAN FRANCISCO. 387-1299. OPEN MONDAY THROUGH FRIDAY 11:30 A.M. TO 3 P.M.; DINNER MONDAY THROUGH SATURDAY 5 TO 10 P.M., SUNDAY, 4 TO 9:30 P.M. BEER AND WINE. ALL MAJOR CREDIT CARDS. 15% NON-SMOKING. NOT WHEELCHAIR ACCESSIBLE. RESERVATIONS ACCEPTED FOR PARTIES OF SIX OR MORE. INEXPENSIVE.

Chiang Mai is a cheerful little Thai restaurant decorated with large fans, carved wood statues, delicate hanging light fixtures, and a window that looks up into a cymbidium garden with a fountain. A visiting raccoon uses the water to moisten his food. He probably wants to get his claws around some of the good stuff being cooked inside. The restaurant is named after a city in northern Thailand where the food is heartier, simpler, and less sweet than the cooking of Bangkok. The area around Chiang Mai is the home of sticky rice, so firm you can scoop it up with your hands, and searing hot beef and pork stews and dips.

At Chiang Mai, the main course curries, seafood-studded coconut custard, and noodle dishes are excellent, but the appetizers and Thai salads are not as interesting. The few regional dishes on the menu are particularly vigorous and intriguing. *Num-Plik-Onge*, a rich, fiery stew of minced pork simmered with chili paste and tomatoes is meant to be eaten like a dip, scooped up by big slices of cool cucumber and chilled raw cabbage. The contrasts in temperature and texture are exhilarating. *Kao-Soy Chiang Mai* is a wonderful northern noodle dish that you can regulate yourself. The heart of the dish is a stew of tender, sweet and sour beef, long cooked in a delicious coconut milk curry sauce. The chunks of meat come on a bed of soft egg noodles, the top scattered with crisp deep fried noodles. You toss in at table some of the hottest, most innocent looking, clear chile sauces and a plate of raw bean sprouts. This net result is absolutely delicious.

Another stand out at this restaurant is a seafood dish called *Hor-Mork*.

If you see it posted on the blackboard, order it, because it's one of the most captivating Thai dishes I've tasted. Coconut milk and curry paste is cooked for hours to form a silky, eggless custard. A mixture of diced seafood and fresh basil is folded into it and then it's steamed to order in banana leaves. The flavors are subtle and the texture as tender as the most delicate creme brulée. A stir-fry of spinach, green beans, Chinese cabbage, and bean cake topped with curried peanut sauce employs the freshest of vegetables and the lightest of sauces, and a roast duck curry gets a lovely, orange, coconut milk sauce.

For dessert you must order a tropical Thai banana split with a deep fried banana, exotic palm fruit, and jack fruit taking the place of pineapple and strawberries. It's perfect after a meal of searing northern Thai specialties.

PATRICIA UNTERMAN

CHINA MOON ★★★

639 POST STREET, SAN FRANCISCO. 775-4789. DIM SUM LUNCH SERVED MONDAY THROUGH SATURDAY, 11:30 TO 2:15 P.M., DINNER SERVED NIGHTLY 5:30 TO 10 P.M. BEER AND WINE. MASTERCARD, VISA. 100% NONSMOKING. PARTIALLY WHEELCHAIR ACCESSIBLE. RESERVATIONS RECOMMENDED. MODERATE.

China Moon is one of the most interesting and personal restaurants in San Francisco. Barbara Tropp, the diminutive chef/scholar, who speaks fluent Mandarin and studied Chinese poetry at Princeton, expresses her own sensibility in every facet of the restaurant, from the witty Chinese/cafe decor to the daily menus of colorful, spicy, Chinese dishes. Though many of the dishes are traditional preparations, you won't find them in quite the same form in Chinese restaurants. Tropp transforms them into her own creations. She loves strong flavors and contrasting textures, noodles, hearty Chinese stews, and crisp Chinese pickles. Her presentations are enhanced by Chinese porcelain, lacquerware, bamboo steamers, and clay pots. China Moon is her way of offering all her favorite dishes in the most appealing ways. I find them to be irresistible.

The tiny cafe itself is a long narrow room with a counter and stools, clearly a converted coffeeshop. Wooden booths for two and four diners have been retained, with a few tables tucked away in the back in a small raised dining area. The high ceilings, full moon shaped hanging lamps, and exotic flower arrangements add another layer of style to the lushly painted and trimmed room.

A menu of both small and entree-size dishes provides one of the most remarkable dining experiences in the city. The meal starts when the wait person brings over a bamboo tray of cold things to choose from, each in a celadon, leaf-shaped bowl. There are glazed pecans, pale green Peking Pickled Cabbage, sweet, hot, and crisp Japanese cucumber fans, aromatically spiced red onion pickles, fat triangles of caramelized tofu, silken Strange Flavor Eggplant, and pearly white cubes of fresh water chestnuts.

The next tier of foods is ordered off the menu. They're brought all together, and when assembled on the table form such a lush, brilliantly colorful landscape that you don't know where to begin. The China Moon Chicken Salad looks like some exotic bird of paradise with bright orange carrot and daikon radish threads, paper thin slices of green chile, black sesame seeds, creamy white chicken breast, and whole Chinese parsley leaves all in a tangy dijon mustard vinaigrette, the plate slashed through the middle with whole chives. Crisp fried noodle pancakes are cut in wedges and lavished with gorgeous stir-fries of peppers, green and yellow beans, miraculously tender strips of marinated pork, tree ears, scallions, and triangles of wok-grilled white onion in a dark, delicious, unthickened sauce.

Strange-Flavor Sparerib Nuggets, a stew of thick meaty pork bones in a dusky black bean sauce, goes with riotously colorful Shanghai Vegetable Rice, smokey pearl rice studded with carrots, egg ribbons, decoratively cut snow peas, and bok choy flowers. Lively by itself, superb with the ribs, there's nothing like this rice dish in town.

I know people who slip into China Moon to sit alone at the counter and eat the fantastic spring rolls filled with curried chicken and glass noodles or with pork and jalapenos, sprigs of Chinese parsley rolled into their impeccably crisp wrappers. The tart, bright green dipping sauce that comes with them is made of pulverized fresh anaheim chiles, yellow wax peppers, and pickled ginger.

I personally am addicted to China Moon's preparation of a homestyle Chinese dish that's rather bland and soft called Pearl Balls. They're long steamed pork balls studded with water chestnuts, coated in pearl rice, and served on a bed of chervil. Crescent Moon Turnovers have flaky pastry and explosive, aromatic lamb curry fillings. Mandarin Dumplings, soft pot stickers filled with spicy pork, come in a bowl of chili-infused sauce. They're wonderful. For those who like fried chicken, China Moon puts out their very own chicken nuggets of tender marinated breast in a sharp, clean sauce seasoned with balsamic vinegar.

For dessert, there's peppery ginger ice cream with dark chocolate sauce and China Moon's array of delicate cookies to be had with espresso or different kinds of tea. A carefully chosen wine and beer list provides many satisfying match-ups with the food.

Though practically every dish is laced with chiles and garlic, they taste and look refined. They boast the detail, brilliant color, and strength of seemingly delicate Chinese silk tapestry.

PATRICIA UNTERMAN

CHRISTOPHER'S CAFE ★★

1843 SOLANO AVE., BERKELEY. 526-9444. OPEN 11:30 A.M. TO 2:15 P.M. MONDAY THROUGH FRIDAY, 5:30 TO 9:15 P.M. SUNDAY THROUGH THURSDAY, UNTIL 10:15 P.M. FRIDAY AND SATURDAY. WINE, BEER. MASTERCARD, VISA, AMERICAN EXPRESS. 100% NONSMOKING. FULLY WHEELCHAIR ACCESSIBLE. RESERVATIONS HIGHLY RECOMMENDED. MODERATE.

When a Hong Kong-born chef strongly influenced by Thai and Mexican cooking opens a restaurant serving California cuisine, you can bet you're not going to get the same old boring cliche dishes. That's what people in Berkeley and Albany have known for years because they've made Christopher's Cafe, on the Solano Avenue border between the two cities, a longtime favorite.

Christopher's obeys all the laws of California cuisine; everything is very fresh and cooked simply and quickly so that the flavors stand out. But there's more to it than that because Christopher Cheung introduces accents from all over the world into his cooking. There will be influences from Thailand, China, Mexico, and the American Southwest. There will be strong-tasting herbs and hot chili peppers. But it's all done with such a skilled hand that the basic tastes of the ingredients are never overwhelmed.

To get an idea of what Cheung can turn out, consider the sauteed, marinated Chinese lamb, his signature dish that always appears on a menu that otherwise changes daily. A high-quality boned leg of lamb is marinated in ginger, cilantro, soy sauce, and sherry. The lamb slices, with red and green peppers and onions, are quickly sauteed in oil that first got a dose of Thai chilis. The heat of the chilis is counterbalanced with the sweetness of a little hoisin sauce, while the texture of the tender lamb contrasts with the crunchy peppers and soft onions. Now let's change nationalities to a Mexican grilled chicken breast. The grilled breast, charred outside but juicy inside, has been marinated in Mexican dark beer, cumin, ancho chilis, orange juice, and cilantro, and it's served with black beans and a really remarkable pineapple chutney on top.

But even the most simple and routine California cuisine dishes sparkle under Cheung's hand. Salmon and tuna are perfectly grilled and come with interesting sauces. A huge bowl of carrot soup is perked up with cilantro and roasted chilis. A chicken salad appetizer comes alive with the flavors of mint, jalapeno peppers, and shallots. Cheung, with his talent for blending together unusual ingredients, does particularly well with pastas. Corkscrew-style fusilli are mixed with slices of rare top sirloin, roasted eggplant, shiitake mushrooms, sweet red peppers and parmesan. A huge platter of spinach noodles, cooked al dente, are tossed with roasted tomatoes, sweet onions, a load of fresh herbs, and olive oil.

Christopher's Cafe stands as proof that California cuisine doesn't have to be boring once the innovation of fresh ingredients has worn off.

STAN SESSER

| CIAO ★½

230 JACKSON STREET, SAN FRANCISCO. 982-9500. OPEN MONDAY THROUGH SATURDAY 11 A.M. TO MIDNIGHT, SUNDAY 4 TO 10:30 P.M. FULL BAR. ALL MAJOR CREDIT CARDS. 60% NONSMOKING. FULLY WHEELCHAIR ACCESSIBLE. RESERVATIONS SUGGESTED. MODERATE.

Ciao was one of the first of the new generation of Italian cafes to open in this country. It broke new ground by offering a menu of housemade pastas in fresh sauces, risotto, charcoal grilled meats with Italian accompaniments, and authentic antipasti. Designed to be casual and bustling, the inspiration for the decor was modern Milan not old world Palermo.

Certainly Ciao, with its authentic approach, was a step in the right direction, but when I reviewed it shortly after it opened, I wasn't wild about it. The kitchen couldn't execute the enticing menu. Ingredients weren't chosen well enough to carry these simpler presentations and I thought the decor sacrificed comfort for artifice. Well, nine successful years later, Ciao is still packing them in. I thought I'd give it another try in light of the Italian food craze that has swept the whole country since then.

The current menu, written on paper placemats set on tiny, white-linen covered tables, sounds as mouthwatering as ever, though now, practically everyone is familiar with the dishes. Fresh pasta and arugula are sold in supermarkets. Olive oil is being touted as the health find of the decade, and every self-respecting urbanite has grazed on carpaccio, fresh mozzarella with tomatoes, and grilled radicchio in many restaurants. The charcoal grilled veal chop is no revelation, and ravioli of varying shapes stuffed with greens and ricotta, sauced with butter and herbs, are de rigueur.

Ciao does all these dishes and they're all competent. Yet, many of them just miss the boat. The restaurant's kitchen has been standing on that pier for almost a decade. On my most recent visits, the carpaccio, paper thin slices of beef, were icy cold and watery. A simple salad of shredded radicchio and watercress, not the promised arugula, with tasteless tomatoes and thin slices of goat cheese, needed better raw materials. Undercooked and flavorless slices of grilled eggplant blanketed with melted smoked mozzarella felt slimy on the tongue. However, a chunky, fresh vegetable soup was as pleasant as it was simple.

The pastas, especially because the noodles are fresh, could be

73

cooked less to give them more texture, the sauces, however, have improved over the years. They're brighter but still not memorable. A fettucine with bolognese sauce was watery. Though I liked the aromatic basil and garlic in a pale, creamy version of pesto, the sauce was monochromatic, lacking the multiple facets that give pesto its character. If a kitchen is going to serve a simple, fresh tomato sauce it has to use good tomatoes. I ate at Ciao during the apex of the tomato season and every tomato I tasted—raw, grilled or in a sauce—was flavorless. However, a filet of salmon wrapped in chard was delicious and perfectly cooked. It needed only a splash of olive oil, not the heavy tomato sauce spooned only on one side, thank goodness.

Most of the decor has remained the same though the white rubber floors have been changed to white tile and the ceiling has lost its fans and become acoustic. Unfortunately, this does not help the sound level much. Tables are extraordinarily tiny and close together, and when the restaurant is full, it is very noisy. At one lunch, background music made the room insanely loud. Also, diners regularly bump their heads on low hanging lamps and knock things off the tightly placed tables as they sit down or leave.

Against this white background, the open kitchen arranged with colorful produce, drying pasta, and cans of tomatoes and olive oil provide a warm focus. Unfortunately, most of the produce so lavishly displayed doesn't taste very good. The problem always has been, and still is, a lack of commitment to substance over style.

PATRICIA UNTERMAN

CITRUS CAFE AND GRILL ★★

2373 CHESTNUT STREET, SAN FRANCISCO. 563-7720. OPEN FOR LUNCH TUESDAY THROUGH FRIDAY 11:30 A.M. TO 3 P.M.; DINNER 5:30 TO 9 P.M.; BRUNCH ON SATURDAY AND SUNDAY FROM 9:30 A.M. TO 2:30 P.M., SATURDAY DINNER FROM 5:30 TO 10 P.M. CLOSED SUNDAY FOR DINNER AND ALL DAY MONDAY. BEER AND WINE. MASTERCARD, VISA, AMERICAN EXPRESS. 90% NONSMOKING. FULLY WHEELCHAIR ACCESSIBLE. RESERVATIONS RECOMMENDED. INEXPENSIVE.

The Citrus Cafe and Grill, a narrow storefront restaurant in the Marina, prepares delicious, spicy, aromatic, Moroccan lamb and chicken brochettes, excellent couscous, trout with lemony *charmoula* and smouldering lentil soup called *harrira*. For dessert, Citrus makes the best homemade apple pie in town.

The seemingly tiny restaurant turns out to have an experienced Moroccan chef whose hospitable American wife runs the front of the house. Her Oregonian mother makes the apple pies. Though Citrus looks tiny from the outside, it offers counter seating, a pleasant garden patio in the back, and a whole mezzanine. The partially open kitchen sends out exotic Moroccan and French vibrations while the front of the house feels like a friendly, homey, country cafe. The Citrus Cafe brings two very different worlds together.

The brochettes of lamb and chicken are juicy, full of flavor, deeply seasoned by a marinade, and expertly grilled. Big chunks of leg of lamb and moist chicken breast are used. The brochettes come with a gently spiced tomato sauce, a pile of buttery, airy, couscous, and a spoonful of warm, Mediterranean vegetable stew. The slowly baked trout on Citrus' menu is transformed by a rich, aromatic spice paste full of cumin, cilantro, and lemon zest. Citrus' version of chicken couscous, piled with turnips, carrots, and zucchini, raisins, caramelized onions, and chickpeas in a bright, saffron seasoned stew is what you hope to get in a Moroccan restaurant.

Often Moroccan restaurants involve so much ritual—sitting on the floor, eating with your fingers, being served a gigantic, prix fixe meal, being entertained by belly dancers—that you have to be in the mood. Citrus is more like the little North African places in Paris,where you can drop in for a plate of couscous. Likewise, Citrus fits into the daily life of its Marina neighborhood.

PATRICIA UNTERMAN

CLAUS HAUS AT DELUXE ★½

1511 HAIGHT STREET (AT ASHBURY), SAN FRANCISCO. 552-1469. OPEN FOR DINNER TUESDAY THROUGH THURSDAY 4 TO 10 P.M., FRIDAY AND SATURDAY UNTIL 11 P.M. SUNDAY BRUNCH 2 TO 8 P.M. FULL BAR. MASTERCARD AND VISA. 100% NONSMOKING. FULLY WHEELCHAIR ACCESSIBLE. RESERVATIONS ACCEPTED. MODERATE.

If you have the right attitude, there's a lot going for Claus Haus, a tiny 24-seat restaurant tucked into the back of the Deco-style DeLuxe bar at Haight and Ashbury.

This quirky restaurant has a personality that makes it easy to overlook some flaws. Partly, it's the unwavering commitment of the chef/owner, Gregory Claus, who was chef at the Avenue Grill in Mill Valley and before that worked as a sous chef at the Rainbow Room in New York. Sparing no expense, Claus insists on keeping his larder stocked with high-quality, mostly organic ingredients such as Niman-Schell meats.

The interior has an authentic Deco look augmented by black and white diner-style chairs. The linoleum floors and the blond wood walls add to the sleek look. WPA-inspired murals are still being installed along the walls.

For inspiration, the 28-year-old chef has gone back to cookbooks and menus from the '20s and '30s, creating what he calls "San Francisco Bohemian Cuisine," which has strong Italian and German influences. He produces some of the best sauerbraten anywhere; it's served with light potato dumplings. Pork Normandy combines apples and a creamy sauce for an old-fashioned rich taste. The California side emerges with the vegetables, which include sugar snap peas and crusty sauteed Brussels sprouts. The housemade spatzle is seasoned with fennel seeds. Moist chicken breast in a green peppercorn sauce is enhanced with braised leeks, strips of garlicky zucchini and bell pepper-scented rice.

Appetizers are equally good. The German potatoes, sauteed slices flecked with red bell peppers, are great. Firecracker prawns do indeed have a dynamite kick. They are served with a confetti of bell peppers, whole tiny yellow chiles, and slices of baguette to soak up the juices. The Mini-Bites Burger, doused with cheese and grilled onions and served on a dense bun, should be enlarged as a full-sized entree. Claus' version of Oysters Rockefeller is superb: plump oysters topped with crispy pancetta, dices of fennel, red and green bell peppers, and a small pile of sauteed spinach.

When you stray off the regular menu, however, you have to be prepared for dishes that don't work. Avoid the pasta and the nightly specials and stick to the small printed menu. Desserts are a disaster, too; there's sometimes only one a night. A bread pudding tasted mostly of bread; an almond torte was dry and lacking in flavor.

One real draw, however, is the help. You have to relax and realize the service won't be very professional. Eating here, in fact, is rather like having dinner at the home of a slightly daffy aunt. So what if we had to ask for refills on water, or if she didn't know where to put the plates, or how to pour the beer? If you want those things, go somewhere else. Personally, I like the ambience at Claus Haus and I can tolerate the sometimes ill-timed, but never ill-willed service. In the right mood, I'd go back in a flash.

MICHAEL BAUER

CYPRESS CLUB ★★½

500 JACKSON STREET, SAN FRANCISCO. 296-8555. OPEN FOR LUNCH MONDAY THROUGH SATURDAY FROM 11:30 A.M. TO 2 P.M.; DINNER SUNDAY THROUGH THURSDAY FROM 5:30 TO 9:30 P.M., FRIDAY AND SATURDAY FROM 5:30 TO 10 P.M.; BRUNCH ON SUNDAY FROM 11 A.M. TO 2 P.M.; BAR MENU SERVED BETWEEN LUNCH AND DINNER AND FROM 10 P.M. UNTIL MIDNIGHT FRIDAY AND SATURDAY. FULL BAR. ALL MAJOR CREDIT CARDS. 80% NONSMOKING. FULLY WHEELCHAIR ACCESSIBLE. RESERVATIONS HIGHLY RECOMMENDED. EXPENSIVE.

From the front door to the bathrooms, the hot, new Cypress Club is a visual, indeed a tactile, spectacle. You have to see this restaurant yourself to get what's going on, but some of the most outrageous features include huge, nipple shaped, blown glass light fixtures that hang from the ceiling next to enormous, blimp-shaped, enameled protuberances, gigantic urn-shaped pillars, pounded copper-covered archways, curved, inlaid, wood paneled walls capped with a continuous wall mural that takes the viewer on a tour of Northern California from the Napa Valley to the 17-Mile Drive, multi-stained wooden floors, stone mosaic floors, overstuffed velvet booths and chairs, and a magnificent cast bronze front door. It's an elegantly constructed baroque work; overfull, overdone, evoking the grandeur of the Old Palace school of dining rooms, but a spoof of it as well. The Cypress Club has reached the end of the restaurant decor road. Decadence has set in. Form and function have split up. The dining room as a decor extravaganza, as theatrical setting, as an imagined space, cannot be taken one step further.

This kind of atmosphere puts tremendous pressure on the kitchen to come up with dishes that carry on the party, and head chef Cory Schreiber has done an admirable job in trying to meet the challenge. There's a very tasty romaine salad dressed with a strong relish of capers, anchovies, minced red pepper, and parmesan, and a re-thought celery Victor that pairs al dente stalks of poached celery with a green salad, sieved egg, and drizzled aioli. A mound of Dungeness crab salad is thick with mayonnaise, but nicely contrasted by a bed of grilled squash with a citrus vinaigrette. Hangtown fry, as interpreted here, is really a warm salad of greens, fried oysters, and pancetta resting on a thin crepe made of egg—a conceptual flourish. One big lamb and potato ravioli with aged Jack cheese and roasted fennel works as a fine, small main course. Everyone likes the red onions wrapped with pancetta and grilled, served with green salad. A very intensely flavored, thick puree of red onion soup, with a buttery little cheddar cheese toast floating on it, provides another good starter.

My favorite main course brings two foods to one plate that I had never tasted before—tiny, mild, crisp lamb sweetbreads in red wine sauce with bacon, and salsify, a root vegetable with an artichoke-like flavor. Another satisfying plate pairs a loin of lamb, roasted on the bone in the Cypress Club's portable tandoori oven, with braised white beans. A saddle and leg of rabbit is moist and tender, served with creamed chard and oversweetened carrots. I also like crisp crab and potato cakes at lunch, served over grilled, citrus-marinated vegetables, a warm replay of the dinner salad.

The restaurant has two sommeliers to administer a twelve page, computer-printed wine list, heavy with some of the best and most obscure California wines including some hard-to-find vintages from the early part of the 80's. An interesting selection of wines by the glass is also available as are some excellent tenths, a boon to tables that want both a white and a red without ordering whole bottles.

Desserts are achingly rich, especially following much-dressed first courses and gigantic, much-sauced main courses. They are highly and skillfully decorative. My favorite, and the one that tastes best after a meal here, is three apple sorbet, bright in flavor and refreshing, dramatically encased in a caramel cage.

Service, for a new place, has been professional and gracious, even if it does take some time for food to come out of the kitchen on the super-busy nights. This civilized treatment of patrons comes as no surprise. Cypress Club's owner/manager, John Cunin, the former maitre d' manager of Masa's, has garnered a loyal following because he knows how to take care of diners so unobtrusively and well.

PATRICIA UNTERMAN

DAR TUNIS ★★½

536 BROADWAY (AT KEARNEY), SAN FRANCISCO. 433-4636. OPEN MONDAY THROUGH FRIDAY FOR LUNCH FROM 11:30 A.M. TO 2:30 P.M.; DINNER NIGHTLY 5 TO 11:30 P.M. BEER AND WINE. ALL MAJOR CREDIT CARDS. 30% NONSMOKING. NOT WHEELCHAIR ACCESSIBLE. RESERVATIONS RECOMMENDED ON THE WEEKENDS. MODERATE.

Dar Tunis feels like one of those narrow Parisian couscous shops with a table at the open front virtually staked out by groups of chattering Tunisian men, smoking and drinking coffee. The stove in the small open kitchen is covered with tall couscoussieres, two-part cooking utensils that allow the fragrant meat and vegetable stews cooking in the lower section to infuse the semolina steaming above on a perforated tray. The clientele is distinctively international. A few oil paintings of North African scenes decorate the white walls. Otherwise, Dar Tunis is furnished with North Beach-Italianate quilted banquettes, velour chairs, wooden trellis partitions, and white linen. Tunisian music hums exotically in the background.

The reason to come here is for the couscous. Order the combination couscous for the whole table. It arrives on a majolica plate, piled high with a marvelous stew of carrots, turnips, chickpeas, and raisins, housemade merguez sausages, chunks of savory lamb on the bone, juicy chicken and, if you're there on the right day, large, Tunisian meatballs called *boulettes*. The couscous underneath it is light and airy, each grain separate, ready to accept the mingled flavors of the cooking pot. The tender vegetables have absorbed these flavors as well, so everything on the platter tastes full and complete, as only foods cooked intimately together do. Each of these couscous toppings can be ordered separately as well.

For starters I liked *mechouia*, roasted peppers and tomatoes mashed with garlic and olive oil, and the merguez platter of grilled sausages surrounding a delicious carrot puree seasoned with hot chiles and coriander. Both of these appetizers were garnished with perfectly cooked, bright-yolked, hard boiled eggs.

The Tunisian chef uses eggs in a number of unusual dishes and they are all excellent. In his version of *breka*, he breaks an egg into filo-type dough stuffed with potato puree, onions, herbs, and garlic and then gently sautees it. When you cut into this crisp turnover, the poached egg oozes out as a lovely sauce. In a versatile Tunisian dish called *chakchouka*, he delicately poaches eggs in a tomato and pepper ragout with a few merguez sausages as well. The whole thing comes out of the pan in a perfectly molded circle. Another fine starter is the daily changing Tunisian soup or *charba*, which, on the night I had it, incorporated chickpeas, rice-shaped pasta, and whole leaves of Italian parsley in a clean, lemony broth.

For dessert, there is baklava, honey-soaked filo stuffed with ground almonds, and a soft, creamy, custard, called crema, too assertively scented with rosewater and covered with ground pistachios and almonds. Cordial glasses of fresh mint tea are refilled many times.

Even though Dar Tunis prepares other dishes, their true specialty is the couscous. The flavors are right on the mark and the textures are sensual and rustic.

PATRICIA UNTERMAN

DOMAINE CHANDON ★★½

1 CALIFORNIA DRIVE, YOUNTVILLE. (707) 944-2892. OPEN FOR LUNCH WEDNESDAY THROUGH SUNDAY 11:30 A.M. TO 2:30 P.M. (EVERYDAY DURING THE SUMMER); DINNER FROM 6 P.M. TO 9 P.M. WINE. ALL MAJOR CREDIT CARDS. 100% NONSMOKING. PARTIALLY WHEELCHAIR ACCESSIBLE. RESERVATIONS RECOMMENDED TWO WEEKS IN ADVANCE. EXPENSIVE.

If you can tolerate the unanswered phones, bored receptionists, and forbidding reservation process, you'll experience excellent wine country cuisine at Domaine Chandon.

This is the third time I've been to the restaurant, and each time I've experienced the same rude to lackluster treatment when trying to book. But once you get in the door, you'll be glad you did. Frankly, if it weren't my job, I'd have given up. Chef Philippe Jeanty, who has been at the restaurant since opening more than 10 years ago, creates some stellar combinations, most on the light side.

A melange of shellfish in a garlic-lemon-thyme broth is superb, as is a filet of rouget served on a bed of artichokes, basil, and with a seductive hint of olives. Jeanty prepares lamb three ways, all arranged around an herb-crusted tart filled with caramelized shallots and garlic: roasted lamb in a natural juice sauce; a lamb chop with a modest dollop of bearnaise; and roasted shoulder with rich braising juices.

Venison is wrapped in pancetta and served with perfect dices of crusted potatoes and an essence of Merlot and juniper. The combinations have a heavy French-California bent, using the products that make the wine country so enticing. Jeanty is such an expert that the food seems tailored to the wine list which offers some excellent California wines at great prices.

Disappointments came at dessert. On the last visit we had a lackluster tart tatin with mushy apples. It was almost saved by a delicious garnish of preserved cherries. An ice cream sandwich of espresso and mascarpone ice cream with a layer of peanut butter and bittersweet chocolate sauce didn't work and was much too simplistic for such a refined restaurant.

The formal French service is strong on technique but, thankfully, weak on pretension. It strikes the right balance for a formal restaurant in a countrified setting. The interior, especially at night, can be magical. The formally set tables with flickering candles look impressive in the sweeping room with high arched ceilings and glass-cornered walls that afford a view of the lush vineyard setting. It all adds up to a refined, peaceful and romantic experience.

MICHAEL BAUER

DOTTIE'S TRUE BLUE CAFE ★½

522 JONES (BETWEEN GEARY AND O'FARRELL) SAN FRANCISCO. 885-2767. OPEN MONDAY THROUGH FRIDAY FROM 7 A.M. TO 2 P.M., SATURDAY AND SUNDAY FROM 7 A.M. TO 3 P.M. BEER AND WINE. CASH ONLY. 30% NONSMOKING. PARTIALLY WHEELCHAIR ACCESSIBLE. NO RESERVATIONS. INEXPENSIVE.

Dottie's is like an old-fashioned fifties coffee shop except that it's cozier, more personal, and the cooking is better. Chef/owner Salvatore Bovoso, who sports a trimmed salt and pepper beard and red suspenders, puts on a one man show. He bakes fine maple-cornmeal and oatmeal-raisin muffins, hand-squeezes the orange juice, and cooks every dish on the menu himself—except on Sunday when his partner, Stefan Reilly from Asta, joins him behind the stove.

Tender pancakes with fruit mixed into the batter, lavished with colorful, ripe fruit salad on top; carefully fried sunny-side up eggs with crisp home fries seasoned with minced bell pepper and onions, and thick-sliced bacon; and softly scrambled eggs, like I do them at home, with spicy, greaseless, housemade sausage patties pretty much make up the breakfast menu—if you throw in a couple of omelets. Buttered English muffins or Oroweat toast come with the egg dishes. Every element of the breakfast service has been thought about and is precisely executed, from juice through freshly brewed coffee.

This modest cafe has blue and white checked oil cloth tablecloths and a bright blue coat of paint. The patterned tile floor looks ancient. Souvenir plates from the fifty states decorate the walls. Each table gets a pair of knick knack salt and pepper shakers and a bottle-diorama, the kind you shake and get a snow flurry. The main waitress is so smart, nice, and efficient she can handle the whole dining room.

Though the superlative breakfast is served all day, a lunch menu also becomes available at 11:30 A.M. Some of the highpoints are a classic grilled cheese, tomato, and bacon sandwich with a pile of toothsome macaroni salad richly dressed in mayonnaise; a tasty Caesar salad; very sweet, toasted lemon poundcake with whipped cream and fresh fruit; and a terrific sundae with chocolate and strawberry ice cream, chocolate and strawberry sauces, whipped cream and nuts.

The basics are in place at Dottie's and for those who want an old-fashioned bacon, lettuce, and tomato, or a chicken salad sandwich made with the freshest ingredients, the walk from Union Square shopping is not that far.

PATRICIA UNTERMAN

DOUG'S BAR-B-Q ★★

3600 SAN PABLO AVENUE, EMERYVILLE (TAKE THE MACARTHUR EXIT OFF I-580). 655-9048. OPEN MONDAY THROUGH THURSDAY 11 A.M. TO MIDNIGHT, FRIDAY AND SATURDAY TO 2:30 A.M., SUNDAY NOON TO 9:30 P.M. TAKEOUT ONLY. NO ALCOHOL, RESERVATIONS, CREDIT CARDS, OR ANY OF THAT STUFF. FULLY WHEELCHAIR ACCESSIBLE. INEXPENSIVE-MODERATE.

For a barbeque lover, Oakland has become something of a mecca, a Kansas City of the Pacific. The appetite of Oaklanders for barbeque rivals that of Berkeley residents for Thai food or San Franciscans for California cuisine. Doug's Bar-B-Q, housed in a tired old building nestled alongside the I-580 San Pablo Avenue freeway overpass in Emeryville, is one of the best. While some purists might object that it's a bit too clean, no one could otherwise fault Doug's for its classic barbeque joint ambiance. It's carpeted in linoleum and bathed in fluorescent light.

Although Doug's is strictly takeout, there are several mismatched chairs for the inevitable long wait. Efficiency here is a foreign word. But the wait makes everything taste even better when you get it home—assuming you can resist the wafting fumes of barbeque sauce in your car.

Doug's is a winner on three fronts: It does the standard stuff terrifically; it offers some unusual choices like barbequed goat and smoked turkey; and it dishes out the rarest of rarities for a barbeque joint—potato salad and baked beans that are actually good.

But for many visitors, the experience will begin and end with the signature dish of barbeque, the pork ribs. And no one serves up ribs juicier and meatier than Doug's. They're wonderful and made even better by an unusually sophisticated hot sauce, a sauce that for once isn't drowned out by the reek of Liquid Smoke. The hot sauce, which has some zing but won't set you on fire, is the only sensible choice here; medium is much too sweet.

The menu at Doug's travels the usual path of beef ribs, brisket of beef, links, and chicken, but also branches out to lamb, smoked turkey and goat. Next to the ribs, my favorite is smoked turkey, which is astonishingly moist, tender, and tasty. Because it's low in fat, it's actually healthy—almost a contradiction in terms for a barbeque.

Doug Keyes didn't exactly go the culinary academy route; he was a cowboy in Texas who moved to Oakland to become a diesel mechanic. "I barbequed all the time on the side anyway," he explains. "I cook a lot of Cajun food, too. That's all I am anyway, a Cajun, but just a black one." The affable Keyes will regale you with stories of his youth if you get him started. And if you want an unusual dinner, you can bring him a whole goat, lamb, or pig and he'll smoke it for you. I couldn't think of a better dinner than one catered by Doug's.

STAN SESSER

E'ANGELO ★★½

2234 CHESTNUT STREET, SAN FRANCISCO. 567-6164. OPEN TUESDAY THROUGH SUNDAY 5 TO 11 P.M. BEER AND WINE. NO CREDIT CARDS. 75% NONSMOKING. FULLY WHEELCHAIR ACCESSIBLE. NO RESERVATIONS. INEXPENSIVE.

E'Angelo is a small, very popular Marina district trattoria that has kept up its standards and low prices over the past twelve years. The very same dishes that this restaurant served when it first opened turn out to be appealing and delicious today.

Getting into E'Angelo is the only trying part of the experience if you come during peak meal-time hours. A long semi-open kitchen shares a small dining room with ten or twelve tables which fill up fast. You have to wait your turn in a tiny lobby since no reservations are taken. Luckily, service by two good natured waiters is efficient.

The tables are tiny and pushed very close together, covered with blue and white checked oil cloth. The wall along the table side of the room is hung with framed garage sale paintings; otherwise there's a fortuitous lack of decor in what is a very cramped room. The feeling, however, is just right for the kind of restaurant E'Angelo is. Without any pretensions, the real charm of the place comes from its solid, neighborhood trattoria style.

E'Angelo specializes in housemade pastas, the old fashioned kind with meat sauces and lots of cheese and savory stuffings. The pasta dough itself has a distinctive flavor and texture, thick, toothsome, satiny and full of character but never heavy. It tastes like the handmade pasta you might get in an Italian home.

Green spinach noodles are layered with mushroom and chicken

liver sauce, fontina and mozzarella, and finished off under the broiler in a mouthwatering Green Lasagne. The same hearty meat sauce with a recognizable chicken liver presence is tossed into egg noodles in Fettucine Ciociara. The eggy white fettucine also get a copious white sauce skillfully constructed with only gruyere and cream. Simple and rich, yes, but balanced perfectly.

Cannelloni usually have such bland, dreadful fillings, but here, you can actually taste the chicken and veal that are rolled into white noodle dough and topped with tomato and mushroom sauce and parmesan cheese. One of my favorite dishes here is another oft abused dish, eggplant parmigiana, which melts in your mouth when prepared by E'Angelo's kitchen. Paper-thin slices of eggplant are layered with mozzarella, tomato sauce and grated parmesan in just the right proportion.

The ricotta and spinach stuffed ravioli are some of the best in the city. They get a haunting cream sauce infused with a demi-glace and mushrooms. For gnocchi lovers, E'Angelo's little dumplings of soft, egg-rich dough, poached in salted water and then napped with tomato sauce and a sprinkling of parmesan cheese, are properly light.

Starters are limited to an antipasto of paper-thin slices of mortadella, prosciutto, and *bresaola* (dry-cured beef) with some snappy house-pickled vegetables in the center, or prosciutto and melon, a dish well worth ordering when melons are in season. A mixed green salad gets a brisk dressing of vinegar and oil as does a plate of tomatoes covered with thinly sliced red onions and anchovies.

Another way to start a meal at E'Angelo is to split a small pizza made only with mozzarella, fresh tomatoes and either mushrooms or salami. These individual sized pizzas on sweet, thin crusts were part of this menu way before the pizza craze swept the country, and you'd be hard pressed to find a better version. Sogginess or oiliness never afflict an E'Angelo pizza. They're about as simple a pizza as you can make, and just about the best.

Being able to depend on a restaurant like E'Angelo year after year makes me, and a lot of other people who wait in line there every night, particularly happy.

PATRICIA UNTERMAN

EDDIE RICKENBACKER'S ★★

133 SECOND STREET, SAN FRANCISCO. 543-3498. OPEN 11 A.M. TO 3 P.M. AND 5 TO 9 P.M. MONDAY THROUGH FRIDAY, 11 A.M. TO 6 P.M. SATURDAY. FULL BAR. ALL MAJOR CREDIT CARDS. 20% NONSMOKING. FULLY WHEELCHAIR ACCESSIBLE. RESERVATIONS RECOMMENDED. MODERATE.

Located in a renovated building just south of where downtown and the Financial District meet, between Mission and Howard, Eddie

Rickenbacker's draws an eclectic crowd. The decor is both ingenious and personal to owner Norman Hobday, built around a collection of authentic World War I photos, guns, and memorabilia. A real World War I bi-plane used to be suspended over the bar until it was sold recently. Mannekins dressed in period soldier's uniforms stand in a group on a ledge above the room. Some fine Tiffany lamps hang in the dining room. The period look continues with white tiled floors, walls paneled with dark stained wood, bentwood chairs, tables covered with white tablecloths and white paper placemats.

Eddie Rickenbacker's can be seen as two separate operations though they occupy the same room. There's the long Victorian bar staffed with the best professional bartenders in the city and frequented by an old-fashioned, hard-drinking crowd. Next to it is the restaurant, run by ex-Balboa chef Chuck Phifer, which may or may not be used by the customers who frequent the bar. The spirit of Eddie Rickenbacker's is of a piece however. The generous portions and straightforward presentations of classic American dishes put out by the kitchen suits the saloon quite well. You can eat and drink with conviction here.

The menu changes each day, though the salads remain a constant. Salad leaves are arranged like the petals on a flower. In a mixed green salad, many different kinds of lettuce leaves are used, scattered with peeled, diced tomato and crumbled blue cheese. The basic vinaigrette is made with good olive oil and vinegar in harmonious balance. A Caesar salad is composed of graduating leaves of romaine, and every one of them is tasty with coarsely grated parmesan, soft-baked croutons, and a fine assertive dressing. The anchovies crisscross in the center of the salad.

Soups are a highpoint of the menu. They're served in large bowls and the kitchen doesn't stint on the ingredients. A cream of mushroom soup was so thick with coarsely chopped Italian field mushrooms, shiitakes and domestic mushrooms that you could practically chew on the wonderful, earthy flavors. A black bean soup turns out to really be a spicy black bean chile.

Rickenbacker's puts out the perfect hamburger. An inch thick, full of flavor and juice, cooked exactly to specification, it sits on a buttered, toasted bun that's just a little bit crusty. The skinny fries melt in your mouth. A rib-eye steak seems more like a New York. It's gigantic, grilled to a turn, and capped with a pouf of garlic butter.

A butterflied slice of swordfish one day, came off the grill juicy, pristinely fresh, perfectly cooked. Its tomato buerre blanc tasted fine with a summery medley of vegetables. A moist grilled chicken breast was dressed up with cheesy, soft polenta and a colorful fresh tomato salsa. A perfect bacon, lettuce, and tomato sandwich is particularly delightful during tomato season.

Phifer goes completely American when it comes to desserts. His fresh fruit crisps and cobblers of apples, peaches, and raspberries, come warm from the oven, achieve the right degree of sweetness, and have truly crisp, buttery tops. I adore them. The hearty shot of liquor in bourbon-pecan pie works to cut its richness in a new way. Eddie Rickenbacker's is a dependable place to get first-rate drinks and really tasty food to go with them.

PATRICIA UNTERMAN

EL FAROLITO ★★

2777 MISSION STREET JUST BELOW 24TH. 824-7877. AND, 2950 24TH STREET ON THE CORNER OF ALABAMA, SAN FRANCISCO. 641-0758. BOTH LOCATIONS OPEN FROM 9 A.M. TO 1 A.M. DAILY. BEER. CASH ONLY. NO RESERVATIONS. FOOD TO GO. INEXPENSIVE.

Taqueria San Jose shops have been favorites of mine since they opened all over the Mission about five years ago. Recently, a new group of taquerias have been sweeping the Mission and they're excellent too. One day when I was shopping at La Palma Mexicatessen and Casa Lucas on 24th Street, hunger overtook me and I walked across the street into El Farolito, a nondescript-looking place with the usual menu of tacos and burritos. I ordered a *carne asada burrito* and ate it in the car. It dripped all over the steering wheel and my arm, but it was so tasty I couldn't put it down—all two pounds of it.

It turns out that this El Farolito is but one of five different branches of this taqueria. If the surroundings of the two I visited are barebones, the salsas, the *tortas* (Mexican sandwiches), the fresh fruit juices, and the *quesadillas suizas* make up for it.

In addition to the usual salsa cruda, made with fresh tomatoes, El Farolito sets out a bright green avocado-tomatillo salsa laced with chiles that's out of this world. For those who like really hot stuff, Farolito makes searing *chiles en escabeche*, pickled chiles, onions, and carrots that look deceptively tame. These condiments, put on the *tacos al pastor*, spit turned pork hacked off in slices and reheated on the flat grill, or the aforementioned charcoally beefsteak burrito stuffed with both beans and rice, add dimension. Farolito also offers a soft, onion-infused beef tongue filling and chorizo fragrant with allspice. No beans are put in the tacos. They're more traditional—just meat, double corn tortilla, and salsa cruda.

Delicious here are the sandwiches served on fresh, soft, white Mexican rolls or *bolillos*. The *tortas* filled with warm *carne asada*, or pork, and grilled onions are surprisingly savory. The juices from the meats are soaked up by the soft rolls but contained by the crisp crusts. *Quesadillas suizas*, flour tortillas folded over *carne asada* and melted cheese, are particularly good swathed in the avocado-tomatillo salsa.

The watermelon drink tastes like the breath of summer and the fresh orange juice has the pedigree of being recently squeezed on a hand machine—a trick most other restaurants should learn.

The 24th Street location is large and roomy with picnic tables, worn linoleum floors, and fake wood paneled walls. The kitchen and dining areas are kept clean and orderly, but I hate the smell of disinfectant competing with the food. That smell is there at both locations, though if you sit towards the front it's not so noticeable. At any rate, you can get everything to go, including many cups of your favorite salsas—so at least you can fill your car with the proper aromas of a great taqueria.

PATRICIA UNTERMAN

ELLA'S ★★

500 PRESIDIO AVENUE, SAN FRANCISCO. 441-5669. OPEN FOR BREAKFAST MONDAY THROUGH FRIDAY FROM 7 A.M. TO 11 A.M.; LUNCH 11:30 A.M. TO 2:30 P.M.; DINNER WEDNESDAY THROUGH FRIDAY 5:30 TO 9:30 P.M., SUNDAY BRUNCH 9 A.M. TO 2 P.M. CLOSED SATURDAY. BEER AND WINE. MASTERCARD, VISA, AMERICAN EXPRESS. 80% NONSMOKING. PARTIALLY WHEELCHAIR ACCESSIBLE. RESERVATIONS FOR DINNER ONLY, AND FOR PARTIES OF 8 OR MORE AT SUNDAY BRUNCH. MODERATE.

Ella's, a pretty, corner storefront near the Muni electric bus barn, puts out a delicious breakfast. The key to the breakfast's success comes from excellent home baking. At Ella's, even the white bread for toast is freshly baked, and what a difference that makes! Eating a couple of Ella's gently fried eggs with a thick slice of this yeasty, buttered, supremely crisp white toast represents one of America's greatest culinary triumphs. The tender home fries, which are why many people go out for a meal as simple as breakfast in the first place, are worth a trip as well.

Ella's assorted baked goods, which are offered by the piece, capture the spirit of American home cooking. Moist banana-nut-cinnamon coffee cake, a stickybun thick with pecans and orange zest, and a light, buttery, sweet potato-raisin muffin are a perfect match for the good coffee endlessly poured here. All the American breakfast foods come to life in the hands of Ella's cooks. Orange juice is freshly squeezed. Buttermilk pancakes are airy and flavorful, especially with an application of the real maple syrup that comes with them. Some southern-inspired breakfast foods, like well-seasoned chicken hash with eggs and toast and fried grits and eggs, are alternatives to the usual omelettes.

I can't imagine a more pleasant place to have coffee and a breakfast roll than Ella's sun filled dining room. Soothed by a warm shade of coral from floor to ceiling, customers sit at small wooden tables or at banquettes along expansive plate glass windows. The shiny open kitchen is part of the decor and diners can sit at a counter in front of it. Each table is tastefully decorated with a small arrangement of dry flowers and a handmade scarecrow. The daily changing menus are elegantly penned.

Ella's also puts out a small lunch menu, enlivened by the home baking. Hamburgers come on freshly baked buns. A chicken pot pie with big chunks of moist chicken and a flaky top crust is preceded by a pretty green salad. Almost everyday there is a different version of a chicken salad and the one I sampled was surrounded by tomato wedges and dressed in a clean, tarragon-scented vinaigrette.

Dinner, which is only offered three nights a week, might start with a delicious warm spinach salad with sauteed mushrooms; a well executed duck and grapefruit salad in a witty mint and honey vinaigrette; or a tartly dressed green salad of tangy lettuces. Most main courses are simply grilled. Save room for desserts like spicy sweet potato pie and tall, judiciously sweetened apple pie. The house-baked dinner rolls are also a treat.

PATRICIA UNTERMAN

EMBARKO ★★½

100 BRANNAN AT EMBARCADERO, SAN FRANCISCO. 495-2120. OPEN MONDAY THROUGH FRIDAY 11:30 A.M. TO 5 P.M.; DINNER NIGHTLY 5:30 TO 11 P.M., FRIDAY AND SATURDAY TO MIDNIGHT. FULL BAR. MAJOR CREDIT CARDS. 90% NONSMOKING. FULLY WHEELCHAIR ACCESSIBLE. RESERVATIONS ACCEPTED. MODERATE.

Embarko's location, right on the Embarcadero across the street from the water, is unusual and fun, though only a hint of a view can be glimpsed from inside the dining room. When you walk inside this sleek, highly conceptualized version of a diner, you are reminded of another Embarcadero success story, the Fog City Diner. The menu format, with a long list of appetizers and dinner entrees running the gamut from meatloaf to paella, suggests a similarly irreverent approach to dining.

Not only is the food wildly eclectic, but the odd shaped dining room has an offbeat edge to it. The glass in tall windows along one zig zag wall are tinted blue and shaded with wide, blue, Venetian blinds. Booths and chairs are pale turquoise. Whimsical, faux, potted palms, each a different surrealistic shape, stand guard along the dining room at the points where the windows triangulate in. An open cooking line in a white tiled kitchen gives people sitting at the counter a show. The large, curved bar at the entryway is crowned by a dropped ceiling outlined with a skinny fluorescent tube that changes color every second. Every kind of shape and angle has been put into play in Embarko's design, yet the decor is cohesive.

The menu, too, offers a multiplicity of choices and its very wackiness turns out to be the unifying factor. Ingredients are good. Portions are large. The food is attractively presented. But what a mix! One meal I ate began with a bowl of matzoh ball soup with light airy balls in a carroty broth; moved on to a crunchy chicken fried steak with dense garlic mashed potatoes, chewy greens, a crumbly biscuit, and authentic bacon-flavored cream gravy with a real skin on top of it; and concluded with a poached pear wrapped in puff pastry with a ginger creme anglaise. Another meal brought a salmon Wellington of nicely underdone fish in a somewhat soggy pastry wrapper on a bed of tomato-flavored butter sauce, and concluded with a gigantic wedge of dense, malty Ovaltine chocolate cake.

One way to approach this menu is to order several of the ample starters as a whole meal. Two of the best choices are juicy chicken satay served with a bright yellow peanut sauce, sharp flavored lettuces, and a little bowl of sweet and sour onions and cucumbers, and crisp, oniony potato pancakes accompanied with housemade apple sauce and sour cream. Tuscan toast, white bread pan-fried in olive oil, comes with a savory garlic, anchovy, and parmesan spread. Another winner brings grilled shrimp slathered with a red spice paste accompanied with greens.

Desserts are monolithic. Huge hot fudge and fresh strawberry sundaes come in banana split dishes. A wedge of chocolate cake weighs in at a half pound. Tennessee black bottom pie, believe it or not, is lighter than the other desserts, with a soft, velvety chocolate layer topped with lots of whipped cream.

The menu is the ultimate culinary free-for-all. If you like rich, spicy, no-holds-barred, ethnically mixed food, you'll love this place. But be prepared for some crazy culinary match-ups.

PATRICIA UNTERMAN

ENOTECA LANZONE ★★

OPERA PLAZA (GOLDEN GATE AND VAN NESS), SAN FRANCISCO. 928-0400. OPEN FOR LUNCH MONDAY THROUGH FRIDAY FROM 11:30 A.M. TO 2:30 P.M.; DINNER MONDAY THROUGH SATURDAY 5 P.M. TO 12:30 A.M. FULL BAR. ALL MAJOR CREDIT CARDS. 85% NONSMOKING. FULLY WHEELCHAIR ACCESSIBLE. RESERVATIONS RECOMMENDED. MODERATE.

Modesto Lanzone understood the pleasures of pungent white Piedmontese truffles, extra virgin olive oil, aged prosciutto and parmesan, porcini, old balsamic vinegars, and fine regional Italian wines well before any of the new crop of California restaurateurs had even tasted them.

So it was no surprise to people who know him when he closed down the formal, eponymously named Modesto Lanzone in Opera

Plaza, to open an *enoteca*, a wine library, that also is stacked with extra virgin olive oils, balsamic vinegars, Italian sparkling wines, and grappas. Arranged on shelves behind a cleverly constructed modern art grapevine, the hundreds of different bottles are proof of the breadth and depth of Italian culinary culture; a culture that Mr. Lanzone has made great efforts to disseminate over the years. He has brought chefs from many famous and not so famous Italian restaurants to his San Francisco kitchen for special meals, and has hosted erudite seminars on grappa and olive oil. The Enoteca, which feels like a completely new operation, puts to use Mr. Lanzone's knowledge and contacts with producers in Italy as the back drop for a thoroughly enjoyable and very smart trattoria.

The black marble bar, canopied with Arnoldo Pomodoro's elegant bronze bas relief, is still the most beautiful in town. A single dining room behind it, with two tiny rooms off to the side, have been painted white and outfitted with shelves for the wines, oils, and vinegars. Etruscan olive oil jars, some original, some reproductions, surround the room. Most of Mr. Lanzone's legendary modern art collection has been consigned to the Hildebrand-Lanzone Gallery which runs down the Golden Gate Street side of the restaurant. A picaresque, wall-sized collage now greets customers as they walk into the restaurant, and here and there is a trompe l'oeil rope carved out of wood or an Harold Paris panorama stuck in an alcove. The fresh, bright look signals a warmer, more casual eating experience.

Prices are about half of what they were, and the menu has been completely reworked. The best part of it are salads, pastas, and the items served at the bar late at night, which are available when you sit down for lunch or dinner, as well. One day at lunch we started with the perfect antipasto plate, a platter of piquant calamari salad, tiny olive oil drenched bay scallops, white bean salad, juicy mushrooms, marinated eggplant and roasted peppers, imported olives, and a slab of fresh mozzarella. Crusty rolls with a saucer of pungent, golden olive oil turns this plate into an ideal light meal. A napkin-lined plate of fried calamari is always worth ordering here as is grilled, quartered radicchio in a tasty balsamic dressing flanked by chunks of mild, moist Italian sausage.

At dinner one night, a classically dressed Caesar salad got the meal off to a fine California start. More Italian, and very delightful, was a clear beef broth studded with vegetables and light tasty meatballs.

The pastas at both lunch and dinner range from plain and simple to rich and complicated and oddly enough, the more complicated pastas are the best. Tagliarini comes in a heavenly, creamy walnut sauce with a julienne of fresh vegetables. A special of venison ravioli explodes with flavor. Another tasty daily creation, called *Cannelloni nere di frutti di mare*, draped a squid ink-blackened rectangle of pasta over scallops and shrimp in a creamy sauce. A simple pasta like cappellini in tomato sauce with basil tasted a bit flat. I felt like grabbing a bottle of olive oil and giving it a shower.

Some main courses seem fancy and formulaic to me, and at dinner one night a couple of them were too salty. The exception was a flavorful, red-fleshed veal chop on a delicious bed of artichokes, porcini, and fennel. A spoonful of crusty scalloped potatoes and some nicely sauteed spinach made this a plate to re-order.

At Enoteca Lanzone, the lightest dessert is a pear stuffed with mascarpone. The rest can all be passed up without great deprivation. But here is your chance to taste some of the 28 different grappas Eugene Lanzone offers behind the bar.

The new Lanzone operation shines because it has become so easy going. Open from 11:30 until after midnight, it is a sophisticated place to stop by for a glass of crisp Ligurian wine and a little plate of food.

PATRICIA UNTERMAN

ENOTECA MASTRO ★★

933 SAN PABLO AVE. (JUST SOUTH OF SOLANO), ALBANY. 524-4822. OPEN 6 TO 10 P.M. TUESDAY THROUGH SATURDAY. BEER, WINE. VISA, MASTERCARD. 100% NONSMOKING. FULLY WHEELCHAIR ACCESSIBLE. RESERVATIONS ESSENTIAL, WELL IN ADVANCE. MODERATE.

A recently opened restaurant in Albany, called Enoteca Mastro, picks you up and transports you to Italy without the price of an air ticket. It's so authentically Italian, so wonderfully Italian, that I'm convinced it would have been a success in Florence or Milan. It gets two rather than three stars because a few too many of the dishes on the ever-changing menu aren't successful. But as soon as you walk in the door you'll fall in love with the place—and quickly realize the occasional flaws don't matter all that much.

What you walk into isn't a restaurant but an "enoteca," a wine store—one that sells exclusively Italian wines. How can anyone make a living selling Italian wines in an area obsessed with the wines of California and France, but paying little attention to those of Italy? For Mark Anthony Mastro, I think it was more a labor of love than a realistic business venture. Now he's expanded into the adjacent storefront to promote an equal love—Italian food. This one, unlike the wine store, should keep him comfortable into old age.

Part of Enoteca's charm is the integration of the restaurant and the adjacent wine store. The restaurant has already become so popular that it has expanded into the wine-selling area, and you might find yourself eating at a table wedged against cases of wine. And the wine store also serves as your wine list.

Enoteca's menu, which changes at least in part every day, is tiny:

■ ANOTHER ASTONISHING STARTER IS NOTHING MORE THAN SAUTEED DUCK LIVERS. BUT THESE LIVERS ARE ENLIVENED BY A COATING OF JUICES FROM THE PAN DEGLAZED WITH MARSALA WINE, AND ONIONS COOKED LONG AND SLOWLY UNTIL THEY'RE ALMOST A PASTE.

five antipasti, three or four pastas, and two entrees. They range all over Italy in origin, but their common theme is simplicity. Similar to what Chez Panisse does with French food, the emphasis here revolves around bringing out the flavors of good ingredients, not on making things fancy. Tuscan bean soup is an example. It's a thick, hearty peasant dish, inspired by a restaurant in Florence, that starts with rich chicken broth and adds beans, greens, vegetables, a chunk of whole-wheat bread, and a poached duck egg on top. Another astonishing starter is nothing more than sauteed duck livers. But these livers are enlivened by a coating of juices from the pan deglazed with marsala wine, and onions cooked long and slowly until they're almost a paste.

Many of the pastas at Enoteca are unusual. Ear-shaped orecchiette, as one example, are baked with a stew-like mixture of spicy sausage, lamb, onions, mushrooms, and chard, the whole thing coated with breadcrumbs. Instead of the normal potato dumplings, fluffy gnocchi come from semolina flour mixed with pureed butternut squash, garlic, eggs, and cheese. Baked pasta shells include a flavorful, spicy blend of fennel sausage, mushrooms, leeks, chard, and parmesan.

The entrees each night include one fish and one meat dish. One night the latter was that old warhorse, stuffed chicken breast. But this time it was a good, juicy piece of chicken, and the stuffing was a delicious mixture of ricotta cheese, prosciutto, and chard. Another night there was steak, hardly my first choice for what I'd order in an Italian restaurant. But this was a thick, tender ribeye steak "battered" on both sides with a coating of fresh herbs and sauteed quickly in olive oil, so you got much more taste than beef alone. On the fish side, a stew of prawns, swordfish, clams, and mussels, all very fresh, comes in a remarkable sauce of sauteed onions and fennel with white wine, tomatoes, and hot peppers.

When you eat at Enoteca Mastro, you get the feeling that Mark Anthony and Diane Mastro are in business primarily to share with you their joy at discovering wonderful Italian food and great Italian wines. In an era when so many new restaurants are coldly calculated commercial enterprises, this is something extraordinary.

STAN SESSER

ERNA'S ELDERBERRY HOUSE ★★½

HIGHWAY 41, AT THE SOUTH END OF OAKHURST ON VICTORIA LANE. (209) 683-
6800. OPEN FOR LUNCH WEDNESDAY THROUGH FRIDAY 11:30 A.M. TO 1:30 P.M.;
FOR BRUNCH SUNDAY 11 A.M. TO 1 P.M.; FOR DINNER WEDNESDAY THROUGH
SUNDAY (AND MONDAY DURING THE SUMMER) 5:30 TO 8:30 P.M. FULL BAR.
MASTERCARD, VISA. 100% NONSMOKING. FULLY WHEELCHAIR ACCESSIBLE.
RESERVATIONS RECOMMENDED. EXPENSIVE.

Taking a long drive for a great meal is a concept much more widely
accepted in Europe than in America. Outside of the wine country,
there are only a few worthwhile destinations in Northern California.
One is Erna's Elderberry House in Oakhurst, a tiny town in the Sierra
foothills on the highway between Fresno and Yosemite.

If ever a restaurant were misnamed, this is it. If you expect to find a
folksy American woman in the kitchen baking berry pie, you're in for
quite a surprise. Instead, you find yourself in Erna's Valhalla, the
palatial realization of the dream of a Viennese woman named Erna
Kubin. Imagine a town that's little more than a collection of gas
stations and fast-food places lining a highway. At one end is the
astonishing sight of a sprawling hilltop chateau of rock and stucco walls
and a red tile roof. To enter, you pass through a gate whose stone
pillars bear the sign Le Domaine Du Sureau, "the estate of the elder
tree."

Kubin, a gregarious woman, greets you at the door, appears constantly at the table, and also acts as co-chef with her partner, Fernando
Madrigal. The two have worked together since 1979 when they ran a
restaurant in Yosemite.

Their food can best be termed Continental cooking adapted to
California cuisine, but it's really much more. Kubin and Madrigal are
far more interested in inventing exciting dishes for their fixed-price
dinner than in reproducing what they've come across elsewhere. The
menu changes often, and you're given no choice on the dinner of a
particular night except to substitute a steak if the entree doesn't appeal
to you.

Consider what they can do to one particular entree as an illustration
of their cooking skill. Tuna on a bed of sauerkraut in a Roquefort
sauce, a most improbable combination if there ever was one, sounds
like a recipe for disaster. Besides, even in a San Francisco fish restaurant,
it's hard to find a piece of tuna that tastes very fresh and isn't
overcooked, since it dries out so quickly.

But Erna's pulled it off magnificently. The sauerkraut had first been
soaked to take the bite out, then sauteed in bacon fat to give it flavor,
and finally sauteed with apples. A delicate and fruity taste replaced the
usual heavy sauerkraut flavor. And the sauce of brown butter, flambéed
brandy and creme fraiche had only a hint of Roquefort taste, enough

to enhance the tuna instead of overwhelming it. Finally, the tuna itself, delivered that day from Monterey, was perfectly fresh and wonderfully moist. The huge plate looked magnificent, with the tuna surrounded by an array of interesting vegetables including spaghetti squash and oyster mushrooms.

That's an example of what Erna's can do to an entree. That particular meal started with what was called beef roulade, but was a clever adaptation of Hungarian goulash to the lightness and delicacy of French cooking. Filet mignon pieces had been sauteed with onions, shallots, and paprika, baked in puff pastry with a bit of spinach and cheese, then served with a seductive sauce of tomatoes and paprika.

There was also a yellow squash soup as good as a pureed vegetable soup can get. A salad dressed with fruit vinaigrette also deserves mention. With some honeydew sorbet and a dessert, this became a country dinner in France transported to California.

STAN SESSER

| ERNIE'S ★★★

847 MONTGOMERY STREET, SAN FRANCISCO. 397-5969. OPEN NIGHTLY FOR DINNER 5:30 TO 10:30 P.M. FULL BAR. MAJOR CREDIT CARDS ACCEPTED. NON-SMOKING TABLES AVAILABLE. PARTIALLY WHEELCHAIR ACCESSIBLE. RESERVA-TIONS ADVISED. VERY EXPENSIVE.

Ernie's represents some of the best elements of traditional San Francisco. Yet unlike people, restaurants aren't allowed to grow old gracefully. They have to change to survive.

Several years ago the owners, Victor and Roland Gotti, realized that tradition wasn't enough for their 56-year-old restaurant. So they transformed the elegant but dated red decor with buttery yellow silk walls and muted tapestry-style upholstered banquettes; the additions mix marvelously with the rich wainscotting and filigreed ceiling.

They also began a "club menu," Sunday through Thursday, consisting of a four-course meal for $36. The choices change nightly but they're drawn from the a la carte menu. They also hired Alain Rondelli, who immediately added a lighter touch to Ernie's French-style preparations. Rondelli has impeccable credentials; he rose to second-in-command during his six years at L'Esperance in Vezelay, France, under Marc Meneau.

The refinement, which is reflected in the dining room and the service, shows up on the menu with a crab timbale with a layer of asparagus in the middle. It is set in a bowl of barely set tomato gelee with three wedges of peeled tomato. The aspic, while delicate, packs loads of flavor. Broiled squab is another amazing dish that showcases the chef's talent. He places a leg and sliced breast in a shallow bowl filled with a smoky broth that's studded with diced carrots, tiny peas and lettuce shreds.

Rondelli has removed much of the butter and cream from preparations here—a style that also works well in a special dish of lobster in a dark broth with Champagne grapes and a frothy dollop of Champagne sabayon. The contrast of sweet grapes, rich seafood, and salty broth was delightful, although the fried sage leaves on top were distracting.

Rustic, less refined flavors emerge in polenta croquettes, filled with Gruyere and positioned on a sprightly tomato coulis. The combination had an old-style Italian flavor. This same homey character is shown in sauteed chicken breast, topped with a crisp blanket of over-salted fried potatoes and served with creamed spinach and shiitake mushrooms.

Other dishes suffered minor flaws. Salmon with a crispy skin was superb, but the red wine sauce tasted fishy and metallic. The potato rosettes served alongside were pasty. Another schizophrenic dish is a smoked salmon tart with asparagus, black olives, tomato, goat cheese, and loads of fresh herbs. It looks like a pizza with a soggy crust, and there's so much going on that no single flavor is dominant: The expensive salmon is wasted.

Ernie's continues its tableside service tradition, but it's best left to another era. It's especially jarring when the waiters rapidly push the carts through the room, conjuring up an image of a freight train. The floors actually vibrate, negating the serene atmosphere the restaurant otherwise evokes.

The major problem, however, comes with desserts. They are consistently mediocre, lacking an artistic spark. You'll probably be more satisfied with a hot, puffy souffle, but be sure to order it ahead of time because the waiter will probably forget to remind you.

The wine list alone is worth a special trip. You'll find more than 350 selections with an inventory of more than 17,000 bottles. There are excellent buys on expensive older vintages, and on some imports.

All in all, an evening at Ernie's adds up to a romantic, gracious experience.

MICHAEL BAUER

ETRUSCA ★★½

RINCON CENTER, 101 SPEAR STREET, SAN FRANCISCO. 777-0330. OPEN FOR LUNCH MONDAY THROUGH FRIDAY 11:30 A.M. TO 3 P.M.; DINNER MONDAY THROUGH THURSDAY 5:30 TO 11 P.M., FRIDAY UNTIL MIDNIGHT, SATURDAY 5 P.M. TO MIDNIGHT, SUNDAY 5 TO 11 P.M. FULL BAR. MASTERCARD AND VISA. 90% NONSMOKING. FULLY WHEELCHAIR ACCESSIBLE. RESERVATIONS RECOMMENDED. MODERATE TO EXPENSIVE.

Etrusca, the ambitious, new restaurant from Italian restaurant mogul Larry Mindel, is meant to satisfy more luxurious and expensive dining out tastes than his Il Fornaio chain. The designers have outdone themselves in creating a stunning, large-scale dining room resplendent with polished birds-eye maple, ox blood mahogany, white marble, onyx, and yards of handpainted frescoes. The pared down menu features a strong list of main courses along with generally excellent pastas and somewhat weaker first courses. The main difference between Etrusca and the Il Fornaio trattorias is service. There is a lot more of it at Etrusca, especially at night, when the white-coated waiters will explicate the best Italian wine list in town, critically describe each item on the menu, split any dish at tableside on carts, and ply you with after dinner grappas and fortified wines from the dessert cart.

Patrons enter at a raised horseshoe bar that offers a breathtaking view of the whole restaurant, and then proceed downstairs into the glowing, high ceilinged dining room that reminds me of a Parisian train station, perhaps because of the scale of decoration and the rectangular shape of the room. Gigantic onyx disks hang from the ceiling softly dispersing light. Golds, yellows and rusts from natural woods, a terrazo floor of crushed marble, and the colors used in ancient-looking frescoes give this massive room warmth. The kitchen is visible behind tall glass walls that frame a three tiered wood burning oven vented by a frescoed hood.

Some of the dishes cooked in this very hot oven have been earthy and delicious, like *riscaldata*, broth-moistened bread topped with cheese, baked in the smoky oven until the top is crusty and all the liquid has been absorbed. Another dish that comes out of the oven is a ramekin of baked rigatoni in a celery-scented duck bolognese sauce with a crust of cheesy bechamel.

The pastas are dependably good and can be shared as a first course. My favorite is a plate of tender fresh pappardelle, wide ribbons of satiny pasta, tossed with a rich meat sauce. *Umbrichelle all'Etrusca* features thick-sided, square macaroni tossed with crumbled sausage, fresh peas, brown mushrooms, and tomatoes. Silky herbed pasta formed into ravioli, stuffed with ricotta and lemon zest and sauced with butter and freshly grated parmesan is delightful as is a perfectly cooked risotto, richly flavored with caramelized onions and bits of lemon zest.

Unlike most other Italian restaurants, the main courses shine here. I loved a gorgeous, rare, grilled filet of beef, bathed in pungent truffle oil, served with a pile of arugula and a spoon of heavenly scalloped potatoes. A thick filet of salmon roasted in the hot oven, comes out smoky and juicy as does a boned-out squab with a loose, savory sausage stuffing and a deep flavored demi-glace sauce. Tasty roasted zucchini and tomatoes, and the stellar scalloped potatoes come with these dishes.

Rather elaborate Italian-accented desserts, presented with two or three different sauces and fresh fruit garnishes, are laid out on a cart so customers can see what they look like. This practice I find to be a little unappetizing, especially since they all look the same. My favorites have been a tender-crusted ricotta tart and an extravagant strawberry semifreddo with a spumoni-like whipped cream folded with chunks of chocolate and chopped hazelnuts.

Like all the bustling Mindel restaurants, Etrusca delivers some extraordinary dishes and some haphazardly executed ones. Turn to the well-trained waiters for menu editing. What makes Etrusca fun, if not a culinary mecca, is its exuberance, style, and superb surroundings.

PATRICIA UNTERMAN

THE FILLMORE GRILL ★★½

2301 FILLMORE (AT CLAY), SAN FRANCISCO. 922-1444. OPEN FOR DINNER FROM 5 TO 11 P.M. SUNDAY THROUGH THURSDAY AND UNTIL MIDNIGHT ON FRIDAY AND SATURDAY; FOR BRUNCH SATURDAY AND SUNDAY FROM 9 A.M. TO 3 P.M. AMERICAN EXPRESS, MASTERCARD, VISA. FULL BAR. 50% NONSMOKING. FULLY WHEELCHAIR ACCESSIBLE. NO RESERVATIONS. MODERATE.

The Fillmore Grill, a bar and restaurant in Pacific Heights, has become the Perry's of the 90's, a place where a lot of straight, single people in their 20's hang out, many of whom live in the neighborhood. The operation is well-focused and well-managed. Half of the space is devoted to a long, polished wood bar with a television mounted above each end. A wooden floor, brass rails, traditional stools, and a high ceiling make bar goers feel at home. Several tables at one end are reserved for drinkers who want to sit down or who are waiting to eat. Since the restaurant does not take reservations, the wait at prime times can be well over an hour.

The dining areas are up a short flight of stairs from the bar, mercifully separating them from some of the noise and the smoke. The simple decor of white walls, green carpet, square white columns, and as much window as possible looking out onto Fillmore and into a garden in the back, provides tailored surroundings for hearty eating. Tables are pushed close together but are large enough to be comfortable, crisply covered in white linen and butcher paper.

The one page, daily printed menu offers a handful of appetizers and salads, and eight or so main courses. They are dishes that break no new culinary ground, but they are what people want to eat when they walk over to their neighborhood pub. Some very crisp, cornmeal-breaded calamari with cocktail sauce go well with beer, and a shellfish and vegetable chowder with garlic toasts is a clean, Mediterranean-style fish stew with mussels and clams in the shell in a tomatoey broth.

The kitchen prepares a barroom interpretation of green salad in that a mix of pretty, small greens are heavily and strongly dressed in your choice of either a very mustardy vinaigrette or a more balanced balsamic vinaigrette with lots of shallots.

The hamburger, with New York cheddar and fries, is perfect—a big, fat, loosely formed patty, grilled exactly to specification, on a soft but crusty bun. Other meat and potato offerings are just as satisfying. A thick, juicy pork chop, nicely grilled, is served with scalloped potatoes and some housemade applesauce and crisp green beans. My favorite meat dish on the menu is roast leg of lamb; three perfect, thin, pink slices on a bed of flavorful couscous, moistened with a natural gravy.

A chicken breast is delicious here, moist and tasty in a ragout of mushrooms, leeks, and peppers, paired with triangles of grilled polenta. One night, halibut braised in an Asian-accented melange of baby bok choy, fresh corn, and basmati rice was velvety and fresh, a surprisingly good dish. Desserts have a barroom heft to them.

It's not an easy task meeting the demands of patrons that have spent an hour or more waiting at the bar, but the staff are pro's; pleasant, efficient, aiming to please. If you're going to the Fillmore Grill to eat, go early or late, as many of the neighborhood regulars do. Otherwise you'll just have to join the party, like you hoped.

PATRICIA UNTERMAN

FINA ESTAMPA ★★½

2374 MISSION STREET (BETWEEN 19TH AND 20TH STREETS), SAN FRANCISCO. 824-4437. OPEN 11:30 A.M. TO 9 P.M. TUESDAY THROUGH SUNDAY. BEER AND WINE. VISA, MASTERCARD. 50% NONSMOKING. FULLY WHEELCHAIR ACCESSIBLE. RESERVATIONS ADVISED. INEXPENSIVE.

Someone really knows how to cook at this Peruvian/Spanish restaurant in the Mission. The food tastes bright and alive; the dishes are colorful and well-balanced. Ingredients of contrasting textures and temperatures work together on practically every plate. You can feel the energy that goes into the cooking. The slightly exotic, carefully prepared food is primally satisfying.

At first glance, it would be easy to dismiss Fina Estampa as another Mission District joint—here today, gone tomorrow. It has the typical long, narrow dining room lined with one row of tables for two and another row of tables for four. Decoration, such as it is, hangs on fake wood paneled walls. Glass covers the tablecloths, but you do get red cloth napkins. A smart black awning on the street gives Fina Estampa a certain cachet, setting it apart from the informal taquerias. Peruvian songs play in the background.

The sole waiter is intelligent, energetic and helpful. The restaurant already has been discovered by families in the neighborhood—on a Sunday afternoon every seat was taken and business was brisk at dinner one night—so he literally runs up and down the dining room, his arms full of plates.

And what savory plates they are—none more so than the traditional

Peruvian appetizer of *anticuchos*, skewers of marinated beef heart aromatically grilled, accompanied by boiled potatoes rubbed with red spice paste and quickly deep-fried. Wonderfully crisp, deep-fried, bone-in chunks of chicken called *chicharron de pollo* come with a bowl of fresh lime juice and chili and a pile of marinated raw onions and tomatoes called *criolla*. The combination is sublime and used often at this restaurant.

A plate of crunchy deep-fried calamari also gets the criolla and a remoulade-like dipping sauce. *Ceviche mixto*, one of the best I've tasted, combines marinated onions and tomatoes with shrimp, squid, and rockfish, along with a healthy dose of chilies. The soft, cold sweet potato and white potato served on the side make the composition Peruvian.

An enormous variety of potatoes is grown in the mountainous regions of Peru and included in many dishes at Fina Estampa. They are the featured attraction of a very typical appetizer called *papas a la huancaina,* boiled, chilled potatoes napped in a bright yellow feta cheese sauce. They also appear in refreshing salads of iceberg lettuce, tomatoes, onions, and radishes or avocado dressed in a delicious garlicky, lemony vinaigrette. Potatoes, cut into sticks and fried, are tossed into a tasty saute of strips of beef, tomato, and onion called *lomo saltado*, served with a big pile of fluffy rice studded with corn.

The restaurant prepares one of the fullest, most interesting seafood soups I've ever encountered. Called *parihuela de maricos*, a deep bowl full of shrimp, squid, mussels, clams, and rockfish comes with a tomato broth seasoned with dried chilies. The menu calls it "Peru's best soup" and I have to agree. Another great seafood dish, *jalea de pescado*, is an elaboration on the fried calamari appetizer, including equally crisp shrimp and chunks of fish served with the marinated onions and tomatoes. The perfectly fried seafood can be dipped into *aji*, a fiery, dark green salsa set at the table. Fina Estampa's *paella marinera*, a gigantic platter of moist, saffron- and tomato-flavored rice studded with seafood, has a depth of flavor so often missing in this dish.

Meat dishes are simple and good, but one stands out. Called *bisteck a la pobre*, it is small, tender, and very juicy grilled steak served on a slice of toast that soaks up all the juices. The steak is piled with sauteed onions and tomatoes, a soft creamy, deep-fried banana and a fried egg. Served with rice, it just might be the most satisfying plate of food in town. *Pollo a la Fina Estampa* runs a close second. A boned-out thigh and breast of chicken are grilled in such a way that the skin, rubbed with red spice paste called *aji panca*, melts in your mouth, and the chicken meat tastes like butter. It is served with a chopped garlic, chili, and parsley sauce and fried potatoes.

Crisp Peruvian beer called Pilsen or either of the two red wines on the menu goes well with the food. Both wines will be poured by the glass. For dessert, there are butter cookie sandwiches with a filling of caramelized sweetened milk, ice cream stylishly served in a parfait glass, and a bright red, fruity, gelatinized pudding called *mazamorra* that tasted pleasantly like spiced crab apples.

The only thing I didn't like at this restaurant was the soft loaves of white bread and scoops of margarine set on the table. Both are very typical of Latin American restaurants here.

Fina Estampa is a small-scale, unpretentious, and unnoticeable operation that distinguishes itself through exceptional cooking. This little place has only its delicious food to offer and it is heartening to see that it has such a loyal clientele.

PATRICIA UNTERMAN

FLEUR DE LYS ★★★★

777 SUTTER STREET, SAN FRANCISCO. 673-7779. OPEN MONDAY THROUGH SATURDAY 6 TO 10 P.M. FULL BAR. ALL MAJOR CREDIT CARDS. 50% NONSMOKING. PARTIALLY WHEELCHAIR ACCESSIBLE. RESERVATIONS RECOMMENDED. EXPENSIVE.

Designed by the late Michael Taylor, Fleur de Lys has never lacked for character or, indeed, drama. It's a created environment, inspired by the idea of a garden tent in the French countryside. Yards and yards of red floral fabric form an interior room. One side of this draped tent is mirrored so cleverly that it gives the illusion that you're in a room twice as large. Visible walls are made of rough wooden planks. Little wicker lamps protrude from the material, giving this soft structure an intimate glow. In the center of the room, under the peak of the tent, a towering arrangement of exotic flowers rises up out of the sea of tables, giving the space a center. The setting uncannily reflects Hubert Keller's cooking which is also highly arranged, but with many references to Provencal country cooking.

Every evening a different prix fixe tasting menu of four or five courses brings forth new dishes from Keller's already large repertoire. One night, fresh American foie gras was set off stunningly by an imaginative stew of endive, sauternes and fresh ginger. This was followed by a flamboyant presentation of spinach packages filled with chunks of fresh lobster and slices of salmon napped with a butter sauce delicately scented with saffron and clam liquor. Next, a lovely piece of tender veal nestled into a savory bed of artichoke hearts and wild mushrooms. For those who attempted the larger "menu prestige," a very strange looking, giant mushroom was delivered from the kitchen as a second main course. It was a hollowed out and lidded baked potato standing on end with a thyme scented squab breast inside. The potato skin served the noble purpose of sopping up a fine red wine sauce. A choice from no less than seven desserts, followed by coffee and a platter of fresh, tiny cookies and chocolate dipped fruit, ends a Keller meal.

Don't fear if you want a smaller repast. Lovely a la carte dishes stud the menu. One of my favorites is an appetizer of a tender corn pancake concealing a thin slice of buttery sauteed salmon, the whole napped with chive beurre blanc and then topped with golden caviar. With each tender forkful, all the elements melt into each other in the most delectable way.

Whenever I see a dish that puts duck breast, duck confit (duck slowly cooked in duck fat) and cabbage on one plate, I have to order it. In this case, the duck confit was wrapped in the cabbage, the rare breast was sliced, and the rest of the plate was decked out in poufs of Hubbard squash puree, peeled sauteed cherry tomatoes, and assorted baby vegetables.

Many dishes, whether they are appetizers or main courses, bring at least two separate main ingredients to the plate and Keller's trick is to bring them together. A custard-like mousseline of scallops accompanies thick medallions of roasted salmon in a ginger-butter sauce. Foie gras on spinach leaves gets thin slices of duck breast. A chunk of grilled swordfish is but one disparate element on a plate that includes a dab of a delicious Provencal relish called Creoja Sauce, five leaves of baby lettuce, croutons, and nicoise olives.

The desserts bring to life my childhood fantasies of what sugarplum fairies eat. My very favorite is a warm, airy, souffled pancake full of warm raspberries with vanilla ice cream in a cookie flower and a little chocolate mousse mouse drinking from a pool of creme anglaise. Bittersweet chocolate souffle cake takes on new flavor dimensions when eaten with a terrine of grapefruit sorbet and fresh mint sauce. A cookie flower with raspberry sorbet center is thrown in for good measure. Other desserts bring chocolate meringue swans, creme brulée, mint-flavored nougats, and all sorts of housemade sorbets and ice creams. The dessert menu certainly holds up its end of the meal. You stagger out of the floral tent, heady from your visit to Hubert Keller's brilliantly imagined world of food and wine.

Chef Keller is unstoppably prolific. Once he gets going on a tasting menu or even a dish, he pours every idea he has into it. There's always something brilliant on the plate, but there's often too much going on peripherally; too many garnishes and flourishes that don't relate to the main structure of the dish. This doesn't diminish the overall effect of his cooking so much as side-tracks it. Hubert Keller is so exuberant, so technically adept, so eager to please, that he doesn't edit. He kills you with kindness.

PATRICIA UNTERMAN

FLOWER LOUNGE ★★★

1671 EL CAMINO REAL, MILLBRAE. 588-9972. OPEN FOR LUNCH MONDAY
THROUGH FRIDAY 11:30 A.M. TO 2:30 P.M., SATURDAY AND SUNDAY 11 A.M. TO
2:30 P.M.; DINNER MONDAY THROUGH FRIDAY 5:30 TO 10:30 P.M., WEEKENDS
STARTING AT 5 P.M. BEER AND WINE. MASTERCARD AND VISA ACCEPTED. 20%
NONSMOKING. FULLY WHEELCHAIR ACCESSIBLE. RESERVATIONS RECOM-
MENDED. MODERATE.

51 MILLBRAE AVENUE (AT EL CAMINO), MILLBRAE. 878-8108. OPEN FOR LUNCH
MONDAY THROUGH FRIDAY 11 A.M. TO 2:30 P.M., SATURDAY AND SUNDAY
10:30 A.M. TO 2:30 P.M.; DINNER EVERY NIGHT 5 TO 9:30 P.M. FULL BAR.
MASTERCARD, VISA, AMERICAN EXPRESS, DISCOVER. 20% NONSMOKING. FULLY
WHEELCHAIR ACCESSIBLE. RESERVATIONS RECOMMENDED. MODERATE.

5322 GEARY BLVD., SAN FRANCISCO. 668-8998. OPEN FOR LUNCH MONDAY
THROUGH FRIDAY, 11 A.M. TO 2:30 P.M., SATURDAY AND SUNDAY 10:30 A.M. TO
2:30 P.M.; DINNER EVERY NIGHT 5 TO 9:30 P.M. FULL BAR. MASTERCARD, VISA,
AMERICAN EXPRESS. 20% NONSMOKING. FULLY WHEELCHAIR ACCESSIBLE. RES-
ERVATIONS RECOMMENDED. MODERATE.

To briefly recap this phenomenal restaurant's history, the original North American Flower Lounge opened three and a half years ago at 1671 El Camino Real in Millbrae. It was the first restaurant to bring high quality Hong Kong style cooking to the Bay Area. The kitchen, headed by Philip Lo, the executive chef of the Flower Lounge chain in Hong Kong, was able to turn out a large menu of dishes so meticulous and subtle that many of us felt we were eating Cantonese food for the first time. The place was packed from the moment it opened and just two years later a second Flower Lounge burst onto the scene.

A mile south on El Camino, this second Flower Lounge offers two floors of dining, a separate cocktail lounge, and two parking lots in a brand new building commissioned by owner/manager Alice Wong. Would the food be as good in this substantially larger venue? It was even better, and once again the dining rooms were constantly full. This Flower Lounge provides the most physical comfort of all the restaurants.

I should add that the menu at the very first Flower Lounge is somewhat different now in that it offers many clay pot dishes and a more family-style kind of cooking. It has kept the same Western name, is still run by the Wong family, but its Chinese name has changed to Fook Lum.

Just a year later, a third Flower Lounge opened and of course the perpetual question hovered about the quality. After several visits at which I ordered directly off the menu (we were the only non-Asian group in the whole restaurant one night), I can only say that the food proved both delicious and completely accessible to anyone who has the perseverance to get a table.

How does the Flower Lounge do it? I asked Dennis Wong, Alice Wong's brother, who manages the Geary Boulevard branch. One obvious answer is that family members are managers. Ms. Wong has always been at the Millbrae restaurants and Dennis Wong spends his time in San Francisco. He told me over the phone that his Geary Blvd. head chef comes from Hong Kong where he has worked with the Wong family for years. The success of these restaurants seems to hinge on bringing top notch chefs to California, and once they are here, keeping them.

The San Francisco restaurant feels small, perhaps because it is narrow. A single room off to the side offers the only seating that looks like it might provide some protection from the clamor. Otherwise two rooms, one in back of the other, are tightly packed with large round tables with many chairs pushed close together around them, all full of people. A bank of lobster, crab, and fish tanks divides the two rooms. Yes, there are carpeting, acoustic ceilings, and white tablecloths, but nothing seems to help the noise level. The decor theme of all the other restaurants, an internal canopy of glazed green tile supported by columns and meant to suggest the feeling of an outdoor pavilion, is also present at 17th and Geary.

The food appears like some miracle out of this chaos. For dinner one night we started with a glistening skinned Peking duck served with hot steamed buns out of which you make little sandwiches of skin, meat, plum sauce, and scallions. What heaven! There was a clean, clear seafood broth with spongy bits of bamboo pith and a plate of nutty slices of geoduck clam, served cold on a bed of spring onions with a gingery dipping sauce. The Famous Roast Chicken is deservedly so, crisp and succulent.

Deep-fried Bones and Sauteed Filet of Sole is a spectacular presentation of delicately sauteed strips of fish and bok choy piled inside the delectably edible deep fried skin and skeleton. Crabmeat sauteed in egg white is one of those delicate Cantonese dishes that depend on the freshest crab meat and a light hand with seasoning. This subtle dish contrasted nicely with a clay pot of star anise-scented Famous Spareribs, another Flower Lounge favorite. A platter of tender baby bok choy seasoned with slivers of Virginia ham is indicative of the careful way this restaurant chooses and cooks vegetables. Of course, no meal would be complete without the glass pie pan of Fook Kin Fried Rice, really a saucy rice casserole topped with scallops and scallions. The only dessert available on this particularly wild Saturday night was a soothing, slightly sweet soy bean soup thickened with beads of tapioca.

At lunch, a large array of dim sum flows from the kitchen including many special ones to watch out for like translucent, rice noodle dumplings in half moon shapes stuffed with bamboo shoots and shrimp. The restaurant makes a fabulous vegetarian dumpling stuffed with cabbage and black mushrooms. You can get individual glass bowls of broth with a gigantic dumpling in the middle. When you break it open, a rich filling of ground pork and shrimp pour out enriching the broth. You season it yourself with a tiny saucer of ginger threads and black Chinese vinegar.

White buns are stuffed with moist, sweet pork; taro leaves are wrapped around sticky rice filled with a similarly sweet pork sausage. Dishes of pure white tripe spiked with red chiles and green onions have a pleasant crunch. Wonderful, lacy, deep-fried taro balls have creamy, savory insides. Large tofu skin-wrapped vegetarian rolls are stuffed with glass noodles, bamboo shoots, and baby corn—a little meal in themselves.

At lunch, a card with special noodle dishes is placed on the table. One of the best is Szechuan, with a hot, red chili-spiked sauce, porcupine cut squid, and fresh scallops all poured over thin vermicelli-style noodles.

For dessert, there are exquisite miniature egg custard tarts, gelatinous sesame balls made out of glutinous rice flour, and all sorts of deep fried pastries filled with red bean paste.

The San Francisco outpost of Flower Lounge adds another jewel to the Wong family crown even though the San Francisco dining rooms can be maddeningly noisy and cramped. The food and service are still impeccable.

PATRICIA UNTERMAN

FLYING SAUCER ★★★

1000 GUERRERO STREET (AT 22ND STREET), SAN FRANCISCO. 641-9955. OPEN WEDNESDAY THROUGH SATURDAY FOR THREE SEATINGS AT 5:30, 7:30 AND 9:00 P.M. BEER AND WINE. CASH ONLY. 50% NONSMOKING. PARTIALLY WHEEL-CHAIR ACCESSIBLE. RESERVATIONS HIGHLY RECOMMENDED.

The Flying Saucer is an eccentric, extremely personal, culinary and artistic statement by two chefs, Albert Tordjman and Donna Meadows, who worked together at Auberge de Soleil in Rutherford. I like everything about it—the "out-of-this-world food," the cozy, corner location, the Bohemian service, the odd wines, the heavy silverplate and gigantic linen napkins, the whole underground cachet this little place has about it. But before I continue, I must issue a few warnings.

The place is very small, with only eight or so sheetmetal topped tables and six or so counter seats in front of the open kitchen. Though the restaurant claims to take reservations by phone, I have only been successful in getting through once—and that was after two visits. Generally, no one answers the phone. On both visits I arrived a little before 6 P.M. and waited until the doors opened. Patrons who come later wait outside on the sidewalk as at K-Paul's in New Orleans.

The wait can be long because the food comes out of the kitchen very slowly. Each dish has about twelve different things on it, all smartly arranged. It's all the two cooks can do to keep up, but the bold and unexpected juxtapositions of ingredients are what make Flying Saucer cooking so distinctive.

The first courses, in particular, are works of culinary magic. An "icy, spicy" squid and shrimp salad was just that, a breathtaking combination of juicy, ice cold, seafood in a super-hot, fruity dressing, piled onto a delicate mountain of mixed baby lettuces sprinkled with fresh mint and roasted peanuts. The salad was clean, refreshing, multifaceted, terrific. The Flying Saucer put out a variation of this salad another night in which the squid was crisply deep-fried in a spicy batter. This time the heat came from a green salsa of cilantro and green chiles and an incendiary red salsa of pureed fresh red chiles.

A spicy, deep-fried, soft-shell crab came with the beautiful greens, the above two salsas, roasted sweet peppers, cooling fresh mango slices, and a sprinkling of sesame seeds. On a preceding visit, the kitchen put out a whimsical sashimi plate with two slices of lovely foie gras, yellowfin tuna, yellow tail, spinach salad, jelly-like agar agar, a fish tartare, pickled ginger, shredded cabbage and carrot, a deep-fried shrimp with head and a pair of chop sticks. Everything on the plate was impeccable. The Flying Saucer is one of the few places in town where you can depend on the freshness of the fish and seafood.

The first courses are so generous they're almost meals in themselves, but there are several main courses that should be ordered if they happen to appear on the daily, changing menu projected onto a wall. One is a peppercorn encrusted, pan seared rib eye steak with big cubes of crusty roast potatoes. Another is a piece of crispy duck confit rubbed with aromatic spices on a juicy bed of black chanterelles and white beans, garnished with a fried quail egg, a sweet little beet, a baby bok choy, a slice of tomato, and a slice of avocado. The Flying Saucer makes the best grilled chicken in town, covered with scallions and an Asian sauce, scattered with a ragout of black chanterelles, garnished with a pile of mashed sweet potato and cumin scented carrots.

One dessert is offered each night. One evening a mound of superb chocolate mousse on top of a buttery crust was the centerpiece of a plate of sliced mango, plum, nectarine, and pureed strawberries. Another evening, two warm triangles of puff pastry came with a variety of fruits, all decoratively cut on a plate dusted with purple powder that tasted like anise, and shaved white chocolate.

If you go to the Flying Saucer, you must have an open mind and be willing to try whatever this passionate and eccentric kitchen is preparing that day. Also, don't expect to get in on your first try, or even to get through on the phone. And finally, don't write to me and say I didn't warn you.

PATRICIA UNTERMAN

FLY TRAP RESTAURANT ★½

606 FOLSOM STREET, SAN FRANCISCO. 243-0580. OPEN MONDAY THROUGH
THURSDAY 11:30 A.M. TO 9:30 P.M., FRIDAY 11:30 A.M. TO 10 P.M., SATURDAY 6 TO
10 P.M. FULL BAR. ALL MAJOR CREDIT CARDS ACCEPTED. 75% NONSMOKING.
FULLY WHEELCHAIR ACCESSIBLE. RESERVATIONS RECOMMENDED. MODERATE.

The Fly Trap is a re-creation of a famous, turn of the century San
Francisco restaurant of the same name. The bentwood chairs, the
wooden floors, the butcher paper covered tables, the wall sconces, the
wooden bar, the very simplicity of the place, are familiar and appealing
to many generations of San Franciscans. A glance at the daily printed
menu conjures up meals taken at Jack's, Sam's, Tadich, and the former
Old Poodle Dog.

One reason the place is so much fun is because of its huge menu, a
list that offers lots of old fashioned salads, chops, steaks, pastas, and
grilled fish with a la carte accompaniments. Yet it has always been
difficult for any restaurant kitchen, old or new, to execute large menus
consistently. The Fly Trap also has that problem.

Happily, there are a number of good bets, especially from the salad
section, like a spectacular Celery Victor, a gigantic, half head of gently
braised celery, chilled, garnished with nicoise olives, anchovies, and
slices of hard boiled egg, all moistened with a mild French dressing.
The classic Caesar salad benefits from high quality anchovies and big
housemade croutons. White Salad brings together hearts of palm,
endive, and mushrooms in a sour cream dressing. A big plate of
vinegary pickled herring filets, served with mounds of sour cream and
pickled red onion, is another fine way to start a meal.

A dinner appetizer special one night brought a square of crisp puff
pastry filled with pungent scallops in a good butter sauce scented with
pernod. Five large, tender snails sizzle in powerful garlic butter, and
brochettes of butter tender sweetbreads wrapped in mild pancetta get
high marks for their texture.

The kitchen prepares some lovely tortellini with wild mushrooms,
large, hand-formed, round ravioli stuffed with minced ham and lavishly
sauced with cream and shiitakes. The tomato sauce on capellini
Napolitana tastes clean and fresh. Two chicken dishes stand out: a
wonderful old creation called Chicken Saute Raphael Weill smothered
in sour cream with lots of mushrooms and big pieces of braised celery,
and *coq au vin* with a rich, red wine sauce full of bacon and mushrooms.

Grilled items, which make up the heart of the menu, can be
inconsistent, both in the grilling and quality. But bright green asparagus or broccoli, both perfectly steamed and napped in hollandaise,
come with them. The simplest desserts are the best, like a chocolate
sundae or a slab of frozen orange mousse with grand marnier sauce.

PATRICIA UNTERMAN

FOG CITY DINER ★★

1300 BATTERY ST. SAN FRANCISCO. 982-2000. OPEN FOR LUNCH AND DINNER
SUNDAY THROUGH THURSDAY 11:30 A.M. TO 11 P.M., MIDNIGHT ON FRIDAY AND
SATURDAY. FULL BAR. VISA, MASTERCARD. 50% NONSMOKING. PARTIALLY
WHEELCHAIR ACCESSIBLE. RESERVATIONS SUGGESTED. MODERATE.

With its glitzy chrome, wood and marble decor, this restaurant
made national news when it opened in 1984. It was heralded as the
return of the diner; a perfect venue for the new American food
combinations. The menu is imaginatively conceived with categories
for breads, soups, small plates, sandwiches, salads, along with large
plates, sides and condiments, desserts and beverages. The diner, which
looks more like a sleek brasserie, has become famous for the housemade
ketchup. It's great with onion rings or fries.

Small plates offer a great cross-cultural mix. Mexican inspiration is
shown in a quesadilla with a slightly crisp flour tortilla outside, and a
mixture of hazelnuts and cheese inside, balanced by a slightly hot
tomatillo salsa. You'll also find a great grilled pasilla pepper topped
with an avocado salsa. The Asian connection is found in prawns with
pickled ginger, or pork satay with papaya chutney. Baked mozzarella
and peppers with pesto have an Italian flair while Buffalo chicken
wings give a nod to America.

Large plates follow the same international theme: Chicken pot pie
is flavored with curry; grilled skirt steak with kobe sauce, and grilled
rabbit with a spicy ancho chile succotash.

The concepts are first-rate, but the execution harks back to another
tradition; a Coney Island roller coaster ride. After my most recent visit
I wondered if Fog City might not also be leading yet another trend—
the '90s version of the greasy spoon. An oil slick covered the barbeque
sauce on the short ribs with mashed potatoes and peas (there were 11),
although the flavor was good. I siphoned off a tablespoon of oil from a
delicious pasilla pepper stuffed with cheese. The Buffalo chicken
wings had little flavor, were undercooked, and saturated with oil. Try
the fried snapper sandwich with avocado, which was excellent and not
the least bit greasy.

Ice cream specialties are always fine, but execution of the baked
goods suffer the same inconsistency as the food. Raspberry pie with
vanilla ice cream also was good. The Turtle, a sundae of vanilla ice
cream, caramel and chocolate sauces, and sugar-toasted pecans, is
super, as is the brownie a la mode. You can also get milk shakes,
malteds, and a wonderful root beer float.

For more grownup palates, the restaurant offers a well chosen wine
list with about 50 selections of mostly California wines.

Since it's part of Real Restaurants (Roti, Mustards, and Tra Vigne), the staff is well trained and efficient. They also maintain a helpful friendly attitude, even when the restaurant is packed to capacity (which it often is). Overall it adds up to a good time in great surroundings.

MICHAEL BAUER

FOOK YUEN ★★★

195 EL CAMINO REAL, MILLBRAE. 692-8600. OPEN EVERY DAY FOR TEA LUNCH 11 A.M. TO 2:30 P.M., DINNER 5 TO 9:45 P.M. BEER AND WINE. MASTERCARD AND VISA. RESERVATIONS ACCEPTED EXCEPT FOR TEA LUNCH ON SATURDAY AND SUNDAY WHEN RESERVATIONS FOR TEN OR MORE ONLY. MODERATE.

At first, the modern two-story Fook Yuen seems unapproachable. The restaurant is so noisy, crowded, and brightly lit, you feel like you're in an airport terminal. But, appointments are basically comfortable, and once the voluptuous food starts arriving you forget everything else. Like most of the new Hong Kong restaurants, Fook Yuen excels at fish and seafood, barbequed pork and fowl, and clean vegetable dishes. A stunning dim sum is offered at lunch. The overall quality of the food is so high that you can take chances. Turn to the ever changing special suggestion page and start ordering there.

One of the most spectacular dishes at Fook Yuen is a whole flounder, fileted, cut into bite sized morsels, dusted with corn starch and deep fried into melt-in-your-mouth nuggets presented in the deep fried skin of the whole fish, a skin that tastes like some kind of fantastic, crisp, bacon. I've never tasted better flounder or better deep frying.

If you've got a group, you shouldn't pass up Fook Yuen's handsome Roasted Peking Duck, carved at tableside by a white-gloved waiter who slices off only the glistening, burnished skin and offers it with tiny white pancakes and black bean sauce with scallion brushes.

A completely different kind of dish from the specials page, braised beef rolls stuffed with Japanese mushrooms garnished with sweet red onions in a rich brown gravy, came off more like an American stew. More exotic, but also comforting, is a braised dish of julienned dry bean curd and mushrooms wrapped in tofu skin. If you're a vegetarian, there are many satisfying dishes to order on Fook Yuen's menu, like a hot pot of all sorts of mushrooms, bamboo shoots, and greens in a tasty broth ennobled by the delicacy of sea moss, a hair-like sea weed.

The seafood preparations are particularly vivid because the kitchen uses uncompromisingly fresh fish. Lightly sauced with red chile paste, sauteed shrimp are practically crisp they're so fresh. Geoduck clam, quickly stir fried with broccoli flowerettes, is sweet, tender and nutty.

A seafood soup with delicate, young peapod shoots has a subtle broth that develops as you sip it. For dessert, fluorescent green honeydew pudding tastes like the essence of melon.

The dim sum lunch offers up superb dumplings and deep-fried rolls. Brought out by waiters on small trays instead of carts, the dim sum are snapped up in the full dining room almost immediately. This means that all the little dishes get to your table still hot from the kitchen. Some of the most interesting ones to look for are skinny, white, deep fried rolls of rice paper stuffed with banana and shrimp; a translucent dumpling filled with aromatic sweet pea sprouts and crab meat; a shrimp cake dipped in egg batter and fried on one side; a small dish of tender squid braised with chiles, ground pork, and ginger; and an airy deep-fried dessert bun filled with sweet egg custard.

PATRICIA UNTERMAN

FORNELLI ★★½

5891 BROADWAY TERRACE, OAKLAND 652-4442. OPEN 5:30 TO 10 P.M. WEDNES-
DAY THROUGH SATURDAY AND 5 TO 9:30 P.M. SUNDAY. BEER AND WINE. VISA,
MASTERCARD. SMOKING ON PATIO ONLY. PARTIALLY WHEELCHAIR ACCES-
SIBLE. RESERVATIONS SUGGESTED. EXPENSIVE.

In the last few years, Italian restaurants have begun to carve out a niche with regional cuisines. The latest addition is Fornelli, (in the former location of the popular Broadway Terrace in Oakland), which is conceived in the spirit of Sicily.

The restaurant is a charming culmination of events that began about 10 years ago when Nancy Vankat, vacationing on the island of Ustica, fell in love with Andrea Caserta, a chef. During their first five years of marriage, they owned a restaurant in Sicily. Then, five years ago, they came to the Bay Area where he worked at such restaurants as Harry's Bar and Grill and Il Gallo.

Caserta's menu has some classics, such as an exquisitely flavored and succulent braised rabbit, studded with pine nuts, raisins, and green olives, presented in a sweet and sour sauce that leans toward the sour. Another classic offering is slices of veal rolled around a mixture of bread crumbs, prosciutto, cheese, and olives. It's then grilled and moistened with lemon dressing.

His innovation shows in a delicious fettuccine alla Tramontana, with shrimp and spinach in a delicate curry cream sauce. He also concocts one of the best preparations of angel hair pasta you'll find, mixing it with tomato sauce, sun-dried tomatoes, basil, chopped arugula, and big slices of pungent garlic. Half-moon ravioli are stuffed with a butternut squash puree that tastes a little like sweetened, canned pumpkin, but the pasta is wonderful and the lemon sauce has a fresh puckery contrast.

Caserta also does a fine job on risotto, which changes nightly. For those who love a strong seafood flavor, his version with clams, tuna, and squid is intense, and the grains are properly creamy and starchy at the same time. Another great way to begin a meal is the eggplant souffle, where the roughly pureed filling is encased in a dome constructed of the vegetable's glossy purple skin. The gutsy flavors are complemented by a tangy marinara sauce with a hint of fresh basil.

The nicely constructed wine list features about 60 wines, almost exclusively from Italy. They're chosen to be easily accessible and ready to drink.

Desserts are the low point. It's not that any are bad, but they don't excite me as they all lack intensity. The best bet is a slice of raspberry and lemon sorbet molded together and served with a slightly tart orange sauce.

The interior of the 42-seat restaurant looks much like it did during the Broadway Terrace days. The ceiling and the top section of the walls are painted blue-gray. Wide louvered shutters give a clean, sleek feel. It's the type of environment and service where you immediately feel comfortable, but because there's little to draw attention, the surroundings recede into the background to let you enjoy the company and the food.

MICHAEL BAUER

FOURNOU'S OVENS ★★★

STANFORD COURT HOTEL, 905 CALIFORNIA STREET AT POWELL, SAN FRANCISCO. 989-3500. 5:30 TO 11 P.M. NIGHTLY. FULL BAR. ALL MAJOR CREDIT CARDS. 80% NONSMOKING. PARTIALLY WHEELCHAIR ACCESSIBLE. RESERVATIONS RECOMMENDED. JACKETS REQUIRED FOR MEN. EXPENSIVE.

The physical surroundings of Fournou's Ovens in the Stanford Court Hotel still represent one of the most unique restaurant designs in San Francisco. A series of small rooms cascade, level by level, down to the magnificently tiled kitchen with wood burning ovens. There, a working chef roasts meats and game under a bower of bay leaves, garlands of garlic, and strings of dried chiles. On one side, a glassed-in atrium with a wonderful view of the cable cars below provides the choicest seating. Terracotta tile floors, wood beamed ceilings, wrought ironwork, and handsome old cabinets and armoires evoke the south of France. It's a space that undercuts the stiff formality of the typical luxurious hotel restaurant with the casualness and warmth inspired by country inns.

The seasonal menus, composed by talented chef Larry Vito, who came to San Francisco via Santa Fe, reads like a primer for the new, sophisticated American dinner house. The long titles of the dishes, really lyrical descriptions, titillate the imagination as well as the taste buds. Combinations both weird and wonderful are spun into appetizers on through desserts. Warm Salad of Barbequed Chicken with Foie Gras in a Smokey Apple Cider Vinaigrette, for example, conjures up images of chicken brushed with red BBQ sauce, hardly what you'd expect with foie gras. Well, the dish turns out to be a dreamy salad of gently smoked chicken and bitter greens in a companionably fruity vinaigrette, with buttery foie gras toasts on the side. In another gorgeous creation, a surprising, crisp, potato pancake is completely concealed by a blanket of mild smoked salmon topped with sour cream and Chinese Osetra caviar—a savory, clever, layered cake.

Simpler but equally successful as a starter is a plate of grilled shiitake mushrooms marinated in a balsamic vinaigrette, or an impeccable salad of mixed greens in a fine sherry vinegar and olive oil dressing. For those who prefer something spicier, the kitchen makes a sharp flavored tomato and red pepper soup, studded with corn kernels and seasoned with dried chiles and cumin. An unusual juxtaposition of crunchy, deep fried calamari on a luscious seafood-infused mayonnaise is paired with small, chilled bay shrimp garnished with minced raw vegetables.

Main courses carry on with the far ranging mix of ingredients and ideas. An exquisite plate brings together grilled breasts of squab, quail, and partridge in a sauce spiked with applejack, accompanied with a pastry cup of tiny sauteed apple balls and baby vegetables. A big, carefully trimmed rib eye steak emerges from the wood burning ovens, cooked exactly to order, with an intriguing smoky flavor. Oak-roasted rack of lamb also is flavored with the wood smoke, a kind of primal seasoning that goes well with the rustic southwestern accents of red pepper-ancho chile sauce and a pozole and corn custard.

Though the meat dishes star at the new Fournou's Ovens, a vegetarian platter of grilled vegetables and mushroom cakes with a fresh tomato puree makes for a light and satisfying alternative, especially when paired with one of the more elaborate appetizers.

The dessert department, newly presided over by a talented American pastry chef, who trained at his grandparents' pastry shop in Switzerland, pairs warm tarts, like caramelized banana or spicy chocolate pecan, with matching housemade ice creams. A lemon spice cake, with thin layers of cake separated by soft layers of lemon curd, is a delight.

You can tell that the relatively new Stouffers management at the Stanford Court is committing themselves to keeping their restaurant competitive with the rest of the city. They have allowed Larry Vito, hired by the original management of the Stanford Court hotel, free rein to buy organic produce and naturally-raised ingredients of the highest quality to use in his lively, Southwest accented menus.

PATRICIA UNTERMAN

FOURTH STREET GRILL ★★★

1820 FOURTH STREET, BERKELEY. 849-0526. OPEN FOR LUNCH TUESDAY THROUGH SATURDAY 11:30 A.M. TO 2:30 P.M.; DINNER SERVED TUESDAY AND WEDNESDAY FROM 5:30 TO 9:30 P.M., THURSDAY 5:30-10 P.M., FRIDAY AND SATURDAY 5:30 TO 10:30 P.M., SUNDAY 5 TO 10 P.M. BEER, WINE. VISA, MASTERCARD. SMOKING IN THE BAR ONLY. FULLY WHEELCHAIR ACCESSIBLE. MODERATE.

Berkeley's venerable Fourth Street Grill seems to get better and better. Under the leadership of owner Susan Nelson, the restaurant has expanded by enclosing what used to be an outdoor patio, and the handsome wooden interior of the restaurant is now decorated with vibrant wall murals of chiles and strings of real ones. Nelson has a real feeling for using rustic Mexican and Southwestern art and artifacts to give her dining rooms character and warmth. Yet, the simple, clean lines of the dining room are never sullied. Though very noisy, Fourth Street offers some of the most handsome rooms on either side of the bay. In the case of Fourth Street, they have evolved organically over the years so that you feel as if you are walking into Ms. Nelson's home.

The kitchen continues to turn out old and new favorites. Some of the dishes date from the opening menu when celebrity chef Mark Miller was at the helm of his first restaurant. I can't imagine Fourth Street Grill without the parmesan dusted, whole leaf "César" salad; the mustardy spinach, bacon, and mushroom salad, currently being made with thumbnail-sized leaves of spinach; incendiary black pepper oysters; and Niman-Schell hamburgers served with the best shoestring potatoes in town.

Other outstanding dishes on the regular menu include a superior version of deep-fried calamari in a cayenne-beer batter and a delicious *pescado en escabeche*, rock fish that is fried, then aromatically marinated, and served chilled with pickled vegetables. Though I don't think of Fourth Street as a place to order ribs, they are exceptionally tender, smoky and flavorful. The housemade barbeque sauce is redolent of dried chiles which suits the baby pork backribs, and the Mexican influence continues with a side dish of black beans. Housemade, white, Yucatan sausages of pork and chicken continue to be a favorite.

Each week the kitchen puts out a separate menu of specials that are supposedly inspired by different world cuisines. Somehow, and happily, the dishes always taste most like Fourth Street Grill cuisine. On a recent Italian night, some fresh Dungeness crab cakes with aioli, and a delicious house-cured roast pork served with baked winter squashes and a piquant onion confit were featured, neither dish being particularly Italian. The restaurant also regularly features several different steaks from Niman-Schell, a Sonoma country ranch that raises organic, range-fed beef.

Desserts are a bit on the heavy side, tending towards mousses, rich chocolate cakes, and creme brulée, but the famous Fourth Street hot fudge sundae is always on hand.

As one of the first of the new generation of restaurants to open in Northern California, it's rewarding to see Fourth Street remain so vital, so true to its philosophy of using only fresh and natural ingredients, and, so much fun.

PATRICIA UNTERMAN

FRANCO'S ★★½

1912 LOMBARD STREET (AT BUCHANAN), SAN FRANCISCO. 929-9595. OPEN TUESDAY THROUGH SUNDAY 5 TO 11 P.M. BEER AND WINE. ALL MAJOR CREDIT CARDS. 40% NONSMOKING. PARTIALLY WHEELCHAIR ACCESSIBLE. RESERVATIONS SUGGESTED. MODERATE.

A pal from Brooklyn told me about Franco's because it reminded him of the Italian restaurants he used to eat at as a kid—the kind with mama in the kitchen and spicy tomato sauce on everything. We all used to like these generic Italian restaurants before *nuova cucina,* but Franco's is a cut above the rest. Though completely dedicated to an antediluvian style, Franco's puts out some delicious dishes from a kitchen that keeps its own set of high standards. Furthermore, this restaurant works hard to please its patrons under a guise of endearing gruffness, mostly in the person of scrawny, mustachioed Franco himself.

Franco works in a chalet, complete with ersatz half-timbered walls, beamed ceilings, and a decor of cow bells and German knick knacks inherited from the former tenant. However, tablecloths, chairs fashioned of solid dark wood, an old wooden floor, and a terracotta tiled entryway lend the cave-like room distinction. Lighting, thoughtfully, is kept to a minimum and the overall effect is coziness.

Franco's is the quintessential pasta and veal house. Happily, the restaurant does them both exceedingly well and Franco, who waits on practically every table himself, will steer you to the best dishes, like a stunningly delicious *pansotti* with walnut sauce made by Franco's Genovese wife. Plump, meat-filled tortellini come napped in an elegant pesto, a suave, well balanced sauce in which garlic, herbs, and pinenuts melt symphonically together. Al dente tagliarini is tossed with imported Italian porcini that make for a surprisingly rich flavored dish.

The restaurant prepares the usual litany of veal dishes using Provimi veal about which there is current controversy, though no one can fault it for not being tender or white. At dinner, scallops of this tender veal smothered in Italian wild mushrooms, made for a memorable dish. Chicken cacciatora brings appealingly browned pieces of chicken in a sauce infused with peppers and tomatoes. A half of a baked chicken

Schiacciata sported a handsomely crusted skin and a simple sauce of olive oil and butter.

There are no desserts to speak of and a barely adequate wine list that offers five or six Italian reds and whites without bothering to note vintages, but this is one of the few restaurants where you can get an excellent cup of espresso.

Everything about this restaurant, especially Franco himself, belies the refinement of the sauces and care with which the food is prepared. The decor wasn't given a moment's thought, and for all Franco cares, the current trends and developments in availability of new Italian foodstuffs might not be happening. Yet, someone at this restaurant really knows how to cook in that rich, old fashioned, Italian–American style, and *ecco*, the eating is good.

PATRICIA UNTERMAN

FRASCATI ★★

1901 HYDE STREET, SAN FRANCISCO. 928-1406. OPEN EVERY NIGHT FROM 5:30 TO 10:30 P.M. BEER AND WINE. MASTERCARD, VISA. 50% NONSMOKING. PARTIALLY WHEELCHAIR ACCESSIBLE. RESERVATIONS RECOMMENDED. MODERATE.

This pleasant neighborhood trattoria, on the corner of Hyde and Green right on the Hyde Street cable car line, offers a typical Roman dining experience. The ceramic tiled floor, simple wooden tables and chairs, a partially open kitchen, two big storefront windows, and a mezzanine for additional seating provide a simple and attractive backdrop for a casual meal. Lots of neighborhood patrons are regulars, though you don't have to wait for a table on the early side of weeknights. The waiters are young and European, and the dining room is happily noisy and alive.

The menu delivers some good dishes, like an unusual antipasto plate of baby pizzas and calzone with delicious red pepper crostini, olives, prosciutto, and marinated artichoke hearts, and a well-handled carpaccio scattered with shaved imported parmesan, capers, olive oil, and lemon. A decent green salad with crisp raw vegetables gets an oil and vinegar dressing.

Some good pasta choices include angel hair pasta tossed in a spicy mixture of wilted arugula, sun dried tomatoes, hot red peppers, olive oil, and garlic, and housemade tortellini in a rich butter and cream sauce with peas, prosciutto, and parmesan. Both the ricotta filled ravioli in copious meat sauce, and housemade noodles in a carbonara sauce of pancetta, eggs, parmesan, and the rather sharp addition of pecorino cheese are competent. A flat bowl of penne smothered in a chili-spiked tomato sauce is tasty .

Fabulous, crusty, new potatoes, fried in olive oil, are served with many of the main courses. You can get them with a nicely grilled filet of beef served with grilled radicchio in a balsamic dressing. The grilled half chicken marinated in herbs is another excuse to get those potatoes.

The inevitable housemade tiramisu, layers of sponge cake and coffee flavored mascarpone, makes for a good conclusion. The restaurant offers a compact but serviceable Italian wine list.

Frascati certainly represents no stunning new development on the Italian restaurant front, but reasonable prices, a congenial atmosphere, a picturesque location, and enough standout dishes to allow for a satisfying meal, make Frascati a welcome addition to the neighborhood.

PATRICIA UNTERMAN

FRENCH LAUNDRY ★★★

WASHINGTON AND CREEK STREETS, YOUNTVILLE. 707-944-2380. OPEN WEDNESDAY THROUGH SUNDAY FOR ONE SEATING BETWEEN 7 AND 8:30 P.M. BEER, WINE. CASH OR PERSONAL CHECKS. 100% NONSMOKING. FULLY WHEELCHAIR ACCESSIBLE. RESERVATIONS REQUIRED. EXPENSIVE.

With new restaurants abounding in the Napa Valley, I was pleased to discover that the twelve-year-old French Laundry, one of the first high quality restaurants to open in the area, is just as wonderful as I remember it. Don and Sally Schmitt run their restaurant in a lovely two story stone house surrounded by trees and a charming garden, just the way they always have. One fixed price meal with some choice of appetizer and dessert is offered Wednesday through Sunday nights at one seating only. 15% service is added onto the bill. An answering service picks up calls during serving hours because all tables are reserved in advance.

One evening's meal began with a cool oeuf mayonnaise, a whole boiled egg in a nest of basil mayonnaise. When you broke into it with your fork, the yolk spilled out, creamy and dark yellow, into the green sauce, a taste sensation. There was a savory new potato salad, German style, with tiny shreds of bacon, juxtaposed with meaty roasted peppers and arugula, and a half fileted smoked trout, dramatically arranged on a plate with head and tail on, topped with pickled red onion rings and sour cream. A sublime, cold, creamy tomato and avocado soup tasted fantastic on a hot Napa evening. The main course was an impeccably roasted poussin topped with a chiffonade of mint, accompanied with buttery green beans and lemony orzo, pasta in the shape of rice. Desserts all centered around ripe, sweet, summer fruits lusciously arranged over meringues, nutty cobbler pastry, or butter and cream-soaked bread in a bread pudding.

A magnificent, all California wine list includes the best bottles the valley has to offer at incredibly low prices, like rare Stony Hill Chardonnay.

Inspired by Chez Panisse, the French Laundry transports you into a world of highly civilized country dining. Walking into the French Laundry for the evening, you feel like you've stumbled upon an oasis where everything reflects the heightened sensibilities of the two owners. Fresh flowers in simple arrangements, soft linen, a leisurely-paced meal punctuated, perhaps, by a stroll around the tree-shaded garden, anticipatory service, wonderful local wines, and simple but carefully prepared food, are still on the cutting edge of dining out, even today. It pleases me immensely that this restaurant has remained so special.

PATRICIA UNTERMAN

THE GANGES VEGETARIAN RESTAURANT ★★

775 FREDERICK STREET, SAN FRANCISCO. 661-7290. OPEN FOR DINNER 5 TO 9:30 P.M. MONDAY THROUGH SATURDAY. BEER AND WINE. NO CREDIT CARDS. 100% NONSMOKING. PARTIALLY WHEELCHAIR ACCESSIBLE. RESERVATIONS SUGGESTED. INEXPENSIVE.

At the Ganges, a modest but very pleasant neighborhood restaurant, you can eat aromatic, strikingly varied Indian dishes without a major commitment of either finances or appetite. The chef/owner of the Ganges, Malvi Dosi, a cookbook author and cooking teacher, makes it very simple to eat at her restaurant. She prepares six to nine curries and a series of appetizers each day as part of an inexpensive fixed price meal. You just sit back as a wonderful progression of Indian dishes is brought to the table.

Papadums come first, those wafer-thin lentil pancakes, full of toasty spices that melt on your tongue as you eat them. You dip them into a little plastic cup of yogurt and cucumber. Golden brown, deep-fried broccoli, and cauliflower *pakoras* are dipped into a tart tamarind-raisin chutney or a bright green, mild chile and fresh coriander chutney. *Samosas*, deep-fried pancakes formed into pyramids, are stuffed with a soft mixture of onions and potatoes seasoned with chiles and a fragrant spice mixture called *garam masala*.

The main part of the meal brings a bowl of dal, a soupy legume puree, and curries. One evening Mrs. Dosi prepared a delicious spinach and white cheese curry. A curry of various dried beans and sweet potato with crisp zucchini and a vegetable curry of potatoes, spinach, and carrots both had distinct textures. They sang of roasted cumin, clove, and coriander. Baked bananas, split into quarters and stuffed with finely chopped fresh coconut, coriander, and green chiles, are another Ganges specialty and point up how nicely fresh herbs and crunchy ingredients work in Indian dishes.

You spoon each of the curries around a mound of nutty, saffron tinted, basmati rice and scoop them up with warm flour pancakes called *chapatis*. A tart, salty medium hot carrot pickle, and a hot red chile puree that tastes like ripe jalapenos brighten all the different foods on the plate. Be sure to ask for them.

Dessert is a high point at Mrs. Dosi's restaurant. She makes dense Indian ice cream scented with cardamon called *kulfi*. A large brown ball of chickpea flour, seasoned with cardamon, pepper, and cinnamon is like a toasty halvah. Don't pass up *ras malai*, a delicate white cheese ball poached in syrup and served in cream. To finish, try a mug of *chai*, hot tea boiled with milk and seasoned with pepper, cloves, and honey.

The Ganges is tucked away in a Victorian building on a residential block next to Golden Gate Park. The immaculate carpeted dining rooms are furnished with wooden tables and chairs, and low tables with cushions. Lighting is kept low. Indian music plays in the background if a sitar player is not performing on a platform in the bay window. Indian artifacts adorn the walls. Mrs. Dosi is visible in the kitchen, separated from the dining areas by curtains, while her husband and a gracious waitress handle the front. There's never any brusqueness or impatience with those who don't know how to proceed. At the Ganges you get Indian home cooking in a home-like atmosphere.

PATRICIA UNTERMAN

GARIBALDI'S ON PRESIDIO ★★

347 PRESIDIO STREET, SAN FRANCISCO. 563-8841. OPEN FOR LUNCH TUESDAY THROUGH FRIDAY FROM 11:30 A.M. TO 2:30 P.M., FOR DINNER TUESDAY THROUGH SUNDAY FROM 5:30 TO 10:30 P.M.; SATURDAY AND SUNDAY BRUNCH 10 A.M. TO 3 P.M. FULL BAR. MASTERCARD, VISA, DISCOVER. 40% NONSMOKING. PARTIALLY WHEELCHAIR ACCESSIBLE. RESERVATIONS ACCEPTED. MODERATE.

The new Garibaldi's on Presidio is a crowd-pleaser. The multinational dishes on the menu are spicy, hearty, and nicely presented—if lacking in coherent style. The fresh looking, white painted dining rooms feature a full bar, tables covered with linen and butcher paper, and big pots of fishleaf ferns. The staff couldn't be nicer or more professional. Garibaldi gives its patrons good value for their money. Those who live near the two blocks of Presidio around Sacramento and California can chalk up yet another winner in their neighborhood.

A bar menu, served at a small but very popular bar on one side of the dining room, offers a generous antipasto plate with a pile of prosciutto, grilled eggplant slices with pesto, roasted peppers, and some flavorful, warm white beans. Another bar dish brings a wholewheat quesadilla filled with hot chiles and melted cheese topped with a chunky tomato salsa. Dishes of green olives are set out at the bar and imbibers also get a basket of baguette toasts brushed with melted butter and dried herbs.

The dinner menu includes soup or salad. The greens in the salad are coated with a creamy balsamic dressing seasoned with ginger, soy, and garlic. An artichoke and celery root soup one day, and a tomato-fresh basil soup another, made smart use of a combination of fresh and conserved ingredients.

The best dish in the house is Garibaldi's *paella*, a luscious plate of moist saffron rice that has absorbed lots of flavor from the browned chicken, spicy chorizo, shrimp, mussels, and clams piled on top of it. Grilled skirt steak, chewy but always tasty, gets a garlic, ginger, coriander marinade and comes with crisp-fried red potatoes and a chunky medley of vegetables.

At lunch, you can construct generous sandwiches yourself by choosing from a list of different main ingredients, condiments, and breads—i.e. house-roasted turkey on sourdough with swiss cheese, aioli, tomato, lettuce, and salsa fresca. Hot entrees are about half the price charged at dinner, and you also get a choice of soup or salad. A boneless chicken breast stuffed with a lot of creamy pesto comes on a bed of those delicious white antipasto beans with a turnip, onion, and green pepper stew and a bowl of excellent fresh tomato salsa—the most generous lunch in town for the price.

The wine list is relatively small and concentrates on California bottles like Vichon Chevrignon, La Crema Chardonnay, and several pleasant choices of wine by the glass at fair prices. Desserts are big and very rich, like white chocolate cheesecake, a wedge of traditional cheesecake studded with white chocolate bits on a chocolate cookie-crumb crust—old-fashioned but irresistible.

PATRICIA UNTERMAN

GAYLORD'S ★★

GHIRARDELLI SQUARE, 900 NORTHPOINT, SAN FRANCISCO. 771-8822. OPEN MONDAY THROUGH SATURDAY FOR LUNCH 11:45 A.M. TO 2 P.M.; DINNER NIGHTLY FROM 5 TO 11 P.M.; SUNDAY BRUNCH NOON TO 2:30 P.M. FULL BAR. MAJOR CREDIT CARDS. 75% NONSMOKING. PARTIALLY WHEELCHAIR ACCESSIBLE. RESERVATIONS RECOMMENDED. MODERATE.

There's something comforting about going to a favorite restaurant from years past and knowing that even though you haven't eaten there in ages, the menu will be unchanged, the food exactly the same. That's how I always remember Gaylord's Indian Restaurant at Ghirardelli Square, which first opened its doors in 1975. You could spend your time looking out at the bay instead of at a menu because you knew everything would be precisely as you left it on your last visit. Gaylord's remains among the best of our Indian restaurants.

Before I get to the food, however, I've got to point to a problem that often casts a pall over a meal at Gaylord's. Service—featuring an

■ **GAYLORD'S USES ITS MESQUITE-FUELED TANDOOR TO GREAT ADVANTAGE, LOCKING IN THE JUICES FROM THE SPICY MARINADES.**

uncomfortable sort of formality—has never been among Gaylord's strongest points. Getting food on the table and then getting the check can be an exercise in frustration. Waiters often seem to disappear completely or else relentlessly avoid eye contact.

The menu at Gaylord's is four pages long; there are 12 breads alone to choose from. And if you order a la carte, you can run up a considerable tab if you want to split several dishes in the traditional Indian style. One alternative is to order the combination dinners called The Maharaja and The Maharani. The Maharaja in particular offers a wide-ranging gastronomic tour of the menu, since you get to sample six different entrees with portions so generous that it's difficult to finish all the food.

Any meal at Gaylord's should include at least a couple of dishes from the tandoor, the cylindrical, clay oven that you can see behind a glass wall as you walk into the restaurant. A tandoor demands real skill on the part of the chef, since the intense heat from the wood or charcoal fire can leave meat tough and dried-out. But Gaylord's uses its mesquite-fueled tandoor to great advantage, locking in the juices from the spicy marinades. Tandoori chicken here is nothing less than sensational. The marinade includes yogurt, lime juice, chilis, paprika, cumin, cloves, and coriander, and these tastes have permeated the flesh, making every bite flavorful and juicy. Moreover, there's no red food coloring, which many Indian restaurants use to give their tandoori chickens a ghastly, neon-red hue. Tandoori fish kabab, sea bass when it's available, emerges fresh-tasting and totally moist. *Booti kabab* offers cubes of high-quality lamb, marinated in spices and grilled.

Some of the curries are as delicious as the tandoor specialties. Chicken *makhanwala* is one of my favorites, boneless strips of chicken cooked in a sauce of fresh tomatoes, butter, and cream, with mild spicing from cumin and coriander. *Sag gosht*, cubes of lamb in a sauce of pureed spinach, features tender lamb and a bouquet of spices to give the spinach an interesting flavor. While some might find it uncomfortably rich, lamb *pasanda*, in a mild cream sauce filled with pieces of cashews, is equally flavorful.

Breads are a good test of Indian restaurants because they so often come out impregnated with oil. But at Gaylord's, no sort of bread is less than delicious. *Nan*, the traditional leavened bread baked on the side of the tandoor, can be ordered stuffed with garlic, onions, and even spiced lamb. Particularly interesting is the *paneer paratha*, a layered, whole-wheat bread filled with homemade farmer's cheese.

STAN SESSER

GEVA'S ★½

482-A HAYES ST. BETWEEN OCTAVIA AND GOUGH, SAN FRANCISCO. 863-1220.
OPEN FOR LUNCH 11:30 A.M. TO 2:30 P.M. TUESDAY THROUGH FRIDAY; FOR SUN-
DAY BRUNCH 11 A.M. TO 4 P.M.; AND FOR DINNER 5:30 TO 9:30 P.M. TUESDAY
THROUGH THURSDAY, UNTIL 10:30 P.M. FRIDAY AND SATURDAY. BEER, WINE.
VISA, MASTERCARD, AMERICAN EXPRESS. 80% NONSMOKING. FULLY WHEEL-
CHAIR ACCESSIBLE. RESERVATIONS SUGGESTED. MODERATE.

The last time I was in the Caribbean, I ate at a restaurant in Guadaloupe whose chef, a young native woman, had just returned from an apprenticeship at a restaurant in France. With spectacular results, she took nouvelle cuisine recipes and adapted them to Caribbean ingredients and spices. I was convinced that this was to be a one-of-a-kind eating experience for me. But no type of cooking is unique when you live in the food-crazed world of San Francisco. Now we have our own nouvelle Caribbean restaurant, a very interesting Jamaican place called Geva's, located on Hayes Street two blocks from Davies Hall.

Geva's is the creation of two Jamaican-born women, Andrea and Opel Baker, who run a catering business and three gourmet food stores. Their mother, Icy Vincent, had trained in New York as a French cook, and was just about to retire from her job as the private chef to a family who live on Park Avenue. Now, instead of retirement, she's working away in her daughters' kitchen cooking lunches five days and dinners six days a week.

With Vincent's French training and her daughters' knowledge of California cuisine, she's been able to do some first-rate adaptations of Jamaican food, taking a traditionally heavy but wonderfully spicy form of cooking and turning it into something much more acceptable in today's weight-conscious world. Not every dish is equally successful; there are enough disappointments on the menu to knock Geva's rating down to below two stars. But the good dishes are excellent.

Everything at Geva's, including the pungent barbeque sauces and two Jamaican non-alchoholic drinks, is made from scratch. Jamaican jerk chicken drummettes are the appropriate way to start, little charcoal-grilled drumsticks bathed in an incendiary marinade. (The word "jerk" isn't meant to be a reflection on the person who orders it; it's the Jamaican word for the marinade.) On the cooler side, but spectacular, are the meaty, fat-free baby back ribs with a dipping sauce that includes ginger, garlic, and tomato paste. Black bean soup is so thick, a spoon could stand up in it; the spicing makes it a satisfying version.

Although the appetizers are all relatively light, they betray their spicy Jamaican origins. But the entrees are much more of a mixed bag. By far the best entree is the curried goat stew, a wonderfully spicy version with high-quality, tender meat. The problem from Geva's perspective is that goat stew is goat stew; there's no way to lighten it up. Their solution—to serve a small portion surrounded by al dente vegetables as well as rice and slices of fried plantain—is totally unacceptable in my book. Curried goat is a hearty dish that's supposed to fill you up, not something you take a few dainty bites of. Another nice Jamaican dish had the same portion problem. A flavorful stew of red peas, rice, chunks of corned beef, and little flour dumplings makes me want much more of it. A fish stew with spicy tomato sauce served over linguine turned out listless and heavy, two surprising defects in view of the rest of the menu. And "calypso" stir-fried vegetables with chicken had a strange, acrid flavor; we left most of it on the plate.

I always have mixed feelings about restaurants that take a wonderful ethnic cuisine and attempt to yuppify it by adding light California touches. Geva's does this successfully in some dishes, less so in others. But the best part of Geva's is pure Jamaican: the jerk chicken, baby back ribs, curried goat, and other dishes that come straight from the Caribbean. For these dishes alone, Geva's is worth a trip.

STAN SESSER

GOLDEN TURTLE ★★★

2211 VAN NESS AVENUE, SAN FRANCISCO. 441-4419. OPEN TUESDAY THROUGH SUNDAY FROM 11:30 A.M. TO 3 P.M., 5 TO 11 P.M. BEER AND WINE. MAJOR CREDIT CARDS. 50% NONSMOKING. FULLY WHEELCHAIR ACCESSIBLE. RESERVATIONS ACCEPTED. INEXPENSIVE.

The unusual interior of this excellent Vietnamese restaurant is practically carved out of wood, with polished columns out of which intertwining tree branches seem to grow. Sconces made of gnarled wood provide soft light. It turns out that wood carving is a hobby of owner-maitre d' Kham Tran, who has put his passion to practical use. He designed and executed the interior himself, with the help of friends.

The food, prepared by Kimquy Tran who co-owns the restaurant with her husband, is wonderful. Every dish that comes out of Mrs. Tran's kitchen exudes freshness. The Vietnamese custom of contrasting hot, savory tidbits with cool, leafy vegetables finds its highest expression in appetizers like *Chao Tom*, charcoal broiled shrimp sticks which are served with silk-stocking-sheer rice pancakes, a plum sauce, and an array of raw vegetables, lettuces, and herbs. You pull the shrimp cake off pared sugar cane sticks and make little packages of them with the vegetables and cold rice noodles in the pancakes. Small, thumb-sized *Chai Gio*, imperial rolls stuffed with a fragrant mixture of minced pork and shrimp, have astonishingly crisp wrappers. These are also eaten in lettuce leaves.

A rice pancake is filled with thin slices of tender pork loin, rice

120

noodles, and herbs, and cut into colorful rounds which you dip into a sweet bean sauce in a dish called Cold Shrimp and Pork Salad Roll. Though many of the same ingredients are used over and over again, the methods of preparation are so different that each dish tastes distinctive. A shrimp and pork salad, composed of the finest julienne strips of pork, cucumber, carrot, and mint, is tossed in a delicate sweet and sour dressing and garnished with lovely pink slices of shrimp. This delightful salad is piled on a crisp, fried, rice pancake shot with black sesame seeds. A similar salad is prepared with threads of beef, radish, cucumber, and carrot, and topped with roasted peanuts. These salads rank high on my list of favored Golden Turtle dishes.

Richly browned quail, flambéed at the table, are succulent and herb-scented. The birds, after their trial by fire, are placed on a green salad laced with threads of onion and fresh mint. You eat the quail and the salad with your fingers, dipping it into a paste of lime juice, celery salt, and pepper served on the side. A whole sea bass is perfectly steamed so that the whole fish remains succulent and flavorful from innermost bone to outermost tail.

The restaurant actually specializes in beef dishes, to the extent of offering a special meal of seven of them which all can be ordered a la carte. One of the best of these is *Bo Luc Lac*, quickly stir-fried chunks of filet in a piquant oyster sauce-like dressing served on a salad. I've never tasted tenderer, more buttery beef. Minced beef wrapped in *lot* leaves are kind of a Vietnamese version of stuffed grape leaves. Both Imperial Beef and Grilled Beef Kabab are skewered with pork fat and charcoal grilled to stunning effect.

The greatest of all Golden Turtle's barbeque dishes is Five Spice Roast Chicken, which has the juiciness and flavor of those incredible barbequed chickens cooked outdoors everywhere in southeast Asia.

Have the creamy, deep-fried, flambeed bananas and Vietnamese coffee for dessert. French white wines, some of which are on the wine list, go uncannily well with the food.

PATRICIA UNTERMAN

GREENS ★★★½

BUILDING A, FORT MASON, SAN FRANCISCO. 771-6222. OPEN FOR LUNCH TUES-DAY THROUGH SATURDAY 11:30 A.M. TO 2:15 P.M.; DINNER TUESDAY THROUGH SATURDAY 6 TO 9:15 P.M.; SUNDAY BRUNCH 10 A.M. TO 2 P.M. BEER, WINE. VISA, MASTERCARD. 100% NONSMOKING. FULLY WHEELCHAIR ACCESSIBLE. RESER-VATIONS SUGGESTED FOR LUNCH, BRUNCH, AND REQUIRED FOR DINNER. MODERATE.

For beautifully prepared, superbly satisfying vegetarian fare, there is no restaurant anywhere comparable to Greens. It has become a national culinary landmark, elevating the cooking of vegetables and grains to a new art form. The view of the Golden Gate Bridge from the long, airy dining room is spectacular; the fruits, vegetables, and every other ingredient used by the kitchen are of the highest quality; the house-baked breads, for which the Tassajara Zen Center is famous, are a delight; and the kitchen, under the leadership of Annie Somerville, consistently meticulous and innovative.

The restaurant serves a popular lunch, enhanced by the fact that you can watch otters and sea lions frolic below in the marina. The menu features crusty pizzas, a satisfying warm spinach salad with feta, mint, olives, and a sherry vinaigrette, terrific black bean chili, grilled tofu brochettes in one of the most luscious sandwiches, and light, flavorful pastas. At weekday dinner, the cafe menu is expanded with several substantial and original main courses and appetizers. For dinner on Friday and Saturday night, the kitchen prepares an elegant, fixed price, five course meal that is inspired by the downstairs format at Chez Panisse. If you've ever doubted that a vegetarian meal could reach the highest culinary levels, you owe it to yourself to try one of these lovely dinners.

A recent weeknight meal was no slouch either. It began with triangles of the best grilled polenta I've tasted, seductively smoky with a soft, creamy interior, served on a thick, fresh tomato and onion sauce. A wonderful sweet and sour cabbage soup with croutons, and a lush antipasto plate starring a white bean salad lightened with vinegary Italian pickled vegetables chopped into little cubes were other enticements. Even something as simple as a green salad takes on new form with a variety of bitter and nutty lettuces and a garnish of sprouted black onion seeds that imparts the most delicate onion aroma imaginable.

For main courses, the kitchen might offer a fragrant Zuni vegetable stew that comes off like an aromatic, meaty chili with chunks of celery root, mushrooms, and potatoes instead of beef. Two triangles of soft corn bread are served with it. More French in character, a leek and butternut squash timbale, enriched with gruyere cheese and napped with a sauce based on creme fraiche, came one night with a compote of apples and dried cherries, and a saute of kale, Brussels sprouts, and chestnuts. The plate tasted like the best Thanksgiving dinner.

Glasses of soft, fruity, rhone red go perfectly with the food. The highly developed wine list features many unusual California and imported wines. For dessert, there are things like housemade chocolate mint- chocolate chip ice cream, subtle tangerine pots de creme with lemon cookies, and banana caramel pie.

Service has improved since the waiters have become professionals, instead of moonlighting Zen students.

PATRICIA UNTERMAN

RISTORANTE GRIFONE ★★

1609 POWELL ST. NEAR VALLEJO, SAN FRANCISCO. 397-8458. OPEN 5 TO 11 P.M.
SUNDAY THROUGH THURSDAY, 5 TO 11:30 P.M. FRIDAY AND SATURDAY. FULL
BAR. MAJOR CREDIT CARDS. 50% NON-SMOKING. FULLY WHEELCHAIR ACCES-
SIBLE. RESERVATIONS RECOMMENDED. MODERATE.

Every time a restaurant closes down temporarily, for whatever
reason, it seems to reopen with—the description is always the same—
"new lighter cuisine using the freshest California ingredients." While
there's nothing wrong with this in principle, the day is fast approach-
ing when every sauce we eat is going to have pureed red peppers in it.
Just for the sake of change, can't any restaurant ever reopen with the
same old heavy, untrendy food?

Ristorante Grifone in North Beach, which used to be one of my
favorite Italian restaurants until it shut down after a fire, has done
exactly that. Putting up a banner saying "the same old heavy, untrendy
food" wouldn't exactly attract a long line of people. But in this case
that same old food also happens to be delicious.

And there's a bonus, too. Grifone's hearty, garlicky cuisine, to my
mind some of the best in North Beach, is served by the nicest, warmest
group of people you could encounter in a restaurant. Grifone was the
creation of the late Bruno Pella, as delightful a restaurateur as you'd
ever want to meet. Now his two sons have taken charge. These two
kids, David and Michael, would make any father proud. They rush
around the restaurant like crazy waiting on tables, apologizing constantly for service that is actually terrific. When you order something,
their eyes light up with joy at the anticipated pleasure of your eating
that dish, and they say, "Beautiful, beautiful."

When you walk into Grifone—a modest-sized restaurant with a
pleasant, homey feel about it—you walk into a wall of garlic. Few
places smell so enticingly Italian. Yet the two chefs are actually
Salvadoran. In the mornings a neighborhood Italian woman comes in
to do the sauces, pastas, and soups, and the Salvadorans take it from
there, according to the recipes Pella taught them from his native
Genoa.

There are fine starters, headed by the gnocchi with pesto sauce.
These potato dumplings, which have the consistency of lead pellets in
so many restaurants, at Grifone come out remarkably light, fluffy, and
tender; a perfect version of pesto, enriched with a little cream, makes
them even better. On the lighter side, calamari salad with marinated
squid, crisp romaine lettuce, celery, and sweet red onions tastes so
fresh it must have been assembled to order; too often salads like this sit
in the refrigerator all day. The minestrone soup is about as good as
minestrone gets—a gutsy, beefy stock loaded with vegetables, beans,
and pasta.

Grifone is one place that avoids the Italian Restaurant Syndrome of good appetizers and pastas but mediocre entrees. About half the entrees are veal—the pink California kind, not the Eastern white stuff from tortured calves. This veal demonstrates that the meat can be tender and delicious without the horrible things that go on to keep the flesh white. The loin of veal is topped with fresh tomato gratin and rests on slices of moist polenta; veal al pesto takes a swim in the restaurant's wonderful pesto sauce. Besides the veal, there is another entree worth noting. Chicken Jerusalem includes half a boneless chicken sauteed in olive oil, lots of good, fresh artichoke hearts, and a cream sauce that's light enough not to smother the dish.

When you leave Grifone, you walk out with more than the pleasure of good food. There's also a glow that comes from being served by a very warm and very Italian family that's so proud of everything they do. This is what Italian restaurants are supposed to be like.

STAN SESSER

GUERNICA ★½

2009 BRIDGEWAY, SAUSALITO. 332-1512. OPEN FROM 5 TO 10 P.M. DAILY. BEER, WINE. VISA, MASTERCARD, AMERICAN EXPRESS. 80% NONSMOKING. PARTIALLY WHEELCHAIR ACCESSIBLE. RESERVATIONS SUGGESTED. MODERATE.

A lot of us—and I'm definitely included—run around checking out the newest restaurants and the latest food fads, and in the process we lose sight of a significant fact: Many people who go to restaurants aren't that much interested in what's new. Instead, they want to go to a comfortable, long-established place where there's an absolute assurance they'll get a good meal at a reasonable price. Guernica, which has been serving French-Basque meals in downtown Sausalito since 1974, fits that description perfectly.

The chef and owner of Guernica, a gregarious man named Roger Minhondo, comes from a Basque village of 700 people in France near the Spanish border. His family and their ancestors have lived in the same house there for 350 years, and his parents run one of the village's restaurants. When Minhondo came to Sausalito, he wasn't much interested in starting a Basque family-style restaurant, which he says is a born-in-America phenomenon unrelated to restaurants you find in Basque country. Instead, he cooks simple French dishes with classic sauces. The good dishes are easily worth two stars, but Guernica gets docked half a star because a couple of the entrees are disappointing.

At the top of the list is the paella. It's a giant platter brimming over with very fresh shellfish, as well as chicken, sausage, peas, red and green peppers, and even some crispy snow peas. When four of us split it as a first course (it has to be ordered a day in advance), there was barely room left for the entrees. Minhondo's paella is the best I've had in the Bay Area. First, he takes care to use good shellfish, and not to overcook any of the ingredients. Second, the rice isn't at all greasy; this has got to be about the most delicate paella ever made. Minhondo says he got the recipe from a Spaniard in his 80's who was a master chef specializing in paella Valenciana-style.

Except for bland quenelles with a texture bordering on rubbery, Guernica's appetizers are completely first-rate. What the menu calls "stuffed clams" is a marvel—little Manila clams done very much like snails, with garlic, butter, and parsley, plus a little lobster sauce and breadcrumbs. They're served on a tray similar to those for escargots, so the indentations catch all the wonderful sauce for bread-dipping. There are escargots also, in little porcelain cups, not as splendid as the clams but still decent. Another good choice is the salad maison, a big plate of lettuces, artichoke hearts, tomatoes, red and green onions, and croutons, with a mustard vinaigrette dressing.

If you're not in the mood for paella or want it as an extra course, three entrees stand out. The sweetbreads come in a tacky metal casserole dish, but they are beautifully braised and served in a rich brown sauce of port, veal stock, mushrooms, and bits of green olive. Chicken Guernica, a Basque dish, is an outstanding bargain, half a chicken baked in chicken stock, Provencal herbs, mushrooms, and garlic. Medallions of lamb came out medium-well when ordered medium-rare, but no one could complain about the sauce *diable*, which includes tomatoes and veal stock.

If you split paella and move on to other entrees, it will be hard to think about dessert. But it's worth saving some room. A chocolate marquis, a slice of rich, very moist cake resting in a vanilla cream sauce, is so good we actually thought about ordering seconds. A tarte tatin for two has a thin, flaky crust and a sweet apple filling.

There's nothing new or innovative at Guernica. It's just good solid French cooking at reasonable prices, with a remarkable paella thrown in.

STAN SESSER

| HAMA-KO ★★½

108B CARL STREET, SAN FRANCISCO. 753-6808. OPEN EVERY NIGHT FROM 6 TO 10 P.M. BEER AND WINE. VISA AND MASTERCARD. 100% NON-SMOKING. FULLY WHEELCHAIR ACCESSIBLE. RESERVATIONS FOR TABLES ONLY. MODERATE.

Hama-Ko, a tiny sushi bar with a few tables, doesn't even have a sign. It seats about twenty- four in a nondescript but cozy, square room. Japanese prints, rice paper lanterns, and a small blonde sushi bar identify Hama-Ko as a Japanese restaurant. Tables are made of plastic made to look like wood. Only two people work here, the chef and his wife, who acts as a very gracious, traditional hostess who does everything perfectly. If more than two or three tables of diners come in at the same time, she does not increase her methodical pace in bringing drinks, setting places, and taking orders. Yet, when she's with you, you bask in her attention.

Hama-Ko is worth some patience. The sushi here has a brightness and flavor that set it apart. Sushi is the only thing that's served, except for a few salads and some comforting miso soup. The *hamachi,* or yellowtail, is rich, fatty, and delicious. *Uni,* or sea urchin roe, is brilliantly fresh, creamy, and nutty, topped with a high-yolked quail egg. The sensations in your mouth when you eat this delicacy confirm that food can be art. The giant clam, or *mirugai,* tastes like a little bite of the sea. An *unagi,* or barbequed freshwater eel handroll, is one way to get enough of this delicately sweet, savory fish. A double-size piece is rolled into a cone of seaweed filled with rice and wasabi.

For a very moderate price, patrons can get a plate of mixed sushi that includes a pair of ccoked shrimp sushi, a pair of *maguro* or red tuna, a piece of giant clam or *mirugai,* one smoked salmon sushi, and *kappa maki,* a roll of cucumber and rice in seaweed that makes for a substantial meal. The Japanese spinach salad is also excellent, a stack of pressed together, stacked spinach leaves, cooked and chilled, sprinkled with sesame seeds and a sharp rice wine vinegar and soy sauce dressing. Even the pickled ginger, pink, thinly sliced, almost delicate, seems special.

The sushi chef, Ted Kashiyama, makes a point of going to the wharf to buy things like scallops and Dungeness crab from freshness fanatics like Paul Johnson of Monterey Fish. If you call ahead and bring a small group, Mr. Kashiyama and his wife will put out a fantastic, multi-course meal of hot and cold dishes for a fixed price. By putting yourself in his hands, you will get one of the highest quality and most unusual Japanese meals in the city.

PATRICIA UNTERMAN

HAMANO SUSHI ★★

1332 CASTRO, SAN FRANCISCO. 826-0825. OPEN TUESDAY THROUGH SATURDAY FROM 5:30 TO 10:30 P.M., SUNDAY 5:30 TO 9:30 P.M. AND MONDAY 6 TO 9:30 P.M. BEER AND WINE. VISA AND MASTERCARD. 80% NONSMOKING. FULLY WHEELCHAIR ACCESSIBLE. RESERVATIONS ACCEPTED. MODERATE.

Hamano Sushi, a charming, new sushi bar and Japanese restaurant in Noe Valley, provides an appealing backdrop for sushi eating. It's a long, narrow restaurant with a hand-tooled blonde sushi bar in the front and a raised dining area in the back. The wooden front door and wall lamps are also beautifully made. The food, sake, and soy sauce all come in handsome Japanese ceramics. Classical music plays in the background.

You can't go wrong ordering anything raw here, including Japanese salads. Clear, yam noodle salad with bits of cucumber in a rice wine vinegar and soy dressing; a refreshing Japanese cucumber salad with surprisingly tender slices of octopus, and the classic *goma ae*, a haystack of cold, boiled spinach sprinkled with sesame seed in a miso dressing, are all wonderful, light, starting tidbits.

The fish in sushi is generously cut, tender, sinew-free; the rice, conservatively swabbed with green wasabi. *Hamachi*, or yellowtail, *maguro*, or red tuna, and unagi, that delectable, barbequed fresh water eel are dependable choices. Exceptional here is giant clam or mirugai, tender, sweet and nutty.

Hamano specializes in *makimono* or rolls of sushi encased by rice instead of seaweed. This makes for colorful rounds filled with such combinations as *unagi* and cucumber, crab, avocado, and crunchy flying fish roe, or vegetarian rolls of pickled burdock, spinach, or avocado and cucumber. My favorite is the spicy tuna roll, a rich California creation of avocado, mayonnaise, and *maguro*, or red tuna, rolled in seaweed, then rice. I couldn't eat at Hamano without ordering one of these.

The prices of sushi and rolls are listed on a separate sushi menu so there's no guessing when your bill comes, a common complaint at some sushi bars. You can reconstruct the bill yourself. This policy, the handsome appointments, and good service make Hamano a dependable, accessible, much frequented neighborhood sushi house.

PATRICIA UNTERMAN

HARBOR VILLAGE ★★★

EMBARCADERO FOUR, SAN FRANCISCO. 398-8883. OPEN FOR LUNCH MONDAY THROUGH FRIDAY 11 A.M. TO 2:30 P.M., SATURDAY 10:30 A.M. TO 2:30 P.M., SUNDAY 10 A.M. TO 2:30 P.M.; DINNER NIGHTLY 5:30 TO 9:30 P.M. FULL BAR. VISA, MASTER-CARD, AMERICAN EXPRESS. 75% NONSMOKING. FULLY WHEELCHAIR ACCESSIBLE. RESERVATIONS ACCEPTED FOR LUNCH AND DINNER. INEXPENSIVE TO MODERATE.

In addition to its downtown location, which affords urban views of the bay and Vaillancourt Fountain from an airy, glassed-in back room, Harbor Village's refined decor and service set it apart. The seemingly labyrinthine dining rooms are lushly carpeted, furnished with lacquered chairs and white damask covered tables. Partially enclosed interior spaces are used as private dining rooms. Shiny brass and Oriental antiques abound. The waiters and waitresses wear formal black and white uniforms and serve out of covered silver platters and tureens. Patrons eat on fragile, rice-shot porcelain. A detail that most impressed

■ MIRACULOUSLY TENDER OCTOPUS SLICES, FRECKLED WITH HOT RED CHILES, COME WITH A MILD, GREEN, WASABI DIPPING SAUCE.

me was the velvety-soft, unstarched damask napkins that lay heavily on the lap. I haven't seen anything like it outside of three star restaurants in France.

Almost in contradiction to its formality, Harbor Village is a huge operation, large enough to put on a full scale dim sum lunch seven days a week. Women in starched white uniforms push carts silently over the carpeting, offering bonafide delicacies. This is one of the few places that makes *shaolin bao*, twisted dumplings filled with shrimp, cabbage, black mushrooms, and a gush of flavorful stock which is put into the dumplings in a cold, gelatinized state. Beautiful shrimp pearl balls, opalescent with pearly rice, are filled with chopped shrimp barely bound together. Elegant slices of cured pork shank rest on a bed of orange soy beans waiting for a splash of vinegary sauce. Miraculously tender octopus slices, freckled with hot red chiles, come with a mild, green, wasabi dipping sauce.

Pork dumplings with rice noodle wrappers surprise you with the crunch of peanuts, dried shrimp, and Chinese celery, while pure-flavored *har gow*, shrimp dumplings, fulfill your highest shellfish expectations. At the end of the meal, sweet curried turnovers with flaky crusts and sandy-crusted egg custards roll out of the kitchen.

At night, the dim sum carts are garaged and dinner menus are hauled out. They offer many delicacies as well. Harbor Village makes an intriguing chicken salad with velvety shreds of chicken breast, bits of crunchy deep fried rice noodle, peanuts, bean sprouts, the traditional jelly fish, as well as Chinese pickles and fresh fruit. It is my favorite dish at this restaurant.

Little broccoli flowerettes stay crisp and bright green inside a pretty pink shrimp ball. Tiny clams must have been startled into opening their shells by a fiery hot wok, because their insides taste like they were just pulled from the sea in a preparation called Fresh Clam Saute with Blackbean and Hot Pepper Sauce. Perfectly fresh crab is infused with the aroma of ginger and scallions. I suggest finishing off your meal with one of Harbor Village's noodle dishes, like Fried Vermicelli Harbor Village Style, angel hair noodles dotted with surprises like little nuggets of shrimp and chicken, bits of sweetened egg, beans sprouts, and shredded carrot. Not a drop of excess oil mars this light, tasty plate of noodles. For dessert, try the cold and refreshing fruit soup of pureed honeydew melon thickened with a little tapioca. It hits the spot.

PATRICIA UNTERMAN

HARPOON LOUIE'S ★½

55 STEVENSON STREET, SAN FRANCISCO. 543-3540. LUNCH SERVED MONDAY
THROUGH FRIDAY FROM 11 A.M. TO 3 P.M.; COCKTAILS UNTIL 9 P.M. FULL BAR.
VISA, MASTERCARD, AMERICAN EXPRESS. 25% NONSMOKING. PARTIALLY
WHEELCHAIR ACCESSIBLE. RESERVATIONS FOR PARTIES OF FIVE OR MORE.
INEXPENSIVE.

Harpoon Louie's comes straight out of *Cheers*—the television
sitcom. Located in an alley between Market and Mission, New
Montgomery and Ecker, the dark, high ceilinged, red brick barroom is
packed, noisy and full of smoke by 11:30 every day. Both the food and
the atmosphere are a throwback to the time when Financial District
workers actually drank cocktails and ate a real meal at lunchtime.

People sit at the long, well-worn wooden bar or at small wooden
tables half covered with condiments. They hang their jackets on tall
oak pillars that bisect the room. The dark wooden floors, bentwood
chairs, mounted stuffed fish, gilt frame mirrors, and old photographs of
historic San Franciscans capture a genuine saloon look. The management, which mails out wacky circulars touting the week's blue plate
specials, somehow has found a staff that combines low key friendliness
with efficiency.

The smallish regular menu offers a good house salad of mixed cut
greens in a tart vinaigrette with variations like peppery grilled shrimp
placed on top. There are hamburgers, a chicken breast sandwich with
chile mayonnaise, and a few grilled items. But the soul of this menu
resides in the daily blue plate special. Typical is a very moist, crisp,
bread crumbed fried chicken with flavorful cream gravy, mashed
potatoes, a couple of crunchy biscuits, and a big tree of perfectly
steamed bright green broccoli. The daily pasta is an excuse to eat large
amounts of sauce as in fettucine carbonara, swimming in a cheesy, egg
yolk thickened emulsion studded with large pieces of bacon and
onion—excessively rich, but tasty.

Dessert has run out every time I've lunched here and the coffee is
typically American and thin. But each week those specials are cranked
out with real conviction. One week brought five different dishes from
the Southern Pacific Railroad dining car; another, hearty grillroom
fare like stuffed pork chops, roast leg of lamb, and chicken with
artichokes and mushrooms. The prices are low and the food satisfies in
a hearty, old-style way.

PATRICIA UNTERMAN

■ **THE SOUL OF THIS MENU RESIDES IN THE DAILY BLUE
PLATE SPECIAL. THE PRICES ARE LOW AND THE FOOD
SATISFIES IN A HEARTY, OLD-STYLE WAY.**

HARRIS' ★★½

2100 VAN NESS AVENUE, SAN FRANCISCO. 673-1888. OPEN FOR DINNER EVERY-
DAY 5 TO 11 P.M., WEDNESDAY LUNCH 11:30 A.M. TO 2 P.M. FULL BAR. ALL MAJOR
CREDIT CARDS. 50% NONSMOKING. FULLY WHEELCHAIR ACCESSIBLE. RESER-
VATIONS RECOMMENDED. EXPENSIVE.

Sometimes even a San Franciscan can get tired of California
Cuisine. There are moments when a person wants to sink her teeth
into a thick, juicy, charcoal broiled steak with a baked potato smothered in butter and sour cream and maybe wash it down with a dry
martini. Ann Harris' steak palace provides this old-fashioned experience.

The large corner building has a gorgeous coat of sand-colored paint
highlighted by green and rust trim. The inside looks like a movie set of
a toney restaurant from the sixties except that everything is real—the
rain forest-sized ferns, the wood paneling, the Barnaby Conrad wall
murals, the gigantic booths, the cozy library, the skylit garden room,
the dark, clubby bar.

The other noteworthy attribute of this restaurant is that it is truly
comfortable. You aren't crammed into hard chairs at small tables
placed too close together. The noise level is civilized, buffered by
miles of thick carpeting, high ceilings, and pounds of drapes. The bar is
in a completely separate room, away from the eating. Finally, gracious
and elegant Ann Harris presides over the dining room, making sure
everyone is taken care of just right.

She is a traditionalist with an eagle eye for detail. Martinis come in
miniature carafes in miniature ice buckets so they stay perfectly
chilled. With drinks you are brought a small portion of the Harris
house paté, made of minced sweetbreads, and a stack of good toast—a
delicious little treat. Start with fresh Blue Point oysters on the half shell
with a horseradish-seasoned red cocktail sauce. Two can split a Caesar
salad. The romaine is crisp and the croutons freshly toasted. The best
salad is a traditional fresh spinach salad with sieved egg. The onion
soup gets its flavor from a real beef stock, not a carapace of melted
cheese and bread. Appetizers such as deep-fried mushrooms or zucchini
come hot from the kitchen, lightly battered and fried in good, neutral
oil.

This is the place for a hefty T-Bone or the wonderful Harris Steak,
a New York with the featherbone left on. Both have been seared over
mesquite to your specifications. The Porterhouse is fine, the Harris cut
superior. It has the most flavor of all the steaks on the menu and
perhaps the most age. The fresh vegetables on the plate are buttery and
bright. The little red potatoes are sweet. A baked potato served with
butter, real sour cream, and real bacon bits must be ordered a la carte,
as must Harris' excellent creamed spinach. The Harris cut of prime rib

served with freshly grated horseradish runs out early. Both the grilled chicken breast and roast duckling are moist and tender. But the steaks are everyone's first choice here.

Ms. Harris used to require a jacket and tie. Recently she has instituted seating in the handsome bar for those more casually dressed. In either attire, patrons get royal treatment at this clubby, traditional, steakhouse.

PATRICIA UNTERMAN

HAYES STREET GRILL ★★★

324 HAYES ST. (NEAR FRANKLIN), SAN FRANCISCO. 863-5545. OPEN FOR LUNCH MONDAY THROUGH FRIDAY 11:30 A.M. TO 2 P.M.; DINNER MONDAY THROUGH THURSDAY 5 TO 10 P.M., FRIDAY UNTIL 11 P.M., SATURDAY 6 TO 11 P.M. FULL BAR. VISA, MASTERCARD, DISCOVER. 70% NONSMOKING. FULLY WHEELCHAIR AC-CESSIBLE. RESERVATIONS RECOMMENDED. MODERATE TO EXPENSIVE.

When I talk to visitors to San Francisco who want restaurant recommendations, the first thing they normally ask about is where to get good fish. I can tell them about a few French, California cuisine, and Chinese places whose fish entrees are generally excellent. But when it comes to restaurants specializing in fish, there's a real problem. My list has but one choice, and that's Hayes Street Grill.

It's difficult for me to write about Hayes Street Grill because one of the partners is Patricia Unterman, the primary author of this book. Yet the fact remains that Hayes Street is the only fish restaurant I've found that really cares. They care whether the fish is fresh and whether it's not overcooked when it comes to your table. They remain interesting and innovative after more than a decade of operation. And, if you're going to the nearby opera or symphony, they get you out on time without your having to glance nervously at your watch all during the meal.

So, while there's a clear conflict of interest in my writing about Hayes Street, I have to write about it anyway, since a restaurant review book for San Francisco would have a huge hole in it without at least one superb fish restaurant. I'd feel better if I could pepper this review with negative comments, but I have only one: I've found the grilled tuna at Hayes Street uniformly overcooked and dried out. Fortunately, there are about two dozen other things on the menu, and I don't think you'll encounter a loser among them.

The menu changes every day to reflect what's fresh, and the centerpiece of the menu is a list of about ten fish grilled over mesquite. You choose the fish (swordfish and salmon are commonly featured, but there are always more exotic choices like spearfish and mako shark); you choose the sauce (tomatillo salsa and Sichuan peanut are nice unusual alternatives). The sauce comes on the side, so there's no danger of the beautiful fresh piece of fish being drowned out. On the side are the best french fries in San Francisco.

If you find the idea of grilled fish not interesting enough, you'll still walk away from Hayes Street satisfied. There are several sauteed fish and shellfish dishes each day that are often quite creative, like angler and clams with white beans, savoy cabbage, and pancetta, or roasted steelhead trout with tomatoes, fennel, and rosemary. And the unusual appetizers are always a treat. I generally can't resist the salads, things like grilled scallops with papaya and mango, or smoked trout toasts with an orange and radish salad. Finally, meat lovers can wolf down a Niman-Schell steak; this is from a ranch in Marin County that produces the best beef in California.

There are always excellent desserts, particularly the deep-dish pies and the crisps. And the extensive wine and beer list shows that Hayes Street cares about what you're drinking. Overall, it's the sort of experience a tourist will love. And, unlike many other fish restaurants that exist largely for tourists, out-of-town visitors to Hayes Street will be rubbing elbows with lots of satisfied San Franciscans who keep coming again and again.

STAN SESSER

HELMAND ★★★

430 BROADWAY, SAN FRANCISCO. 362-0641. OPEN FOR LUNCH MONDAY THROUGH FRIDAY 11:30 A.M. TO 2:30 P.M., DINNER MONDAY THROUGH THURS- DAY, 6 TO 10 P.M., FRIDAY AND SATURDAY, 6 TO 11 P.M. FULL BAR. MASTERCARD, VISA. 60% NONSMOKING. FULLY WHEELCHAIR ACCESSIBLE. RESERVATIONS RECOMMENDED FOR DINNER. INEXPENSIVE.

The Bay Area boasts so many different ethnic restaurants that it is hard to get excited about one more—and a seemingly exotic Afghani one at that—but the Helmand, a new restaurant on Broadway between Montgomery and Kearny is the best restaurant of any nationality I've encountered in a long time. The cooking, which is unique but reminiscent of elements in Persian, Indian and Middle Eastern cuisines, is so lovingly and skillfully prepared that every dish on the menu provides a revelation about how wonderful food can taste. The gracious professional service, well chosen wine list and simple, tradi- tional dining room are all worthy of the food.

The five spectacular appetizers define the breadth of the cuisine. Several of them are offered as main courses as well. *Aushak*, large, tender skinned ravioli filled with sauteed leeks, are served on a bed of yogurt speckled with fresh mint and then topped with a mild, buttery, meat sauce. The dish is so delicately constructed that the raviolis seem to melt in your mouth. Another textural thrill comes with *kaddo borawni*, pumpkin that has been deep fried and roasted, then moistened with garlic scented yogurt. Pan fried then roasted eggplant also achieves a superb creaminess underscored by yogurt, but the dish takes on a Mediterranean flavor from smoky roasted tomatoes and peppers.

In *mantwo*, the housemade noodles are filled with buttery onions and chopped beef and topped with a delicious sauce of carrots and slightly al dente yellow split peas. In one more noodle permutation, noodle dough is stuffed with either Indian spiced potatoes or leeks and cleanly deep-fried, accompanied by a dollop of thick yogurt sprinkled with mint.

You can't pass up any of the three soups, a small portion served in a big, deep bowl. *Aush* is like a liquid version of those addictive raviolis in *aushak*, in that tender noodles are served in a minted yogurt soup drizzled with the meat sauce. *Mashawa* is a warm, delicious yogurt soup full of mint and dill, studded with legumes like mung beans, chick peas, black eyed peas, and chunks of beef. *Shorwa*, a vegetable soup, features a clear, elegant lamb broth with green beans, cauliflower, black eyed peas, carrots, and potatoes.

Main courses are heartier, meatier, more rustic. Most of them come with big portions of light airy rice, seasoned either with cumin seeds or with meat broth and cinnamon. *Koufta challow* (challow refers to cumin-scented rice) are large, soft meatballs in hot, cinnamon-scented tomato sauce strewn with green peas while *sahzy challow* brings chunks of braised beef napped in spicy spinach puree. Marinated, grilled chunks of chicken breast called *mourgh kabab*, skewered with smoky vegetables, stand out for their superb texture.

Lamb gets a number of interesting treatments. *Dwopiaza*, medium rare chunks of grilled lamb, are sauced with vinegared onions and yellow split peas and presented on a square of Afghani flat bread that soaks up all the juices. Juicy rack of lamb chops come with a chopped salad. The Afghani version of *theeka kabab* gives yogurt-marinated beef kebabs a sweet and sour twist with golden raisins. Oddly enough, the Italian wines on the short wine list go marvelously with the food.

The desserts are unusual and wonderful like a cardamon scented, basmati rice pudding and a velvety, reduced milk custard served on a flat plate. Both are sprinkled with crushed pistachios. *Burfee*, an ice cream also made from reduced milk, is superb. A big chunk of it towers over an ice cream glass filled with frozen clotted cream.

The long, narrow dining room is furnished with polished antique cabinets displaying glass bowls of colorful spices and Afghani costumes. Blue carpeting and blue upholstered chairs, white walls hung with framed oil paintings, and a red brick wall hung with an intricately woven Oriental rug give the space elegance. Tables are covered with real white linen and decorated with fresh red tulips, appointments that would suggest a much more expensive restaurant.

From the moment you walk into the Helmand and are greeted by a serene, dark haired hostess, to the paying of the miraculously small check, you are embraced by people who both know and care about what they are doing. I can't recommend the Helmand highly enough.

PATRICIA UNTERMAN

HING LUNG RESTAURANT ★★½

674 BROADWAY, SAN FRANCISCO. 398-8838. OPEN EVERY DAY FROM 8 A.M. TO 1 A.M. BEER AND WINE. MASTERCARD AND VISA. 50% NONSMOKING. PARTIALLY WHEELCHAIR ACCESSIBLE. RESERVATIONS NOT ACCEPTED. INEXPENSIVE.

Very Chinese and unique to San Francisco, Hing Lung specializes in *congee*, rice noodles, and Chinese fried bread. This bill of fare may seem exotic to the uninitiated, but the food served at Hing Lung is light, tasty, and satisfying for anyone who gives it a try. Also, the price can't be beat.

Everyone orders *congee* or *juk* here, a milky white rice porridge kept hot in a gigantic sunken vat at one side of a wildly active glassed-in kitchen at the entrance to the restaurant. Exactly the right amount of congee to fill one bowl is ladled into sauce pans and brought to a rolling boil over a high flame. Then the porridge is poured over finely shredded ingredients waiting in the serving bowls. Cilantro, ginger, and scallions are usually part of the seasoning but the overall effect of congee is soothing and restorative. Congee is eaten for breakfast and late at night, though hundreds of bowls of it are served at lunch as well.

My favorite version, called Fresh Sliced Hard Head Porridge, is flecked with tiny strips of a trout-like fish, mushrooms, scallions and slivers of ginger. Earthy Sampan Porridge comes with shrimp, scallions, bits of fish, lettuce and roasted peanuts—the strongest flavored of all the congee. The congee for which Hing Lung is famous, Pork Giblet Porridge, is a miraculous preparation in which the sweetest, most velvety pork liver, freshest pork kidney, pork meatballs and tripe are simmered in the congee to exactly the right degree of doneness, leaving the porridge both rich and clean flavored. Anyone who likes foie gras should try it.

The other special dish made here is fried bread, which looks like a long, oblong doughnut. Yeasty, airy, crisp and unsweetened, they are irresistible hot from the fryer. You can order them wrapped in a freshly steamed rice noodle, cut into sections, topped with sesame seeds and seasoned with a soy, ginger, and peanut oil dipping sauce.

One chef in the kitchen is constantly forming shrimp dumplings and wontons which go into a fairly mundane broth. But the fascinating thing to watch and eat, besides the congee, are the pearly sheets of rice noodles being made from a thin batter on a special rectangular steamer covered with oiled canvas. That amazingly sweet pork liver, or barbequed pork or shrimp, to name just a few items, are cooked right into them.

On the flip side of the menu are such dishes as super-crisp, deep-fried tofu squares, bland and creamy inside, but topped with a little shrimp paste. They're texturally wonderful and come with a tart dipping sauce to perk them up. There's also a long list of Hong Kong style crispy fried chow mein noodles topped with an abundance of satiny chicken breast, whole black mushrooms, baby bok choy, and thin slices of canned abalone, to name one satisfying variation.

Hing Lung is a madhouse on the weekends, but during the week, the turnover in the large, cheery, utilitarian dining room is so fast, that the wait is never too long. If worse comes to worse, you can get a hot doughnut to eat at the kitchen window while you wait, watching the unceasing dance of the cooks. You can see how fresh the food is here because the kitchen can barely keep up with the orders.

PATRICIA UNTERMAN

▌ HONG KONG EAST OCEAN ★★½

3199 POWELL STREET, EMERYVILLE. 655-3388. OPEN FOR LUNCH MONDAY THROUGH FRIDAY FROM 11 A.M. TO 2:30 P.M., SATURDAY AND SUNDAY 10 A.M. TO 2:30 P.M., DINNER 5 TO 9:30 P.M NIGHTLY. FULL BAR. MASTERCARD, VISA, AMERICAN EXPRESS. 40% NONSMOKING. FULLY WHEELCHAIR ACCESSIBLE. RESERVATIONS RECOMMENDED. MODERATE.

Everyone likes to eat seafood by the water, as restaurateurs at fisherman's wharves everywhere will attest, but often shore meals served in scenic waterfront locations harvest from the freezer rather than the fishing boat. The Hong Kong East Ocean restaurant in Emeryville offers an alternative for people who want fresh seafood, and a view of the bay. This new branch of a Hong Kong restaurant specializing in seafood has a nifty location right on the water's edge, and a Hong Kong-Cantonese sensibility that truly respects foods from the sea.

The large, freestanding building, with an ample parking lot in front of it, has a pagoda-style green tile roof and a sleek modern interior that is dominated by floor to ceiling windows framing an unobstructed view of the city and the Bay Bridge. The location of this restaurant, on a piece of Emeryville that extends right into the bay, couldn't be more dramatic. Floral carpeting, lacquered chairs, white tablecloths, crystal chandeliers throwing out twinkling light from the low ceilings, and a strategically placed cocktail lounge with wonderful views give Hong Kong East Ocean the props to be a serious, full-service restaurant.

The dinner menu offers several unique dishes that the restaurant considers its specialties, and justifiably so. A big filet of black cod, smoked and marinated in a slightly sweet, Japanese-style sauce, arrives at the table warm, satiny, and rich. Squid is crisply deep-fried dusted in a spicy salt and pepper seasoning, and topped with finely chopped chiles and scallions. The crunchy, bite-size pieces are more addictive than potato chips. A juicy stir-fry of diced scallops, shrimp, and water chestnuts comes in a pinked iceberg lettuce cup. A clean but luscious clay pot dish with scallops, shrimp, squid, glass noodles, and lots of Napa cabbage is like a delicate seafood stew. Fresh Dungeness crabs are given noble treatment here, stir-fried with ginger and scallions.

Hong Kong East Ocean's many vegetable dishes have the delicacy and savoriness of their excellent seafood preparations. The classic Cantonese tofu combination of black mushrooms, Virginia ham, and big white cubes of tofu comes on a bed of tender mustard greens subtly seasoned with just the right amount of dried scallop.

Tea lunch is served during the day. Trays of little dishes are carried from the kitchen by a corps of waitresses, eager to distribute their wares. The trays include a series of steamed dumplings in different wrappers with fillings of fresh shrimp and pork. A Shanghai-style dumpling of white bread dough, pan-fried, with a juicy pork filling is a rarely prepared specialty here. *Yee mein*, a phonetic translation of the Chinese word for soft, wide, fresh noodles, reminds me of fresh Italian pasta, sparingly tossed with sauce. Ordered off a separate soup and noodle menu, the tender noodles themselves are the star of the dish. A triangular dumpling of translucent rice noodle is stuffed with a variety of Chinese greens, a vegetarian treat. The chicken feet are exceptional here, extremely tender and gently smoldering with red chile. Crisply baked miniature pork *bao*, with a golden brown top crust sprinkled with sesame seeds, are another passing fancy you don't want to let go by.

PATRICIA UNTERMAN

HOUSE OF NANKING ★★★

919 KEARNY STREET, SAN FRANCISCO. 421-1429. OPEN MONDAY THROUGH FRIDAY FROM 11 A.M. TO 10 P.M., SATURDAY NOON TO 10 P.M., SUNDAY 4 TO 10 P.M. BEER. NO CREDIT CARDS. 10% NONSMOKING. PARTIALLY WHEELCHAIR ACCESSIBLE. RESERVATIONS FOR LARGE PARTIES ONLY. INEXPENSIVE.

A passer-by would never notice this small, nondescript restaurant on a transitional block of Kearny. Half the steamy front window is blocked by sheet metal where a tiny kitchen has been installed. A counter with stools and six tables take up the rest of this very modest dining room owned and worked by Peter and Lily Fang. A passer-by would not think anything very special would come out of a bare bones set up like this, but he would be wrong.

The food at House of Nanking is extraordinary and Peter Fang is a natural, if unschooled, chef. His Shanghai-style dishes taste like the best home cooking—the honest kind of cooking done by people who shop every day and only buy what is best; the kind of cooking in which the flavors are so clean and clear they jump out at you; the kind of cooking that comes from people who love to cook.

In order to sample Peter's food, you will have to exercise patience. Not only do the dishes come out one at a time with possible long breaks between courses, but you almost always have to wait to get in. The restaurant is so small that people line up outside the door. The inconvenience is worth it for Fang's delicious Shanghai dumplings alone. For each order, he pulls out a ball of soft yeast dough and carefully makes six beautiful meat or vegetable filled buns. Then he pan fries them so that they are crisp on one side, or he steams them so the sweetness and tenderness of the delicate yeast dough is emphasized. They are truly the best Chinese buns I've ever tasted. Another spectacular starter hides behind the mundane title of Fried Squids, lacy fritters of the tenderest squid inside a crisp, scallion-studded crust. Shanghai Eggplant Salad is made with long, pale purple Chinese eggplants cut into long strips in a hot and sour dressing. The Nanking fish soup is dreamy, clean, peppery fish broth, ever so slightly thickened and full of bits of kingfish, cucumber, fresh tomato, black mushroom, and peas.

Noodles are a specialty here and one of the most brilliant preparations is a crisp noodle pancake topped with baby eggplants, crunchy but tender green beans, and velvety chicken, called Shanghai Crispy Noodles. Shanghai Special Fried Noodles are soft, wider noodles generously sauced and topped with snow peas and the lovely, baby Chinese eggplants.

The stir-fries look like food magazine centerfolds because the vegetables are so fresh and of such deep color when they arrive at the table. Chicken Filet with Tsing-Tao Beer Sauce contrasts the pure white of chicken breast with dark brown tree ears. A simple plate of crisp/tender, stir- fried long beans seasoned with garlic and oyster sauce is perfection itself.

Peter Fang's skill with doughs is further demonstrated by the thin, chewy white pancakes served with an exquisite stir-fry of handpicked bean sprouts, precisely julienned duck breast, and slivers of black tree ear called Lean Duck and Beansprout Pancakes. You smear the pancakes with a dab of black bean sauce, pile on the duck and roll the pancake up. Two of the pancakes are also used for a dessert called Crispy Sweet Beanpaste Buns. They are spread with sweet beanpaste, pressed together and deep-fried. The restaurant serves them with a saucer of fresh kumquats.

House of Nanking is the ultimate family restaurant. The food is so homespun, in the best sense, that it moves you. You can't find food so personally and honestly prepared in restaurants anymore. Peter Fang

■ THE NANKING FISH SOUP IS DREAMY, CLEAN, PEPPERY FISH BROTH, EVER SO SLIGHTLY THICKENED AND FULL OF BITS OF KINGFISH, CUCUMBER, FRESH TOMATO, BLACK MUSHROOM, AND PEAS.

does every step of the cooking himself, with absolutely no shortcuts. A cook has to be inspired to do what he is doing; he has to have a passion for being in the kitchen. At House of Nanking, you can taste that soul, that understanding of food, in every bite.

PATRICIA UNTERMAN

HYDE STREET BISTRO ★★½

1521 HYDE STREET, SAN FRANCISCO. 441-7778. OPEN NIGHTLY FOR DINNER 5:30 TO 10:30 P.M. BEER AND WINE. VISA AND MASTERCARD. 100% NONSMOKING. FULLY WHEELCHAIR ACCESSIBLE. RESERVATIONS ADVISED. MODERATE.

Hyde Street Bistro is one of those cozy neighborhood places offering food that would be at home in much higher priced surroundings.

Not that the surroundings are bad, mind you. The white-clothed tables are covered with butcher paper, an irregular-shaped piece of granite, and a glass of crispy chile breadsticks. The tables are a bit close together, giving a casually informal feel, augmented by the service, which is low-key, efficient, and friendly.

Chef/owner Albert Rainer uses his Austrian background and California sensibilities to produce some gutsy but light combinations. For starters try the vegetable strudel, a flaky casing of pastry surrounding crunchy vegetables, served with a salad of baby greens. Sausage with warm creamy polenta will satisfy a hearty appetite.

If tuna is on the menu, don't miss it. It's always done in a simple manner but Rainer consistently excels in preparation. Sonoma chicken is smeared with cumin and other spices and comes out of the oven tasting barbequed. It's served with potato pancakes and vegetables that might include roasted onions and carrots. Spatzle also accompanies some entrees, and it's always delicious. Pasta is worth ordering, one of the best bets being penne with sausage and eggplant.

Desserts are masterminded by Rainer's brother, Klaus. All plates are dusted with cocoa with the outline of a fork on one side and a spoon on the other. Don't miss the frothy torte flavored with Anchor Steam beer, a clever melding of local products and European techniques.

In all, Hyde Street is one of the shining examples of the emerging small chef-owned restaurants in the city.

MICHAEL BAUER

IL FORNAIO ★★

LEVI'S PLAZA, 1265 BATTERY STREET, SAN FRANCISCO. 986-0100. OPEN FOR
BREAKFAST MONDAY THROUGH FRIDAY 7 TO 10 A.M.; LUNCH AND DINNER
MONDAY THROUGH THURSDAY 11:30 A.M. TO 11 P.M., FRIDAY UNTIL MIDNIGHT,
SATURDAY 9 A.M. TO MIDNIGHT, SUNDAY 9 A.M. TO 11 P.M. FULL BAR. VISA AND
MASTERCARD. LIMITED SMOKING SECTION. FULLY WHEELCHAIR ACCESSIBLE.
RESERVATIONS ADVISED FOR LUNCH AND DINNER. MODERATE.

One of the advantages of living in a city is that the population can
support cosmopolitan, large scale cafes and restaurants. Larry Mindel,
the force behind Il Fornaio bakeries and trattorias and the elegant
Etrusca, revels in being able to produce these multi-faceted food
operations. Since his favorite cities are Milan and Florence, the
sprawling, sparkling, bustling Il Fornaio in Levi Plaza translates everything into Italian. The San Francisco Il Fornaio looks like it was
airlifted from some magic city in northern Italy.

For breakfast his chefs have invented a calzone filled with fresh
apples and raisins, fried eggs with pancetta instead of bacon, and a
panoply of Il Fornaio sweet rolls. For lunch and dinner, pastas, thin
crusted pizzas from a wood burning oven, and grilled meats and fowl
flow out of the open kitchen. On top of all this, a commercial bakery
turns out a wide variety of Italian breads, cookies and sweets; a
salumeria sells cheeses, hams, sausages, sandwiches and Italian coffees to
go. If you don't want full table service, you can order coffees and rolls
from a marble topped bar and sit outside in the morning sunshine on a
little patio furnished with Italian street furniture. If you want full
service outside, you can sit at yet another outdoor eating area right on
the plaza. Frankly, Il Fornaio gives people anything they could conceivably want for breakfast, lunch, or dinner and then some, outdoors,
indoors, or to go. The scope of the operation is breathtaking!

The design of Il Fornaio makes me want to move in. No expense
was spared on marble, hand-painted wall murals, terracotta tiles,
wrought iron, and majolica. The lyrical dining rooms are warm, cozy,
and beautiful, enhanced by the light that pours in through a whole
wall of soaring arched windows. In the dining rooms full of white
tablecloths and dark wooden chairs, Il Fornaio caters to the full
appetite as well as the peripheral one. The long menu in Italian, with
English explanations, has something for everyone.

The standouts are the crisp and rich pizza with four cheeses, the
pizza margherita with tomato sauce and basil, and an unusual, engag-
ing, pizza Mediterranean with fresh tomatoes, shrimp, zucchini, and
feta. A puffed pizza called Luna Piena gets a simple topping of tissue
thin smoked prosciutto and olive oil.

One of the most delicious pastas on the long menu is ravioli stuffed
with spinach, chard, and basil sauced in ground walnuts, pinenuts and

cream. Much simpler but wonderful are al dente tubes of pasta tossed in a fresh, well balanced tomato sauce enriched with pancetta. Cappellini with fresh tomatoes, basil, and garlic is transformed by flavorful extra virgin olive oil.

Once you leave the pasta and pizza sections of the menu, the going gets a bit more risky. Though chickens, rabbits, and ducks appetizingly turn on the mechanized spit above a wood-burning fire, getting a perfectly cooked one is hit or miss. Timing is such that they're removed from the spit, held, and finished off in the oven or on a grill. A giant veal chop and a beef steak for two with white beans both come off the grill dependably juicy and well cooked.

The wine list gets an A for the many and varied Italian bottles on it and the waiters get a pat on the back for knowing what most of them taste like. This selection does much to enhance the food.

The scale of Il Fornaio is so far reaching that it goes beyond mere restaurantdom. It provides every conceivable Italian food service in one spot with great conviction. If a bit of inconsistency afflicts the food, it's almost to be expected. The overall scheme of things is so exciting, and the place is so much fun, that it fulfills Mr. Mindel's dream of opening the ultimate Italian food center. As the crowds there attest, the concept fits San Francisco like a soft, stylish, Italian leather glove.

PATRICIA UNTERMAN

IL POLLAIO ★★½

555 COLUMBUS AVENUE, SAN FRANCISCO. 362-7727. OPEN MONDAY THROUGH SATURDAY 11:30 A.M. TO 9 P.M. BEER AND WINE. MAJOR CREDIT CARDS. 25% NONSMOKING. FULLY WHEELCHAIR ACCESSIBLE. NO RESERVATIONS. INEXPENSIVE.

Il Pollaio, which means the chicken coop in Italian, is a great find for those who want a simple, nourishing, tasty, and inexpensive meal. The main attraction is chicken, mildly marinated and grilled until its skin gets golden brown and crispy. Sweet, fine grained, Italian sausage, specially made for Il Pollaio, goes beautifully with the chicken in an impromptu mixed grill.

What I like in particular are Il Pollaio's salads of crisp, cold greens or freshly cut coleslaw, both dressed in tangy Italian dressing. Also good is the vinegary marinated eggplant which acts like a pickle. Each day a different soup is offered like a hearty lentil, split pea, or vegetable minestrone, all made with real stock. Glasses of soft Italian and Spanish wines go wonderfully with everything.

The pleasant little dining room looks onto Columbus Avenue. A cheerful, husband and wife team run Il Pollaio together and seem to know everyone who walks in the door. Much Italian is spoken over many bottles of wine. You can call ahead for take-out or enjoy the welcoming ambience of this popular North Beach spot while you eat your chicken there.

Patricia Unterman

IRONWOOD CAFE ★★★

901 COLE STREET, SAN FRANCISCO. 664-0224. OPEN FOR LUNCH MONDAY THROUGH FRIDAY, 11 A.M. TO 2:30 P.M., DINNER MONDAY THROUGH THURSDAY 5:30 TO 10 P.M. FRIDAY, SATURDAY 5:30 TO 10:30 P.M. BEER AND WINE. MASTERCARD, VISA, AMERICAN EXPRESS, DISCOVER. 50% NONSMOKING. PARTIALLY WHEELCHAIR ACCESSIBLE. RESERVATIONS ACCEPTED. MODERATE.

Besides having one of the most pleasant dining rooms in town, the Ironwood kitchen is turning out inventive and exciting food that is always well-prepared. The early American look of the cafe lets you settle in immediately. The commodious pine booths with cushions confer complete privacy, while a cozy row of tables along a balcony railing afford a perch for viewing the whole room. Homey print wallpaper, ceiling fans, Colonial-style lanterns and chairs, and paintings of quilt patterns all fit naturally into the uncluttered, square dining room with windows along two sides. The tiny kitchen is tucked away in a corner of the room and takes advantage of a narrow, outdoor courtyard for its charcoal grilling. The food tastes homemade too, in the best, made-from-scratch way.

Begin with the coarse textured housemade paté, bursting with flavor, served with housemade red wine mustard, some of the best I've ever tasted. Paired with Ironwood's just baked French bread, yeasty, chewy, and full of character, and a side order of house-pickled cucumbers, Jerusalem artichokes, onions, and searing hot pepper pickles and you have reason enough to come back to this restaurant. A salad of watercress with mushrooms and red onions grilled over rosemary branches has the most extraordinary aroma. Some tiny artichokes, sweet, tender, and crisply deep-fried surround a ramekin of well made garlic mayonnaise. Avocado and bright red blood oranges are set off by tangy lettuces and a tart vinaigrette.

As main courses, crusty, golden brown pieces of chicken are sprinkled with feta cheese, roasted onions and grilled Japanese eggplant, and a perfectly cooked piece of halibut sauced with dill sour cream stunningly shares the plate with dark green, deep-fried chard leaves.

The most delicious dish of all is Ironwood Cafe's buttery seafood stew loaded with clams, mussels, big chunks of juicy fish, new potatoes, and spinach. The broth is a dream, rich with fresh herbs, shellfish liquor and good, clean fish stock. When you dunk Ironwood's housemade crackers into it, you're in heaven.

At lunch, the kitchen puts out a remarkable warm spinach and baby artichoke salad with toasted walnuts, shaved parmesan, and a delicious walnut dressing. Another salad matches slices of cantaloupe and avocado with arugula, in a mustardy, poppyseed dressing. A grilled chicken breast sandwich on Ironwood's incomparable housebaked rye bread brings into play grilled red onion, swiss cheese, sauteed mushrooms, and the deep, richly flavored red wine mustard. You couldn't ask for a more savory sandwich.

Though the house-baked breads rival any I've tasted, the desserts are a bit clunky. My favorite is a fresh strawberry pie with a thin cream cheese layer above a thick, hard crust. Pineapple cobbler and chocolate layer cake are just plain heavy and unsweetened strawberry short cake tasted flat. The small wine list has some excellent and unusual bottles, including some lovely Oregon pinot noirs.

When I had eaten at Ironwood years ago, I felt that the food was so home-grown that it was amateurish. Now, that made-from-scratch inspiration has turned into a conceptual framework for some graceful and sophisticated dishes.

PATRICIA UNTERMAN

IZZY'S STEAK AND CHOP HOUSE ★½

3345 STEINER STREET, SAN FRANCISCO. 563-0487. OPEN MONDAY THROUGH SATURDAY FOR DINNER 5 TO 11 P.M., SUNDAY, 5 TO 10 P.M. FULL BAR. MAJOR CREDIT CARDS. 75% NONSMOKING. FULLY WHEELCHAIR ACCESSIBLE. RESERVATIONS ACCEPTED. MODERATE.

Izzy's is a meticulously recreated period piece that serves updated chophouse food. Restaurant impresario Sam Duval took a neighborhood bar called Mulcreavy's and transformed it into an elaborate stage set of a run-down, turn-of-the-century saloon. There are wooden floors, painted wood wainscoting, wooden booths, and an old looking, solid wood bar. The ceilings and upper walls have been textured and painted to look like distressed leather. White tablecloths stand out pristinely against the many different shades of brown. The walls are hung with period photos and memorabilia; hundreds of bottles of steak condiments line wooden ledges that encircle Izzy's two dining areas. The mirrors, ceiling fans, and hanging schoolhouse light fixtures project a Gold Rush ambience that puts you in the mood to have a shot of whiskey and a steak.

The menu is simple, straightforward, and manageable for the kitchen. There are steaks and chops which come with a choice of potato and vegetable, a few salads and appetizers, and a selection of non-meat entrees. What Izzy's really has down is the classic chop house plate—a charcoal grilled steak or chop, lightly creamed spinach, and scalloped potatoes layered with onion, leek, and cheese.

The filet is the best cut of steak to order here, delivering the most tenderness and flavor. The New York, even though dry aged for 21 days, isn't quite as tasty, though chewy skirt steak in a sweet, teriyaki-style marinade, is. Loin lamb chops, cut nearly two inches thick here, are a good buy. For those who like lighter meat, a gigantic veal T-bone chop has a more delicate, young animal flavor.

Included in the price of these steaks and chops is a choice of vegetable and potato, the best being the scalloped "Izzy's Own Potatoes" and the bright green creamed spinach. Neither of these is heavily laden with cream or butter. The potatoes have more melted onion than butter and the spinach really tastes like fresh spinach. Delicious roasted onions with sweet carrot chunks offer a third choice. You can also get a baked potato, unexceptional shoestrings or bland, thickly battered deep-fried zucchini.

For starters I recommend a crisp house salad of butter lettuce with a punchy garlicky dressing, or a halved head of romaine, blanketed in crumbled blue cheese and doused in vinegar and oil.

Order the marvelous Cajun Fried Oysters with Jalapeno Sauce as a first course, split. Briny, fresh, sweet oysters are barely coated with corn meal and get only the briefest of cooking before being placed on shells dabbed with a spicy green puree of jalapenos and scallions.

Somehow a meal of red meat always requires something sweet to end it and Izzy's doesn't let you down. A chocolate rum pecan pie is rich without being cloying. Key Lime Pie has a soft, creamy filling brightened by lime zest, but a soggy graham cracker crust. English Sherry Trifle, served in a wine goblet, happily combines sherry-soaked cake with lots of softly whipped cream. The wine list offers California bottles at fair prices and includes a large assortment of wines by the glass.

PATRICIA UNTERMAN

JACK'S ★½

615 SACRAMENTO, SAN FRANCISCO. 986-9854. OPEN MONDAY THROUGH FRIDAY 11:30 A.M. TO 9:30 P.M., SATURDAY AND SUNDAY 5 TO 9:30 P.M. FULL BAR. AMERICAN EXPRESS. 30% NONSMOKING. PARTIALLY WHEELCHAIR ACCESSIBLE. RESERVATIONS RECOMMENDED. COAT AND TIE REQUIRED. MODERATE.

Times have changed, even at Jack's, where generations of San Francisco's old-line families have held Sunday supper, where generations of Montgomery Street lawyers established themselves through years of devoted attendance, where men are still required to wear coat and tie and are the only ones deemed capable of tasting the wine. Now the dining room at night is only scattered with well-to-do senior citizens; the new generation of Auchinclossian characters that would frequent Jack's, prefer salads and yogurt instead of chops and hollandaise. Also, other restaurants have learned well from Jack's and taken the concept of the San Francisco grill a step or two higher, using better ingredients and more modern preparations. But, as far as I'm concerned, I'd rather go to Jack's than most of the trendy restaurants that have opened in San Francisco in the past five years. You can eat and drink honestly there in an atmosphere palpably linked to the past.

The dining room looks like it hasn't been touched since the fifties, the era that saw the installation of the acoustic ceiling and the graying white linoleum floor. Otherwise, the high ceilinged room looks pre-earthquake, with trimmed walls decorated with gilt floral plasterwork, narrow, shoulder-high mirrors, a border of coat hooks and sconces that encircle the room, bentwood chairs, small tables covered with white linen, hanging schoolhouse lamps, and a tiny, ancient wooden bar at the front of the room. Fraying curtains of a singular mustard color hang inside the front door.

The menu, printed daily but rarely changing, is a long white card offering over a hundred dishes. You sense it is a minefield of culinary disasters, especially considering that the dining room is relatively small. But, many of the least ordered items are simply unavailable and the waiters will suggest, strongly, what can be ordered safely that day. The heart of the menu offers high quality grilled chops, steaks and fish, and an appealing range of vegetable side dishes. Salads could use better lettuces, but are acceptable in an old fashioned way.

Begin with Celery Victor, a plate of chilled braised celery napped with vinaigrette and topped with anchovies, my favorite Jack's dish. Asparagus vinaigrette features sweet, first of the season stalks with some bite left in them. Vichyssoise comes well chilled and not too creamy, just the right texture for a cold potato soup.

A rump steak has terrific flavor while still being lean; a thick, juicy veal chop would cost dollars more any place else. The meats are grilled perfectly as is an unadorned broiled half chicken. All these foods come on small oval plates, ungarnished, a refreshing and honest presentation. As an accompaniment, order Jack's famous deep-fried eggplant, crisp outside and creamy in, or the excellent creamed spinach.

The wine list is particularly well chosen with emphasis on reasonably priced French bottles. Half bottles are also represented, a boon at lunchtime when one or two glasses of good wine will suffice. Desserts are awful at Jack's, the best bet being warm, thick zabaglione for two, preferable to doughy apple pie or bland caramel custard.

Though Jack's kitchen has certainly not kept up with recent developments in the market regarding produce and imported foods, the quality of the main ingredients has remained high and it is these that Jack's specializes in. You still can have a meal at Jack's that makes you appreciate the simple pleasures of life. Even if Jack's sometimes feels like an aging men's club, I hope it keeps going for people who relish a meal of celery Victor, a rare rump steak, and a good bottle of wine.

PATRICIA UNTERMAN

JACKSON FILLMORE ★★½

2506 FILLMORE, SAN FRANCISCO. 346-5288. OPEN FOR DINNER TUESDAY THROUGH THURSDAY 5:30 TO 10:30 P.M., FRIDAY AND SATURDAY UNTIL 11 P.M., SUNDAY 5 TO 10 P.M. BEER AND WINE. MAJOR CREDIT CARDS. 50% NONSMOKING. PARTIALLY WHEELCHAIR ACCESSIBLE. RESERVATIONS FOR THREE OR MORE. MODERATE.

From the street, Jackson Fillmore looks like any storefront restaurant. Once inside, assaulted by the aromas of cooking and packed surroundings, you know there's something marvelous going on.

The interior is clean and bright, with blue and white checked tablecloths overlaid with white. There's only one row of tables and a diner-style counter, where you're tempted with a mouth-watering array of antipasti that really gets you in the mood to eat.

Yet, there's a catch. The restaurant has developed a not unfounded reputation for rude, uncaring treatment of diners who are, nevertheless, willing to fork over the bucks so they can spoon-up the delicious sauces and main courses. So, you might ask, what's the deal? It's the food. Period. It's probably the best moderately priced Italian restaurant in the city. All the food is consistently prepared in the gutsy, full flavored fashion that eludes most other cooks.

The gnocchi is without equal, fluffy almost mousse-like pillows of potato dough, doused with different sauces such as a creamy tomato mixture, contrasted with pieces of slightly bitter chard. Roast chicken, served with natural juices, is simple, but it's done to perfection. Pastas are always cooked to the proper stage of al dente and the sauces are simple but brimming with character; penne is doused in a tomato sauce with coins of sausage and ground veal.

On one night, the traditional *ribollita,* a minestrone style soup thickened with bread, was absolutely delicious. The base tasted like it had simmered for hours, but the vegetables still had character. With the bread and an added sprinkle of cheese, it could be a hearty meal in itself.

Two desserts rank among the best in the city; tiramisu—a large square of rum-soaked ladyfingers with chocolate and fluffy mascarpone cheese—is the standard for which other versions should be judged. So should the classic zabaglione, served in a stemmed glass, with the frothy, intensely flavored mixture spilling over and pooling on the doily-covered serving plate. It's swirled with just a hint of strawberry puree that barely tames the intensity of the marsala-laced egg mixture.

145

However, there's another catch to tasting this culinary magic—getting a table. No reservations are taken, so if you aren't a regular you should go early or late.

The wine list, which is confined to a page, is in the tradition of an Italian trattoria—there's not a lot of selections, but the wines are quaffable and stay in the lower price range.

And, wonders of wonders, on our last visit the service was surprisingly cordial. I know people who forgo the fabulous food for the sometimes degrading task of getting a seat. However, last time there was a cheerful hostess greeting patrons, and the waiter was extremely pleasant and efficient.

Maybe there's hope after all. It may wind up being the perfect restaurant. Then it's going to be impossible to get a seat.

MICHAEL BAUER

JANOT'S ★★

44 CAMPTON PLACE, SAN FRANCISCO. 392-5373. OPEN FOR LUNCH 11:30 A.M. TO 2:30 P.M.; DINNER 6 TO 10 P.M. MONDAY THROUGH SATURDAY. FULL BAR. AMERICAN EXPRESS, VISA, MASTERCARD. NONSMOKING TABLES AVAILABLE. PARTIALLY WHEELCHAIR ACCESSIBLE. RESERVATIONS RECOMMENDED. MODERATE.

French cooking has become so light in the Bay Area that butter and cream have gone the way of canned white asparagus. Fortunately Janot's, a cute little brasserie around the corner from the Campton Place Hotel, continues to serve simple, delicious preparations with classic sauces.

Although the food doesn't weigh on the palate, you'll find butter incorporated in most dishes. A moist grilled breast of chicken glistens with a butter sauce infused with horseradish and chives. Steamed fillet of sole is rolled around a mixture of spinach and tarragon, enriched with a plain butter sauce. A mix of prawns, scallops, and oysters in cabbage leaves is accented with a fennel butter sauce and grilled wild salmon is served with a cabernet butter sauce.

Janot's also does one of the best versions of calves liver sauteed with onions and bacon. You'll also find stellar versions of two continental classics, onion soup and snails in herb butter.

Janot's collection of salads, often topped with warm ingredients, are sure-fire winners though most are priced only slightly less than the entrees. Seafood sausage shines when paired with a warm vinegary cabbage salad. Grilled quail and smoked bacon make a perfect duo for sturdy spinach leaves. However the one dish to order is the confit duck leg on a perfectly dressed bed of endive and watercress. The food is accented with a small, unpretentious wine list with California and French selections.

Desserts come off a standard looking pastry tray but most are better than you find at other establishments. One of the best is the strawberry tart with loads of berries and a thick crust.

The dining room, located on two levels separated by a brass railing, has a European feel. The exposed brick wall and the cramped bar-entry area adds a homey charm. The long narrow room is broken up with banners hanging from the ceiling. As you look around at the clientele, you'll see a lot of people smoking Gitane's over coffee. Now, you know you've discovered a true brasserie. The service, however, is much warmer than you'd expect in Paris and generally efficient.

MICHAEL BAUER

JENNIE LOW'S CHINESE CUISINE ★★

38 MILLER AVENUE, MILL VALLEY. 388-8868. OPEN FOR LUNCH 11:30 A.M. TO 3 P.M. MONDAY THROUGH SATURDAY; DINNER 4:30 TO 9:30 P.M. EVERY NIGHT. BEER AND WINE. MASTERCARD, VISA, AMERICAN EXPRESS. 100% NONSMOKING. FULLY WHEELCHAIR ACCESSIBLE. RESERVATIONS RECOMMENDED. MODERATE.

When you eat at Barbara Tropp's China Moon or Bruce Cost's Monsoon in San Francisco, the chefs' visions are clearly evident. Each has created Asian-style food with a highly personalized touch. That same feeling is shown at Jennie Low's Chinese Cuisine in the Mill Creek Plaza in Mill Valley.

In some ways, Low has followed a path similar to Cost's and Tropp's. Low was a cooking teacher 20 years before realizing her dream of opening a restaurant, with co-owner David Lau, in 1987. The author of two books, *Jennie Low's Szechuan Cookbook* and *Chopsticks, Cleaver and Wok*, Low wanted to create a simple homestyle food.

She's crafted a personalized restaurant with a few quirky elements that make it endearing and enduring. Low's favorite color is lavender—you'll find it everywhere, from the type on the menu to the shirts on the staff. She's so committed to the color that she hasn't worn any other for more than 20 years. Her lucky number is eight, so all prices end in that number.

The interior is Marin modern with taupe-mauve walls and matching plaster beams crisscrossing the ceiling. The sleek look is completed with Japanese-style screens and a bustling kitchen visible behind glass.

Many might argue the cuisine isn't authentic, and it does seem tailored to American tastes. But it's good, and that's what matters. Sauces generally have a sweet note but always taste lively. One of the best combinations is Snow White Chicken. The meat has an amazing velvety texture that mirrors the sauce, contrasted by crunchy snow peas and big, meaty mushrooms.

Also memorable is Hot Spicy Eggplant, featuring long wedges of the stewed vegetables, accented with slivers of wood-ear mushrooms. The spicy sauce creates an exciting layer of contrasts—first comes the velvety texture in the mouth, a quality characteristic of all her sauces, then sweetness, and finally a spicy kick.

She does a fine job with noodles, too. Jennie's Noodle Soup is a generous portion of Chinese noodles barely floating in a thickened broth with shrimp, snow peas, bok choy, Chinese cabbage, carrots, chicken, and water chestnuts.

A few dishes just don't work. Jennie's Calamari, fried squid in a spicy garlic sauce, on my visit tasted of batter only. Sizzling Rice Soup did indeed sizzle, but the rice was mushy rather than crispy. However, the full, rich chicken broth was first-rate.

The main flaw in Low's style, however, is that all dishes seem to have the same consistency; most items are stir-fried and a few are deep-fried or roasted. No steamed dishes are on the menu although they are available upon request.

There's not much to end the meal save for lychees and fortune cookies. No coffee is served although the house tea is superb, a fragrant lychee and black tea that she also markets commercially.

MICHAEL BAUER

JUST WON TON ★★

1241 VINCENTE STREET (BETWEEN 23RD AND 24TH AVENUES), SAN FRANCISCO. 681-2999. OPEN TUESDAY THROUGH SUNDAY FROM 11 A.M. TO 10 P.M. NO ALCOHOL. NO CREDIT CARDS. 75% NONSMOKING. PARTIALLY WHEELCHAIR ACCESSIBLE. NO RESERVATIONS. INEXPENSIVE.

People often tell me that they return to a restaurant for a favorite dish. Even though the menu may be long, just one preparation pulls them back. I understand this phenomenon completely because it often happens to me.

A little place in the Sunset that devotes itself entirely to making won ton has found a permanent locus on my culinary map. Appropriately named Just Won Ton, this place puts out some of the best won ton I've tasted. The skins are gossamer thin, tender, and flavorful, and the filling is sublime; a combination of big chunks of sweet, impeccably fresh shrimp bound with a little ground pork and restrained seasoning. I could eat bowls of them. They come in soup with noodles, without noodles, with fish balls, roast duck, barbequed pork, spicy chicken, different cuts of beef, different kinds of innards, and pig's feet. And, for a pittance more, you can get extra won ton, a terrific culinary value.

Though the menu runs on for four pages, this is clearly a noodle house. Most of the entries are variations on a theme. I love the chow fun noodles here. These thick, pure white, soft rice noodles are delicious with bright green bok choy and bits of tenderized beef in a broth-based sauce.

This place is also known for two non-won ton appetizers. One is called Vegetarian Duck because the dish resembles a plate of roast duck. It satisfies like a plate of duck as well, even though it is made with ribbons of tofu skin rolled around a filling of savory mushrooms. This restaurant's famous Chinese tamale turns out to be a gigantic mound of sticky rice with a center of braised Chinese sausage, and taro paste, all wrapped and steamed in a taro leaf—a larger, more filling version of the wrapped rice packets you find at Chinese tea lunch.

All the food here is clean, fresh, and nicely seasoned. The noodles have texture and flavor, and the won tons are simply the best. They merit a special trip and offer the possibility of presenting a fabulous dish at home—by making your own rich chicken broth or fish broth and buying won ton and noodles to go into it. Invite me over for that meal.

PATRICIA UNTERMAN

KABUTO ★★★

5116 GEARY BOULEVARD (NEAR 14TH AVE.), SAN FRANCISCO. 752-5652. OPEN TUESDAY THROUGH SATURDAY 6 P.M. TO 1 A.M., SUNDAY 6 TO 11 P.M. BEER AND SAKE. AMERICAN EXPRESS, VISA, MASTERCARD. 30% NONSMOKING. PARTIALLY WHEELCHAIR ACCESSIBLE. RESERVATIONS ACCEPTED FOR DINING ROOM BUT NOT AT SUSHI BAR. MODERATE.

Sachio Kojima, the sushi chef/owner of Kabuto, one of the best sushi bars in San Francisco, is behind the counter at his sushi bar every minute it is open, from late afternoon to the wee hours of the morning, and he never stops moving for one second. He has hired an assistant who plays the tortoise to his hare, but it is brilliant Sachio who puts together every piece of sushi at his sushi bar. He's a marathon athlete, a warrior wielding knives, a cowboy who never leaves the saddle. He could have been the star of *Tampopo* if it were a movie about sushi bars instead of noodle houses. I have never walked into Kabuto when he hasn't been there.

Sachio himself gauges the appetites and tastes of everyone who sits down at the bar. He lets new customers order themselves and then gives them a few things he thinks they'd like. For regulars, Sachio creates the meal. He keeps track of fifteen diners, all of whom get many different things. The charge is by the meal, more for an elaborate sitting, less for simpler foods and fewer delicacies. His patrons feel they have a private relationship with this sushi chef—that

■ SACHIO KOJIMA, THE SUSHI CHEF/OWNER, IS A MARA-
THON ATHLETE, A WARRIOR WIELDING KNIVES, A COW-
BOY WHO NEVER LEAVES THE SADDLE.

he knows what they want. And indeed, his personal control of the
sushi bar is almost as important as his preparations. Sachio has mastered
the theater of the experience. Without him, Kabuto would be just
another sushi bar.

One evening he started everyone at the counter with a deep
celadon bowl holding a little salad of marinated kelp followed by a
glazed pottery bowl arranged with two slices of monkfish liver, with a
texture like foie gras, resting on a pile of pickled shredded onions and
a shiso leaf. Then came a gray bowl beautifully composed with
sashimi—thick slices of meaty red bonito seared on the outside looking much like filet mignon and thin slices of iridescent mackerel with
pearly skin and pink flesh. A tiny carrot flower with a salmon roe
center, strings of white radish, and a separate dipping sauce with grated
fresh ginger accompanied.

After these composed things came a mild piece of toro sushi, the
fat, buttery stomach meat of the tuna, then a contrastingly assertive
piece of mackerel sushi, and a very fresh yellowtail jack sushi. From
the kitchen emerged a red lacquer bowl with a broiled tofu dumpling,
a fried potato dumpling, and a slice of seafood-stuffed squash. Next
came an oval of seaweed stuffed with rice and topped with creamy
orange *uni*, or sea urchin roe, then a raw, East Coast shrimp split and
garnished with a few grains of flying fish row and a chiffonade of shiso
leaf.

Next, the kitchen sent out a tiny pottery tea pot, about three inches
high. A tiny flat bowl was tucked under the straw handle. Diners pour
the clear bonito stock enriched with oyster mushrooms, chicken,
cabbage, and fish into the little saucer and then eat the solids from the
teapot with chopsticks. A sushi of broiled fresh water eel, painted with
teriyaki, banded with seaweed, and topped with toasted sesame seeds
followed and the meal ended with a sushi roll stuffed with the slimy
textured raw mountain potato, an acquired taste.

What most people want when they go out to dinner is some special
attention and that is the attraction of sitting in front of Sachio, as
opposed to the tables at Kabuto, where the menu is more predictable.
Of course, the popularity of the sushi bar means you might have to
wait. The sushi bar gets more crowded in the late evening, turning
into a hot spot around midnight. The scene there is fascinating. You
get to see a slice of the Japanese underworld sharing the same bar with
aging hippie sushi eaters and chain-smoking Japanese students. Sachio
treats everyone with equal respect.

PATRICIA UNTERMAN

KANSAI ★★

325 SACRAMENTO ST., SAN FRANCISCO. 392-2657. OPEN FOR LUNCH 11:30 A.M. TO 2:30 P.M. MONDAY THROUGH FRIDAY; DINNER 5:30 TO 10 P.M. MONDAY THROUGH SATURDAY. FULL BAR. MAJOR CREDIT CARDS. 50% NONSMOKING. FULLY WHEELCHAIR ACCESSIBLE. RESERVATIONS RECOMMENDED FOR DINNER. MODERATE TO EXPENSIVE.

Sometimes it takes awhile for the word to get around. Kansai, a big, two-floor Japanese restaurant on Sacramento Street directly across from Embarcadero Center, has been in business more than a decade. Yet I'd never even heard of it until someone casually mentioned it to me. Did I know, he asked, that there's a San Francisco restaurant whose chef used to cook for the Japanese embassy in Washington? That bit of information was enough to tempt me to visit.

The chef, Kiichiro Imanaka, grew up in Osaka and moved to Kyoto, where he ran a branch of his uncle's Osaka restaurant for 30 years. In 1963 he left for Washington; in six years at the Japanese Embassy he went to the White House to cook for Presidents Kennedy and Johnson a couple of times.

While the menu starts with 28 appetizers, many of them hardly ever seen in these parts, it also offers all the standard Japanese-American dishes, like *tempura, teriyakis,* and *sukiyaki* cooked at your table. The food at Kansai isn't cheap. If you really want to splurge, you can order a kaiseki dinner where the chef chooses all the dishes. You get to pick the price you want to pay for this dinner (the higher the tab, the more courses and the more exotic the food).

No one should pass over the appetizers which strike me as the best thing about the restaurant. It's hard to believe that so much food could appear on the table that's so interesting and so good. There are delicious skewers of grilled chicken *yakitori* bathed in a gingery brown sauce. *Oshitashi* is the conventional cold boiled spinach with sesame sauce, bright green and crunchy. *Chawan mushi*, the egg custard with bits of vegetables and shrimp, is nowhere more creamy or more tasty.

But many of the appetizers are things I had never had before. *Maguro yamakake* presents raw shavings of Japanese mountain potato over chunks of raw tuna. *Kushi-age* are bite-sized pieces of chicken, beef, shrimp, and vegetables, dipped in rice flour and deep-fried, to emerge delicate and absolutely greaseless. Tofu cooked in broth comes with a special dipping sauce that includes shavings of bonita, spring onions, ginger, and seaweed.

Among the entrees, *yosenabe*, the Japanese seafood stew, has an assortment of impeccably fresh fish and shellfish, plus chicken and vegetables, all in an enticing broth of fish stock with a little sweet rice wine. The *tempura* couldn't be better, the batter light, the frying greaseless. *Shabu-shabu*, the beef and vegetable concoction similar to *sukiyaki*, is all so superbly light and fresh that it makes the paper-thin, fat-free beef slices seem like a health-food dish. The chicken *teriyaki*, normally a dish to skip, here is flavorful and juicy with a light, rather than cloying sauce.

At the second meal I decided to order a kaiseki dinner, throwing in an extra $10 over the $40 minimum in the hope that the chef would do something really special. But although everything tasted fine, this $50 kaiseki dinner wasn't nearly as interesting as our selection of appetizers the meal before. While kaiseki dinners are supposed to be a series of small courses demonstrating the inventiveness and talent of the chef, two of our dishes were sashimi and tempura, which anyone could order off the regular menu. I think the strategy was to keep a Westerner happy; next time I do this, I will insist on being served exactly what a Japanese customer would get.

STAN SESSER

KAPPA ★★½

1700 POST ST. AT BUCHANAN, SAN FRANCISCO. 673-6004. (CLIMB THE WOODEN STEPS OUTSIDE DENNY'S). OPEN FOR DINNERS MONDAY THROUGH SATURDAY. BEER, SAKE. VISA, MASTERCARD. DINNERS BY RESERVATION ONLY. EXPENSIVE TO VERY EXPENSIVE.

It can be more expensive than Chez Panisse, but you'll probably have to eat your meal sitting at a counter. The only California wine offered is Almaden chablis. Although four of us spent $281 (including beers and tip), I left hungry. And the food just happens to be exquisite.

This is the story of a place called Kappa, which has to be the most unusual restaurant in San Francisco. A husband-wife team named Toshiaki and Rumiko preside over 11 counter seats and one table for four at a Japanese restaurant so hidden away that you likely couldn't find it if you knew the address but didn't have precise directions. The menu is written on a scroll of paper tacked onto the wall, and it's only in Japanese. The theme is small dishes to go with sake.

Getting to eat at Kappa is more than a matter of directions. Dinners are by reservation only, and reservations are hard to come by since the restaurant is already largely filled by Japanese businessmen. Moreover, although Rumiko speaks excellent English and was very helpful translating the menu at my two visits, she fears an influx of non-Japanese Americans sampling food that's not familiar to them. I think she has visions of loud Americans pounding the table and demanding their sukiyaki and sushi.

Since so many of the dishes are likely to be unfamiliar, the best thing to do is put yourself in Rumiko's hands. You'll get a procession of courses, mostly fish and vegetables, all elegantly arranged and served in little lacquer bowls or on beautiful pottery. Portions are small; most of the dishes are between $10 and $20, and a $25 plate of sushi barely made a dent in my appetite.

All the fish is flown in fresh from Japan; I don't know what makes fish from Asian waters more Japanese than fish from American waters, but every bite tastes impeccably fresh. Deep-fried stonefish with a dried persimmon slice, grilled yellowtail topped by a heap of daikon shavings, and herring roe with seaweed and bonita flakes all sparkle. Stewed eel comes tossed with scrambled eggs and barely cooked Napa cabbage in a light broth. A big pancake of crab, tofu, and yam comes in a bowl of broth, a really unusual combination of tastes. The most spectacular presentation is reserved for the conch, a shellfish of moderate size that resides in a giant shell. Rumiko brings out one of these shells on a big plate decorated with rocks and salt, with a little flame burning on one side. Inside is the conch meat—two bites worth, but flavorful and tender—in a hot broth with bits of green onion.

The vegetable dishes are equally good. Tofu, tofu skin, and orange-colored burdock root are all crumbled together in a bowl, a wonderful taste combination. Japanese potato is mashed with seaweed, compressed, and served on a beautiful clear glass plate. *Mitsuba* turns out to be a spinach-like green, barely cooked and chopped aesthetically like spinach *oshitashi*; it has a stronger, more assertive taste than spinach. *Miso* soup might be a standard dish, but this one is like no other, powerful but not salty.

With no rice, no dessert, and many dishes seen nowhere else, a meal at Kappa is an absolutely unique experience. I couldn't quarrel with a single ingredient or a single preparation. But there was a subtlety to the food that made it more refined—and for me a bit less satisfying—than a meal at a very good, regular Japanese restaurant. Someone who is Japanese would no doubt respond that refinement is the name of the game.

STAN SESSER

KENWOOD RESTAURANT AND BAR ★★

9900 HIGHWAY 12, KENWOOD. 707-833-6326. OPEN TUESDAY THROUGH SUNDAY FROM 11:30 A.M. TO 9 P.M., FRIDAY AND SATURDAY 11:30 A.M. TO 10 P.M. FULL BAR. MASTERCARD AND VISA. 80% NONSMOKING. FULLY WHEELCHAIR ACCESSIBLE. RESERVATIONS RECOMMENDED. MODERATE

The Kenwood Restaurant is conveniently located next to some of Sonoma's best vineyards and wineries, in the heart of the wine producing area. It inhabits its own spacious wooden building with an outdoor patio, two indoor dining rooms, and a bar. It stays open all day, offering the same versatile menu for lunch and dinner augmented by daily specials. Prices are moderate; the wine list proudly local. Most important, the cooking is modern, tasty, and personal, very much the product of Frenchman Maxime Schacher who owns the restaurant with his American wife Susan. The restaurant brings a professional, full service operation to a part of Sonoma that has needed one.

The dining rooms have high pitched wooden ceilings, polished wooden floors, off-white, linen-covered walls, and a clean, spare look. A few unframed large oils and some framed drawings of plants are scattered here and there. The requisite dramatic French flower arrangements look fabulous against this simple background. Ceiling fans keep the air moving. Double French doors are thrown open to verandas and patios, the largest being off the main dining room next to a horse pasture. White canvas umbrellas shade the marble tables from the sun.

There are such simple items as hamburgers, club sandwiches, and marvelous, authentic pommes frites, but also an elaborate salad of crisply sauteed sweetbreads with capers, mushrooms, and endive finished off in a demi-glace. You can choose an excellent, peppery Caesar salad with garlicky croutons or a perfectly poached filet of salmon presented with a salad of endive, frisee, and tomatoes in a creamy feta cheese dressing, dotted with nicoise olives. A round of goat cheese is breaded and fried until it browns on the outside and gets warm and creamy inside. Strewn with julienned sun-dried tomatoes, toasted pinenuts and served with a salad, Mr. Schacher proves that he, too, can put out California classics.

That my two favorite dishes at Kenwood have been cold and refreshing, perhaps reflects how warm it gets in Sonoma in the summer. A chilled gazpacho, a smooth, thin, flavorful, fresh tomato puree, is garnished with finely minced vegetables which are stirred into the soup for texture. Mr. Schacher's interpretation of Hawaiian sashimi is just as eloquent. A generous portion of neatly sliced, firm, red tuna filet is topped with a relish of minced ginger and scallions and arranged on a soy sauce and wasabi-painted plate.

Kenwood is one restaurant where the main courses are as lively as the starters. A magnificently crisp, half Petaluma duck with a subtle orange sauce came with a tomato stuffed with deliciously seasoned wild rice. A moist pork tenderloin was sliced over a bed of meltingly tender, sweet and sour red cabbage fragrant with caraway seeds and hot with black pepper. A grilled filet of tuna, a little over done, was topped with a salsa of fresh tomato, onions, and cilantro while it sat on a fresh tomato puree. Desserts are not as polished as the rest of the menu, so you don't have to worry about saving your appetite. This is a place to enjoy the great local wine with appropriate food.

PATRICIA UNTERMAN

KIMBALL'S EAST ★★

5800 SHELLMOUND STREET, EMERYVILLE. 658-2555. OPEN FOR DINNER AT 6:30 P.M. WEDNESDAY, THURSDAY, SUNDAY, 7 TO 9:30 P.M. FRIDAY AND SATURDAY. FULL BAR. MASTERCARD AND VISA. 70% NONSMOKING. FULLY WHEELCHAIR ACCESSIBLE. RESERVATIONS RECOMMENDED. MODERATE.

The Bay Area finally has a first rate supper club and it happens to be located in Emeryville instead of San Francisco. Such a hip, tuned-in, well planned venture naturally belongs in the City, but the owners, who also own the San Francisco Real Foods stores, gambled on the developing Emeryville Public Market area. They built their club, Kimball's East, on the second floor of a spacious brick building and opened a Real Foods branch next door. The result is one of the most comfortable, audio-visually successful rooms in recent club history, with the added attraction of an excellent full scale dinner service that draws on the organic food sources of the health food chain.

Customers choose from a small, regular menu of California/Caribbean style dishes augmented by a printed page of daily specials. There is a compact but well chosen wine list offering both glasses and bottles, many different imported and local beers, a full bar, as well as freshly squeezed fruit juices and sparkling waters. On top of all this the service is professional. Our waiter could describe every dish on the menu. He was able to discuss the merits of several different wines, and though the staff has to traverse a space akin to a small, sloped football field to get from the kitchen to the tables, the food arrived promptly and hot. My one objection is that the drab plastic table tops are not covered with tablecloths or placemats for those having a full meal.

The best starter was a plate of imported olives, grilled vegetables, and a mound of marinated feta cheese, better spread on the dense white bread brought to the table instead of the commercial crackers that came with the plate. Peanut soup, an intense, thick puree, brought to mind melted peanut butter.

The Niman-Schell hamburger is worth the price of admission alone. Fresh, juicy, amazingly flavorful, this locally raised organic beef makes the perfect hamburgers. Served on a soft but gently crusty bun with thick-sliced applewood smoked bacon and melted jack cheese, the much abused hamburger becomes a luscious meal, especially when accompanied with a delicious, tartly dressed sweet potato salad. Jamaican Jerked Duck is not poultry that has been subjected to some awful torture, but a spicy marinade applied to a tender breast of duck that has been grilled and sliced and set on a pleasantly sweet molasses rum sauce. Red-tinted achiote rice and sauteed greens completed the lively plate. One evening roast leg of lamb smothered in a red wine and rosemary-scented gravy was cooked through, but still tender and tasty, especially with a mound of garlic mashed potatoes. Steamed salmon needed more soy-rice wine sauce to save it from austerity, but its freshness was evident. Ginger-scented rice and steamed baby bok choy came with it. The only dish that really was a mess turned out to be overcooked spaghetti swimming in mussel cream sauce studded with chunks of andouille sausage and mushrooms.

Desserts have a homey feel to them, like a spoonful of pleasantly tart, warm rhubarb compote surrounded by orange custard cream, and short-crusted sweet potato-pecan pie with bourbon whipped cream. Full bodied espresso and coffee are a pleasure.

By the time the show begins, food service stops. Too bad you can't have dinner at Kimball's East without paying for the show. That hamburger is so good, I'd stop by just for that.

PATRICIA UNTERMAN

KIRALA ★★★

2100 WARD ST. AT SHATTUCK AVE., BERKELEY. 549-3486. OPEN 11:30 TO 1:45 P.M. TUESDAY THROUGH FRIDAY, 5:30 TO 9:30 P.M. TUESDAY THROUGH SATURDAY, AND 5 TO 9 P.M. SUNDAY. WINE, BEER. MAJOR CREDIT CARDS. RESERVATIONS ESSENTIAL. INEXPENSIVE TO MODERATE.

There are dishes at Kirala, a Japanese restaurant next to the Berkeley Bowl produce market, that I've never seen before on a Japanese menu. There are subtle flavors I've never encountered before. The food is so good I ate at Kirala five times before I could get myself to write this review.

Kirala is housed in one of those old warehouse-type buildings that can become a dramatic restaurant setting at the hands of the right architect. With its high beamed ceiling, white walls, and gray carpet, Kirala is rescued from trendiness only by red vinyl chairs that look like they came from a dinette set. All the food is served on a breathtaking array of pottery crafted in Emeryville by a man named Ryusei Arita.

Kirala's menu features two pages of robata specialties. These are among the most sensational appetizers I've ever encountered in a restaurant—and many of them cost just a couple of dollars. In terms of innovation and taste, you can get things that would blow away any California cuisine restaurant and its $7.50-to-$10 appetizers. To begin with, the robata menu features several varieties of chicken, one better than the next. There's skewered chicken wrapped in shiso leaves, like little juicy grilled dolmas. There are chicken meatballs, blended with egg and flour and magnificently spiced. That same ground chicken meat can be ordered stuffed into mushrooms and green peppers, with a teriyaki sauce glaze. The grilled chicken wings are fine also.

But don't stop there. Crunchy asparagus wrapped with razor-thin slices of beef, tender pieces of calamari battered and impeccably deep-fried, cold, marinated, bright-green chopped spinach and juicy deep-fried oysters all make satisfying starters. *Sakamushi*, clams steamed in sake, couldn't have been fresher or tastier. And the *gyoza*, the little dumplings that are on almost every Japanese restaurant's menu, have never been better than at Kirala. They're stuffed with a delicate mixture of ground pork, black mushrooms, bamboo shoots, chives, sesame oil, and pepper.

For entrees, Kirala offers many of the standard dishes found on Japanese menus, including teriyakis and sukiyaki. There are also some unusual things I've seen nowhere else. If my sampling is any indication, whichever you choose you're in for a treat. In my book the single best entree is the *unaju*, freshwater eel served over rice in a lacquer box. Although much less unusual, salmon teriyaki is another entree to consider, the salmon absolutely fresh and perfectly cooked, the teriyaki sauce—like almost everything else at Kirala—made from scratch. Chicken *katsu*, a huge portion of deep-fried cutlets surrounded by an array of vegetables, is a bargain. A sizzling platter of ginger pork on a bed of shredded vegetables presented very tender meat absolutely infused with the flavor of fresh ginger. *Yosenabe*, the Japanese fish stew, has a sparkling array of fish and shellfish served in a rich, aromatic broth.

Who is the Bay Area's newest three-star chef? Yoshi Murakami, after years of training in Osaka, came to Berkeley just a few years ago. He holds a license to prepare *fugu*, the fish that can be fatal if any residue of the internal organs remains on the flesh. While the U.S. hasn't joined Japan in the fugu-eating game, Murakami is getting plenty of chance at Kirala to display his other talents.

STAN SESSER

▌ KULETO'S ★★

221 POWELL STREET, SAN FRANCISCO. 397-7720. OPEN 7 A.M. TO 11 P.M. MONDAY THROUGH FRIDAY, AND 8 A.M. TO 11 P.M. SATURDAY AND SUNDAY. FULL BAR. 25% NONSMOKING. FULLY WHEELCHAIR ACCESSIBLE. MAJOR CREDIT CARDS ACCEPTED. RESERVATIONS ADVISED. MODERATE TO EXPENSIVE.

Kuleto's is one of the most popular restaurants in the city, featuring a warm, inviting interior that looks like an upscale Italian trattoria. The mahogany bar, which you walk by to get to the reservation stand, is always packed. Combined with the rich wood and brass appointments, the white-clothed tables and the rich marble floor, you get a lot of ambience for the buck.

There's always something going on, especially in the open kitchen. You'll see cooks throwing spoonfuls of this and that into hopelessly warped saute pans and then tossing it all with precooked pasta. And therein lies the biggest problem with the food. The pasta consistently tastes waterlogged and mushy. It's too bad because the kitchen has a knack for sauces, although they're often ladled on too generously and overpower the pasta.

You'll find such things as penne with ground lamb, a zesty marinara sauce with a dollop of soft cheese in the center or linguine that combines the oceanic flavor of clams with the meaty nuances of salty prosciutto.

One of the best appetizers is a heaping portion of mild fennel sausage with roasted peppers and marinara sauce on a slab of baked polenta and cheese. Although grilled radicchio tends to be bitter, the chefs at Kuleto's overcome the problem by charring the outside and dousing it in a Caesar-pesto sauce with loads of crumbled feta cheese. There's also great fried calamari with caper aioli and marinara sauces.

On occasion, the combinations can get a little outlandish, such as halibut on a bed of spinach with a sauce of cherries and apricots. Although some work, I'd stick to the proven path. Grilled items are the best bets. One of the best items is thick and meaty lamb chops served on an under seasoned but nicely cooked risotto with artichokes and a chunky tomato sauce.

The efficient and unintrusive service, which sometimes slows at busy times, and the bustling atmosphere all add up to a pleasant evening. There's such a style and spirit to Kuleto's that the problems with the food are easily overlooked.

MICHAEL BAUER

L'AVENUE ★★★

3854 GEARY BOULEVARD, SAN FRANCISCO. 386-1555. OPEN FOR DINNER MONDAY THROUGH SATURDAY 6 TO 10 P.M., SUNDAY 5:30 TO 9:30 P.M. FULL BAR. ALL MAJOR CREDIT CARDS. 100% NONSMOKING. FULLY WHEELCHAIR ACCESSIBLE. RESERVATIONS RECOMMENDED. EXPENSIVE.

Nancy Oakes, the chef/owner of L'Avenue, is largely self-taught, but her talent has taken her to the top. Without a doubt, she's one of the brightest chefs in the city.

She made a name for herself by turning Pat O'Shea's Mad Hatter, an unrefined crowded pub, into a gourmet stop by creating new twists on old American favorites. Before long she was working with squab and other items that seemed incongruous with the surroundings. Then, about three years ago, she moved next door creating a charming personal restaurant that is the perfect understated platform for her talents.

Oakes is a master at creating sauces and vegetables that harmonize with everything else on the plate. The menu changes nightly, and so do the vegetables and sauces. You'll discover such combinations as grilled salmon on a bed of sweet white corn and onions, dressed in a vinaigrette and accompanied by potato pancakes and pencil-thin stalks of asparagus.

Standard roast chicken is given a fresh treatment with buttermilk mashed potatoes, garlicky chard and tomato slices under Fontina cheese and applewood-smoked bacon. Boneless rabbit is served with a melange of artichokes, roasted potatoes, shallots and garlic, green beans, and red and green bell peppers.

Appetizers may include delicately breaded and fried soft-shell crab on a bed of fried greens, or mussels with andouille sausage in a powerful broth with diced tomatoes and herbs. One of the most clever twists on tradition is the oyster BLT—an appetizer of crisp puff pastry, breaded fried oysters, applewood-smoked bacon, tomatoes, and peppery baby greens all drizzled with a mayonnaise-based sauce.

Desserts, created by Marlene Hazeltine, are some of the best in the city. All have a homey bent such as rhubarb and pear crisp, raspberry huckleberry pie with a crunchy buttery topping, or a rich mud cake teamed with espresso ice cream.

The interior, like the service, is a peaceful mix of pale yellow walls, wood floors, and tables draped in white cloths. There's a small bar tucked into the front of the room that offers a dozen seats for those who come in at the spur of the moment without reservations.

The focal point of the restaurant is a large oil painting of people crowded around the table, eating and drinking and having a good time. And that best sums up the allure of L'Avenue.

MICHAEL BAUER

| LA BERGERIE ★★

4221 GEARY BLVD. AT SIXTH AVE., SAN FRANCISCO. 387-3573. OPEN 5 TO 10 P.M. NIGHTLY. BEER, WINE. VISA, MASTERCARD, AMERICAN EXPRESS. 20% NON-SMOKING. FULLY WHEELCHAIR ACCESSIBLE. RESERVATIONS SUGGESTED. MODERATE.

Remember when French restaurants always had onion soup, escargots, and paté for appetizers, and the menu would inevitably include entrees like *coq au vin* and duck with orange sauce? When you could eat a good French dinner for $10 to $15, and that would also be the price of a bottle of wine? When there were little neighborhood French restaurants with absolutely no pretensions, just a friendly neighborhood feel?

Walking into La Bergerie is nothing less than stepping into a time machine and being transported back to those days. The full-course dinners, whose price depends on the entrees you choose, and the excellent wine list, are outstanding bargains.

And, most amazing of all, the food is actually good. The classic French onion soup, made absolutely from scratch starting with beef bones for stock, is the best I've had outside of France. Several of the entrees, with very sophisticated sauces, are wonderful. Even the salad is something special.

If you stick with the fixed-price dinner, you'll get the soup of the day to start, and this isn't just some mediocre dishwater. Cream of broccoli and cream of carrots, the two soups I tried, are both extraordinarily light and flavorful. Several of the a la carte appetizers are worth trying, too. The escargots in a garlicky butter sauce are identical in quality to those you'd get in a little bistro in Paris. The spicy shrimp bisque imparts a briny shrimp flavor with every bite. Paté is tastier than most versions.

Three of the entrees are so outstanding that you could almost consider them miraculous, considering the price. Very tender, fresh-tasting sweetbreads come in a rich brown sauce that includes Madeira wine, cream, and mushrooms. Rack of lamb is a beautiful piece of meat and a generous portion; a crust of bread crumbs and garlic on top and a sauce that is basically a reduction of lamb stock and red wine makes it even better. Finally, seafood in cream sauce turns out to be a very fresh mixture, mainly salmon and scallops, in a remarkable fish stock veloute, all resting on a bed of mashed potatoes that are browned under a broiler.

Who gave San Francisco such a bargain of a restaurant? The owner and chef of La Bergerie is Cambodian, Andy Try. When Try bought La Bergerie, he found the perfect restaurant to match his cooking. It's a pleasant '50s sort of room, with tan banquettes and coats of arms on the walls—just the kind of place you might remember eating escargots and onion soup in 20 years ago.

But La Bergerie is more than an exercise in nostalgia. Try reminds us how good hearty, classic French cooking can be when done properly, even though it might be considered hopelessly outdated today. It's so good I sense it could someday be resurrected as the trendy new cuisine of the future.

STAN SESSER

LA CREME ★★

2305 IRVING ST., SAN FRANCISCO. 664-0669. OPEN TUESDAY THROUGH SUNDAY 6 TO 10 P.M. BEER, WINE. VISA, MASTERCARD, AMERICAN EXPRESS. 90% NON-SMOKING. PARTIALLY WHEELCHAIR ACCESSIBLE. RESERVATIONS RECOMMENDED. MODERATE TO EXPENSIVE.

La Creme, a little French restaurant in the Sunset, is a remarkable exception on the restaurant scene—a venture of amateurs that has succeeded where most other beginners have failed. Steve Weich prepared for the restaurant business in a most unusual way; as an engineer and manager in the micro-electronics industry, the last 15

160

years in London. Meanwhile, his wife Judy was getting an advanced sociology degree at the London School of Economics. Now in their fifties, they're both working seven days a week at La Creme doing everything from busing tables to discussing pedigrees of wines with their customers.

The Weichs have a roaring success on their hands, a pleasant neighborhood restaurant with reasonable prices and food so satisfying that people come from way beyond the neighborhood to eat there. Their success is largely attributable to a very sound decision: they found a talented chef named Richard Plaskett and had the good sense to let him run the kitchen the way he wanted. Plaskett's cooking is nouvelle French but in his own style; very simple dishes with light and elegant sauces, often based on citrus, that are sparingly applied. The sauces are mostly made-to-order with each individual dish. There's nothing cloying or heavy on the menu; even the chicken liver paté manages to be refreshingly light. I found only one problem: a few of the red meats were unpleasantly dry and didn't have much flavor, a defect I'd attribute more to the quality of the raw material than the cooking.

Plaskett succeeds best in vegetarian and fish dishes; that's about all you have to know to have a wonderful meal at La Creme. Among starters in these categories, a perfect fettuccine with barely cooked asparagus comes in a sauce of white wine, lemon juice, and nutmeg, with a bit of creme fraiche stirred in. Asparagus appears in another form as a flan, a custardy mixture of asparagus, eggs, and cream baked in a mold lined with blanched leek leaves. Escargots in their classic preparation of garlic butter and parsley couldn't be better balanced— not too garlicky, not too oily, with very tender snails.

Then it's time for the fish. For each of my two dinners I had the fish special of the day, and, despite the presence of other good entrees, these soared above everything. Salmon in a ginger-lime sauce features as nice and fresh a piece of salmon as you can get, with a sauce heaven-sent for it. First the salmon is rubbed with lime juice and cayenne, then wrapped in foil and baked. The sauce, with subtle sweet-and-sour flavors, consists of lime juice, shallots, fresh ginger, port wine, creme fraiche, and the liquid shed by the cooked fish. Equally fine is the grilled tuna Provencal, pink and juicy inside, with a delightful tomato sauce that includes onions, butter, garlic, and thyme.

For meat lovers, I'd recommend both the duck and chicken. Grilled breast of duck slices, pink and meaty with almost no fat, benefits from a sauce of reduced chicken stock with porcini mushrooms and shallots, plus port and a bit of cream. Juicy sauteed boned breast of chicken comes with an abundance of garlic cloves roasted for two hours with sugar and butter, and a simple but excellent sauce of white wine, chicken stock, and creme fraiche.

From talking with Steve and Judy Weich, I get the impression that they're willing to learn as they go along, that they haven't let go to their heads the fact that many nights are filled to capacity. La Creme is right now well worth a visit. Any improvements could produce a restaurant with a city-wide reputation.

STAN SESSER

LA CUMBRE ★★

515 VALENCIA STREET, SAN FRANCISCO. 863-8205. OPEN MONDAY THROUGH SATURDAY 11 A.M. TO 10 P.M., SUNDAY NOON TO 9 P.M. BEER, WINE. CASH ONLY. 70% NONSMOKING. PARTIALLY WHEELCHAIR ACCESSIBLE. NO RESERVATIONS. INEXPENSIVE.

La Cumbre sets itself apart from the numerous and excellent taquerias that dot the Mission by its cheerful, wrought iron and red-tile interior and its *carne asada* deluxe burrito. This burrito causes long lines to form in front of the grill where the burritos are constructed to order. Thin slices of beef are charred over hot rocks and then cleaved into strips. They go into a warm flour tortilla covered with melted jack cheese. Whole red beans, a creamy avocado sauce, and a big spoonful of fresh tomato salsa are added and then the whole thing is wrapped up into a fat roll. The smokiness of the meat, the juiciness of the salsa, and the richness of the avocado, beans, and cheese make one terrific dish. La Cumbre is famous for this particular burrito and after you try one, you'll understand why. Another popular burrito is the vegetarian cheese with green chile.

Though people can take their burritos to go, the dining room is so pleasant that many stay to eat. Clean wooden picnic tables and benches set with several different salsas are one incentive to eat your food immediately. A colorful folk mural along one wall, arching adobe doorways, imported Mexican beers and sodas, and the fact that the place is so lively and bustling give this self-service Mexican fast food place a cafe-like feel. One draw back is that the ventilation system seems to falter when the windows aren't open—a conjunction of events that only happens on the rare cold day.

PATRICIA UNTERMAN

LA FIAMMETTA ★★

1701 OCTAVIA AT BUSH, SAN FRANCISCO. 474-5077. OPEN 6 TO 10 P.M. TUESDAY THROUGH THURSDAY, UNTIL 10:30 P.M. FRIDAY AND SATURDAY. WINE, BEER. VISA, MASTERCARD, AMERICAN EXPRESS. 90% NONSMOKING. FULLY WHEEL-CHAIR ACCESSIBLE. RESERVATIONS REQUIRED. MODERATE TO EXPENSIVE.

I was thinking about the question of salt—so frequently overused at so many restaurants—after two otherwise first-rate meals at La Fiam-

162

metta, a San Francisco Italian restaurant located where Restaurant Robert used to be, at Bush and Octavia. Several of the dishes here were so overwhelmed by salt I couldn't eat more than a couple of bites. Yet almost everything else that escaped the onslaught was completely delicious. So I find myself in the unprecedented position of giving a restaurant two stars when there were at least a half-dozen things I couldn't manage to eat.

La Fiammetta is an appealing little place, a pleasant room lined with white shelves and cabinets that's comfortable and quiet even when it's filled. The small menu is appealing too, with Tuscan food very much of the sort you'd find in Italy—interesting appetizers and pastas, lots of grilled meats, and no gloppy sauces. In addition to the regular menu, there's a mimeographed sheet of about five specials each night.

The chef is a marvel when it comes to seafood and soups, which makes for some very interesting starters. I love the marinated shellfish salad with clams, mussels, scallops, and shrimp all tasting totally fresh. And a mussels appetizer is a knockout—perfect mussels on the half shell in a garlic-cream sauce. As for soups, there's one that shouldn't be missed, despite the mundane-sounding description of "pasta, beans, seafood." Broad noodles, an array of perfectly cooked shellfish, and a heap of kidney beans are smothered in a thick and spicy tomato-based broth. There are some other good starters too, including prosciutto with buffalo-milk mozzarella cheese and a copious and interesting antipasto misto. But several of the pastas suffered from the salt problem.

La Fiammetta, fortunately, isn't among those many Italian restaurants where entrees prove the weakest part of the meal. Almost all the charcoal-grilled meats are delicious, particularly the veal with mushrooms. Thick, tender grilled veal slices are served in a zesty sauce of Italian field mushrooms sauteed with garlic, thyme, a broth of porcini mushrooms, and veal stock. The mixed grill is another good choice, with a slice of that veal, a wonderful lamb chop, a piece of rabbit and a shiitake mushroom.

Rabbit is often a special, and it's terrific. It comes in an interesting sauce of field mushrooms, pancetta, pearl onions, and rabbit stock. Another successful special is grilled halibut in a spicy tomato sauce filled with garlic and olives. But a duck leg with sausage and beans was intensely salty, and charbroiled chicken breast with herbs pressed into it by a heavy weight emerged much too dry.

La Fiammetta is one of the new-style Italian restaurants popping up these days, serving much more of what you find in Italy rather than the leaden, heavily sauced Italian food traditional in America. To pull it off, you need a skilled cook and first-rate ingredients. Fiammetta has both—if someone would only hold the salt.

STAN SESSER

LA FOLIE ★★★

2316 POLK STREET, SAN FRANCISCO. 776-5577. OPEN 6 TO 10:30 P.M. MONDAY
THROUGH SATURDAY. BEER AND WINE. 80% NONSMOKING. PARTIALLY
WHEELCHAIR ACCESSIBLE. MAJOR CREDIT CARDS. RESERVATIONS RECOM-
MENDED. VERY EXPENSIVE.

La Folie is one of the prettiest, intimate chef-owned restaurants in
the city. The sky-blue ceiling is painted with billowy white clouds and
crisscrossed with natural oak beams. The yellow printed chintz fabric
on the French-paned windows and doors give the dining room an
understated elegance. The slightly cherubic chef/owner, Roland
Passot, can be seen toiling in the kitchen, visible through the window-
like opening into the kitchen.

Although the French-style food is produced with a minimum of
butter and cream, Passot has impeccable classic training. He was a
protege of Jean Banchet at Le Francaise near Chicago. He then
opened the opulent French Room in Dallas and quickly brought it to
national prominence, at prices that ranked among the highest in the
nation. At this restaurant, however, Passot's prices are much gentler.
In fact, he creates a three course fixed price menu Monday through
Thursday that ranks as one of the best fine dining bargains in the city.

His highly stylized food combines the flavors of France and California with a little Southwest thrown in for contrast. One of the signature
dishes, for example, is a creamy yet sprightly cream of tomatillo soup,
given a refined twist with silken tomato quenelles.

Another zesty dish is the perfect round medallion of salmon topped
with a crusty mixture of horseradish and celery root, presiding over a
sauce of cucumbers in yogurt. In Passot's art-directed presentations,
the white sauce is surrounded by concentric rings of tomato, carrot,
and spinach purees. The colors are so vibrant that often his main
courses look as splashy as dessert presentations.

A succulent breast of chicken is fanned on the plate between large
diagonally cut potato chips, looking like a surrealistic butterfly in
flight. Rich foie gras is presented in a terrine layered with potatoes and
chanterelle mushrooms, all encased in leeks. It is warmed and served
with a hazelnut vinaigrette.

Each meal begins with a complimentary appetizer: an egg-shell
filled with a layer of tomato concasse, creamy scrambled eggs, herb
sauce and a dollop of caviar. Even the decidedly homey dishes take an
upscale turn. An utterly delicious Lyonnaise salad is updated with
quarters of warm potatoes, both yellow Finnish and purple varieties,
and a perfectly poached egg nestled in the tender greens.

Desserts offer familiar tastes with a French flair. A carrot cake is
presented like a terrine with multiple layers of cake and cream cheese

frosting, presented on a pumpkin cream anglaise. A hot pear feuillete is served with ginger sauce and airy quenelles of chocolate mousse.

The service is first-rate. Any pretension is negated by Jamie Passot who greets guests with a Midwestern down-home friendliness. It's a perfect blend of high style dining and down-home comfort.

MICHAEL BAUER

LA LANTERNA ★★½

799 COLLEGE AVENUE, KENTFIELD. 258-0144. OPEN FOR LUNCH TUESDAY THROUGH FRIDAY NOON TO 2 P.M.; DINNER TUESDAY THROUGH SUNDAY 6 TO 9 P.M. BEER AND WINE. MASTERCARD, VISA. 80 TO 100% NONSMOKING. FULLY WHEELCHAIR ACCESSIBLE. RESERVATIONS RECOMMENDED. MODERATE.

La Lanterna, a family operated Italian restaurant in Marin County, came to my attention through a long letter and a computer printout of a year's worth of the restaurant's dishes. Risotto, housemade pasta, fish soup, osso buco, braised rabbit with polenta, grilled veal loin, and fried calamari represented just a few of the dishes that perked my appetite on the six page list. The letter talked about nearby gardens supplying the restaurant, quoted from my favorite Italian cook book writer, Marcella Hazan, and included a biography of the chef, a 53-year-old high school teacher who left teaching to pursue his passion to cook. I couldn't resist the story and made the short trip to Kentfield. I'm happy to report that La Lanterna does fulfill the promises of its correspondence. Its fresh, authentic, Italian cooking shines all the way to San Francisco.

Like most Marin County restaurants, La Lanterna is part of a small shopping center. It occupies a low ceilinged space with some interior red brick walls and lots of windows that look out to a manicured lawn rimmed with gorgeous flowers, where at lunch, outdoor tables are set up. Though the interior is unpretentious and comfortably suburban, varying floor levels and an irregular shape create separate dining areas and alcoves. Commodious blond wood, dowel-backed chairs, white linen tablecloths and reproductions of famous Italian paintings set the stage for the main attraction, the food.

You can tell that the food is prepared by someone who loves to cook from your first bite. The appetizers are shining examples of the Italian way of presenting especially fresh and interesting ingredients with ingenious simplicity.

Fresh squid, velvety and tender, get the merest battering and the quickest, cleanest deep frying. House cured *bresaola,* tissue thin slices of aromatic, air-dried beef is drizzled with lemon juice and extra virgin olive oil. La Lanterna puts out a basic and, I think, superlative version of carpaccio. Almost translucent slices of raw beef are sprinkled with olive oil, shavings of parmesan and a few spikes of fresh rosemary. A Caesar salad is loaded with rough cut croutons which soak up a tart, garlicky, anchovy-rich dressing. A pile of sliced ripe tomatoes, topped with first-rate anchovies and rings of red onion crown a bed of piquantly dressed lettuce.

The risotto absorbs the requisite quantity of good chicken stock, butter, and olive oil to give it the perfect creamy yet toothsome texture with various combinations of seafood and vegetables stirred in. An extended menu of housemade pasta has supplanted some of the best veal dishes anywhere. Sometimes, the expertly grilled veal chop, thick and juicy, reappears as a special.

Also, for non-meat eaters, eggplant parmigiana is every bit as satisfying as a meat dish. Big, pear shaped slices of eggplant cut lengthwise, are battered, deep-fried and sauced with a spritely tomato puree.

A homey creme caramel with satiny, gently set custard, and zuppa inglese, a special dessert of molded layers of liqueur soaked cake and custard, are lovely.

The dining room is staffed by young, fresh-faced men and women who are well informed, eager to please, and efficient—an extended restaurant family. For the past year, the La Lanterna has instituted a series of heart-healthy menus as well as daily dishes that appear on the menu. A newsletter keeps customers up to date on Italian wines and new happenings. This energy has kept the restaurant a vital part of the Bay Area culinary community.

PATRICIA UNTERMAN

LA MEXICANA ★★½

3930 EAST 14TH ST., OAKLAND. (TAKE THE HIGH STREET EXIT FROM I-880 AND TURN LEFT ON EAST 14TH.) 436-8388. OPEN 11 A.M. TO 8 P.M. WEDNESDAY THROUGH SUNDAY. (YOU GET SERVED IF YOU'RE IN THE DOOR BY 8.) BEER, WINE. VISA, MASTERCARD. 100% NONSMOKING. PARTIALLY WHEELCHAIR AC-CESSIBLE. NO RESERVATIONS. INEXPENSIVE.

I've written many times about the dearth of real Mexican cuisine in the Bay Area—the wonderful, sophisticated cooking you see in major cities in Mexico, as opposed to the Tex-Mex food we eat here. Enchiladas, tacos and the like—which in Mexico are normally con-signed to sidewalk stands—might be tempting on occasion, but I usually find them so heavy, greasy, and salty that I regret it afterwards.

This is what makes La Mexicana, a nondescript restaurant on a street in east Oakland a few minutes north of the Coliseum, such a remarkable place. You'd never suspect it when you walk in the door, but La Mexicana elevates Tex-Mex to an art form, leagues above any other such food I've eaten. Did you ever hear of a Mexican restaurant in these parts where nothing comes from cans, where everything is made from scratch, where nothing is leaden, oversalted, or greasy?

La Mexicana has been around for more than three decades, run by Francisco and Olympia Gudina and their family. Now their son Arthur and his wife Lilia have taken over. Lilia, who speaks perfect, unaccented English although she's a Mexican citizen, has become the chef. The key to this restaurant's success starts with the homemade tortillas, which have to be tasted to be believed. These tortillas become the casing for the enchiladas and tacos, and they're cut up and deep-fried into chips to go with the spicy red and green salsas and the guacamole.

The menu is simple: enchiladas, tostadas and tacos with a choice of chorizo, chicken, or cheese filling, plus a few other items like tamales, steak, green chiles with pork, and a couple of egg dishes. All three fillings are fine, but the chorizo, the spicy Mexican sausage, is really unique. This isn't sausage in a casing; it's just the ground meat and spices. La Mexicana uses both pork and beef and adds to it oregano, chiles, cumin, and vinegar. It comes out deliciously spicy but not fatty. Try it also with scrambled eggs as the huevos con chorizo.

Among the other dishes, the chile relleno is unparalleled. For once it's a fresh anaheim chile, not from a can, and it's stuffed with jack cheese, battered with a delicate eggy coating, and deep-fried. Then there are the tamales stuffed with shredded pork; they actually have the flavor of corn. Try also the pork with green chiles, which is pieces of pork leg, strips of green chiles, and onions in a sauce that's nothing more than the juice of the meat. Finally, the tender *menudo* in a beautiful broth represents absolute heaven for those of us in the Bay Area—we must number at least five—who are tripe lovers.

Everything fresh, nothing leaden, sauces so light that there's not a globule of grease floating on them—this is the sort of cooking that could threaten to elevate Tex-Mex into haute cuisine.

STAN SESSER

LA TAQUERIA ★★★

2889 MISSION STREET BETWEEN 24TH AND 25TH STREETS, SAN FRANCISCO. 285-7117. OPEN EVERY DAY 11 A.M. TO 8 P.M. BEER. CASH ONLY. PARTIALLY WHEEL-CHAIR ACCESSIBLE. NO RESERVATIONS. FOOD TO GO. INEXPENSIVE.

Open since 1975, La Taqueria was one of the first food operations to prepare burritos and tacos exclusively, much in the tradition of Mexican food stalls. Customers stand in line at a counter in front of an open kitchen where beef is grilling, cheese is melting into tortillas on a griddle and a couple of cooks are putting together the tacos and burritos. You can order chicken, chorizo, carnitas, carne asada, or cheese in either taco or burrito form. There are beers and fresh fruit

■ **FOR HEAT, YOU SQUEEZE ON A STUNNING, MEDIUM HOT, FRESH GREEN CHILE AND TOMATILLO SALSA IN PLASTIC BOTTLES SET AT THE TABLES.**

juices, and that's it. When you get to the cash register, which takes about five minutes at peak times, you pay, and get a numbered receipt, then find a spot to sit down in the pleasant tiled dining room. A few minutes later your number will be called. The whole system works fast and efficiently. The tacos and burritos are prepared exactly the way you want them and the time elapsed is less than it takes at the large McDonald's on the corner.

The tacos are made with two soft, warm corn tortillas. They're piled with big shreds of chicken simmered with tomatoes and chiles or aromatically spicy Mexican sausage that's been crumbled and fried. The *carne asada*, or thin slices of grilled beef, is grilled on the rare side here and stays a little chewy if more moist. But the glory of La Taqueria's menu is their greaseless carnitas, pork slowly cooked in boiling lard, which turns out moist, savory and soft. It has all the succulence that pork usually loses when it's cooked any other way. La Taqueria is one of the few restaurants or taquerias that prepares it every day.

In addition to the meat, a spoon of whole, creamy textured red beans and a spoon of mild salsa cruda, chopped red tomatoes, onions, cilantro, and chiles goes onto the tacos. You may also request cheese and/or avocado at a small surcharge. I feel it's unnecessary on the tacos. For heat, you squeeze on a stunning, medium hot, fresh green chile and tomatillo salsa in plastic bottles set at the tables.

The burritos start with a large white flour tortilla and get the same fillings, but twice as much. I like avocado in the burritos and recommend that the hot green chile sauce be applied by the cooks during construction. That way you get a more even distribution in the filling.

Besides the delicious carnitas, and the extremely fast, well organized service, the appointments of this taqueria set it apart from all the others. The white adobe building has a tiled front patio under an arched arcade with iron grillwork gates. Inside, terracotta tile floors, glazed tile walls, skylights, an acoustic ceiling that really does cut down on noise, and an immaculate open kitchen make the Taqueria a pleasant place to eat. A vibrant folk mural along one wall and rustic, dark wood tables with woven leather stools, some of which are placed outside on the front patio, remind me of those pretty half-indoor half outdoor restaurants in Mexico.

I rank this white adobe taqueria very high on my personal list of favorites. The place is exemplary because it does what it does perfectly on every level, day after day, year after year.

PATRICIA UNTERMAN

LA TRAVIATA ★★

2854 MISSION ST. (BETWEEN 24TH AND 25TH), SAN FRANCISCO. 282-0500. OPEN
FROM 4 TO 10:30 P.M. TUESDAY THROUGH SUNDAY. VISA, MASTERCARD. BEER,
WINE. 30% NONSMOKING. FULLY WHEELCHAIR ACCESSIBLE. RESERVATIONS
NECESSARY. MODERATE.

La Traviata, the splendid Italian restaurant in the Mission with an
opera motif and wonderful veal and pasta, has literally risen from the
ashes. In July 1988 a fire gutted the place, destroying not only a good
restaurant, but also hundreds of signed photographs lining the walls of
opera singers who had eaten there over 13 years. This was the sort of
warm, atmospheric, old- fashioned Italian restaurant that San Francisco does so well, but with one major difference from most of the
others—the food was excellent.

I had such fond memories of La Traviata that I dreaded what I'd
find now that it's reopened. I feared a new trendy menu to replace the
dishes I had come to love over the years and stratospheric prices to
match. I shouldn't have worried. The decor is a little nicer, but
everything else is exactly the same. The same waiters, the same chef,
the same food and reasonable prices—even the signed opera photos
lining the walls. (Zef Shllaku, the owner, says that some opera singers
and opera-loving patrons helped him replace his collection.)

La Traviata's menu is largely pasta, veal, and chicken. There are
some fish dishes too, but, except for the admirable calamari with
capers and mushrooms sauteed in butter and tomato sauce, don't fool
around with them. Don't worry about the appetizers either, particularly the boring antipasto plate for two which is mainly tasteless,
refrigerator-cold slices of delicatessen meats.

Instead, the idea at La Traviata is to pig out on pasta, keeping in
mind only that you should save a little room for the chicken or veal
that follows. Don't be deterred by the fact that the entrees themselves
come with a choice of pasta as a side dish; it's all so good that one pasta
dish followed by another is the only logical progression here. And the
good-natured, accommodating waiters make sampling the pasta even
more fun. If you want pesto on your gnocchi instead of tomato sauce,
if you want a half-order of spaghetti, if you want a pasta dish split in
the kitchen for two or three people, it's all no problem.

The pastas you can choose with your entree take no back seat to
the a la carte pastas; that's why it's essential at La Traviata to have at
least two rounds of pasta courses. At Italian restaurants that give you
free pasta with your entree, what appears on your plate normally tastes
worse than what comes from a Franco-American can. But the ravioli
stuffed with cheese, beef, and spinach in a tomato sauce are fantastic—
until you taste the tortellini, which are even better. These tortellini,
ethereally light, come in a sauce of half-and-half, butter, parmesan
cheese, and nutmeg.

Then it comes time for the veal or chicken. The two favorites are veal Traviata and chicken Beverly Sills. The tender, pounded slices of veal are topped with a bit of prosciutto and mozzarella, and served in a brown sauce that's tasty, but seems to always lack the extra minute that would be needed to cook out the wine. Beverly comes boned and rolled with pancetta, mozzarella, and mushrooms.

Its vaulted wood ceiling, track lighting, and comfortable, fabric-covered banquettes and booths make La Traviata even more pleasant than before. With the food as good as ever and the prices as reasonable as ever, it's hard to believe this restaurant could come back from a destructive fire in such fine fashion.

STAN SESSER

LAGHI ★★★

1801 CLEMENT ST. (AT 19TH AVE.), SAN FRANCISCO. 386-6266. OPEN TUESDAY THROUGH SUNDAY FROM 5 TO 10 P.M. BEER AND WINE. MASTERCARD AND VISA. 100% NONSMOKING. FULLY WHEELCHAIR ACCESSIBLE. RESERVATIONS REC-OMMENDED. MODERATE.

Of all the restaurants where Gino Laghi has cooked, this little corner storefront in the Richmond may be the most satisfying for both him and his patrons. Everything is made from scratch on the daily menu and the food is absolutely delicious.

What sets his cooking apart from the many neighborhood pasta houses that dot the city, is the authenticity of the food and the passion behind its preparation. Gino's cooking reminds me of meals I've eaten in tiny regional restaurants in Italy that are barely extensions of the home kitchen. The prepared food fills your mouth with long, deep flavors. The contrastingly simple composed dishes work because of high quality Italian ingredients. Finally, his choice of dishes on the daily changing menu is a relief from the manufactured-tasting Italian fare you get with slight variations at so many of the Italian spots in town. The Laghi preparations are unique.

His pink, veal carpaccio is strewn with shaved parmesan, capers and truffled olive oil. It's wonderful. A hot, flat bread resembling a tortilla, called *piadina*, from Mr. Laghi's native Emilia-Romagna, is folded over a slice of imported prosciutto. One night a basket of these hot flat breads appeared and were lovely with a pepperonata, a cold salad of roasted peppers, eggplant and onions. Radicchio loses its bitterness when cooked and nothing is more delectable than a plate of braised quarters with crisp pancetta in warm olive oil and vinegar. Little bowls of marinated wax beans come as a treat for everyone.

If cappellacci alla crema di parmagiano are on the menu, order them. I've never tasted anything like these delicate meat dumplings, barely encased in the tenderest noodle dough, sauced with a heavenly

■ RADICCHIO LOSES ITS BITTERNESS WHEN COOKED AND
NOTHING IS MORE DELECTABLE THAN A PLATE OF
BRAISED QUARTERS WITH CRISP PANCETTA IN WARM
OLIVE OIL AND VINEGAR.

parmesan cream seasoned with nutty truffle oil. Two simpler pastas of
very finely cut, housemade semolina noodles absorb a bright green
pesto, perfumed with basil, and a fresh tomato sauce with its own share
of basil and garlic in a characteristically Italian way. Both are good
choices as shared antecedents to a main course. One of my favorite
pastas features hand-rolled tubes of housemade pasta tossed with fresh
tomato sauce and fresh fava beans.

Gino Laghi has a source for porcini, those much sought after,
meaty boletus mushrooms, and he uses them generously in a number
of different dishes. His toothsome risotto with domestic mushrooms
and porcini is infused with their flavor. Squares of gnocchi, a chewy
dumpling made from eggs, butter and flour, are sauteed with porcini,
pine nuts and fresh tomato in one interesting version.

Only four main courses are prepared each night and most of them
have been exceptional. Four little rib lamb chops, pounded, breaded
and crisply pan fried are tender, tasty, a dream. Two quail braised in a
game stock with red wine and grappa are presented in a small white
casserole on a bed of creamy polenta, a stunning dish. A filet of halibut
takes on the most amazing, velvety texture, baked in a hot oven with
herbs, olive oil, and lemon. An individual casserole of veal stew with
potatoes and peas served with grilled polenta was satisfying one night,
if not as exciting as the other main courses.

Mrs. Laghi makes the desserts, when she can. The two I tasted were
very homey, a little messy but good. The wine list offers a small
selection of excellent Italian bottles.

The tiny restaurant has a cheerful, mostly inherited decor. Booths
and floors are made of varnished knotty pine. French impressionist-
style oils in heavy frames hang on the walls, covered in tiny flower
print wallpaper. A pine bar displays bottles of Italian wine and an
espresso machine behind a big picture window that lets in lots of light.
In all, there are only about fifteen tables in this generically cozy-
looking restaurant.

In this era of 200-seat restaurants, with cooks ultimately responsible
to the portfolios of investors, the tide may be turning to the small
neighborhood place—not run by beginners or amateurs—but by experienced cooks who have spent lots of time in other people's kitchens
and finally want to cook for themselves. They get to express their own
cooking voices and their patrons get the inspired results at refreshing
neighborhood prices.

PATRICIA UNTERMAN

LARK CREEK INN ★★★½

234 MAGNOLIA AVENUE, LARKSPUR. 924-7766. OPEN FOR LUNCH MONDAY
THROUGH FRIDAY 11:30 A.M. TO 2:30 P.M., BRUNCH SATURDAY AND SUNDAY
11:30 A.M. TO 2:30 P.M. DINNER SUNDAY THROUGH THURSDAY 5:30 TO 10 P.M.,
FRIDAY AND SATURDAY 5:30 TO 11 P.M. FULL BAR. MASTERCARD, VISA, AMERI-
CAN EXPRESS. RESERVATIONS ADVISED. MODERATE.

Chef Brad Odgen, who put the restaurant at Campton Place on the map, has come through again, this time as owner of his own place. He and his partner bought the fading but beautiful old Victorian Lark Creek Inn, gave it a face lift and started turning out imaginative American dishes at moderate prices. The combination of location, physical surroundings, and food couldn't be more inspired.

The romantic wooden building is located in a stand of redwoods in the middle of Larkspur, about a twenty-five minute drive from San Francisco, barring rush hour traffic. There is a spacious main dining room with a skylit ceiling, a light filled patio room, and wonderful outdoor seating area, seemingly in the middle of wilderness. The restaurant has a luxurious, country feel to it. Tables are placed generously apart and the noise level is bearable. One of the nicest sights in the main dining room is the red brick, wood burning oven out of which emerge aromatic stews, suckling pig and roast chickens.

What is surprising about this handsome new restaurant is that the menu is so reasonably priced. Tariffs are half what they were at Campton Place and yet the operation offers almost as many amenities, like an extensive and interesting all-American wine list, baskets of warm housemade biscuits and breads, a well-set table, and layers of staff to take care of you.

Of course, the best part of the experience is the rustic, colorful, and multi-faceted food. Just reading the menu whets your appetite and the meals do a great job of satisfying it. At lunch you eat vine ripe tomatoes of all hues, napped with a delicious creamy onion dressing and a napkin basket of deep-fried squid and clams with a peppery garlic mayonnaise dipping sauce. Yankee pot roast comes in a hand-thrown pottery plate with lots of gravy, airy onion dumplings and an array of roasted root vegetables. The fried egg sandwich here defines the genre, with Hobbs Shore's thick sliced smoked bacon, ripe tomatoes, and lots of good mayonnaise. Even a more esoteric dish like ravioli with shredded ham hocks in a roasted tomato broth has a homey feel. Served in a pottery bowl, the thick, tasty noodle wrappers stand up to the smoky meat just fine.

Everything on the menu is made in-house—dill pickles, corned beef, BBQ suckling pig, breads, cocktail sauce, and of course, dessert. The desserts are gigantic and very American. There are tall glass dishes of nutty butterscotch pudding with thick, lemon sugar cookie stars, warm, gooey brownie sundaes with hot fudge pudding sauce, and deep bowls of old fashioned shortcake swimming in fresh berries, whipped cream, and soft buttermilk ice cream. More restrained and even better are a rich, tart, apple crumb pie with vanilla ice cream and an end of summer nectarine and fresh fig compote with creme fraiche. A spectacular banana cake has many layers with lots of frosting and mashed bananas in between, and a peach dumpling comes neatly wrapped in buttery pastry with cinnamon ice cream and warm caramel sauce.

At dinner there are field lettuce salads with lovely, warm, potted cheese toasts, or tomato salad with goat cheese mozzarella, an array of assorted oysters, or a stew of lobster, vegetables, and thick egg noodles.

With main courses, the dinner menu gets homier. I adore butter tender slices of braised pork shoulder served in a pottery bowl with white beans and kale, and a juicy, spit roasted chicken with chive flecked mashed potatoes and a whole ear of white corn slathered with red pepper butter. A New York strip steak with a bone is topped with buttermilk-battered, onion rings. A plate-sized grilled lamb steak is strewn with fresh peas and irresistible scalloped potatoes and turnips.

Bradly Ogden finally has the chance to cook with his own voice and it turns out to have a distinct Midwestern twang. His best dishes remind me of dishes I grew up with—or wish I'd grown up with. Of course Ogden knows how to present his dishes beautifully, to find great ingredients, and to compose an intriguing menu, but he knows, as well, the power of a juicy roast chicken with a plate of mashed potatoes. With so many derivative new restaurants opening all the time, it is exciting to get an original.

PATRICIA UNTERMAN

LE CASTEL ★★½

3235 SACRAMENTO (NEAR PRESIDIO), SAN FRANCISCO. 921-7115. OPEN FOR DINNER 5:30 TO 10 P.M. TUESDAY THROUGH SATURDAY. SUNDAY 5 TO 9 P.M. WINE AND BEER. MAJOR CREDIT CARDS ACCEPTED. JACKETS REQUIRED FOR MEN. 30% NONSMOKING. NOT WHEELCHAIR ACCESSIBLE. RESERVATIONS ADVISED. EXPENSIVE.

There are times when you want to go to a restaurant to have a quiet, relaxed meal. It is in this context that Le Castel shines. In a converted house on Sacramento Street near Presidio, the three dining rooms of the 60-seat restaurant are cozy and intimate, with stucco walls, shaded candles, and little silver vases with fresh flowers on each table, lamps in the corners, and service that is classy and understated.

The restaurant offers an almost cocoon-like setting, perfect for either a romantic evening or for a serious business dinner, an ideal setting for classic French food. This restaurant, conceived by Fritz

Frankel who owned La Mirabelle for 15 years before opening Le Castel six years ago, is about the only place in town where you can get bone marrow on toast or sauteed calves' brains with brown butter and capers. Both dishes are first-rate. Emile Waldteufel, an American chef who was trained in France and has been at Le Castel since it opened, has a master's touch with sauces. All of them have good structure and depth. Sometimes they are subtle and seductive, at other times they are brassy and boisterous, but they always are harmonious with the other ingredients.

For example, the chef lightly sautees thin portions of tender veal and tops each with slices of artichoke hearts that are cooked so tender they could be spread on toast. He ties the elements together with a delicate lemon butter sauce made with just a hint of veal stock.

You can get crusty beef tenderloin, decadently topped with rounds of bone marrow and glistening with a red wine sauce. Tuna is cooked rare, sliced, and served with a red pepper sauce that has a velvety texture of cream. A salad of warm prawns is dressed with a creme fraiche-based dressing that gives a pleasant reprieve from the traditional vinaigrette.

The menu, which consists of about eight regular main courses, five appetizers and generally about three or four specials, is as understated as the chef's creations. It's not innovative in the sense of American restaurants, but it's perfectly executed and supported by a first-rate wine list, which features 15 sparkling wines and Champagnes. The list is large without being intimidating, well organized with good depth in older California and French red wines. There's also a nice selection of sauternes and a good representation of 10 rhone red wines and two whites, including Condrieu. Many of the desserts are good partners to the 18 sauternes and barsac.

Desserts include a rhubarb tart, topped with phyllo dough, and a walnut tart that has a grand dose of maple syrup. Generally, the other desserts sampled were good, but not nearly as well conceived as the rest of the meal. In all, the restaurant still offers unwavering consistency in both food and service. It's enough to make you forget your troubles, sit back and enjoy.

MICHAEL BAUER

LE CENTRAL ★★

458 BUSH STREET, SAN FRANCISCO. 391-2233. OPEN MONDAY THROUGH SATUR-DAY 11:30 A.M. TO 3:30 P.M.; DINNER 5:30 TO 10:30 P.M. FULL BAR. ALL MAJOR CREDIT CARDS. 50% NONSMOKING. FULLY WHEELCHAIR ACCESSIBLE. RESERVATIONS ACCEPTED. MODERATE.

Much beloved as the first authentic French brasserie in San Francisco, the food at Le Central took a dive when its energetic owners, the Cappelle brothers, sold out majority interest to a group of investors. The famous roast chicken started coming out of the kitchen soggy, as if rewarmed, and the pommes frites went limp. Well, thank goodness an original owner, Pierre Cappelle, is back, and the restaurant has returned to its former level of consistency.

It's so much fun to sit at Le Central's tiny, crowded tables and banquettes, eating on butcher paper, perusing the mirrors for daily specials written in grease pencil, looking around at all the celebrity lunchers strategically seated at the tables by the front windows. If you hadn't walked down Bush Street to get there, you'd think you were in Paris.

What the food lacks in brilliance, it makes up for in dependability and pure French ethnicity. Salads of butter lettuce with walnuts, or plates of long braised leeks with tasty green tops, or a plate of crisp, julienned celery root make for authentic starters.

The roast chicken is now juicy and crisp as I remembered it and comes with the traditional sprig of watercress, grilled tomato half, and french fries. *Boudin noir,* or blood sausage, are still excellent here and still from master charcutieres Marcel and Henri. The fat, black sausages are sauteed to the bursting point with lots of caramelized onions, whose sweetness goes so well with the allspice in the sausages. The restaurant also offers another dish rarely encountered outside of France, poached skate wing with capers. The soft, white meat of the skate wing, divided by a layer of cartilaginous bones, reminds me of sea scallops and tastes wonderful with the slightly vinegary butter sauce.

With first-rate fresh fruit and nut tarts from TARTS and excellent espresso, a bottle of decent French wine or a better bottle of Le Central's specially labeled house chardonnay from Chalone, all a diner's needs are met in a thoroughly French way.

PATRICIA UNTERMAN

LE CHEVAL ★½

1414 JEFFERSON ST. AT 14TH ST., OAKLAND. 763-8495. OPEN 11 A.M. TO 9:30 P.M. MONDAY THROUGH THURSDAY, 11 A.M. TO 10 P.M. FRIDAY AND SATURDAY, 5 TO 9:30 P.M. SUNDAY. BEER, WINE. VISA, MASTERCARD, AMERICAN EXPRESS. 60% NONSMOKING. FULLY WHEELCHAIR ACCESSIBLE. RESERVATIONS ACCEPTED. INEXPENSIVE.

ALSO AT KAISER CENTER, 344 20TH ST., OAKLAND. 763-3610. OPEN 11 A.M. TO 3 P.M. MONDAY THROUGH FRIDAY.

To call Le Cheval unique in an era of cookie-cutter restaurants is something of an understatement.

It's a Vietnamese restaurant with a French name serving food that's almost Chinese in character. To get to it, you have to park in one of the seediest areas of downtown Oakland, and walk into a building covered with scaffolding made necessary by the earthquake—scaffolding that seems to shelter a large homeless population. But once inside, you find yourself in a room with the ambiance of a long-established steakhouse, with old wooden tables, starched white tablecloths, and wisecracking waiters nattily attired in vests and ties. And you see an obviously devoted clientele that looks like a who's who of downtown Oakland law firms.

Now there's a choice of locations: Le Cheval has opened a branch for lunches only in the shopping mall of Kaiser Center. It's a sleek modern place with blond wood walls and tweed carpeting, and it does a booming business. I found the food very similar at both, but I'd vote for the original location at 14th and Jefferson, which certainly isn't your ordinary Asian-restaurant ambiance. How many Vietnamese restaurants have walls covered with displays of beer bottles (you can choose from 60 beers), and a big earthquake-induced crack in the plaster labeled in red paint: "7.1 was here"?

In general, you'll have to like heavy and pungent-style Asian food to like Le Cheval, since no one can accuse the sauces of being in any way delicate. While that's not characteristic of Vietnamese restaurants, Le Cheval clearly has plenty of fans, as my mail over the years can attest to. Here's the best of what I tasted, starting with appetizers. There's a fabulous soup called creamy carrot chowder, the most French-like thing on the menu. Several interesting eggroll-type creations are good choices, including the deep-fried imperial rolls, with a ground beef and mushroom stuffing, the chicken rolls, and the shrimp rolls, which incorporate shrimp, rice noodles and fresh mint, and are steamed instead of fried. A traditional Vietnamese dish, ground beef wrapped in an Asian leaf called *lot* and grilled, is done expertly here; the filling includes garlic, lemongrass, ground peanuts, and green onions.

When it comes to entrees, there are some wonderful dishes that are also unusual. *Be thiui*, the only thing on the menu not translated or explained, turns out to be thin slices of veal, quickly roasted so that they come out rare, spread with shreds of ginger, roasted rice powder, and Thai basil. Two claypot dishes proved hearty and satisfying: pork in claypot, stewed in soy and fish sauce; and claypot rice, a combination of beef, shrimp, chicken and mushrooms, that are first wok-fried and then baked in the pot with rice.

One dish that got universal raves at my table was beef in orange flavor, with the very tender slices of flank steak smothered in onions and served in a thick brown sauce flavored with orange peels. Crisp chowmein with eggplant and vegetables is a rewarding vegetarian offering of celery, carrots, eggplant, and broccoli served in a bird's nest of deep-fried noodles. There are two tasty versions of boneless chicken, one in a spicy, rich coconut milk sauce with lots of vegetables, the other in a roaring-hot lemongrass sauce with ground peanuts, hot peppers, and onions.

STAN SESSER

LE PIANO ZINC ★½

708 14TH ST. (NEAR THE INTERSECTION OF CHURCH AND MARKET), SAN FRANCISCO. 431-5266. OPEN 5 TO 11 P.M. NIGHTLY. BEER, WINE. VISA, MASTERCARD, AMERICAN EXPRESS. NONSMOKING EXCEPT FOR THE BAR. PARTIALLY WHEELCHAIR ACCESSIBLE. RESERVATIONS ACCEPTED. MODERATE.

There's a very appealing notion of restaurant economics that unfortunately is tried out by only a small minority of non-Asian restaurants. The principle is this: since so many costs, like rent and utilities, are the same whether two people come for dinner or two hundred, why not cut prices to increase patronage—and hopefully increase profits at the same time?

This is what has happened at one of my favorite San Francisco French restaurants, Le Piano Zinc. Prices are substantially lower than when I first wrote about it several years ago. With a wine list that emphasizes excellent low-priced French wines, this means you can eat a first-rate French dinner for neighborhood restaurant prices.

And at Piano Zinc you sacrifice nothing—except, unfortunately, the piano that gave the restaurant its name and provided some good music at late hours. That piano is gone, replaced by a takeout operation that sells the entrees for one dollar less than menu prices. Warm duck paté in puff pastry to go? Why not? Except for that piano, it's the same old Piano Zinc, a comfortable room with pretty place settings and two long rows of tables spaced only a few inches apart, just like you find all over Manhattan.

Most of the appetizers at Piano Zinc sound interesting and come out beautifully executed. For anyone who likes sweetbreads, call Piano Zinc and find out when they're featuring them, because their sweetbreads are second to none. Sweetbreads sauteed with cognac sauce are blanched, sliced, lightly breaded, then sauteed in butter to produce a crusty outside and a creamy interior. Sweetbreads baked in a tartlet with escargots and slices of fresh goose liver is a dish so stunningly delicious I could hardly believe it.

Other first-rate appetizers include a curried cream of mussel and clam soup served in an attractive tureen, the soup, rich, bisque-like, and filled with shellfish. Two salads, a warm breast of duck salad on boutique lettuces, and warm goat cheese with baby lettuces from Santa Rosa are enticing, the duck slices tender, the lettuces crisp, and the dressings sparingly applied.

The entrees are a much more varied experience, and most desserts can be skipped. The cassoulet, with its delicate white beans and sauce and good duck confit, is marred by disappointing smoked pork and sausage that tastes too much like an American hot dog. Aiguillette of rabbit in a forceful red wine sauce has good tender rabbit and the puff pastry that Piano Zinc does so well. Tender osso bucco with noodles features high-quality veal shank and an interesting sauce that includes vegetables, raisins, and citrus.

Le Piano Zinc's recent round of price cutting and its new takeout operation are clearly designed to make it less of a formal restaurant and more of a neighborhood brasserie. This restaurant is so wonderfully French, and so much of the food is so good, that I can envision lines out the door.

STAN SESSER

LE ST. TROPEZ ★★★

126 CLEMENT STREET, SAN FRANCISCO. 387-0408. OPEN TUESDAY THROUGH SATURDAY FROM 5:30 TO 10 P.M. FULL BAR. VISA, MASTERCARD, AMERICAN EXPRESS. 50% NONSMOKING. FULLY WHEELCHAIR ACCESSIBLE. RESERVATIONS ACCEPTED. MODERATE.

I have always liked Gerald Hirigoyen's cooking. As a pastry chef during the dizzy first year at Le Castel, he turned out whimsical-looking cakes and confections that actually tasted as good as they looked. As the opening chef at the Pacific Avenue location of Lafayette (which recently closed after ten years), he put together a tasty menu of very reasonably priced bistro fare for the downtown crowd. At Le St. Tropez, Hirigoyen has developed into a full fledged French chef. Each dish has a focus, a star ingredient that is always perfectly cooked, and around which everything else revolves. It occurs to me that Hirigoyen must like simple food because all his handsomely arranged plates never subvert the qualities of the main ingredient. His cooking has substance and logic.

Each week he puts out a different, moderately priced, prix fixe meal and the one I sampled was gorgeous, taking advantage of all the wonderful spring produce around. It began with a shallow bowl of delicate cream of asparagus soup followed by a warm salad of baby artichokes and scallops sprinkled with hazelnuts and dressed in a hazelnut oil vinaigrette. A delicious, golden crusted roast poussin had been cut into quarters and arranged around a pile of morels napped in cream and shallots. Sweet little carrots added slashes of color. For dessert, three bright-flavored sorbets came with a plate of tiny madeleines and chocolate truffles. Even though there were no sauces, the dishes had an elegance and lushness of flavor that only the best French cooking seems to achieve.

The regular menu offers many opportunities to put together your own fine meal. One night the soup of the day combined mushrooms and fennel in a silky puree. The tender meat of Pacific lobster is the center of a pretty green salad strewn with tiny fava beans, diced tomato, and a lively vinaigrette. A huge slab of foie gras is gently warmed through with some apples and Calvados. A plate of poached oysters napped in a lovely vermouth cream sauce comes on a bed of julienned, braised endive.

The reasonably priced main courses don't let up on quality one bit. A special one night brought a thick steak of rare, marinated venison served with pears poached in red wine. It was tender, buttery, exotic but not too gamey. Three marinated lamb chops come with a spec-tacular potato gratin. A thick filet of fresh tuna is smothered under a pile of sweet and sour onions and garnished with tiny squash.

You can tell that Hirigoyen still loves to make desserts. Plate after plate of beautiful, light, well balanced sweets flow out of the kitchen like an ethereal pistachio cream cake and an airy cocoa cream cake with raspberries.

The wine list is strong on California bottles but I appreciate the ten or so moderately priced bordeaux which go so well with Hirigoyen's excellent meat dishes. The restaurant itself looks like a little Swiss chalet with half-timbered walls and a large open hearthed fireplace which begs the question of why it is named after a beach town on the Mediterranean. The service, by an all French staff, is smooth and professional.

PATRICIA UNTERMAN

LICHEE GARDEN ★★

1416 POWELL, SAN FRANCISCO. 397-2290. OPEN 11:30 A.M. TO 9:30 P.M. EVERY DAY. BEER AND WINE. VISA AND MASTERCARD. 30% NONSMOKING. FULLY WHEEL-CHAIR ACCESSIBLE. RESERVATIONS RECOMMENDED. INEXPENSIVE.

One of the best restaurants in the city for homey, simple, family-style, Cantonese fare is the Lichee Garden, a bustling, medium-sized restaurant just on the edge of Chinatown. Everyone brings their kids and grandparents, uncles, aunts, and friends. Most of the round tables seat eight or ten people and most of the time they're full. A lazy susan in the middle of linen-covered tables makes it simple for each person to serve himself from large platters, and the kitchen is used to adjusting amounts of each dish to the number of people eating.

Begin a meal with a platter of big, juicy, salt and pepper shrimp with flavorful shells and heads. A crisp, glistening, whole roast chicken, gaily decorated with melt-on-your-tongue shrimp chips, has velvety, succulent flesh. Custardy, handmade, fresh tofu cakes with slivers of fileted steelhead, scallions, and a light, clean sauce of ginger, soy, and clear fish stock, appeals to the most subtle palate. A platter of simple snap peas in the cleanest of sauces, emphasizes the vegetable's sweetness.

A dramatic, large, deep-fried catfish, slit down the middle, sits on a pile of wilted scallions sauced with ginger and soy sauce. The catfish is wondrously crisped to a deep brown color which seems to make its white flesh even moister. A spectacular preparation of boned duck, topped with taro paste and then deep-fried, produces a brilliant Cantonese interplay of textures. Each piece has a lacy tempura-like crust, a layer of creamy taro, a layer of dark duck meat, and then another ultra crispy crust on the bottom.

Frogs legs are a rarely served treat in San Francisco, but Lichee Garden does a smashing version, cut through the bone into nugget size pieces and tossed with garlic chives, fresh straw mushrooms, and carrots in a translucent sauce. It's a dish that the finest French chef would admire, full of subtle flavor and lovely colors. Other strong suits at Lichee Garden are saucy House Special Ribs, all the duck dishes, impeccable and barely sauced greens of all sorts, hairy melon soup, fresh eel, and catfish-tofu hot pots.

Lichee Garden is a little more expensive than many Chinatown places, but the quality of the ingredients and skill in preparation is well worth it. Many knowledgeable Chinese families in San Francisco consider Lichee Garden to be one of their most dependable and pleasurable restaurants.

PATRICIA UNTERMAN

LITTLE JOE'S ON BROADWAY ★½

523 BROADWAY, SAN FRANCISCO. 433-4343. OPEN EVERY DAY FROM 11 A.M. TO 10:30 P.M. BEER AND WINE. NO CREDIT CARDS. 25% NONSMOKING. FULLY WHEELCHAIR ACCESSIBLE. NO RESERVATIONS. INEXPENSIVE.

When I revisited this North Beach institution after a hiatus of five years, I was pleasantly surprised to find the restaurant still vital—and a lot of fun. The prices, miraculously, seem just as cheap as ever and the menu exactly the same. The broad, San Francisco-Italian-style dishes come off the famous, open cooking line with the old fervor.

At Little Joe's customers sit at long formica tables, shared with other people, often after waiting in line in the middle of the restaurant, watching the cooks slap the food around the flaming stoves. The waitresses, in Little Joe's T-shirts, have a gum-chewing, off-hand manner. They get the food to the tables as it comes off the line, sometimes dish by dish. You're lucky to get the bottle of wine you ordered before the middle of the meal and you rarely can get their attention.

Yet, when a bottle of absolutely delicious, full-flavored chianti for an amazingly low price finally arrives along with an oval platter full of tender, buttery beef tongue slices served with a piquant green sauce, you can't help but be pleased. The food here tastes honest, the value is extraordinary, and the complete lack of pretension, a breath of fresh air.

Other old favorites on the menu include a chicken liver and onion saute in a red wine and tomato sauce (if you order the livers "pink", they'll come out perfectly) and a quickly cooked calamari saute finished off with copious amounts of garlic, white wine, and tomato sauce. Little Joe's signature *caciucco*, an Italian fish stew of fresh squid, snapper, clams, and mussels in a broth of red wine, tomatoes, and lots of garlic is always worth ordering.

With your entree you get huge portions of vegetables, spaghetti, or rigatoni. Plates of lightly sauteed cauliflower, zucchini, carrots, and chard are always crisp if a little bland. Ask for vinegar and oil to dress them up. The spaghetti, for reasons of expediency, has been pre-cooked and is heavily doused in a tomato and meat sauce. For a small surcharge you can get plump, doughy ravioli stuffed with something akin to library paste, also covered with the meat sauce. For some reason, many people love them.

Little Joe's offers San Franciscans the opportunity to eat in a timeless, noisy, egalitarian dining hall. The scenic mural that covers one long wall could have been painted by a WPA art crew, who probably would have eaten this exact North Beach-Italian fare sixty years ago.

PATRICIA UNTERMAN

LO COCO'S ★★½

510 UNION STREET, SAN FRANCISCO. 296-9151. OPEN MONDAY THROUGH THURSDAY FROM 5 TO 11 P.M., UNTIL MIDNIGHT ON FRIDAY AND SATURDAY, FROM 4 TO 11 P.M. SUNDAY. BEER AND WINE. NO CREDIT CARDS. 100% NON-SMOKING. FULLY WHEELCHAIR ACCESSIBLE. NO RESERVATIONS. MODERATE.

Lo Coco's is a true Sicilian restaurant with a menu of spicy, aromatic, traditional dishes. Giovanni Lo Coco, the chef and a man who clearly likes to eat and cook, takes particular pride in his *pasta con sarde*, a recipe that dates from 831. It does taste like something from another age—a combination of saffron-infused, curly spaghetti tossed with sardines, anchovies, fennel with a lot of very licoricey fennel greens, pinenuts, currants, and breadcrumbs. Though the first bite tastes almost medicinal, the second bite becomes less strange and somehow compels you to take a third, then a fourth....

More accessible and absolutely delicious are *mezza zita alla Norma*, tubular pasta in an unabashedly rich sauce of tomatoes, eggplant velvety with olive oil, much, much garlic, basil, and grated parmesan. Everything melts together in an extraordinary way. The *mezza zita* also comes with Lo Coco's bright tasting Napolitana tomato sauce and

■ THE CHEF, A MAN WHO CLEARLY LIKES TO EAT AND COOK, TAKES PARTICULAR PRIDE IN HIS *PASTA CON SARDE*, A COMBINATION OF SAFFRON-INFUSED, CURLY SPAGHETTI TOSSED WITH SARDINES, ANCHOVIES, FENNEL WITH A LOT OF VERY LICORICEY FENNEL GREENS, PINE-NUTS, CURRANTS, AND BREADCRUMBS.

two large, soft, fine-textured meatballs studded with currants and toasted pine nuts. These represent the evocative cooking of Sicily at its best. Other pastas are lighter. Capellini with tomato sauce, arugula, and basil almost seems like a salad in comparison.

The plainest pizzas at Lo Coco's best show off the exceptionally airy, crisp crusts. Pizza Napolitana, blanketed with thinly sliced mushrooms over the excellent tomato sauce and mozzarella, makes me want to move to Naples. The pepperoni on a pizza with green onions comes out of the oven all crispy around the edges. Whichever of the many toppings you choose, the yeasty, chewy, but delightfully thin crust is the main attraction. The pizzas cook fast, so they can be ordered as a quick meal.

To begin a meal, there are several appealing salads like *Insalata Emancipata* which brings together a Sicilian combination of currants, pecans, blue cheese, and olives with romaine lettuce in a simple vinaigrette. A large salad of whole leaves of arugula, endive, radicchio, and fresh fennel scattered with tiny black olives is beautifully arranged on the plate and refreshing.

There are two desserts and they are both terrific. A homemade *cannoli* brings a crunchy, deep-fried shell, filled with sweetened ricotta and bits of preserved dark cherries, dusted with powdered sugar. These same cherries are spooned over vanilla ice cream in a dish called *Amarone*.

Customers can see the kitchen from the small dining room and the cooks can see if you are enjoying what you are eating. The red brick walls, sliding front window, and terracotta tile floors give the little restaurant a cafe-like feel. Tiny Italian lamps made out of colorful blown glass hang from wires above the glass covered tables. Mr. Lo Coco's daughter and an effusive Italian waiter, who makes up in gestures what he lacks in English, work the dining room, though Mr. Lo Coco himself likes to make the rounds and talk about the food.

I didn't think I could get excited by another Italian restaurant in North Beach but Lo Coco's produces a number of heartfelt, regional dishes. Some of the overly long menu reads all too predictably, but by choosing the Sicilian dishes and the Napolitana pizza, you will get to the fine rustic cooking this restaurant has to offer.

PATRICIA UNTERMAN

MADRONA MANOR ★★★

1001 WESTSIDE ROAD, HEALDSBURG. 707 433-4231. OPEN EVERY NIGHT FROM 6
TO 9:30 P.M., SUNDAY BRUNCH FROM 11 A.M. TO 2 P.M. BEER AND WINE. ALL MA-
JOR CREDIT CARDS. NO SMOKING. FULLY WHEELCHAIR ACCESSIBLE. RESERVA-
TIONS RECOMMENDED. EXPENSIVE.

The Madrona Manor in Healdsburg reminds me of country inns
and restaurants in wine producing areas of Europe. It inhabits a
Victorian mansion built in 1881, meticulously renovated by the Muir
family eight years ago. The son, Todd Muir, who cooked at Chez
Panisse for a year before he left to run the kitchen in Healdsburg, has
developed the Madrona Manor dining room to the point where it is
the equal of any restaurant in the city. Instead of following the current
trend of making his menu more informal and less expensive, he has
gone in the opposite direction, moving from pizzas and smoked trout
plates to an elegant five course prix fixe menu along with a substantial
choice of a la carte dishes. Prices are still reasonable by San Francisco
standards, but the cooking has become more complex, with multiple
elements in each dish.

The fixed price meal I had one weekend evening was worth the
65-mile trip from the city. It began with house-smoked salmon on
buckwheat blini spread with sour cream, chives, and black caviar.
Muir has always been interested in smoking and has set up a small
smoker behind the kitchen. This delicate smoked salmon has a freshness one doesn't find in vacuum packages and the presentation with
the yeasty pancakes set that off nicely. A bright green artichoke
timbale that tasted intensely of artichokes—a difficult flavor to capture—was colorfully arranged on a bed of prosciutto, endive, and
artichoke leaves. Campbell Ranch lamb, very tasty, red, and rich,
came with alternating slices of roasted tomato, eggplant, and peppers
forming a composed version of ratatouille. A salad of small, pretty
greens in a vinaigrette, made with strong local olive oil, was garnished
with a little round of warm, breaded goat cheese. For dessert, a
heavenly warm chocolate cake called Chocolate Velvet lived up to its
name, accompanied by sublime, dried cherry ice cream.

The wine list at Madrona Manor stands as a model of its kind,
offering the best Sonoma bottles from the likes of Kistler, Lytton
Springs, La Crema, Sonoma-Cutrer and Lyeth, to name a few.

The parlor-like dining rooms are decorated with Victoriana—
antique fireplaces, marble mantels, gilt framed mirrors, tall, draped
windows, print wallpaper, chandeliers, and commodious wicker-
backed chairs. The three-story mansion in a grove of trees looks like
the setting for a romantic Victorian novel; indeed, after dinner you
want to walk upstairs and fall right into bed.

There are many other excellent dishes on the menu, like radicchio marinated in olive oil and wrapped in thick slices of deep red, imported prosciutto. Greens from the Madrona Manor garden are tossed with gorgonzola and a mustardy dressing. Similar greens are topped with crisply breaded and fried sweetbread nuggets, garnished with baby golden and red beets and asparagus. A moist pork loin is stuffed with dried cherries, rosemary and garlic, and served with grilled polenta and asparagus. A juicy grilled squab comes on a bed of braised greens, white beans, and a delicious red wine sauce; and a smoky filet of beef wrapped with prosciutto and sage is served with fresh fava beans and a stack of peeled sweet peppers, baby eggplant slices, and fresh basil. Fish and seafood dishes have not been as successful.

A very talented pastry chef turns out ethereal creations like a strawberry and coconut napoleon with pastry so light and crisp it practically lifts off the plate. A banana split ice cream sandwich with crisp chocolate cookies, banana pecan nougat ice cream just out of the ice cream maker, and warm, buttery, chocolate and caramel sauces gives this classic dessert a new dimension. A sophisticated frozen mascarpone souffle, with layers of raspberry puree topped with a half poached pear, is both rich and refreshing at the same time.

Sometimes country restaurants compromise on staff, menu, ingredients, or service because they can't consistently draw enough business. The Madrona Manor, on the other hand, is committed to running a first-class restaurant all the time. Excellent, professional people staff the dining room as well as the kitchen, and customers feel everyone's dedication to creating a serious and interesting restaurant.

PATRICIA UNTERMAN

MAHARANI ★★½

1122 POST STREET (BETWEEN POLK AND VAN NESS), SAN FRANCISCO. 775-1988. OPEN FOR LUNCH MONDAY THROUGH FRIDAY 11:30 A.M. TO 2:30 P.M.; DINNER SUNDAY THROUGH THURSDAY 5 TO 10 P.M., FRIDAY AND SATURDAY 5 TO 10:30 P.M. BEER AND WINE. MAJOR CREDIT CARDS. 50% NONSMOKING. FULLY WHEELCHAIR ACCESSIBLE. RESERVATIONS ACCEPTED. MODERATE.

Maharani has given Indian cooking in San Francisco a fresh look. The dishes are garnished with colorful vegetable salads and relishes. Ingredients are cooked less, including tandoori items, making them juicier and more flavorful. Fish appears on the menu in three or four different places and a greater variety is promised. Unusual chutneys and pickles add piquancy to the meals.

The double storefront dining room off Polk Street has been decorated in a warm shade of rose with sea green carpet. Intricate Indian prints framed in gold and a huge metal peacock adorn the walls of the long, narrow room. Seating is on two levels with a food counter at the back from which buffet lunch is served. There are no tablecloths, but linen napkins add a touch of luxury as do the fresh flowers. A fantasy-like draped room is available for parties who want to sit Indian style on the floor at low tables in private compartments, but the regular dining room strikes a nice balance between comfort and casualness.

Dinner begins with crisp *papadums* and four excellent chutneys: a prune-like tamarind chutney that is subtley sweet, sour, and hot; a sour lemon pickle, suitably fierce and strong; a smouldering yogurt-mint-cilantro chutney; and a wonderful jam-like combination of fresh pineapple, mango and grapefruit seasoned with whole coriander seeds. They all are great with crisp, greaseless potato and pea *samosas*. Deep-fried butterfish *pakoras* are magnificent, golden on the outside, smooth as silk inside, served with a slaw of shredded carrots, golden raisins, zucchini and tiny Zante currants.

Raita, that simple but absolutely necessary cooling agent during an Indian meal, combines smooth, housemade yogurt with cucumber and roasted cumin. A bowl of diced cucumbers and tomatoes with cilantro and onions also provides a refreshing contrast. A basket of mixed breads, some sprinkled with black onion seeds, others with garlic and cilantro, some stuffed with nuts and raisins, some multi-layered with butter, serves the purpose of scooping up rich curries and succulent meats.

The roasted foods from the tandoori oven at Maharani have deep flavor from marination and the juicy, velvety texture that is achieved through this clay oven method of cooking. The lamb, poultry, and fish come out on sizzling metal trays strewn with onions and shredded peppers moistened by lemon and the juices from the roasted meats. Tandoori chicken, kebabs of rare, satiny leg of lamb, and big chunks of Chilean sea bass are all superb.

Goa fish curry features Chilean sea bass in a spicy tamarind and tomato sauce that turns out to be unexpectedly tame. If you really like chiles, you must tell the kitchen to turn up the heat, since many curries are offered both spicy and mild, though some, like a creamy, pale orange, lamb korma with butter-tender meat and a delicately seasoned yogurt sauce, are always mild and comforting. The kitchen shows particular conviction for rich legume dishes fragrant with many layers of spices, like *dal makhni*, creamed lentils or chickpeas seasoned with tamarind and spice paste. The irresistible spinach curry with cubes of fresh white cheese, *saag paneer*, is perfumed with a medley of sweet spices while *bangan bharta*, mashed eggplant with tomato, is seasoned mostly with lemon.

Save room for dessert because this restaurant freshly prepares them. Warm *galub jamin*, light, round, doughnuts steeped in syrup sprinkled with pistachios; *ras malai*, patties of white cheese in cream, which are too grainy here; little triangles of Indian "fudge" or halvah-like candy; and an absolutely gorgeous plate of sliced fresh fruit surrounding a scoop of Double Rainbow blackberry ice cream are some of the choices. The plates are fancifully decorated with rose petals.

There is an audience now for more exotic, regional and homestyle Indian dishes and the restaurant-wise, chef/owners of Maharani have the confidence and skill to put them out.

PATRICIA UNTERMAN

MALTESE GRILL ★★½

20 ANNIE STREET (BEHIND THE SHERATON PALACE), SAN FRANCISCO. 777-1955. OPEN MONDAY THROUGH FRIDAY FOR LUNCH 11:30 A.M. TO 3 P.M., FOR DINNER MONDAY THROUGH THURSDAY 5 TO 9:30 P.M. FRIDAY AND SATURDAY 5 TO 10 P.M. PASSATEMPI BAR OPEN CONTINUOUSLY. FULL BAR. ALL MAJOR CREDIT CARDS. 60% NONSMOKING. FULLY WHEELCHAIR ACCESSIBLE. RESERVATIONS SUGGESTED. MODERATE.

The location of the Maltese Grill, in the basement of the old Monadnock Building in an alley just off Market near Third, is a curse and a blessing. The Maltese Grill has become a popular lunch spot but seems more difficult to find at dinner. The interior design takes advantage of some lovely old marble floors but has to deal with the drawbacks of a cellar. Colorful hand-painted murals, a diversity of rooms, some of which are paneled in clubby dark wood, an overall peachy pink coat of paint, and an acoustic ceiling which really does keep the noise under some control, all work well. A large arched window looks right into the kitchen and serves to open up the main dining room, while a marble bar at the entryway, where you can eat as well as drink, feels intimate.

I've had lots and lots of dishes at the Maltese Grill and I've liked almost every one. Especially delicious has been the grilled vegetable *escalivada,* a plate of thinly sliced eggplant, squash, onions, and peppers all charcoal grilled and served warm in a tart vinaigrette with a sprinkling of salt cod. Another excellent starter comes in the form of a beautiful antipasto platter of house-cured dried beef and pork, prosciutto, tiny, tender balls of fresh mozzarella, peppers, dried bean salads, cured olives, and assorted lettuces. Every element is perfect. *Suppli,* rice fritters stuffed with cheese, nest on a bed of braised kale; a brochette of mussels is presented on fennel salad. The green salad is composed of an assortment of lettuces with fresh croutons in a well balanced vinaigrette.

The hamburger served at the bar on freshly baked focaccia with grilled onions and fontina is one of the best in town. You can get some crusty pizzas there too, like one dotted with housemade duck sausage.

The main courses continue in the hearty, spicy, ethnically mixed style of the starters. A luscious choice is leg of lamb marinated in garlic and rosemary, cooked slowly on the restaurant's rotisserie until pink and juicy. It comes with grilled leeks and roasted potatoes. The Mediterranean fish soup boasts a clean fish stock, an assortment of sweet, fresh clams, mussels, and rock fish, and a garlicky aioli that pulls the thing together. Good spit-roasted garlic chicken comes with a marvelous endive, red pepper and onion saute and skinny french fries. Braised rabbit prepared in a Spanish country-style has a dark brown sauce that's so spicy it tastes like a curry. The current chef is Spanish, and prepares a wide range of tapas, small plates of savory Mediterranean foods that go well with wine or sherry.

To this end, the restaurant offers many good wines by the glass, on a list that's been selected to match the full flavored food. A slice of fresh lemon tart and excellent espresso finishes the meals with a flourish.

On top of all this good cooking, generous portions, and very reasonable prices, patrons are treated so warmly at the Maltese Grill that they want to come back. The waiters are pro's, and owner Jo Policastro's enthusiasm and professionalism informs every aspect of this excellent restaurant.

PATRICIA UNTERMAN

THE MANDARIN ★★

GHIRARDELLI SQUARE, 900 NORTHPOINT, SAN FRANCISCO. 673-8812. OPEN EVERY DAY NOON TO 11 P.M. FULL BAR. ALL MAJOR CREDIT CARDS. 60% NON-SMOKING. PARTIALLY WHEELCHAIR ACCESSIBLE. RESERVATIONS RECOMMENDED AT NIGHT. MODERATE TO EXPENSIVE.

When Cecilia Chiang opened the elegant Mandarin in 1968, she was the first to offer the rich and spicy dishes of Sichuan and Hunan provinces in the United States. (Last year, she sold the restaurant.) These days many neighborhood restaurants prepare the same dishes, but not in comparable surroundings or with formal service.

The look of this second-story restaurant, in an old chocolate factory, is as stunning today as it was twenty years ago, especially after a recent repainting and sprucing up. Its rough brick walls, plastered over in some places, thick wooden structural beams, high ceilings, and tiled floors, have been the inspiration for practically every stylish conversion of industrial space to commercial use in the country. Much of the raw space has been kept, yet you feel engulfed in luxury. That wonderful juxtaposition of rustic and refined has never worked more timelessly. Oriental antiques, calligraphy, and paintings seem more resonant against the background of red brick and unfinished wood. Of course the tables are large, the chairs soft and comfortable, the lighting, subtle. Though the restaurant is almost monumental, the space is divided into intimate dining areas.

The list of specials on the menu will lead you to some of the best

187

dishes in the house. Pot stickers are deliciously filled with juicy pork and Chinese cabbage, and the noodle wrappers are thin and tender. The minced squab, which isn't on the menu for some reason, is always fun to eat. Black mushrooms, water chestnuts, and the squab are finely chopped and stir-fried together to make a juicy stuffing with crunchy fried rice noodles for cold, crisp head lettuce leaves.

A soup of pureed chicken and corn with a sesame-scented broth is as notable for its silken texture as its comforting, mild flavors. A smoked tea duck, which no one does better than the Mandarin, distills the most sensual aspects of Chinese cooking. The amazingly crisp skin is contrasted by velvety flesh infused with the perfume of smoke and the flowery aroma of jasmine tea.

Your waiter will construct four little Spring Crepes with shreds of richly sauced pork, cucumber, bean sprouts, and scallions. He will also bone a whole, miraculously crisp, deep fried rock fish in a spicy brown Sichuan sauce studded with incendiary, dried red chili halves. Spinach and glass noodles in a clear sauce is a fine foil for the rich fish. A soothing Shanghai dish of baby bok choy braised in a delicate, clear sauce, topped with straw mushrooms is another good choice. A serious wine list featuring California bottles provides many wines that go well with the food.

On busy nights I have encountered lapses in both the service and the cooking, like cold Peking duck served with unwarmed white pancakes, which at these prices can be annoying. The best bet, for a party of six or eight, is to plan a menu ahead with the maitre d' when you make a reservation. Few restaurants can put out such delicious food for larger parties and do it with such elegance.

PATRICIA UNTERMAN

MANKA'S INVERNESS LODGE RESTAURANT ★★½

ARGYLE AND CALLENDER (RIGHT OFF SIR FRANCIS DRAKE), INVERNESS. 669-1034. DINNER THURSDAY AND MONDAY 6 TO 9 P.M., FRIDAY AND SATURDAY 6 TO 10 P.M.; SUNDAY BRUNCH 9:30 A.M. TO 1 P.M.; DINNER 5 TO 9 P.M. BEER, WINE. VISA, MASTERCARD. NONSMOKING DINING ROOM. NOT WHEELCHAIR ACCESSIBLE. RESERVATIONS RECOMMENDED. EXPENSIVE.

When you walk into the main dining room at Manka's Inverness Lodge Restaurant, you're confronted with a large central pedestal surrounded by tables and topped with a glorious arrangement of sunflowers, calla lilies, gladiolus, unusual greens and other blooms. Then you notice the walls of long-paned windows that overlook lush tree tops. The chairs look a bit too early American for the rest of the room and the burgundy tablecloths a bit too bold, but they are

■ **AS THE SUN SETS, THIS BECOMES ONE OF THE MOST ROMANTIC RESTAURANTS YOU'LL FIND. BOTH THE SERVICE AND THE FOOD SUPPORT THE MOOD.**

tempered by a single white taper on each table flickering atop a silver holder. As the sun sets, this becomes one of the most romantic restaurants you'll find. Both the service, which achieves the proper balance of casualness and formality, and the food support the mood.

The combinations are fresh, lively, and well prepared. The changing menu orchestrated by chef/owner Benjamin Grade features eight appetizers and eight main courses, each featuring great combinations with an unexpected twist. Roasted corn soup, in a thick cream swirled with red pepper puree, is given a spicy punch with lots of ground white pepper. The salad, a mix of baby greens and Sweet 100 tomatoes, is dressed in a balsamic dressing enhanced with rosemary. Walnut and rabbit sausage is another magnificent blend, served with braised red cabbage, a red pepper and onion relish, and a dollop of mustard.

Most chefs pair roast duck with a sweet fruit concoction, but Grade successfully veers from the proven path with a caraway sauce that works beautifully. His creativity doesn't work as well in the wild boar with sun-dried cherries and a red pepper chutney. The plate is filled with black beans, Chinese long beans, and a strip of bacon. While all the ingredients are packed with flavor, they don't quite come together.

Other combinations might include sea scallops with shrimp and mussels, accented with sun-dried tomatoes and tasso, a spicy Cajun cured pork; poached salmon with a golden caviar butter sauce, or an appetizer of onion and cheese pudding with a wild mushroom ragout.

The wine list is pared down, but you'll find some unusual selections at reasonable prices.

Desserts could use a little boost. The texture of the creme brulée is great, but it needs a little more sugar to bring out the richness, and the topping tastes gritty. The lemon meringue pie is actually layers of meringue spread with a lemon pie filling and topped with whipped cream and chocolate shavings. If you like things on the sweet side, this will satisfy. But then, anything would show well against the rich coffee, some of the best restaurant blend you'll find.

If you don't want to drive home, the eight rooms at the inn are waiting. I fell in love with the room above the restaurant, featuring a large deck overlooking the trees and Tomales Bay. The city's so close it almost seems you should be able to see it from the balcony. Fortunately, all that's in view are millions of stars and the gently swaying trees.

MICHAEL BAUER

RISTORANTE MARCELLO ★★

2100 TARAVAL (AT 31ST AVENUE), SAN FRANCISCO. 665-1430. OPEN TUESDAY THROUGH SATURDAY FROM 5 TO 10:30 P.M., SUNDAY 4 TO 10 P.M. FULL BAR. MASTERCARD AND VISA. 20% NONSMOKING. PARTIALLY WHEELCHAIR ACCESSIBLE. RESERVATIONS ACCEPTED. WALK-INS CAN SIT AT THE BAR. MODERATE.

Marcello is just the kind of no nonsense restaurant that makes native San Franciscans happy—it's one of the last and best San Francisco-style Italian eateries. The spirit of raffish old Vanessi's must have ascended over the city and come down near the ocean at Taraval and 31st. The food, the customers, the look, the feel of the place takes San Franciscans back to another moment in dining out history.

Typical of these restaurants, Marcello has a long and active bar where people eat when the adjacent dining room is full. The dining room is outfitted with red vinyl banquettes, padded wooden chairs, tables pushed too close together covered with white tablecloths, and waiters in tuxedos, all adding up to a classic Italian dinner-house look.

When you dig into a basket of dense, soft, San Francisco sour dough sliced from long, fat loaves, and press on some nice, salty butter pats, the memories of past meals come floating back. When a Caesar salad arrives, torn romaine in a tart but rich dressing with an undercurrent of anchovy, you are happy to be eating this food today. The salads definitely come from the pre-arugula period, but they're terrific, mainly because they are dressed in a shalloty, mustardy, relishy remoulade. Even out of season tomato halves, draped with thinly sliced red onion and anchovies perk up under a blanket of this dressing, as do liberally dressed half heads of romaine surrounded by thinly sliced marinated mushrooms.

The pasta tastes like it comes from a Tuscan home kitchen. *Spaghettini Bolognese* has a celery-scented sauce, authentically gravelly with finely chopped beef, chicken livers, and prosciutto. Housemade ravioli, plump with seasoned ricotta cheese, were deliciously moistened by a little of the bolognese. Tender green pasta is used for housemade *panzotti*, filled with spinach and ricotta and topped with a clean flavored tomato sauce. Don't pass up *Cannelloni della Casa* because you think it's old hat. Made with hand-rolled dough stuffed with a distinctive filling of finely chopped veal, spinach, and prosciutto and sauced with tomato tinged cream, they are absolutely gorgeous. Rustic *Spaghetti alla Matriciana*, has a lively sauce of bacon, tomatoes, and onions.

Three main courses stand out: a marvelously crisp skinned, flattened, half chicken called *Pollo ai Ferri*; roasted leg of lamb sliced thin and slathered with a restrained brown marsala and mushroom sauce; and a gigantic veal chop called *Lombatina* with enough flavor to sustain interest. It, too, gets the pleasant brown mushroom sauce. All entrees come with crisp edged scalloped potatoes baked in chicken stock and braised white chard. Both accompaniments add pleasure to the plates.

One disappointment at Marcello is the wine list. Bottles, as well as wines by the glass, are not particularly well-chosen. Also, dessert is the neglected child on a large and otherwise well-executed menu.

The dining room is full of people of all ages and nationalities, and everyone dresses up a little for dinner. You might find me there, happily chatting with the old-timers and exploring the pasta menu. I have the carbonara, the homemade tortellini, the pasta primavera and the housemade gnocchi to get to.

PATRICIA UNTERMAN

MARNEE THAI ★★½

2225 IRVING ST. (AT 23RD AVENUE), SAN FRANCISCO. 665-9500. OPEN WEDNESDAY THROUGH MONDAY 11:30 A.M. TO 10 P.M. BEER, WINE. VISA, MASTERCARD, AMERICAN EXPRESS. 30% NONSMOKING. PARTIALLY WHEELCHAIR ACCESSIBLE. RESERVATIONS RECOMMENDED ON WEEKENDS. INEXPENSIVE.

Thai food is readily available all over San Francisco now. But Marnee Thai still offers some splendid and unusual dishes not found elsewhere; from fresh corn cakes as an appetizer to fresh mango with sweet sticky rice for dessert.

Marnee Thai is one of those rare restaurants that makes up in little touches for anything it might lack in expensive decor. The place is virtually carpeted in fresh flowers, with bouquets on every table. The waitresses joke with you, fuss over you, and will insist on giving you something else or not charging you if they see you didn't like a dish.

The dishes here are perfumed by a long list of herbs and spices. They're commendably light on cooking oil. You don't have to go further than the appetizers to know you're in an extraordinary restaurant. Spicy angel wings are chicken wings that are first deep-fried, then sauteed in a curry paste loaded with chili and garlic. They emerge perfectly crisp with a fiery, delicious glaze. Corn cakes are a special during fresh corn season and they're an absolute must. Patties are made from corn flour, wheat flour, fresh corn kernels, and eggs, then deep-fried. They come out light and fluffy and without a speck of grease.

After the appetizers, try the sinus-clearing soup called *potak*. A variety of very fresh seafood floats in spicy chicken stock perfumed by lemongrass, galanga, and ginger. The place to start for entrees is with the sensational *hor mok*. Red snapper is blended with curry paste, coconut milk, and eggs, then steamed in a banana leaf to emerge as a fluffy fish mousse that rivals anything you can get in a French restaurant.

The curries at Marnee Thai are excellent, too. Green pork curry, succulent with coconut milk, has the unusual touch of eggplant slices. Red chicken curry is so subtly perfumed that the coconut milk broth tastes almost French. Another winner is the spicy duck, which is roasted first, then boned and sauteed with tomatoes, onions, garlic, and chilies. It's completely tender and fat-free.

Did you ever hear of an Asian restaurant with good desserts? Wait until you try the roti, an Indian-style fried bread sauced with a little sweetened milk. And if they've found mangoes in the market, you can have them in the traditional Thai style, accompanied with sweetened glutinous rice flavored with coconut milk.

Chaiwatt Siriyarn, perhaps the world's only Thai chef who holds an MBA, presides in the kitchen, while his wife, Muaynee, runs the dining room with unrelenting good humor. They've created a Thai restaurant that stands out even today, when there's one on almost every block.

STAN SESSER

MASA'S ★★★★

648 BUSH STREET, SAN FRANCISCO. 989-7154. OPEN TUESDAY THROUGH SATUR-DAY 6 TO 9:30 P.M. MAJOR CREDIT CARDS. FULL BAR. 100% NONSMOKING. FULLY WHEELCHAIR ACCESSIBLE. RESERVATIONS REQUIRED (CALL THREE WEEKS IN ADVANCE). VERY EXPENSIVE.

It was with some skepticism that I marched into Masa's at 6 P.M. on a Thursday night. Normally, I would never sit down to an elaborate French dinner at that early hour, but it was the only opening the restaurant had for the following three weeks.

No restaurant in the United States has received higher national and international praise than Masa's, and I had not eaten there since the late Masa Kobayashi was at the helm eight years ago. The restaurant had gone through one other chef and was now in the hands of former sous chef Julian Serrano. Did Masa's really deserve its reputation? Under Masa himself, I felt that some dishes were too rich and too fussy, though the dining room, under the enlightened management of John Cunin, now the owner/manager of the Cypress Club, did much to transform the experience of haute cuisine into something democratic and approachable.

My recent experience at Masa's took me completely by surprise because it was better than anything I expected. In fact, I have to join the crowd of critics who consider Masa's to be the best French restaurant in the United States. The food, the service, and the wines were fantastic, an amalgam of classic French culinary wizardry of the highest order with California warmth and lack of pretension in the dining room. Perhaps because Masa's current chef is a culinary tradi-

■ MAIN COURSES ARE SO WELL PREPARED THE MAIN IN-GREDIENT ALWAYS REMAINS THE STAR, SUPPORTED BY INGENIOUS LITTLE SIDE DISHES.

tionalist and a Spaniard, the restaurant has maintained such an unusual and authentic tone.

The small, square dining room is anything but unique. Kept too dark, simply appointed with comfortable chairs, soft linen, and elegant silver, crystal, and china, the dining room works as an empty canvas to be painted by the beautiful food and the wines.

Most people opt for one of the two prix fixe menus, at $68 and $75. Waiters will spend as much time as each table requires explaining and recommending dishes, indeed, working out the whole meal. A sommelier administers the wine list like a coach, planning wine to go with each course. Because only one of us at the table was drinking, he suggested a play-by-play attack, a different glass for each dish. He brought cold amontillado sherry for a lobster bisque, a Bonny Doone chardonnay with a lobster salad, a soft red burgundy for squab, a Qupé marsanne, a white rhone-style wine produced in California, to go with a salad of seared scallops, a sercial madeira with dessert—the interesting match-ups went on and on.

As for the food, it just couldn't have been better. If anything Mr. Serrano has simplified and lightened dishes that he inherited from Masa himself and his own dishes, which come slowly onto the menu, are brilliantly conceived and meticulously executed. In his latest creation, a warm salad constructed of slices of potatoes and slices of lobster in a sharp, saffron-scented vinaigrette topped with a beehive of deep-fried leek threads, the ingredients seem to melt together in a dreamy way. Another deceptively simple salad brought a little cake of lobster slices encased in paper thin rounds of turnip dressed in a honey-sweetened vinaigrette.

Main courses are so well prepared that the main ingredient always remains the star, supported by ingenious little side dishes. A roasted squab, in its own juice, melts in your mouth. Lamb stays velvety and moist under a coating of scented bread crumbs. Tiny onion tarts, corn custards, bundles of asparagus tips, miniature whole squashes are chosen to complement the plates and they are equally well prepared.

Desserts strike the same balance of luxury and simplicity that distinguishes everything about this restaurant. You can't go wrong choosing any of them, from the warm apple galette to a grand assortment of different cakes, mousses, and ice creams.

A meal here is a major investment, but it is one that continues to pay back high dividends of pleasure.

PATRICIA UNTERMAN

193

THE MATTERHORN SWISS RESTAURANT ★★

2323 VAN NESS AVENUE (BETWEEN VALLEJO AND GREEN), SAN FRANCISCO. 885-6116. OPEN WEDNESDAY THROUGH SUNDAY FROM 5:30 TO 10 P.M. FULL BAR. MASTERCARD, VISA, AMERICAN EXPRESS. 85% NONSMOKING. PARTIALLY WHEELCHAIR ACCESSIBLE. RESERVATIONS ACCEPTED. EXPENSIVE.

For those who are looking for a restaurant that serves unabashedly rich Swiss-German dishes served in a rustic, Swiss setting, the Matterhorn fits the bill. It puts on the whole production—from costumed waiters and waitresses in embroidered floppy-sleeved shirts to a handcrafted, all wood, Swiss chalet interior—with jolly conviction. The ebullient owner, builder, and host of the Matterhorn has done everything he can to re-create a Swiss restaurant from his childhood in Canton Wallis, on Van Ness Avenue.

The style of the food hearkens back to a kind of fancy cooking that exemplified fine dining in America about thirty years ago. Everything has a sauce. Vegetables come in deep fried potato baskets, and many of them are swathed in butter sauce. One or two starches come with each main course, both soup and salad are included in the price. Desserts are decoratively presented.

The soups are fabulous. A thin, cream of asparagus afloat with bright green asparagus tips is second only to a delicious, bacon-scented puree of mushroom and potato. A clear, oxtail consomme with a browned custard topping, served in a little crock, is traditional and wonderful. The salad course brings thinly sliced cucumber vinaigrette, garlicky roasted eggplant in sour cream, red cabbage salad, and dressed butter lettuce.

Swiss appetizers on the menu include a generous plate of tissue thin slices of semi-dried beef called *Bundnerfleisch*, and creamy Swiss cheese fritters served with fruit sauces. *Raclette*, a plate of melted cheese with boiled new potatoes, cornichons, and pickled onions, is fun on a cold night.

Main courses feature lots of tender veal—sliced into strips, sauced with cream and mushrooms, served with crisp, pan fried potatoes as well as vegetables napped with hollandaise. Also good are the restaurant's tournedos, thick slices of beef filet topped with white asparagus and bearnaise.

True to Swiss reputation, the desserts are luscious and fanciful. A swan made out of cream puff pastry, filled with vanilla ice cream, swims on a raspberry pond. Fat slices of apple strudel are sprinkled with chopped nuts and sauced with creme anglaise decorated with swirls of raspberry puree.

What sets the Matterhorn apart is the whole-hearted participation of its owner, who is always there. He greets everyone with a little joke. He's wonderful with older patrons, but most important of all, he keeps the food at his restaurant solid and consistent. Just what you would expect at a Swiss restaurant. The Matterhorn adds one more piece of exotic geography to San Francisco's far ranging landscape of restaurants. When that urge to eat food from the Swiss alps hits you, the Matterhorn is there.

PATRICIA UNTERMAN

THE MERMAID ★★

824 UNIVERSITY AVENUE, BERKELEY. 843-1189. OPEN MONDAY THROUGH THURSDAY FOR LUNCH FROM 11:30 A.M. TO 2:30 P.M., DINNER SUNDAY THROUGH THURSDAY 5 TO 10 P.M., UNTIL 11 P.M. FRIDAY AND SATURDAY. BEER AND WINE. MASTERCARD, VISA, AMERICAN EXPRESS. 100% NONSMOKING. FULLY WHEEL-CHAIR ACCESSIBLE. RESERVATIONS ACCEPTED. INEXPENSIVE.

The Mermaid, a Cambodian restaurant that specializes in fish and seafood dishes, operates in one of the most visible spots in the East Bay, the freestanding building at the foot of the University Avenue freeway entrance. For some reason that location, even with a convenient parking lot, has had trouble drawing people, but if there were ever a time to make a visit, this is it.

The Mermaid offers a menu of Cambodian fish and seafood stews, and curries that are absolutely delicious. The Mekong Fish Chowder, a house specialty, boasts a clear, sweet smelling broth; fresh, tenderly cooked squid, clams, rockfish, and shrimp; rice stirred into the soup, porridge-style, for texture, and bright, aromatic seasoning from fresh ginger and mint. It's a dish that's so satisfying yet light, I could eat it every day. Another dish worth traveling the freeways for is the Mermaid's Fisherman's Stew, a spicy, fragrant, coconut milk enriched yellow broth, full of catfish, scallops, shrimp, and crab with big chunks of pumpkin, straw mushrooms, zucchini, and spinach.

For starters I love the shrimp and green papaya salad, a tart and crunchy julienne of the crisp fruit with bean sprouts and a mint-infused dressing. It's juicy and refreshing. A seafood crepe is excellent here with a stuffing of bean sprouts, onion, and the usual mix of seafood piled into a thin, omelet-like pancake. A sweet and sour dressing is poured over it. Fish cakes come as one large, spongy pancake cut into strips, with pickled vegetables and the sweet and sour dipping sauce. Children like the tiny spring rolls filled with mild ground pork. A richer, more elegant beginning to a Cambodian meal calls for *Amok*, a firm, velvet-textured fish mousse that is steamed in a banana leaf. I didn't like some of the dishes, like squid salad, which are dressed in too much fish sauce for my palate.

For non-fish eaters, practically all the preparations on the seafood menu are made with vegetables only, or with chicken or beef. A half broiled chicken, marinated in a red Cambodian barbeque sauce, and a plate of saucy stir- fried noodles with spicy chicken and lots of vegetables are both likeable dishes. For dessert, deep-fried banana fritters are served alongside dishes of chunky, coconut ice cream.

Wine goes amazingly well with this Cambodian food and several, carefully chosen wines at rock bottom prices turn out to be a real pleasure. Service couldn't be more gracious and the red carpeted dining rooms are clean and well kept. A mirrored mezzanine, a lower dining area, and a small bar with a small television feel very homey after a couple of visits. Lots of families come here and the staff goes out of their way to be nice to the kids.

PATRICIA UNTERMAN

MESCOLANZA ★½

2221 CLEMENT STREET, SAN FRANCISCO. 668-2221. OPEN MONDAY THROUGH THURSDAY 4:30 TO 10 P.M. BEER AND WINE. MASTERCARD AND VISA. 100% NON-SMOKING. PARTIALLY WHEELCHAIR ACCESSIBLE. RESERVATIONS RECOM-MENDED. INEXPENSIVE.

Pasta and pizza may be beating out the hamburger and hot dog as the nation's favorite foods, if the proliferation of restaurants that serve them are any indication. While health and nutrition experts advocate olive oil, complex carbohydrates, and fresh vegetables as corner stones of a better American diet, consumers are pleased that pasta and pizza are relatively cheap. This makes the new, down-scaled, Italian trattorias that are popping up everywhere instantly popular. Now we have Mescolanza, a small, pleasant, Richmond district cafe that brings thin crust pizzas and rich, sauce laden pastas to the avenues.

Opened in a Clement Street storefront between 22nd and 23rd avenues, Mescolanza is a clean, white room with linoleum floors, bentwood chairs, ceiling fans, tables covered in checked plastic cloths with linen napkins, and a decorative stack of olive oil cans next to the espresso machine on a counter in the back of the restaurant. Majolica plates and copper pots adorn the walls. A large wooden china cabinet has been placed in front of the door to block off cold drafts. The room is cheerful and well lit, especially in the early evening when the two front plate glass windows on each side of the door let in the last light.

The menu is as straightforward and simple as the decor, offering a few salads and appetizers, pasta themes and variations, a good handful of different kinds of pizzas, and some fish, chicken, and veal dishes. The pizzas have thin, crisp crusts and are about the size of a large dinner plate, so they can be ordered individually or shared as appetizers. The basic unit, *pizzetta Toscana*, covered with mozzarella, tomato sauce, and fresh basil, is light and appealing with bright red dabs of juicy tomato sauce placed here and there. The *Mediterraneo* brings salty anchovies, capers, tons of garlic, and oregano. The *pizzetta al Mescolanza*, throws in gorgonzola, prosciutto, and artichoke hearts. All the pizzas are intentionally sparsely topped, which emphasizes the almost cracker thin crust. These easy to eat pizzas are fresh and appealing.

The pastas move in the opposite direction, with ladles of sauce submerging a small amount of noodles. I love spaghetti the way it's served in Italy, almost naked with a little, very flavorful sauce tossed in. High quality al dente pasta is so tasty it doesn't need a lot of sauce. Restaurateurs in America must think their customers feel cheated if their noodles aren't swimming in sauce—perhaps because Americans serve pasta as the main part of the meal instead of an introductory course. At any rate, the capellini with fresh tomatoes and basil brings enough tart, bright flavored tomato sauce for twice as many noodles as are on the plate, and meat-filled *agnolotti*, tiny doughnut shaped pasta, float in a pool of cream with walnuts.

A handsome green salad has a vinegary dressing and the Caesar salad, a pre-mixed-style dressing shot with hot garlic. The competent wine list offers appropriate bottles in the inexpensive range. For dessert, the kitchen makes an excellent hazelnut–infused flan, while it buys other desserts from North Beach bakeries.

The service can be a bit slow, but it is friendly. The hostess takes a proprietarial interest in her patrons, many of whom she recognizes. Mescolanza draws crowds from the immediate neighborhood, and outer Clement Street is the happier for it.

PATRICIA UNTERMAN

MICHELANGELO CAFE ★½

579 COLUMBUS, SAN FRANCISCO. 986-4058. OPEN MONDAY THROUGH SATURDAY FROM 5 TO 11 P.M. SUNDAY 3 TO 10 P.M. BEER AND WINE. CASH OR CHECKS. 10% NONSMOKING. FULLY WHEELCHAIR ACCESSIBLE. RESERVATIONS ACCEPTED. INEXPENSIVE.

Though it would seem that North Beach hardly needs another pasta house, Michelangelo has joined the line-up on Columbus near Union. It draws in passers-by with big front windows that look out to Washington Square, Coit Tower, and St. Peter and Paul Cathedral. The purposely uncluttered dining room features a black and white checkerboard floor, tables covered with white linen and small vases of flowers, and one wall hung with a gallery's worth of small, representational oils.

The menu centers on pastas with an emphasis on seafood and appetizers. Starters worth ordering are a garlicky calamari salad on a bed of lettuce and tomatoes in a copious olive oil and lemon dressing, and lightly floured, deep-fried calamari tossed with chopped garlic. The prosciutto is cut tissue thin and the accompanying melon is juicy and ripe in the classic pair-up. The restaurant has the good sense not to offer it when good melons can't be found.

Some of the pastas here are over sauced, like a mounded plate of penne in a Bolognese-style meat and mushroom sauce, and fettucine in too much bland pesto. But a bowl of pasta tubes in a sharp, thick, tomato sauce infused with garlic and flavored with the juices of clams is delicious, as are terrific housemade potato gnocchi in a parmesan and cream enriched tomato sauce. They have the desired heft while not being heavy.

Fish dishes, offered as specials, are not exceptional. Large, thick, pounded calamari steaks, breaded and sauteed, taste like generic processed seafood. Some Pacific rock cod, treated much the same way, is swathed in a tart, unsalted butter sauce. Both are accompanied with crisp but gray tinged vegetables.

The crusty, very fresh San Francisco sour dough served here is a pleasure, as are imported amaretti cookies brought to the table with coffee. Fresh raspberries in a thick, sweet, chilled sabayon makes for a swell, if predictable, dessert. The wine list is abbreviated but the ebullient Italian reds on it never fail to please.

Service can be brusque, informal, and a little off-handed, but it fits with the casual, North Beach style of the place. The prices are cheap, the pastas good, and the room appealing and unpretentious. Believe it or not, Michelangelo proves that there's room for another Italian dining room in North Beach.

PATRICIA UNTERMAN

MISS PEARL'S JAM HOUSE ★½

601 EDDY, SAN FRANCISCO. 775-5267. OPEN FOR LUNCH MONDAY THROUGH FRIDAY 11:30 A.M. TO 2:30 P.M.; DINNER MONDAY THROUGH WEDNESDAY 6 TO 10 P.M., THURSDAY THROUGH SATURDAY UNTIL 11 P.M.; SUNDAY BRUNCH 10:30 A.M. TO 2:30 P.M.; SUNDAY DINNER 5:30 TO 9:30 P.M. FULL BAR. MAJOR CREDIT CARDS. 90% NONSMOKING. FULLY WHEELCHAIR ACCESSIBLE. RESERVATIONS RECOMMENDED. MODERATE.

If you're looking for the gorgeous young crowd, and a noise level that feels like you're inside a pounding bass drum, Miss Pearl's is the place to be.

It's equipped with two bars and a whimsical decor that looks like a Gilligan's Island set. A boat hull is suspended over the bar to act as a canopy. Peeling doors in an array of colors are fitted together to make wainscoting.

In the front of a 50s style motel, there's outdoor dining around the pool—just the thing for a nice-weather brunch or lunch. You'd swear you're in Florida, with the bright color scheme carried off on the well-maintained motel that attracts visiting rockers.

It's the brainchild of Julie Ring, who first brought the crowds back to the South of Market area with Rings, and then brought the 50s back at Julie's Supper Club. This time she takes a fantasy trip to the Caribbean orchestrated by chef Joey Altman, who went to the islands for vacation and fell in love with the electric flavor combinations.

Therefore, the menu consists of a whole list of tongue-tingling, tropical-styled tapas including spicy black-eyed pea fritters, deep-fried fingers of catfish with a pepper-cilantro sauce, or eggplant layered with duck confit, mushroom risotto and served with a tomato-coriander sauce.

Island flavors emerge on hearts of palm and jicama salad with a green onion and coconut dressing. In all, there are about 30 items, including larger-portion dishes. Don't miss the blackened fillet of beef, fanned over black beans and roasted peppers. There's also duck breast strewn with shards of fried sweet potatoes and served with spaghetti squash and a tamarind-cherry sauce, or grilled swordfish with yellow bell pepper sauce and Chinese long beans.

Other dishes on the changing menu might include chicken breast with artichoke, eggplant, red beans, and a creole hollandaise sauce, or salmon with pink and black peppercorns with lentils and a Jamaican curry sauce.

The cooking is interpretive to be sure, and at times the combinations don't work, but eating at Miss Pearl's is a lot of fun.

Service is good natured and it's amazing the staff keeps their cool—and their voices—with the noise level as it is. Before the end of the night, I gave up trying to converse with my dining companions. I just sat back and watched the show of people.

MICHAEL BAUER

| MO'S ★★

1322 GRANT AVENUE, SAN FRANCISCO. 788-3779. OPEN SUNDAY THROUGH THURSDAY 11:30 A.M. TO 10:30 P.M., FRIDAY AND SATURDAY 11:30 A.M. TO 11:30 P.M. BEER AND WINE. NO CREDIT CARDS. NO RESERVATIONS. FOOD TO GO. INEXPENSIVE.

Mo's makes one of the best hamburgers in the city: thick, juicy, soft, and delicate in texture. You can watch the grillman scooping up a big handful of bright red, freshly ground meat and gently forming it into a patty. He places it on a round, revolving, cast iron grill above red hot lava rocks. When the burger is done to specification, he places it on a pale but slightly crusty bun dressed with a generous smear of creamy housemade mayonnaise. A decent dill pickle quarter, tomato slice, red onion, and romaine lettuce garnish the plate. This basic hamburger can be ordered with a slice of sharp cheddar, a generous portion of imported blue cheese, or apple-smoked bacon for an additional charge. To go with the hamburgers, Mo's makes old fashioned milkshakes, serving them in tall metal containers with glass and straw on the side. The mocha shake made with coffee ice cream and chocolate syrup is a dream.

Mo's also prepares a tasty, spicy, chicken breast sandwich. The breast is marinated in Thai chili paste and packs quite a wallop. Like the hamburger, it is grilled carefully and served on a bun with mayonnaise. A tart, very thinly sliced red cabbage salad served on the side also works well piled into the bun. This sandwich comes with skinny, skin-on, french fries. Pita chicken, a juicy marinated kebab with a spoonful of roughly chopped cilantro, onions, and tomatoes comes in pocket bread, a great multinational invention. Skip the salads made with tasteless vegetables and unseasoned dressing.

Mo's minimalist decor is not the most inviting. All the surfaces are white tile, chrome, or black Formica, and the stark lighting gives the small room all the warmth of a public bathroom. Loud music blares until someone asks that it be turned down. The best seats are at the counter where you can watch the cooking. But if you're in North Beach, or anywhere in town for that matter, and feel like a hamburger, this is the place to go.

PATRICIA UNTERMAN

MOM IS COOKING ★★½

1192 GENEVA BOULEVARD, SAN FRANCISCO. 586-7000. OPEN EVERY DAY FROM 10 A.M. TO 10 P.M. BEER AND WINE. NO CREDIT CARDS. 30% NONSMOKING. PARTIALLY WHEELCHAIR ACCESSIBLE. NO RESERVATIONS. INEXPENSIVE.

The Mexican food slowly coming out of the kitchen at Mom Is Cooking is home-cooking at its truest. Being able to get it in a restaurant at all presents a rare opportunity that requires compromises you don't normally have to make when you go out to eat. The main drawback, and of course, asset, is that one diminutive woman, Abigail Murillo, does all the cooking. She makes everything—tortillas, sauces, chorizo and stocks—from scratch and she personally cooks each plate of food to order. With only one person in the kitchen, the food comes out slowly, especially if more than a few tables are occupied. The slow pace is also exacerbated by the fact that only one waiter works the floor, Ms. Murillo's ebullient brother, Rick.

The small place looks like it was airlifted from the suburbs of Mexico City. There's metal grating over the windows, brown imitation wood tables, brown imitation wood paneled walls, fluorescent lighting, and a fake brick counter with stools. The food is served on unmatched plastic plates, but beer and wine are served in chilled glasses. A vintage jukebox, a Victorian back bar, and genuine warmth and hospitality counterbalance the drabness. By the time you finish eating, you can't imagine Mom's being anyplace else. The place does feel like home.

The long menu in a loose leaf binder is another surprise. The list of dishes goes on for pages and you wonder how this little restaurant could put them all out. Yet every dish I sampled had that tastiness and lightness that comes from conscientious preparation. Quesadillas arrive as folded over packets of tangy, creamy white Mexican cheese melted into very fresh tortillas. The chips for salsa and chips are hot, crisp triangles of thick corn tortilla, and the thin red salsa for dipping is piquant and smouldering with chiles, the kind of balance all those bottled enchilada sauces never achieve.

You can get Mexican dishes here unavailable anyplace else, like authentic chicken *mole*, a quarter of a juicy bird blanketed in a dusky brown chocolate sauce infused with dried chiles and toasted spices. The hot, slightly bitter sauce goes particularly well with the creamy red beans and moist rice, enriched with lard, that are Mom's signature. Another unusual ethnic dish is *pozole*, a soup of soft kernels of hominy in a dried chile-reddened, cumin-scented beef broth with big chunks of meat. Chopped raw onion, radishes, and lettuce go in at the last minute. You finish the soup at the table with a squeeze of lemon.

Ms. Murillo makes her own intensely seasoned chorizo and then demonstrates how best to use it, as a seasoning with eggs or chicken. Her unique chicken with chorizo marries long simmered, shredded chicken with the spicy, vinegary sausage crumbled into it. In most neighborhood restaurants I would never think of ordering seafood, but Mom's inspires confidence. *Camarones fritos*, small, fresh shrimp, are marinated, split down the back and deep-fried for a second in hot oil. Presented on a bed of radishes and lettuce with roughly chopped fresh tomato and onion salsa, they are a revelation of how tasty shrimp can be. The delicacy of crab enchiladas would make a French chef proud. Thin corn tortillas are stuffed with a small amount of seasoned crab and then topped with a clean-flavored green tomatillo salsa, chunks of the pale, green, squash-like chayote, and melted, creamy white Mexican cheese.

The same light touch makes chiles rellenos so special. They are thin and flat—fresh chiles stuffed with just the right amount of white cheese, lightly egg battered and fried, and topped with a fresh tasting tomato sauce. Tamales can be the heaviest food on earth, but a small chicken tamale here proves how interesting they are when well prepared. The airy cornmeal steamed in a cornhusk is stuffed with spicy chicken and fresh tomato. Mildly hot, all the flavors and textures run into each other in a deep, country-style way. A flour tortilla stuffed with a savory beef stew and then cleanly fried, called a *chimichanga*, offers yet a different play of textures, served with the salad-like tomato salsa, guacamole, and creamy beans. Though nothing is formally made for dessert, some deep-fried bananas, unsugared but naturally sweet, topped with rich, housemade sour cream, turns out to be one of the best around.

PATRICIA UNTERMAN

MONSOON ★★★★

OPERA PLAZA AT 601 VAN NESS, SAN FRANCISCO. 441-3232. OPEN 5:30 TO 10 P.M.
SUNDAY THROUGH THURSDAY, UNTIL 11:30 P.M. FRIDAY AND SATURDAY. FULL
BAR. VISA, MASTERCARD. 90% NONSMOKING. FULLY WHEELCHAIR ACCESSIBLE.
RESERVATIONS RECOMMENDED. EXPENSIVE.

There are undoubtedly lots of people who could happily live out their lives never seeing the words "East-meets-West cuisine" again. What started out as an interesting food trend has lately become pretty much of a cliché. But now I've got to trot out this phrase yet one more time, because there's a restaurant that breathes new life into these words.

I'm talking about Monsoon in Opera Plaza, the restaurant of Bruce Cost, a Westerner with extensive training in Shanghai-style cuisine, who has given many Asian cooking classes and written a highly praised Asian cookbook. With a largely non-Asian staff, Cost has attempted to resurrect classic Chinese recipes rarely seen in these parts, improvise other dishes derived from the cooking of Thailand and elsewhere in Southeast Asia, and base his menus on the California-cuisine principle of using only what's available in the markets that day.

This a pretty big order, but Monsoon succeeds. Although the kitchen does wonderful things with pork and with fowl, the seafood is so fresh and so brilliantly prepared that it provides the fondest memories. Sweet, barely cooked sea scallops are enlivened by the crunch of fresh water chestnuts and an aromatic sauce that includes diced pork, coconut milk, fresh turmeric, freshly ground cumin, fennel and coriander seeds, along with ginger, galangal and chiles. A whole Dungeness crab turns out to be the only completely successful preparation of this San Francisco favorite that I've experienced in an Asian restaurant. For once, it isn't overcooked, and the sauce isn't overly salty. Instead, the crab is quickly wok-fried, then tossed in a sauce of ground pork, black beans, ginger, garlic, scallions, chicken stock, and eggs. Cost says this is the true version of the Cantonese "lobster sauce" that's massacred in so many restaurants.

There are lots of other great dishes. Grilled lemon duck has a crisp skin, not a speck of fat, and a non-sweet, intensely lemony sauce. Tea-smoked squab, at other restaurants so often acrid and greasy, comes out lightly smoked and deliciously tender. Tea-smoked duck is simply the best there is. Red-braised pork shoulder is a marvel, a butter-tender stew of pork and sliced daikon flavored by cinnamon and star anise. And the list has to include one of the most spectacular Asian noodle dishes ever, yellow curry noodles from a homemade curry paste, tossed with pork and Chinese chives.

Many of the starters are equally good. A saté of venison brings three skewers of tender grilled venison and a spicy, delectable peanut-coriander dipping sauce. A Thai seafood salad of shrimp, squid, and octopus has a freshness rarely seen this side of Bangkok. And deep-fried taro-flour dumplings stuffed with ground pork, mushrooms, and bamboo shoots come out greaseless and delicate.

If all this food sounds wonderful, the desserts of pastry chef David Lebovitz, who comes from Chez Panisse, make it even better. Rather than serving Panisse-style French desserts, he tries to invent things that would be appropriate for an Asian meal. This means lots of tropical fruits—ranging from fruit ices, to passion fruit and shaved coconut in a bowl of custard-like Thai tapioca. Poached pears with star anise, tea-poached prunes, ginger cookies, and an Asian "tiramisu" of coconut custard, sponge cake, tropical fruits, and rum would alone be enough to bring me back to Monsoon for additional meals.

STAN SESSER

MUSTARDS ★★½

ONE MILE NORTH OF YOUNTVILLE ON HIGHWAY 29, YOUNTVILLE. (707) 944-2424. OPEN DAILY FROM 11:30 A.M. TO 10 P.M. FULL BAR. VISA, MASTERCARD, DINER'S CLUB. 75% NONSMOKING. FULLY WHEELCHAIR ACCESSIBLE. RESERVATIONS RECOMMENDED. MODERATE.

I hadn't visited Mustards, the very first of the new generation of restaurants to open in the Napa Valley, for eight years, but I wasn't surprised to find it as popular as ever, this summer, a must-stop in practically every tourist guide book. That's because the food is as good as ever. At a late lunch in Mustards' airy porch room, I gobbled down a huge plate of signature deep-fried onions threads, all in a crisp tangle, and an order of deep-fried green tomato slices with a corn meal crust, moistened by a creamy tarragon aioli.

The menu has just changed for the first time since opening. Though many of the favorites like barbecued baby back ribs and chef Cyndi Pawlcyn's flavor-packed Asian-marinated skirt steak are still on it, two excellent new additions bring chipotle chile marinated quail cooked to a dark glistening turn in the wood burning oven served with deep fried plantains and chili flecked mango slices; and a refreshing Asian chicken salad, served in a bowl with romaine, chicken skin cracklings, roasted peanuts, a tahini/sesame dressing, and shredded grilled chicken. Don't leave the restaurant without having the definitive strawberry, peach, and nectarine shortcake, in season.

PATRICIA UNTERMAN

NAN YANG ★★★

301 EIGHTH ST. (AT HARRISON), OAKLAND. 465-6924. OPEN TUESDAY THROUGH THURSDAY 11 A.M. TO 9 P.M., FRIDAY TO 9:30 P.M., SATURDAY NOON TO 9:30 P.M., SUNDAY NOON TO 9 P.M. BEER, WINE. VISA, MASTERCARD. 30% NONSMOKING. FULLY WHEELCHAIR ACCESSIBLE. RESERVATIONS FOR PARTIES OF FOUR OR MORE. INEXPENSIVE.

The Bay Area now has a group of Thai, Cambodian, and Burmese chefs—often skilled professionals in other fields in their native country—who take creative cooking as seriously as any three-star French chef ever did. Philip Chu of Nan Yang is a perfect example of this. He's a Burmese architect who believes that both food and architecture can be made into impressions of art. He loves to talk about the relationship between the two.

At first, Nan Yang was a sideline to Chu's work as an architectural engineer. Now it's a booming restaurant that requires his full-time attention. The Burmese food is positively exciting and finds a ready audience. It resembles in some ways Thai and Indian cooking, particularly in its profusion of herbs and spices. But it's much more subtle and delicate than either of these.

Start out with the ginger salad, or for greater adventure, the green tea salad. Both include hot peppers, ground dried shrimp, peanuts, sesame seeds, fried garlic, and split yellow peas. But the secret of the latter is marinated tea leaves from Burma, suspended in a river and then buried until they taste like a tender vegetable. The Eight Precious Bean Curd is also very much worth ordering as a starter. The dish is actually fried milk—milk, cornstarch, crab and shrimp meat, and little pieces of ham are made into a paste, formed into squares, lightly breaded, then deep-fried. And above all, don't miss the Burmese cold noodles, one of the most interesting noodle dishes anywhere.

Fish noodle curry soup, called *mohinga* in Burma, is the Burmese national dish and very much worth ordering at Nan Yang. So are all the curries—the fish, beef, and both versions of chicken curry. Each has a distinctive sauce, very aromatic and tasty, but not nearly as hot as Indian curries.

The atmosphere at Nan Yang is informal but very pleasant, reflecting its architect-owner's hand. While you're eating, Phil is always delighted to explain to you what's in each dish. His great love of Burmese food shows in everything that's served. A restaurant like Nan

Yang illustrates how the Bay Area's ethnic diversity makes eating such an exciting experience.

STAN SESSER

NOB HILL RESTAURANT ★★½

MARK HOPKINS HOTEL, 1 NOB HILL, SAN FRANCISCO. 392-3434. OPEN EVERY DAY FOR BREAKFAST FROM 6:30 TO 10:30 A.M.; LUNCH FROM 11:30 A.M. TO 2:30 P.M.; DINNER FROM 6 TO 10:30 P.M. DINNER-DANCING WEEKENDS. FULL BAR. ALL MAJOR CREDIT CARDS. 90% NONSMOKING. FULLY WHEELCHAIR ACCESSIBLE. RESERVATIONS RECOMMENDED. EXPENSIVE EXCEPT FOR MODERATE PRIX FIXE LUNCH.

I have to take my hat off to the Nob Hill Room in the Mark Hopkins Hotel. Several months ago I attended an all cheese dinner put on in conjunction with the Parisian Androuet cheese store and restaurant. The meal was gorgeous and flawlessly executed. Though the recipes, the cheese, and a couple of chefs came straight from Paris, the fact is that the local staff headed by Ward Little and Tony Breeze prepared a difficult meal for a dining room full of people.

I was so impressed that I returned to the Nob Hill Restaurant three times, and at one of those meals, a lunch, had a transcendent experience. The lobby-level restaurant has always been a favorite room of mine. Richly paneled in walnut with tall windows that look out onto the top of Nob Hill, the dining room is small enough to feel like a club, but spacious enough to provide comfortable distance between tables.

I discovered that for a moderate sum you can get the best lunch in town. That day, the Complete Express Lunch, which is served within 45 minutes, consisted of a lovely green salad lightly tossed in a mustardy vinaigrette; a pink, juicy, crisp skinned grilled squab, neatly sliced with braised coins of young ginger, pearl onions, baby carrots, and mashed potato in a mild, ginger-scented sauce; and a superb poached pear tart on flaky puff pastry with a little baked almond cream. The restaurant even throws in a cup of coffee.

Some other delicious dishes that day included a seafood salad of crabmeat, quickly griddled scallops, crisply fried shrimp, cold lobster, and marinated mussels all in a tart, fruity chopped tomato vinaigrette. In another stunning appetizer, the chefs piled a deep-fried vegetable basket with chanterelles sauteed with bacon, thyme, and red wine. As a main course, roast free-range chicken with a seductively crunchy skin came in an elegant pan gravy with a savory potato cake. The meal was gracefully served—the waiter gently steering us to the stellar seafood salad.

While patrons can indulge in lunch for a relatively reasonable sum, dinner represents a major investment that may not compete with independent restaurants in the same price range. The kitchen does have a way with foie gras, especially in a sweet, velvety, cold terrine, or quickly sauteed with an artichoke, onion, and sorrel ragout. They also show an aptitude for cooking birds. Juicy free-range chicken comes crisply sauteed with green olives and garlic, and squab arrives perfectly roasted with fresh pears in oregano-scented natural juice. You can dine very well here, but you must select the right dishes from a large, rather daunting menu for any kitchen to prepare perfectly.

PATRICIA UNTERMAN

NORTH SEA VILLAGE ★★

300 TURNEY STREET, SAUSALITO. 331-3300. OPEN FOR DIM SUM LUNCH MONDAY THROUGH FRIDAY 11 A.M. TO 3 P.M., SATURDAY AND SUNDAY, 10 A.M. TO 3 P.M., DINNER EVERY NIGHT 5 TO 10 P.M. BEER AND WINE. VISA, MASTERCARD, AMERICAN EXPRESS. RESERVATIONS ADVISED. MODERATE.

The wave of Hong Kong restaurants washing up on the shores of the Bay Area has extended to Sausalito. The North Sea Village, a branch of a Hong Kong house, has found itself a spectacular location right on the marina in Richardson Bay. Gazing out the floor-to-ceiling windows of this wooden dock building, you can imagine yourself in Hong Kong's Aberdeen harbor, except that the masts sprout from sailboats instead of sampans. This restaurant brings a level of Cantonese cooking to Marin that has not existed before.

North Sea Village shines on seasonal vegetable and seafood dishes. The raw materials are impeccable and the technique solid. One can dine on true delicacies here, like raw, thinly sliced geoduck clam, presented on an escarole-lined platter covered with bean threads and straw mushrooms. Wasabi and a chili-scallion-soy dipping sauce come on the side. You can eat the delectably sweet clam raw or you can dip it in boiling broth at the table in a gold mesh basket. When everyone is finished, the lettuce goes into the enriched broth and the table ends up with a heavenly bowl of melted lettuce soup.

The restaurant maintains lots of tanks for live fish and shellfish. A rock fish plucked from one of them, and steamed with ginger and scallions, had flesh so firm and juicy, I actually think it worth the price. (By the way, always ask the price when you order live fish in Chinese restaurants.) Lobster Supreme brings live lobsters cut into chunks and stir fried with garlic and ginger in a scant sauce that is enriched with the red coral, or roe, of the lobster.

Other unusual dishes include *ung choy*, a seasonal, hollow-stemmed watercress-like vegetable with pointy leaves, aromatic with garlic, ginger, and red pepper, and a crisp skinned half chicken, treated like Peking duck, that boasts velvety flesh. Moist Fukien rice comes in a glass pie plate topped with a tasty mixture of black mushrooms and dried scallops.

Eggrolls are small, crisp and simply filled with ground pork and sprouts. Deep fried wonton, unfilled, come as a crunchy chip to dip in a sweet and sour stew of squid and green peppers. Big, lavishly battered shrimp are notable for being cleanly deep fried. Pieces of flounder are dusted with seasoned corn starch and deep-fried momentarily to become golden nuggets. A hotpot of fatty, delicious, pork "spareribs" comes in a sauce flavored with lots of onions. Contrastingly lean, though full flavored, is a striking presentation of white bean curd topped with steamed scallops and black bean sauce, one of my favorite dishes at North Sea Village.

Meals end with bowls of warm, delicately sweetened red bean soup, or chilled, fresh cantaloupe pudding laced with pearls of tapioca and bits of melon.

Though the service is not up to the standards of the great Hong Kong houses on the Peninsula and in the city, the wonderful setting, the nicely appointed interior, and easy parking make the North Sea Village well worth a journey over the Golden Gate Bridge.

PATRICIA UNTERMAN

O CHAMÉ ★★★

1830 4TH STREET, BERKELEY. 841-8783. OPEN MONDAY THROUGH SATURDAY FOR LUNCH 11:30 A.M. TO 2:30 P.M.; TEA 2:30 TO 5:30 P.M.; DINNER 5:30 TO 10 P.M. BEER., WINE, AND SAKE. MASTERCARD AND VISA. 100% NON-SMOKING. FULLY WHEEL-CHAIR ACCESSIBLE. RESERVATIONS RECOMMENDED FOR DINNER. MODERATE

O Chamé is a Japanese restaurant that invokes peace. The food is soothing, balanced, and easy to digest. The handcrafted interior emphasizes light, air, and natural materials. The service is quiet and sincere. When you eat there you feel refreshed.

You enter the restaurant through a small courtyard with a bench and a low stucco wall. At lunchtime, a wooden cart there dispenses bento boxes to go. The whole front of the restaurant is a gently curved arch fitted with little French doors. The pale orange walls have designs drawn into the plaster. The rooms glow from the light of handmade copper lamps. Terracotta tile floors extend the use of clay from Japanese vases; hand-thrown sake jugs and bowls are neatly stored behind a charming tea and sake bar. All the tables, booths, and chairs are made of wood and have cushions upholstered with hand-dyed material. The dining rooms of O Chamé are graceful, restful, and very much a whole.

The food carries on these themes. Lunch is served in two-tiered, lacquered, red bento boxes, each section holding a different food. At dinner, a series of little dishes comes on a stunning assortment of

Japanese pottery. The color, texture, and placement of foods on each plate makes each dish look inviting. Usually only one or two elements make up the preparations, and this simplicity makes you taste each ingredient more deeply.

The prix fixe dinner consists of a progression of cold, steamed, simmered, and grilled dishes. You choose one from each category. I would not eat a meal at O Chamé without having a bowl of miso soup because it is the most soothing and full flavored miso soup I've tasted. One night the smoky broth held big cubes of yellow Kabocha squash, rings of leek, and shiitake mushrooms. At lunch one day, a slightly lighter broth was rich with soft, daikon radish slices and shredded scallion. Sashimi of the day can also be ordered a la carte and usually brings two types of raw fish, like red tuna with geranium-like shiso leaves, and fingers of impeccably fresh, briny sea urchin roe.

I particularly like the simmered dishes. Tender, roughly textured white fish dumplings come in a clear broth with pale green winter melon, bright orange Kabocha squash, and slices of shiitakes. Sea scallops are split and inserted with a slice of kiwi and seasoned with a garlic flower. Tea-flavored, hard boiled eggs, velvety chicken livers, and diced tomatoes make for a buttery stew in rice wine. Bulging tofu skin pouches are filled with braised carrot, shiitakes, and burdock root in an amazingly delicious combination. All these dishes balance a protein rich element with colorful vegetables or fruit in a way that makes them sing together.

The steamed dishes taste a bit more esoteric, but they are completely accessible. One of the nicest is fish cakes, lovely rectangles of ethereally light fish custard studded with chunks of pink shrimp and white fish served in a clear broth.

The cold dishes defer most directly to California influences, like a salad of organic mixed greens in a mild vinaigrette that uses rice wine vinegar, and endive, watercress, and roasted pepper salad with sweet geoduck clam. Vinegared seaweed, octopus, and cucumber salad reminds me of a calamari salad.

From the grilled category comes a buttery chunk of crisp skinned yellowtail with marinated spinach, and tiny slices of marinated beef filet with enoki mushrooms. All meals come with individual bowls of fabulous, chewy pearl rice dotted with bits of carrot, shiitake, and scallion. The rice rounds out the meals wonderfully.

At the prix fixe lunch you get to choose from six entrees to go with your bento box. One of my favorites is something called wheat gluten, which turns out to be a hearty stew with braised carrots, tender burdock root, and chunks of juicy brown wheat gluten which looks just like meat and offers similar satisfactions in its savory, brown gravy.

With the food, I like drinking sake; either Berkeley-produced, Shochikubai medium sweet sake served hot in jugs, or dry or very dry Japanese sakes served cold by the 4 oz. glass.

For dessert, you must order a cup of Japanese tea individually brewed in tiny brass pots to go with O Chamé's famous, super-crisp, wafer-like tea cakes full of peanuts. This exquisite combination can be enjoyed throughout the afternoon.

PATRICIA UNTERMAN

OLIVETO ★★★

5655 COLLEGE AVENUE, OAKLAND. 547-5356. OPEN FOR LUNCH MONDAY THROUGH SATURDAY 11:30 A.M TO 2 P.M.; DINNER MONDAY THROUGH SATURDAY 6 TO 10 P.M. BEER AND WINE. MASTERCARD AND VISA. 100% NONSMOKING. FULLY WHEELCHAIR ACCESSIBLE. RESERVATIONS RECOMMENDED. MODERATE.

Oliveto is the inspiration of Maggie Klein, a woman who loves olives—not just olives, of course, though she has written a whole book about them called the Feast of the Olive, but of cuisines based on olive oil and the products of the Mediterranean. Her airy, two-story restaurant evokes a Mediterranean villa. Terracotta colored walls, high ceilings, beautifully framed windows and doors that open wide to let in the breezes, an immaculate open kitchen, soft lighting, and a location next to a European-style market that sells fresh fish, vegetables, cheeses, and pasta, match the rustic but stylish food. A popular cafe/tapas bar takes up the ground floor with the full-scale restaurant upstairs.

A plate of marinated olives—green and black, large and small—greets customers at each table covered with linen and white paper, along with two kinds of Acme bread and a slab of sweet butter. No beginning to a meal could be more inviting. At that point, you can decide how you want to eat by choosing large or small dishes from a daily printed menu of tapas-like first courses, pastas and risotti, and hearty main courses. A list of wines from Italy, Spain, France, and California offers dozens of intriguing bottles including many tenths. This is one of the most sophisticated restaurants in the Bay Area at bringing together regional wines and foods.

You can take advantage of a half bottle of medium dry Manzanilla sherry to drink with little plates of spicy and savory foods offered as antipasti—such as excellent prosciutto on a plate with blue-grained Morbier cheese, toasts rubbed with olive oil, and roasted garlic cloves.

With a velvety Spanish red wine, you can continue with a pasta course—a perfect wild mushroom-infused risotto, or fusilli tossed with deliciously charred squash, caramelized onions, turnip greens, and mozzarella.

Oliveto makes its own boudin noir and lamb sausages and puts them into a kind of cassoulet with white beans and a crisp bread crumb topping that's one of the best dishes around. If this "gratin of housemade sausages" appears on the menu, order it. A main course salad of pink grilled duck breast, sliced over greens with radishes and shaved pecorino cheese, and a hearty, melt-in-your-mouth osso buco have also been wonderful.

The imaginative menu continues with desserts like a rich, bitter-sweet chocolate and espresso paté in a pool of creme anglaise, or apricot tiramisu with layers of almond cake alternating with apricot compote and mascarpone.

Oliveto is one of those rare, unified, fully realized restaurants. The food, the wines, the ambience, all work together in an exhilarating and very satisfying way. The waiters are terrific. They know the wines and the dishes; they express opinions about both; and they steer you to the best the restaurant has to offer. The food is beautifully presented, takes risks that pay off, and is ever changing. You can sense the dedication behind it all. Ms. Klein is still celebrating the olive, day after day, at her own restaurant.

PATRICIA UNTERMAN

ON LOK YUEN ★★

3721 GEARY BLVD. NEAR ARGUELLO, SAN FRANCISCO. 386-6208. OPEN FOR LUNCH WEDNESDAY THROUGH SUNDAY FROM 11:30 A.M. TO 3 P.M.; DINNER SUNDAY THROUGH THURSDAY 5 TO 9:30 P.M., FRIDAY AND SATURDAY 5 TO 10:30 P.M. BEER, WINE. VISA, MASTERCARD. 50% NONSMOKING. FULLY WHEEL-CHAIR ACCESSIBLE. RESERVATIONS SUGGESTED. INEXPENSIVE.

I'm a great fan of mom-and-pop Asian restaurants, and On Lok Yuen, with wonderful Burmese food and reasonable prices, illustrates why. Until not long ago, Burmese food was pretty esoteric in these parts, represented only by Mandalay in San Francisco and the superlative Nan Yang in Oakland Chinatown. But lately it seems to be taking off.

On Lok Yuen, like virtually every restaurant in Burma, is run by Burmese of Chinese origin. David Chou, who came from Burma in 1975, employs an extended family; everyone who works there is his relative, and their kids play around in the back room. Chou's wife and brother-in-law are the cooks. The menu includes both Burmese and Chinese dishes. In a wonderful switch from the past, when restaurants run by Southeast Asians used to pretend that their food was Chinese so people wouldn't be afraid to order it, On Lok Yuen puts the word Burmese in front of several of the Chinese dishes to make them seem more exotic.

What makes Burmese food so interesting is that it combines in one package some of the nicest things from its neighbors. There are curries from India, frequently accompanied by *paratha*, the Indian bread. There are spices and chili peppers from Thailand. There are lots of noodle dishes inspired by Chinese cooking—but none of the grease.

The place to start for Burmese food is with the salads. With their contrasting textures and tastes, they'll be like nothing else you've ever eaten before. On Lok Yuen does a superb ginger salad, blending fresh shredded ginger with the crunchiness of peanuts, fried garlic, and sesame seeds. There's also a pickled tea leaf salad, a great Burmese specialty, where the tea leaves are actually buried in the ground for several months until they taste like a tender vegetable. Don't miss the *samu sa* either, a crisp, deep-fried dumpling like the Indian *samosa* with an aromatic filling of curried potatoes and ground beef.

Next get the Burmese fish chowder, a great Burmese specialty that's done superbly here. With its thin noodles, rich, peppery broth, and crunchy fried beans, it's a melding of beautiful flavors and textures. Many of the best entrees are curry dishes; the Burmese variety is much milder and more subtle than the Indian version. Among the curries, I'm particularly impressed with the squid, unusually fresh and tender. Curried fish balls are interesting also, not at all rubbery like fish balls in so many Chinese restaurants. Curried, hard-boiled eggs cooked with sauteed onions, and a bowl of surprisingly tender curried beef with potatoes are both excellent.

Then there's what the menu calls Burmese chicken, nuggets of chicken battered and deep-fried, emerging crisp and greaseless, and served in an incredible sauce loaded with diced green onions and chilies. Equally good is the *nan gyi dok*, one of the best noodle dishes anywhere. The soft egg noodles are tossed with shredded coconut, bits of chicken, fried onions, fried garlic chips, green onions, sesame seeds, and lemon juice. Each bite of noodles has wonderful flavors clinging to it.

STAN SESSER

ORIGINAL JOE'S ★★

144 TAYLOR STREET (NEAR MARKET), SAN FRANCISCO. 775-4877. OPEN EVERY DAY FROM 10:30 A.M. TO 1:30 A.M. FULL BAR. DINERS CLUB, VISA AND MASTER-CARD. 50% NONSMOKING. FULLY WHEELCHAIR ACCESSIBLE. RESERVATIONS FOR PARTIES OF 6 OR MORE. INEXPENSIVE.

Original Joe's, celebrating its 53rd anniversary this year, serves incredibly generous breakfasts, lunches, and dinners every day of the year for amazingly low prices. One sitting at Original Joe's supplies enough good food to carry you through the whole day and into the next.

A wide stratum of San Francisco society frequents Original Joe's specifically for their monumental and delicious hamburgers; three quarters of a pound of freshly ground beef grilled exactly to specification slapped between hollowed out, thickly buttered slabs of french

■ ORIGINAL JOE'S OFFERS A SLICE OF LIFE FROM THE PAST. THE PEOPLE WHO LIKE IT, WHETHER THEY BE 70 OR 30, LEAVE THEIR MODERN PRETENSIONS BEHIND. I BREATH A SECRET SIGH OF RELIEF WHENEVER I WALK IN.

bread positioned next to a stack of gigantic, soft french fries. Original Joe's buys sides of beef, ages and breaks them down. The beef must be chosen for its hamburger potential, because I've never tasted any better. Purists who don't want the distraction of bread order the mammoth hamburger steak, a handsome slab of meat pressed into chopped onions and grilled. With it comes a choice of spaghetti with meat sauce or a mountain of cauliflower, chard, zucchini, and carrots cooked through but not mushy.

It's amazing to see seemingly frail old ladies happily nibbling at man-sized fried ham and cheese sandwiches made with thick rashers of ham and inches of cheese. Each day of the week brings a different special like a two pounds or so serving of braised, butter-tender oxtails smothered in vegetable thickened sauce on Saturdays, or savory short ribs on Tuesdays. A plateful of moist corned beef and cabbage is available on Thursdays. The kitchen puts out a gargantuan slab of lean, tasty roast beef everyday, but prime rib is served on Saturdays only.

The restaurant has remained exactly the same for the mere twenty years I've been going there. The wood paneled bar room is kept mercifully dark day and night, with booths at the back and along one wall. The main dining room has more red vinyl booths with plastic veneered tables of large and small proportions, and the famous open cooking line with counter seats in front of it. Original Joe's claims to be the oldest of the existing "Joe's-style" restaurants in the country. It was using a mesquite grill in 1937 to cook its meats and wasn't shy about exposing the kitchen to the public; concepts that since have been adopted by the nation's most trend setting restaurants.

The major drawback of the restaurant is its neighborhood, which can get pretty dicey in the early evenings for some reason. Luckily, there are inexpensive parking lots next to the restaurant and directly across the street. But, in some ways, Original Joe's Tenderloin location is O.K. It takes a certain kind of person to go there, those who go to eat big and hearty rather than to be entertained. Original Joe's offers a slice of life from the past. The people who like it, whether they be 70 or 30, leave their modern pretensions behind. They smoke, they drink, they eat too much food, they eat too much fat, and they don't care. I breath a secret sigh of relief whenever I walk in.

PATRICIA UNTERMAN

ORITALIA ★★

1915 FILLMORE ST. (NEAR PINE), SAN FRANCISCO. 346-1333. OPEN MONDAY
THROUGH THURSDAY 5 TO 11 P.M., UNTIL 11:30 P.M. FRIDAY AND SATURDAY, 4:30
TO 10 P.M. SUNDAY. FULL BAR. VISA, MASTERCARD, DINERS CLUB. 70% NON-
SMOKING. FULLY WHEELCHAIR ACCESSIBLE. RESERVATIONS RECOMMENDED.
MODERATE.

One of the most interesting examples of East-meets-West cuisine
at the moment is to be found at Oritalia, a slickly designed but
comfortable restaurant that serves only small-portion, Italian-oriented
dishes cooked by two Japanese chefs. Much of Oritalia's food is
absolutely first-rate in concept, execution, and presentation. A typical
menu (several things change every couple of weeks) will have purely
Italian dishes (for instance, prosciutto and melon), Italian dishes with
a Japanese touch (spicy *mabo-tofu* pasta with shiitake mushrooms and
sun-dried tomatoes) and a scattering of appetizers from all over
Asia (Imperial rolls, Indonesian chicken satay). It's a real culinary
adventure.

The last category is my favorite. I didn't taste a loser among any of
the Asian dishes. The chicken satay is permeated with an outstanding
marinade, made even better by the spicy peanut and pickled vegetable
salad that accompanies it. Imperial rolls, stuffed with chicken and
shrimp, have a crisp, thin, greaseless skin and a host of interesting
ingredients. Japanese satsuma potatoes, sliced with the skin and topped
with creme fraiche and flying fish roe, look ravishing on a plate
decorated with red and yellow peppers cut in diamond shapes.

Pastas are perfectly made, although on some you might wish the
sauces were a bit more assertive. Al dente angel hair pasta comes with
impeccable clams in the shell. Spaghettini with eggplant and anchovies
in a pesto-mint sauce is surprisingly subtle, considering the ingredients. The most interesting pasta is the spicy *mabo-tofu*, a plate of
spaghettini tossed with tofu, ground chicken, sun-dried tomatoes,
black mushrooms and some Asian spices.

Among the other dishes, fried brown rice with Italian sausage tastes
much better than it sounds, an absolutely greaseless blend of wonderful
sausage, mushrooms, carrots, celery, ginger, and green beans. Spicy
marinated cucumbers come in a great salad of fried peanuts, bean
sprouts, ginger, cabbage, and carrots. Sweet and fresh-tasting scallops
are in a soupbowl of a thick orange-ginger-cilantro sauce.

The interesting food and pleasant surroundings at Oritalia could
still have turned into a disaster had service not been perfectly paced.
When two people order eight or ten dishes, you'd think it would be
almost impossible to get the timing right, so that not too many dishes
come at once, and so that everything is hot. But the waiters and the

kitchen have it orchestrated like a ballet; they do the job so easily you never even think about how hard it must be. This restaurant is a welcome addition to the San Francisco food scene.

STAN SESSER

OZONE ★★½

1654 HAIGHT STREET, SAN FRANCISCO. 255-0565. OPEN TUESDAY THROUGH FRIDAY FROM 11:30 A.M. TO 10 P.M., SATURDAY AND SUNDAY FROM 10 A.M. TO 10 P.M. BEER AND WINE. MASTERCARD AND VISA. 100% NONSMOKING. PARTIALLY WHEELCHAIR ACCESSIBLE. NO RESERVATIONS. MODERATE.

Ozone is a south of market style restaurant that opened in the Haight. It's got a witty look, an up-to-the-minute menu that oddly combines the cooking of Stars Cafe with a Jewish deli, and a spiky, urban cast of characters working and eating there.

If you were to imagine what the ozone looks like, the expanses of sponged, lavender-swirled gray walls of this restaurant might be it. Graceful, painted figures float in it, peeking around corners and perching on ledges. Though small, the uncluttered decor, clean materials, and high ceilings make Ozone feel spacious.

The menu, created by Sharna Gross an alumna of Stars and Stars Cafe, certainly owes some of its conception to her alma mater. Lots of different things go on each plate, often a juxtaposition of the raw and the cooked with creamy mayonnaise sauce drizzled over all. She brings her more personal cooking voice to the menu in the guise of refined Jewish dishes, like chicken soup, and excellent braised brisket, an unusual treat for San Franciscans. Everything is made from scratch like catsup, pickles, and relishes. Breads come from Semifreddi's and the kitchen makes a different, olive oil-rich vegetable conserve to pile on the bread instead of butter.

A recent dinner brought slices of raw yellowfin tuna, outlined in crushed coriander berries and seared on the outside, dramatically topped with a mountain of crunchy deep-fried onions rings. A crisp noodle pancake supported a pile of fried rock shrimp tossed with a chunky, bright green, tomatillo salsa. A thick filet of salmon came off the grill moist and velvety, accompanied with a crisp cake of thinly sliced potatoes and turnips and a mound of tender Swiss chard. Juicy, sliced duck breast on a bed of tiny French lentils, drizzled with a creamy mayonnaise sauce and sprinkled with deep-fried beet shavings and parsley leaves would have done her mentor proud.

One technique the kitchen really has down is deep-frying. A fried chicken salad at lunch one day featured delicate nuggets of the crispest, moistest chicken breast on greens with a buttermilk dressing. Deep-fried calamari, as addictive as popcorn, is regularly paired with parsnip ribbons and mint-chile salsa verde.

214

Desserts are homey in a refined sort of way, and delicious, like an airy, custard-filled Boston Cream Pie coated with a thin layer of bittersweet chocolate. Hot fudge sundaes with roasted peanuts and a fabulous chocolate mousse-filled tart topped with caramel will satisfy anyone's sweetest tooth.

Industry trend forecasters are saying that small places with labor intensive menus like Ozone won't succeed, but it seems to me that Ozone is both manageable, interestingly personal, and of a scale that fits the small shop ethos of the Haight. This good little restaurant brings a breath of fresh air to the neighborhood.

PATRICIA UNTERMAN

PACIFIC HEIGHTS BAR AND GRILL ★½

2001 FILLMORE STREET, SAN FRANCISCO. 567-5226. OPEN DAILY FOR DINNER 5:30 TO 9:30 P.M., UNTIL 10:45 P.M. ON WEEKENDS. OYSTER BAR OPEN UNTIL 11 P.M. ON WEEKDAYS AND MIDNIGHT ON WEEKENDS. SUNDAY BRUNCH 10:30 TO 2:30. FULL BAR. MASTERCARD, VISA, AMERICAN EXPRESS. 15% NONSMOKING. FULLY WHEELCHAIR ACCESSIBLE. RESERVATIONS RECOMMENDED. EXPENSIVE.

Pacific Heights Bar and Grill is one of the best places to go for oysters. At peak season you'll find up to 20 varieties, generally from the West Coast, including Washington and British Columbia. The sit-down oyster bar surrounds a picture window, manned by a friendly, efficient shucker. To the left is a great view of the sidewalk and street traffic. On the other side is the long, natural-wood bar and a lounge area that has become a hangout for single, young, conservatively dressed types. (The restaurant, however, attracts an affluent older crowd.)

In the main dining room, you'll have the best luck with simple preparations. As with the oysters, the seafood is fresh, but the execution of the finished dish can be amateurish. The Australian baked lobster tail served with drawn butter, is seductively sweet and meaty, although the risotto that accompanies it is mushy and gluey. A mixed grill is nothing short of weird. The sea bass is excellent, but it's topped with an acidic chunky pineapple salsa that doesn't work with the fish. Scallops are overpowered by a coarse tomato salsa. Shrimp, however, hold up to a chunky tomatillo salsa.

Grilled Fanny Bay Oysters are exquisite, lightly doused in a spicy sweet barbecue sauce. However, a tombo tuna pate with pistachio has the look of canned fish with an unpleasant pasty consistency.

Desserts are respectable enough to win some accolades. Creme brulée is simplistically sweet and could be a bit creamier. Pumpkin pie has a creamy custard-style filling and a crust that is a bit too brittle. I'd recommend the oatmeal spice cake with coconut cream cheese frosting encrusted with chopped pecans, and a chocolate torte that is like a flourless chocolate cake with a pleasantly bitter edge.

Although the food quality is uneven, I enjoy the low-key atmosphere with friendly service, though it can be a bit slow when busy. As for decor, the pastel, flame-stitch fabric on the chairs, banquettes, and large windows gives an airy feel, while two draped dining alcoves at the back have an intimate appeal. Most important, lighting is wonderful, giving off a glow that lifts the spirits.

MICHAEL BAUER

PACIFIC'S EDGE AT HIGHLANDS INN ★★★

FOUR MILES SOUTH OF CARMEL ON HIGHWAY 1. (408) 624-0471. OPEN 11:30 A.M. TO 2 P.M. FOR LUNCH MONDAY THROUGH SATURDAY, AND 6 TO 10 P.M. FOR DINNER SUNDAY THROUGH THURSDAY, UNTIL 10:30 P.M. FRIDAY AND SATURDAY; SUNDAY BRUNCH 10 A.M. TO 2 P.M. FULL BAR. ALL MAJOR CREDIT CARDS ACCEPTED. 75% NONSMOKING. PARTIALLY WHEELCHAIR ACCESSIBLE. RESERVATIONS REQUIRED. VERY EXPENSIVE.

The theory that views and fine food are mutually exclusive is disproved at Pacific's Edge restaurant, in the exclusive Highlands Inn in Carmel. Chef Brian Whitmer, a graduate of Campton Place, has miraculously created food that equals the view.

Perched on a ruddy pine-strewn cliff overlooking the irregular coastline, there's a breath-taking panorama of splashing waves, shimmering waters, and soaring birds. This has to be one of the prettiest spots in California.

Whitmer's combinations are fresh, light, and innovative. The continually changing menu features such combinations as salmon on a bed of artichokes and asparagus moistened with pesto, crispy duck in a soy-based sauce with intensely scented ginger noodles, and creamy raspberry "purses" made of phyllo and presented with a scoop of ice cream and shavings of chocolate and splatters of raspberry sauce.

Whitmer also offers homier selections such as roast chicken with whipped potatoes and garlic, or pan roasted veal chop with chanterelle mushrooms, cabbage, and pancetta. Even the more standard items have an intriguing twist such as the loin of lamb with eggplant cannelloni, or a fillet of beef served on black pepper ravioli with Roquefort.

The Sunset Dinner menu featuring four courses is an excellent value. Each savory course is matched with wine for an extra charge. You get a good selection of wine from an impressive list, which could occupy a connoisseur for hours. There's a full page devoted to

German wines, an excellent Italian list, and one of the most impressive California and French lists to be found. There's a particularly good selection of older California red wines. For example, you'll find Chateau Montelana Cabernet Sauvignon from 1977 to 1986; and good depth in Clos du Val and Caymus, to name a few. The number of producers and vintages represented on the French list can overwhelm as it features a series of older vintages from most of the big names, and a surprising number of other areas such as Chateauneuf du Pape, Volnay and Nuits St. Georges.

The interior and the service are quietly elegant, letting the food and the view hold center stage. The tables, set with white cloths, and first-class china and crystal, are arranged on several levels so most diners have a good view of the ocean. Although it might seem chic to dine late, I'd go for an early seating when it's still light.

You can also drink in the view at lunch which features a buffet and a la carte items. However, at night you can watch the sun go down, and the softly lighted trees cast an eerie, romantic glow.

MICHAEL BAUER

PALIO D'ASTI ★★

640 SACRAMENTO STREET, SAN FRANCISCO. 395-9800. OPEN MONDAY THROUGH SATURDAY FROM 11:30 A.M. TO MIDNIGHT, SUNDAY 4 TO 10 P.M. FULL BAR. MASTERCARD, VISA. 80% NONSMOKING. FULLY WHEELCHAIR ACCESSIBLE. RESERVATIONS ACCEPTED. MODERATE

Palio d'Asti shimmers in the stodgy old Financial District like a Milanese dream. Installed in the marble-lined 505 Montgomery building, its design cleverly takes advantage of the raw cement pillars and unfinished ceilings of new construction, while featuring an alleyway of sophisticated, open cooking stations. When you walk into Palio, the first thing you see is a tiled, wood burning pizza oven and then a glassed-in pasta kitchen, a separate grill room, and finally a station with a shiny pasta machine. It's the most appetizing decor a restaurant could have.

The vision behind Palio d'Asti comes from Gianni Fassio, whose family owned the original Blue Fox, a restaurant he recently bought and refurbished. At Palio d'Asti he's going after a more casual multi-faceted Italian experience.

One of his ideas with the most potential is an antipasti cart full of delights like marinated *chioggia* and golden beets, moist *caponata*, roasted eggplant and peppers, salt-cured anchovies dressed in parsley and lemon, barely cured, mild green olives, red onions roasted in balsamic vinegar, and crisply blanched fennel. There are about twelve different antipasti which revolve and come into sight three at a time. Serving from the cart has been cumbersome.

There are other good starters on the menu like a *frittura di mare,* a pile of deep-fried squid, small shrimp, smelt, and sardines of varying consistency. When the seafood is fresh and crisp, it's magnificent. A plate of sliced roma tomatoes and fennel in olive oil and vinegar will be clean and refreshing.

Pizzas from the wood burning oven are another possibility. Pizza *Margherita* with tomato sauce, mozzarella, and basil on a chewy crust hits the spot. Pizza *alla Scozzese,* scattered with smoked salmon, goat cheese, ricotta, and red onions, tastes like a warm canape. I'm not sure that goat cheese and smoked salmon really belong together.

My very favorite dish at Palio is a plate of wide noodles with arugula, tomatoes, and black olives. The flavors are clean, distinct, and earthy. And they go together. Richer, but very nice, are tri-colored strands of pasta in a lot of smooth, buttery, not too strong gorgonzola sauce with roasted pine nuts. A huge amount of tasty pesto practically submerges the *tagliolini* it is served with .

If you order a second course, like a gigantic veal chop stuffed with prosciutto and fontina, or a delicious slab of rib eye steak, you won't be able to eat much more. Sensitively grilled fish is available on a daily basis. Rabbit, though tender and juicy, had the typical, soapy flavor that afflicts most commercially raised animals. A brochette of rose-mary-marinated shrimp comes with a big, moist triangle of grilled polenta and a pile of chewy chard and mustard greens. There is a long and excellent Italian wine list with which to increase your knowledge of Italian wines.

The best desserts are a baked fresh peach, in season, sprinkled with crumbled amaretto cookies with mascarpone on the side, and a gelatinous but still velvety *panna cotta*, or vanilla flan, with fresh berry sauce.

Palio has real possibilities, but its large size and complicated menu, both to serve and to execute, has been a problem. Perhaps as more and more meals are served, this smart, ambitious, Financial District spot will grow more consistent.

PATRICIA UNTERMAN

| RISTORANTE PARMA ★½

3314 STEINER ST. BETWEEN LOMBARD AND CHESTNUT, SAN FRANCISCO. 567-0500. OPEN 5 TO 10:30 P.M. NIGHTLY EXCEPT SUNDAY. BEER, WINE. VISA, MASTERCARD, AMERICAN EXPRESS. 100% NONSMOKING. PARTIALLY WHEEL-CHAIR ACCESSIBLE. RESERVATIONS RECOMMENDED. MODERATE.

As anyone who travels in Italy quickly finds out, the food is considerably different from a meal in a typical San Francisco Italian restaurant. Here, the style of cooking is much heavier and it relies much less on fresh ingredients from the daily market. Moreover,

■ THE GARLICKY SMELLS THAT FILL THE DINING ROOM ARE ENTICING.

there's a homogeneous stamp to a San Francisco Italian restaurant: It's "everyone's favorite Italian dishes," including lots of veal and lots of melted cheese and tomato sauce.

Ristorante Parma certainly fits into this category, but in the most positive way. This place is so user friendly that you tend to overlook the fact that some of the dishes aren't quite as good as others. Prices are reasonable, including those for the small but very interesting Italian wine list. Portions are huge. The garlicky smells that fill the dining room are enticing. And never have I seen waiters enjoying their work so much; their spirit is infectious.

Almost all the appetizers are terrific, including one of the best minestrone soups ever, with the vegetables so fresh and firm-textured you'd almost think the soup had been made to order. Caesar salad is a delight; the romaine crisp and the assertive dressing, tasting of garlic and anchovies, lightly applied so that it isn't overwhelming. Mussels and clams Maria, cooked in tomato sauce, onions, white wine, and garlic, taste very fresh. Prosciutto and melon, the simplest of dishes but one that depends on the quality of ingredients, here features very sweet canteloupe and a flavorful prosciutto imported from the restaurant's namesake, Parma, Italy.

These excellent appetizers are followed by a mixed bag of pastas; you do well only if you order the right thing. Linguine alle vongole has good al dente noodles, clams and mussels as fresh-tasting as those in the Maria appetizer, and a light garlicky sauce mainly of shellfish stock. Ravioli stuffed with ricotta and spinach, tasty and tender, can be ordered with pesto, cream sauce, or Parma's homemade tomato sauce. By mistake, the waiter brought us *penne all'arrabiata,* and it was so wonderful I wouldn't let him take it away. The little tubular noodles come in a zingy tomato sauce of hot red peppers and garlic.

Like the pastas, the entrees—which revolve around veal and chicken— demonstrate a need to choose wisely. The thinly-sliced veal is tender and flavorful, but some preparations are far better than others. I'd recommend the scaloppine del chef, with eggplant and a thin layer of Monterey jack and reggiano cheese, the *scaloppine capriccio,* featuring nice artichoke hearts and mushrooms in a rich brown sauce, and the *cocconcini di casa,* rolled around a stuffing of spinach, cheese, prosciutto, and mushrooms.

Ristorante Parma reminds me very much of Ristorante Grifone in North Beach and La Traviata in the Mission. At all three it's like being welcomed by a warm, Italian family: no pretensions, lots of fun, and good, hearty food.

STAN SESSER

PEARL CITY ★★½

641 JACKSON STREET, SAN FRANCISCO. 398-8383. OPEN EVERY DAY FROM 9 A.M. TO 9:45 P.M. FULL BAR. AMERICAN EXPRESS, MASTERCARD AND VISA. 15% NON-SMOKING. FULLY WHEELCHAIR ACCESSIBLE. RESERVATIONS AT DINNER ONLY. INEXPENSIVE.

Pearl City is a relatively new Chinatown sensation, a very inexpensive, rustic, dim sum house that is practically unapproachable on the weekends, it's so busy. Portions are huge, the ingredients very fresh, some of the dim sum newly invented, the style, earthy. All the rage here are deep fried rice paper rolls stuffed with shrimp and banana, a startling combination. Pearl City's sticky rice–stuffed taro leaf packets are exceptional; moister and more savory than most. Vegetarian rolls wrapped in crisply deep fried tofu skin stuffed with mushroom are also a winner.

The *sui mai* here have roughly chopped fillings, composed of big tender chunks of shrimp and pork barely held together. Shark's fin-shaped dumplings get a similar chunky filling. Very popular in dim sum houses now are gigantic dumplings in glass bowls of broth. When you break them open, a rich filling of ground pork, shrimp and black mushrooms pours out into the broth. You add gingery Chinese vinegar at the table. My favorite dumpling at Pearl City is a fresh tasting, vegetarian one filled with chopped greens, garlic chives, and a little pork wrapped in a translucent rice noodle. Tripe is clean and tender. Egg custard tarts have pasty crusts.

At $6 a person, Pearl City delivers more than any table can eat. That the dim sum is shiningly fresh, conscientiously prepared, and distinctly rustic gives this restaurant its own niche in the ever growing supermarket of Chinese eateries in San Francisco.

PATRICIA UNTERMAN

PHNOM PENH HOUSE ★★

251 EIGHTH ST. (BETWEEN HARRISON AND ALICE), OAKLAND. 893-3825. OPEN MONDAY THROUGH THURSDAY 11 A.M TO 9:30 P.M., FRIDAY AND SATURDAY 11 A.M. TO 10 P.M. BEER, WINE. MASTERCARD, VISA. 100% NONSMOKING. FULLY WHEELCHAIR ACCESSIBLE. RESERVATIONS FOR PARTIES OF FOUR OR MORE. INEXPENSIVE.

It's no wonder that the Bay Area is now supporting about a dozen Cambodian restaurants. Because it's more exotic than most Chinese food, but less oily and less hot than Thai food, Cambodian cuisine is proving very appealing to lots of people.

At Phnom Penh House in Oakland's Chinatown, the food not only is delicious, but prices are so low that people can eat out for little more than it costs to cook at home. It's a bright, cheerful place, with cloth napkins, Cambodian decorations on the walls, and very attentive service. Dishes are brought out one at a time by a waiter who's delighted to explain what's in the food.

One of the best dishes here is a double-cooked, deep-fried pompano. The whole fresh fish is first deep fried, then poached in chicken stock. It emerges really juicy, with the skin crisp and greaseless. Then it gets a sauce that includes ground pork, ginger, green onions, red bell peppers, and green chilies. Close seconds are two barbecued dishes, the pork and the chicken. The thick strips of pork are moist, tender, and beautifully spiced. The chicken, served in boneless strips, is unlike any other Asian barbecued chicken I've had. It's marinated overnight in a long list of sauces, herbs and spices until the flesh turns brown. So the strips end up looking like pork but tasting like flavorful chicken.

There are several good choices to start. In the spicy squid salad, fresh, tender squid is mixed with baby ginger, mint leaves, carrots, lemongrass, green onions, red bell peppers, and shredded red cabbage, and it forms a dazzling array of colors. The very tasty Cambodian version of an egg roll, delicate and greaseless, is stuffed with ground pork, bean threads, and mushrooms.

Beef soup with lemongrass is a great choice. Slices of beef and little green Asian eggplants are cooked in chicken broth with lemongrass, fish sauce, preserved fish, and tamarind powder to produce an aromatic, flavorful broth.

Now that Cambodian food is well established here, it's time to bring up one problem that exists at Phnom Penh House and elsewhere. Cambodians, and many Thais, think Westerners only want to eat beef, pork, chicken, and shrimp, so their menus tend to be confined to those areas and to repeat each other. We miss out on tripe and other innards, and on wild game, frog legs, snails, and all the other things sold in Chinatown at all the grocery stores that surround Phnom Penh House. They do such a good job on conventional foods here that they should try some others.

STAN SESSER

PIATTI ★★

6480 WASHINGTON STREET, YOUNTVILLE. 707-944-2070. OPEN MONDAY THROUGH FRIDAY 11:30 A.M. TO 2:30 P.M. FOR LUNCH; 5 TO 10 P.M. FOR DINNER, SATURDAY AND SUNDAY NOON TO 10 P.M. FULL BAR. VISA, MASTERCARD. 100% NONSMOKING. FULLY WHEELCHAIR ACCESSIBLE. RESERVATIONS REQUIRED. MODERATE.

Piatti which was opened in 1988 by Claude Rouas of Auberge de Soleil, has now replicated itself eight or nine times up and down the state of California. The original in Yountville is an airy, white, red-tiled restaurant with two outdoor patios and an open kitchen with a wood fired rotisserie and pizza oven. As can be expected from Mr. Rouas, his designers captured just the right summery, breezy look in this rambling one story wood frame building with windows that look out to the Yountville hills ridged with vines.

The menu concentrates on pizzas and pastas, some interesting appetizers, and chickens and rabbits cooked on the rotisserie. A savory cheese-stuffed pizza called *schiacciata al formaggio* and a chewy-crusted small pizza with tomato, mozzarella, and basil make for good shared starters. Also appealing as appetizers are pristinely white, tender sweet-breads and mushrooms in a sharp, winey sauce, and crisply grilled radicchio wrapped in pancetta and scattered with fresh herbs.

The pastas have their ups and downs. A bowl of little ear shaped pasta with cabbage, pancetta, and fontina is smoky and delicious. Tubes of pasta with slices of potato and green beans in a pesto sauce comes to life with a grating of parmesan cheese. Ravioli stuffed with ricotta in a lemon cream sauce are well-made.

Piatti's wood burning rotisserie kitchen produces an excellent, hot, juicy grilled chicken and a similarly tasty rabbit. Potatoes roasted in the wood-fired oven come out crusty and irresistible. For dessert, there's a delicate, coffee-flavored tiramisu with creme anglaise, and two slices of nutty semifreddo, an almost chewy Italian version of ice cream, in a lovely fresh strawberry sauce.

PATRICIA UNTERMAN

PIER 23 ★★

ON THE EMBARCADERO, SAN FRANCISCO. 362-5125. OPEN TUESDAY THROUGH SATURDAY 11:30 A.M. TO 10 P.M. AND SUNDAY 11 A.M. TO 3 P.M. FULL BAR. VISA, MASTERCARD. 30% NONSMOKING. FULLY WHEELCHAIR ACCESSIBLE. RESERVA-TIONS RECOMMENDED. MODERATE.

Owned by San Francisco character at large, Flicka McGurrin, Pier 23 is the quintessential San Francisco waterfront shack. The outside of this small, freestanding building is white stucco with blue trim around the windows. The interior is trimmed with worn wood. Gigantic stuffed marlins and sail fish are mounted on the walls. An ancient copper topped bar looks straight out to Treasure Island. About twelve tables with sturdy wooden chairs fill up the rest of the room. White tablecloths and big bowls of spring flowers don't intrude on the sanctity of waterfront naturalism. No attempt has been made to transform Pier 23 into anything chic or touristy. In good weather, people sit outside on the cement pier in the back, right by the water.

The food reflects this same down-to-earth attitude as the ambience. A floppy Caesar salad with a thick, lemony dressing is distinguished by delicious buttery croutons. The house green salad amply coats both Belgium endive and butter lettuce in a tart, creamy dressing with a sprinkling of pinenuts. A lively version of Chinese chicken salad has lots of shredded poultry balanced by celery, cucumber, and scallion, all tossed in a chile-infused peanut sauce. The dark-bake Boudin sourdough and big pats of salted butter brought to the table immediately endears this restaurant to old-time San Franciscans.

For main courses I like the thick slices of Cajun meatloaf made with lean beef, slathered with a hot, smoky barbeque sauce, served with real mashed potatoes, or a half pound hamburger topped with asiago cheese. A lighter choice is a beautifully grilled trout, crisp and brown on the outside but still moist inside. Big spears of bright green asparagus and mashed potatoes make the trout plates look like an American still life.

Pier 23 also serves an excellent and popular Sunday brunch. Vividly seasoned corned beef hash is hand-chopped and made with freshly boiled corned beef and potatoes, topped with two perfect poached eggs. An equally impressive set of poached eggs crowns Pier 23's version of eggs Benedict with rivers of classic hollandaise, slices of Canadian bacon, and a base of baked potato. Eggs any style come with crusty chunks of herbed new potatoes and buttered Boudin toast and can be accompanied with squeezed orange juice, a strawberry, melon, and orange fruit plate, and big cups of aromatic Graffeo coffee.

PATRICIA UNTERMAN

PLEARN THAI CUISINE ★★★

2050 UNIVERSITY AVE., BERKELEY. 841-2148. OPEN DAILY 11:30 A.M. TO 10 P.M. BEER AND WINE. NO CREDIT CARDS. 100% NONSMOKING. PARTIALLY WHEELCHAIR ACCESSIBLE. RESERVATIONS FOR SIX OR MORE ONLY. INEXPENSIVE.

Plearn is my favorite Thai restaurant in the Bay Area and that's because it reminds me so much of Bangkok. The food is bounteous, wonderful, and inexpensive; the service is so efficient that a party of twenty gets served just as quickly as a table of two. Just like at all good restaurants in Bangkok, there are constant crowds and constant bustle. And everyone—from students out for a cheap meal to Thai food aficionados—seems to be enjoying the food.

Plearn Kundhikanjana, the charismatic chef, and owner along with her husband Visut, oversees both the kitchen and dining room with a firm hand. When you see her supervising every aspect of the operation, you understand why the restaurant has maintained its quality over the years.

Lots of her dishes are fiery hot, but the heat never drowns out other flavors; there's always a bouquet of aromas and tastes. The fact that a dish can be both hot and complex at the same time to me is the great miracle of Thai cooking.

If you're a hot food fan, two salads are so wonderful it's essential to start out with them. *Yum-nua* presents slices of tender barbecued beef on a bed of mint leaves, onion, ground chilies, lime juice, and lettuce—a host of wonderful tastes with fire underneath. There's also *yum-pla-muek*, a similar salad made from squid; the squid at Plearn is always superb. For less adventurous palates, the grilled chicken and pork satays with their peanut curry sauce, and the thick, tasty spring rolls stuffed with pork and cabbage never disappoint.

The soups at Plearn are not to be missed. *Po-tak* is a variety of seafood in a hot-and-sour broth with the strong perfume of lemon grass. *Tom-kha-gai* is chicken soup in a thick coconut broth.

Then you're ready for the entrees. Beef in red curry and pork in green curry are two dishes that will shock anyone who thinks a curry dish has no taste beyond the overwhelming sensation of curry powder. The barbecued chicken and pork are each fantastic, tasting heavily of their spicy marinades. If your taste buds want a little more sweetness and a little less heat, consider Plearn's duckling, tender chunks of fat-free duck meat with pineapple and vegetables in plum sauce. There's also *pad-thai*, the noodle dish tossed with shrimp, pork, and chicken that many people consider their favorite dish at Plearn.

Lately, a number of new dishes have been added to the menu; many of them are vegetarian. But my two favorites among these are for fowl and fish eaters. Deep-fried quails are enhanced by their marinade of garlic and ground pepper. Salmon baked in a banana leaf is flavored by ginger, green onions, and a thick, red spicy sauce.

When Plearn started up a decade ago, there were very few choices for a Thai meal. Today there are dozens of choices, but Plearn Thai Cuisine remains as tempting as the day it opened.

STAN SESSER

POSTRIO ★★

545 POST STREET, SAN FRANCISCO. 776-7825. OPEN MONDAY THROUGH SATUR-DAY FOR BREAKFAST FROM 7 TO 10 A.M., LUNCH 11:30 A.M. TO 2:30 P.M., DINNER EVERY NIGHT FROM 5:30 TO 10 P.M. ; SUNDAY BRUNCH 9 A.M. TO 2 P.M. FULL BAR. ALL MAJOR CREDIT CARDS. 80% NONSMOKING. FULLY WHEELCHAIR ACCES-SIBLE. RESERVATIONS REQUIRED FOR EVERY MEAL EXCEPT BREAKFAST. EXPENSIVE.

From the moment Postrio opened two years ago, the restaurant was a hit. A cooking trio consisting of Los Angeles cooking star Wolfgang Puck and Anne and David Gingrass, a married couple who worked in Puck restaurants and moved up here to run Postrio, were responsible for the menu. The opening meals, served in a carefully managed dining room with restricted reservations, were spectacular. The restaurant was reviewed very early on and got the highest rating.

Recently I returned to Postrio for several visits and found that the food had slipped. Under the relentless pressures of full houses seven days a week, three meal a day, the kitchen seemed to be performing on automatic pilot.

Of course, people love Postrio for reasons other than the food. It really is a tourist hot spot. Celebrities, local and southern Californian, find their way here. When people book a room at the Prescott Hotel, in which the restaurant is located, they get preferential reservations at the restaurant. This policy, plus its local popularity, make it difficult to get a table for dinner during prime hours. If you want to eat dinner at Postrio within two weeks or so of calling, it will be at 5:30 or 9 p.m. Lunch is an easier ticket. However, the bar area, the only place where you can order wood-fired pizzas and desserts, is always an alternative.

The cavernous main dining room down a dramatic flight of stairs has a La Coupole feeling to it. Like the famous Parisian cafe on the boulevard Montparnasse, noise bounces off the walls and high ceiling at a deafening pitch. Huge, pendulous light fixtures with serpent-like appendages hang from the ceiling, with other design curlicues super-imposed on a wooden, Victorian structure. Comfortable booths take up the center of the restaurant, but tables along the perimeter are too small and pushed too closely together.

The best Puck dishes, in my estimation, are the Chinese-French creations served at his Santa Monica restaurant Chinois. Several of these found their way onto the Postrio menu and they were prepared beautifully during opening weeks. Recently, they were a pale re-minder of their former glory. The Peking style roast duck, in my favorite salad at lunch, had a wonderful texture, but absolutely no seasoning, and the mango relish served next to a pile of tangy greens was astringently tart. At dinner, the soy vinaigrette on a salad of scallops with potato chips and greens was so salty, it was all I could taste. A lunch appetizer of stir-fried Hunanese-style lamb with mint and garlic in radicchio leaves was again so salty that I couldn't eat it and too vinegary as well. Was anyone tasting in the kitchen?

Other dishes on an intriguing and ambitious menu came out much better. A salad of thumb-sized leaves of young romaine, with garlic vinaigrette and parmesan croutons, impressed me as a produce buying coup. A dinner pasta of a grilled quail surrounded by delightful ravioli filled with soft cooked egg showed off some real kitchen wizardry. Smoked veal and parmesan tortelloni with pools of creamy, rosemary tomato sauce were tasty but achingly rich.

The wine list, printed on one long page, takes a magnifying glass to read, and it is weighted towards pricey wines. Desserts are intensely sweet and served in very large portions, real restaurant confections. Service on all occasions has been exemplary.

I know that Postrio's kitchens are capable of turning out better food because I've tasted it. Yet, the restaurant is full all the time, no matter what it serves. The cooks must feel like they are mass producing dishes when they need to be individually preparing them, to taste right. This kind of overwhelming popularity has affected the quality of the food, at one time or another, at every highly regarded restaurant that has opened in the past ten years. These kitchens have had to take a hard look at their menus and their staff in order to keep their cooking on track. From my recent experiences at Postrio, it's time for this kitchen to start from scratch on a lot of the dishes they are currently cranking out.

PATRICIA UNTERMAN

POZOLE ★★½

3337 MARKET STREET, SAN FRANCISCO. 626-2666. OPEN FRIDAY, SATURDAY, SUNDAY NOON TO 4 P.M., DINNER NIGHTLY 4 P.M. TO MIDNIGHT. BEER AND WINE. CASH ONLY. 100% NONSMOKING. PARTIALLY WHEELCHAIR ACCESSIBLE. NO RESERVATIONS. INEXPENSIVE.

Pozole takes the concept of a taqueria to new heights. This whimsically decorated storefront shop puts out the most imaginative menu of burritos, quesadillas, Mexican soups, and salads in the city. Chef/owner Jesse Acevedo's use and understanding of authentic, regional Mexican ingredients keeps his cooking deliciously rustic while his signature flair for color and presentation gives these usually humble dishes a fantastic new set of clothes.

When you order at the muraled counter at the back of the restaurant, you are given a numbered stand which you set on your table. Someone from the kitchen runs out the dishes you order, course by course, so you get some of the convenience of table service even if you have to order and pay before you sit down.

Every dish has a new twist, a different look, a spectrum of flavors. *Sopa Tarasca*, a smooth puree of pinto beans is subtly seasoned with smoky *chipotles* and a palette of other dry red chiles. It is served in a pottery crock with crumbly *queso fresco* and warm tortilla strips, drizzled with Mexican crema. Pozole is a lighter soup based on a tomatoey chicken broth seasoned with lime and roasted green chiles. Big white kernels of hominy, or pozole, and the tortilla strips give this refreshing soup texture.

Ensalada do Brazil, a beautiful pale green salad of jicama, hearts of palm, and cucumber slices on a bed of perfect baby romaine leaves is dressed in a *mezcal*, lime, and oregano vinaigrette perked up with roasted chiles; a juicy and delicious way to start a meal here.

The quesadilla, a Mexican version of a grilled cheese sandwich except that flour tortillas are used instead of bread, takes on new forms here. Quesadilla Baja oozes with mild Mexican cheese, mushrooms, black beans, corn, and tomatoes. Like many of the dishes here, the quesadilla is served with a colorful pile of salsa/salad of cucumber, tomato, black beans, corn, red onion, and chiles on shredded romaine.

Burritos are another main taqueria item and Mr. Acevedo's have lighter fillings. Burrito Maya, for example, is filled with a luscious mixture of tender pork stewed in an achiote-orange-tequila sauce mixed with a few black beans, fresh corn kernels and rice, which makes for a savory, juicy, slightly fruity filling.

The kitchen works wonders with *masa harina*, or cornmeal, used in tamales and Salvadorean *papusas*. An unusual *papusa*, a fluffy, hand-patted pancake of cornmeal is stuffed and topped with braised pork and served on a bed of black beans and fried bananas with Pozole's wonderful, smoky chipotle chile salsa on the side. Airy, soft, Oaxacan tamales are stuffed with prunes and topped with a chunky fresh mango salsa and sliced bananas. They rest on aromatically seasoned black beans scattered with *queso fresco* and garnished with the chipotle salsa and a chile-spiked salad. The whole, sweet, savory, highly unusual combination works like an Indian charm. The non-tortilla based dishes aren't quite as exciting.

There are well chosen drinks to accompany the food. The fruity, refreshing sangria is one way to go; imported Mexican beers another. You can get bottles or glasses of excellent Spanish wines as well. For dessert Pozole makes fabulous ice creams, some of the best I've tasted.

Mr. Acevedo has opened a place that meets his own high standards of originality and fun. Pozole is a brilliant, well run, fast-food restaurant that draws on the best of traditional, ethnic, and avant garde culinary ideas in a highly personal way.

PATRICIA UNTERMAN

PRIMA ★½

1522 NORTH MAIN ST., WALNUT CREEK (TAKE THE WALNUT CREEK EXIT OF 24, GO STRAIGHT FOR SEVERAL BLOCKS, TURN LEFT ON MAIN ST.). 935-7780. OPEN FOR LUNCH MONDAY THROUGH THURSDAY FROM 11:30 A.M. TO 3 P.M.; DINNER FROM 5 TO 9:30 P.M., FRIDAY AND SATURDAY 11:30 A.M. TO 10 P.M. FULL BAR. VISA, MASTERCARD. 75% NONSMOKING. PARTIALLY WHEELCHAIR ACCESSIBLE. RESERVATIONS ESSENTIAL. MODERATE.

What first caught my eye about Prima in Walnut Creek was not the menu but the wine list. Prima has a wine store in the back, a comfortable, attractive Italian restaurant in the front, and a tasting bar in between. The first bit of news is that Prima demonstrates that the tasting of wine in a restaurant can be as appealing a prospect as the ordering of food. The wine prices here are outright bargains. Moreover, if you're a twosome, you have a good alternative to getting a whole bottle of wine and then worrying about driving home.

■ EGGPLANT THAT IS ROASTED IN OLIVE OIL MAINTAINS ITS TEXTURE, AND THE DISH IS ENLIVENED BY A LIGHT SAUCE THAT INCLUDES GOAT CHEESE.

Consider this: You can choose from a list of about twenty wines, mostly from Italy and California, by the glass or by the taste. There's also a special comparative tasting each night; my first dinner it was tastes of six different California and Oregon pinot noirs for $9.95.

Prima turns out to be a very pleasant place to eat, decorated in grays and pinks, with a pianist playing soft jazz, and with several tables outdoors for lunches and balmy nights. The menu consists mainly of appetizers and an interesting list of pastas; there are only a couple of meat entrees. I had problems with about half the dishes here; some were too bland and others, I felt, needed higher-quality ingredients. But the other half I found both interesting and well-executed, and you can have a completely first-rate meal if you order some of these.

Pasta prima, a vegetarian dish rivaled in that category only by the cooking at Greens, heads the list. Each vegetable is done separately, some steamed and others sauteed. Meanwhile, homemade angel hair noodles are tossed with pesto sauce. Then the vegetables—including carrots, mushrooms, broccoli, snow peas, eggplant, yellow squash, and sun-dried tomatoes—get mixed with the pasta. Finally, the pasta and vegetables are laid on a bed of marinara sauce. Another perfect combination of ingredients comes with the lasagne. Lasagne noodles are baked with goat and ricotta cheeses, onions, garlic, ground beef, tomato sauce, herbs, and spinach Florentine, which includes basil, nutmeg, and parmesan cheese. Delicacy is the keyword here; you can pick out almost every ingredient in the bouquet of flavors. A third pasta to consider is the tortellini stuffed with ground veal and herbs, and served in a commendably light gorgonzola cheese sauce with prosciutto and snow peas.

There are a couple of simple but satisfying starters. A whole boiled artichoke comes with a great aioli, the garlic mayonnaise flavored with fresh tarragon and dijon mustard. Eggplant that is roasted in olive oil maintains its texture, and the dish is enlivened by a light sauce that includes goat cheese.

The excellent homemade Prima desserts include an unusual version of tiramisu; it's a chocolate-rum sponge cake with a cream cheese frosting. A light and creamy cheesecake has a strawberry sauce capturing the essence of fresh strawberries, while a walnut tart avoids the pitfall of being too goopy.

STAN SESSER

228

R & G LOUNGE ★★

631 KEARNEY (BETWEEN CLAY AND SACRAMENTO), SAN FRANCISCO. 982-7877.
OPEN 11 A.M. TO 9:30 P.M. MONDAY THROUGH SATURDAY. BEER. MASTERCARD
AND VISA. 60% NONSMOKING. NOT WHEELCHAIR ACCESSIBLE. NO RESERVA-
TIONS. INEXPENSIVE.

A perpetual hotspot in Chinatown turns out to be a small, claustro-
phobic restaurant in a basement with the unlikely name of a corner
bar. The kitchen, three times the size of the dining room, manufac-
tures wholesale dim sum, but it also prepares a mean deep-fried catfish
and a glorious crab for sit-down diners. Owned by a former dim sum
chef from the Canton Tea House, the R & G Lounge has become
wildly popular for fresh seafood and low, low prices.

Because of its popularity and small size, customers are allowed as
little time at table as possible. The dining room has a few small square
tables, the rest being large rounds. If your party is less than six or eight,
chances are you will end up sharing a table, especially at lunch when
financial district workers pour in.

The discomfort is assuaged by the sparkling freshness of the fish and
seafood. The catfish, kept in a tank in the dining room, put up such a
fight when they are netted that they splash the nearby tables. In Hong
Kong the best cooks use live seafood and can make distinctions
between the fish swimming in the tank. The liveliest fish of the right
size and age for its particular species cost the most. I'd say that the R &
G catfish netted for us was at its optimum. The good-sized fish,
expertly fileted, crisply deep-fried and seasoned with wilted scallions,
ginger and soy sauce, had sweet, pure flesh without a trace of muddi-
ness. Likewise, a whole crab stir fried with ginger and scallions had
remarkably succulent, delicate meat that almost melted in our mouths.

Whole shrimp butterflied in their shells, dusted with white pepper
and salt and deep-fried are spicy and rich. A beautiful dish of bean
sprouts and Chinese chives, tossed with paper-thin slices of conch and
geoduck clam, is one of the nicest dishes, though it isn't on the menu.
You have to ask for it because geoduck is not always available. On the
menu is the fantastic Braised Catfish with Double Bean Curd Stick, a
hearty clay pot stew of big chunks of catfish braised with fresh bacon,
pork cracklings, and browned rectangles of tofu that absorb the
marvelous cooking juices. Notable for their tenderness and sweetness
are sliced sea scallops, coated with a spicy salt and pepper mixture, and
deep-fried. Bright pink shrimp steamed whole with head and shells
look gorgeous on a platter of subtle garlic sauce tinted pale pink by the
shrimp.

R & G is a very simple restaurant, specializing in catfish, crab and
shrimp. Don't expect great noodles, soups, or poultry. If you know to

order from the small selection of perfectly fresh fish, you too will be joining the cognoscenti jockeying for a table.

PATRICIA UNTERMAN

REGINA'S ★★½

490 GEARY BLVD., SAN FRANCISCO. 885-1661. OPEN DAILY FOR CONTINENTAL BREAKFAST 6 TO 9 A.M.; LUNCH NOON TO 2 P.M.; DINNER 6 TO 11 P.M., UNTIL MIDNIGHT FRIDAY AND SATURDAY; BRUNCH SATURDAY AND SUNDAY 10 A.M. TO 2 P.M. FULL BAR. ALL MAJOR CREDIT CARDS. 50% NONSMOKING. FULLY WHEELCHAIR ACCESSIBLE. RESERVATIONS ACCEPTED. EXPENSIVE.

Regina's serves rich New Orleans-style dishes in a clubby dining room across the street from San Francisco's two major theaters. While sitting down to deep-fried seafood napped in butter sauce may not be conducive to staying awake through the first act, this restaurant represents a true outpost of Creole cooking. Nothing is "Californiaized," or lightened to local tastes. The chef, Regina Charbonneau, flies ingredients up from the Delta and prepares the dishes with pure conviction.

Located on the first floor of a small hotel, the lobby-like, el-shaped dining room is comfortably furnished with substantial chairs and decorated with potted plants and lithographs. One wall displays a collection of Mardi Gras masks. A bar at the entryway is much used as a meeting place for theater-goers.

Regina's weekend brunch offers an extensive menu of New Orleans favorites like *beignets,* warm, square doughnuts dusted with powdered sugar; and *Pain Perdu,* slices of delicately orange-scented French toast made with brioche bread, smothered in warm strawberry and blueberry compote. Eggs Hussarde brings together thin slices of smoky ham, a tomato slice, a tomatoey meat glaze, two perfectly poached eggs, and a blanket of bearnaise on top of toasted French bread. Regular eggs served with apple-cured ham or bacon are dressed up with a side of corn grits topped with melted cheese, a small stack of pancakes made with corn meal and corn kernels served with molasses syrup. A large filet of pan fried catfish in a crunchy cornmeal breading comes with three silky-centered crab and eggplant fritters.

On top of all this, everyone gets a warm, buttery, buttermilk biscuit and an elegant, yeasted, fresh blueberry muffin, the best I have tasted. The buttermilk biscuits are the first thing that comes to you at dinner, as well, along with light, crumbly corn muffins. Any kitchen that can bake like this makes a great first impression.

Dark brown corn and crab bisque, a chunky soup made with a smoky brown roux and lots of crab is an excellent starter. So is Regina's shrimp remoulade, which employs large, fresh, chilled shrimp in a shalloty mayonnaise seasoned with Creole mustard.

One of the tastiest main courses features large shrimp split and stuffed with seasoned spinach, then battered, deep-fried and topped with toasted almonds and butter to create a kind of shrimp amandine. A whole spectrum of crunchy textures happens in each bite. Chicken breast is handled well in *Poulet Acadien*, staying moist and juicy in a ragout of spinach, cream, crawfish tails, and reduced stock. Eggplant Lafayette brings thin slices of fried eggplant topped with a mound of garlicky creamed shrimp and crab, surrounded by a tomato *coulis*.

If you can even think about dessert after a meal here, warm *beignets* stuffed with ice cream topped with praline sauce, old fashioned vanilla custard-filled chocolate eclairs or bananas Foster, that delicious classic of bananas sauteed in butter, brown sugar, and rum, will satisfy the urge—for the whole week.

PATRICIA UNTERMAN

RICE TABLE ★★★

1617 FOURTH STREET, SAN RAFAEL. 456-1808. OPEN THURSDAY THROUGH SATURDAY, 5:30 TO 10 P.M., SUNDAY 5 TO 9 P.M. BEER, WINE. MAJOR CREDIT CARDS. 25% NONSMOKING. FULLY WHEELCHAIR ACCESSIBLE. RESERVATIONS RECOMMENDED. INEXPENSIVE.

In the restaurant world, when some places stay the same year after year it is cause to rejoice. The Rice Table in San Rafael is one of those places. When I first visited this little Indonesian restaurant over ten years ago, I couldn't believe how pretty and tasty the food was. It turned out that all the cooking was done by a diminutive and very energetic woman named Leonie Hool. Ms. Hool is still in the kitchen, putting out the rainbow of dishes that make up a traditional Dutch-inspired rice table.

The dining room is, as ever, clean and well kept up. Rattan matting serves as wall paper and rattan screens separate the batik covered tables from each other, making each one into a separate booth. Painted across one whole side of the room are the myriad islands that make up the country of Indonesia, the Spice Islands. When you taste the fragrant spices that are woven into the different dishes, the mural reminds you that the inhabitants of these islands were cooking with spices thousands of years before Europeans even knew of them.

The menu is short and simple. There are 11 dishes on it which can be ordered separately with accompanying soup, Indonesian salad, rice, and dessert. But the real way to eat here is to choose the Rice Table Dinner for two or more people which brings you all the dishes, as well as *lumpia*, pickles, and toasted coconut; or the Rice Table Special which gives you all of the above plus two more dishes thrown in. When every inch of the table is covered with little dishes of food, you wonder how you can ever come close to tasting it all. But sure enough, it disappears.

**■ THE RICE TABLE EXISTS BECAUSE OF MS. HOOL'S PAS-
SION TO COOK THE DISHES OF HER NATIVE ISLANDS. HER
CUSTOMERS BECOME PART OF AN EXTENDED FAMILY AND
THE FOOD GOES BEYOND DELIGHTING AND ENTICING.**

Try not to make a meal of a basket of extraordinarily crisp shrimp
chips brought to the tables with three *sambals*. One is a warm, creamy
peanut sauce spiked with chiles and cooled with ginger. A medium
hot, vinegary, fresh green chili and onion salsa, and a searing hot red
chili paste each take the level of hotness a notch higher. The meal
begins with a bowl of thin, celery-scented split pea soup, like a
flavorful Indian-style *dahl*.

The *lumpia*, deep-fried, noodle wrapped, mini-cigars, are stuffed
with savory pork and served with a creamy tomato sauce. An Indonesian cole slaw of shredded Chinese cabbage and carrots dressed with
tiny threads of orange peel and fresh mint leaves, and a salad of
crunchy bean sprouts and raw zucchini slices with chopped peanuts
also awakens the palate.

Next come the satays, a spectacular chicken brochette in sweet
sauce, and pork satay in a creamy peanut sauce. Shrimp, stir-fried with
whole pieces of tamarind with big, very hard square seeds, is one of the
best shrimp dishes I've tasted, but beware of the seeds. The combination of garlic and tamarind in a sharp, buttery sauce is superb.

Mushrooms sauteed with hot red chiles, tamarind, and butter are
velvety. A delicious beef stew called *semur* is aromatic with cloves; a
mild chicken curry in a coconut milk-based sauce is the most familiar
and Indian influenced of all the curries. Just to show how varied
Indonesian cuisine can be, the kitchen one night sent out crab and
bean sprout pancakes held together with eggs—kind of an Indonesian
egg foo young, with a tangy, sweet and sour tomato sauce. Filling out
the table are saucers of condiments like toasted, grated coconut,
pickled julienned vegetables, and cold, deep-fried potato sticks coated
in hot red chili paste. Both saffron rice and a nutty, white rice are
intrinsic to the meal, though thin fried rice noodles, lushly sauced and
studded with bits of pork and vegetables, are happily included too.

Dessert brings miraculously creamy, deep-fried bananas sprinkled
with powdered sugar, and cinnamony Indonesian coffee.

I feel so appreciative when a restaurant is able to keep up its
standards, energy, and spirit year after year. The Rice Table exists
because of Ms. Hool's passion to cook the dishes of her native islands.
Her customers become part of an extended family and the food goes
beyond delighting and enticing. It nourishes, in the deepest possible
way.

PATRICIA UNTERMAN

RODIN ★★

1779 LOMBARD STREET, SAN FRANCISCO. 563-8566. OPEN MONDAY THROUGH SATURDAY 3:30 TO 10 P.M. BEER AND WINE. ALL MAJOR CREDIT CARDS ACCEPTED. 75% NONSMOKING. FULLY WHEELCHAIR ACCESSIBLE. RESERVATIONS SUGGESTED. VERY EXPENSIVE.

Nouvelle French with Japanese overtones best describes the light, bright foods at Rodin, under the hand of Morgan Song.

The interior is elegantly understated in grays with light natural wood chairs. Lighting, bubble-style candle holders on the table, and black and white photos on the walls give a dramatic flair. Service is low key and efficient. In an almost Japanese-style, glasses are filled without pretense and dishes are brought to the table and placed before diners without interrupting the flow of dinner conversation.

The food is just as dramatic. Every presentation is crafted. Sauces are intense and used sparingly, and combinations often take the yin-yang approach balancing sweet and sour. However, the overall effect of the dish is subtle. Long tubes of squid stuffed with salmon and tied with chives are presented in a tomato and red pepper sauce that is so minimally used, it's difficult to distinguish flavors. The intense sweetness of papaya sauce on perfectly sliced duck breast is just the opposite. Although used as judiciously, the sweetness is 100 proof.

The wine list has less style than the food, though some good current-vintage wines by well-known producers are available. A good selection of pinot noir matches the lighter style of the food.

Desserts, including a delicious apple tart with nougatine ice cream, are rich without the corresponding nod to lightness, thank goodness.

MICHAEL BAUER

ROSALIE'S REDUX ★½

1415 VAN NESS AVENUE, SAN FRANCISCO. 923-1415. OPEN FOR LUNCH 11:30 A.M. TO 2 P.M. MONDAY THROUGH FRIDAY; DINNER 5:30 TO 11 P.M. NIGHTLY WITH A SUPPER MENU FROM 11 P.M. TO 12:30 A.M. TUESDAY THROUGH SATURDAY. FULL BAR. ALL MAJOR CREDIT CARDS. NON-SMOKING TABLES AVAILABLE. FULLY WHEELCHAIR ACCESSIBLE. RESERVATIONS SUGGESTED. EXPENSIVE.

Rosalie's Redux, even more than the first time around, is an ego restaurant. The flamboyant owner, Harry de Wildt, took the restaurant as his toy after it ran into financial snags and closed, thus resurrecting one of his favorite hangouts.

He's turned the place into a stage, with diners becoming both actors and audience. You'll notice many looking unabashedly into the mirrors, striking glamor poses, laughing a little too loudly, and tossing hair with extra flair. It's a place to be seen, and the Continental food is designed so as not to draw too much attention.

The surrealistic setting—aluminum palm trees, pink shaded lamps, and Pepto Bismol-colored walls—casts a blushing glow that makes the crowd look robustly healthy. Multilevel dining areas and mirrors that line the back wall afford a complete view of the room from just about every table.

The staff is well-trained, pleasant, and businesslike in their approach, so they don't compete with the decor or diners. It all adds up to a lot of fun. The crowd is affluent and eclectic: a black man with the sides of his hair shaved up to a loose wild mop on top is with an exotic, elegant Asian woman with hair a la Veronica Lake. An aging society matron with a Dina Merrill hairstyle caught in a gust of wind couldn't decide what to wear—so she wears it all: a thick gold chain around the neck (Nancy Reagan), a strand of pearls (Barbara Bush), and long dangling earrings (Cher, perhaps?).

The only thing without ego is the food. It's some of the most basic Continental I've seen since the '60s, with a little down-home thrown in for warmth. It's obvious the menu isn't the main attraction, but the execution is generally good, save for a chef who needs half the holes in his salt shaker blocked, and save for desserts that make you want to go on a diet.

A cramped presentation of prawns in an herb sauce with shallots and a dollop of anemic tomatoes tasted fine, except for the power dose of salt. Carpaccio, thin slices of raw beef, couldn't have been simpler. The ribbons of sauce tasted like mustard straight from the squeeze bottle, liberally sprinkled with capers.

Other appetizers broke no new culinary ground: cold poached salmon with horseradish cream, fried calamari with a raw flour taste, and more anemic tomatoes with mozzarella, and basil practically devoid of olive oil or other flavors. For main courses, the roll of sea bass with a chile-citrus butter was respectable, though it didn't shine— although the array of vegetables did: Brussels sprouts, red cabbage piquant with vinegar, corn, and julienned carrots. Thin slices of veal weighed down with wild mushrooms would have been much better if the salt had been restrained.

The one page wine list follows the same tried-and-true pattern as the food: It has drinkable selections, culled from well-known producers such as Jordan, Beringer, Sterling, Acacia, and Simi, all with a no-bargain markup.

For dessert, the only thing worth ordering is tiramisu. All other desserts suffer basic technical flaws. There's only one comment appropriate for such a dismal way to end a meal, and it's a quote from the bottom of the charge slip: "Really Harry."

MICHAEL BAUER

ROYAL THAI ★★★

610 THIRD ST., SAN RAFAEL (TAKE CENTRAL SAN RAFAEL EXIT FROM HIGHWAY 101).485-1074. OPEN MONDAY THROUGH FRIDAY 11 A.M. TO 2:30 P.M., SUNDAY THROUGH THURSDAY 5 TO 9:30 P.M., FRIDAY AND SATURDAY 5 TO 10 P.M. BEER, WINE. MAJOR CREDIT CARDS. 60% NONSMOKING. FULLY WHEELCHAIR ACCESSIBLE. RESERVATIONS RECOMMENDED ESPECIALLY ON WEEKENDS. INEXPENSIVE.

Royal Thai, in San Rafael, is housed in one of the most unlikely settings imaginable for a Thai restaurant. It's in one of the cutely restored Victorians that comprise a little shopping development called the French Quarter. No one from New Orleans—and certainly no one from Bangkok—would feel that they had been transported to their native city.

Pat Disyamonthon was a banker in Bangkok who came here to get his MBA. But he decided he was too old and too poor to be a student, so he took the first of what turned out to be seventeen different jobs at restaurants. One night he was working at a French restaurant when a friend, who owned San Francisco's Khan Toke Thai House, asked him to help out for an evening. He took one look at the dancer who was performing that night and fell in love.

Pat married the dancer and discovered he had also married a great cook. His wife Jamie runs the kitchen at Royal Thai. She tends to use less oil and less salt, and there's a cleaner feeling to the food. Thai food normally speaks of complexity, but at Royal Thai you get a sense of the ingredients—all of them impeccably fresh—standing out individually.

If you order the squid salad, you'll learn that when the menu says something is going to be hot, it's not fooling. Tender, fresh squid—mixed with lime juice, onions, lemongrass and lots of fresh mint—is roaring and raging. Less fiery but equally good is the Thai crepe. A rice flour wrapping, cooked to crispness and without a speck of grease, encloses a tasty blend of shrimp, pork, shredded coconut, tofu, and peanuts. There's a wonderful contrast of textures and tastes.

There are some great entrees at prices you'd pay at any dumpy Thai restaurant in San Francisco. Roast duck curry presents a big bowl of tender, fat-free chunks of duck with tomatoes and green peppers in a light, aromatic sauce. Sliced pork stir-fried with eggplant and lots of Thai basil in a black bean sauce features eggplant that retains its texture and isn't a bit oily. And the barbecued chicken once again demonstrates that the Thais can do this dish better than any American restaurant.

You should also try the stir-fried vegetables with garlic and yellow curry. All the vegetables at Royal Thai are impeccable; nothing is ever overcooked.

If you were seeking a great Thai dining experience, a cutesy New Orleans-style development under the freeway in San Rafael would hardly be the first place you'd look. But in that unlikely location, Royal Thai manages to turn out some of the best Asian food in the Bay Area at real bargain prices.

STAN SESSER

SAMUI ★★

2414 LOMBARD ST. NEAR SCOTT, SAN FRANCISCO. 563-4405. OPEN 11:30 A.M. TO 2:30 P.M. MONDAY THROUGH SATURDAY AND 5 TO 10:30 P.M. NIGHTLY. BEER, WINE. MASTERCARD, VISA, AMERICAN EXPRESS. 40% NONSMOKING. FULLY WHEELCHAIR ACCESSIBLE. RESERVATIONS RECOMMENDED ESPECIALLY ON WEEKENDS. INEXPENSIVE.

Samui Island (Koh Samui) is off the east coast of Thailand, a member in good standing of the International Hippie Beach Circuit. That means you can stay in a bungalow for two dollars a night right on a beautiful, unspoiled beach, gazing at the crystal-clear water and thinking how lucky you were to have given up your job selling vacuum cleaners. But it doesn't necessarily mean you eat well; while I found the food on Samui quite decent, it was nothing compared to what goes on in the rest of Thailand.

I guessed I missed the best place, however, because a Samuian (if that's the word for it) restaurant has transplanted itself to San Francisco, and much of its food is absolutely wonderful. It's appropriately called Samui, next to Scott's on Lombard Street. Samui looks like it could be a steakhouse—a very pleasant place to eat, but about as Thai as a Denny's. But the menu makes up for the lack of Thai atmosphere. Anyone who complains that the menu of every Thai restaurant is exactly the same should try Samui, where there are several dishes I've never seen before, either here or in Thailand.

Some of the most interesting and most successful dishes at Samui appear among the appetizers. It's worth a trip alone for the crispy fried catfish. The catfish is minced, deep-fried, then tossed with lemon juice, fresh chilies, shallots, bean sprouts, peanuts, and red onions. A close second is the chopped roast duck. This is the essence of duck; little pieces of tender meat with no fat or skin, mixed with toasted rice, red onions, mint leaves, lemon juice, and a lime sauce that adds considerable heat to the enterprise. Other outstanding appetizers include the fluffy Thai crepes with shredded coconut in the batter, stuffed with shrimp, pork, bean curd, and ground peanuts; roaring-hot squid tossed with lime juice, chilies, onions, lemongrass and mint leaves, and fabulous eggplant mixed with minced prawns in a spicy lime sauce.

Samui's curries are the high spot of the entree list. The boneless duck curry served on a bed of bright green New Zealand spinach is near miraculous, the meat without a hint of fat, the spicy aromatic sauce a pretty orange color from the blending of coconut milk and tomatoes. Slices of boneless chicken with yellow curry and chunks of sweet potatoes are outstanding also. The Samui seafood combo is very much worth sampling, particularly if you like dishes that will send you running to the nearest fire extinguisher. This is a three-alarm special, with a variety of fresh-tasting fish and seafood, green beans, carrots, and what must be the Bay Area's hottest red chilies.

STAN SESSER

SAN BENITO HOUSE ★★½

356 MAIN STREET, HALF MOON BAY. 726-3425. OPEN FOR DINNER THURSDAY THROUGH SUNDAY 6 TO 9 P.M., FOR BRUNCH SUNDAY 10:30 A.M. TO 1:30 P.M. FULL BAR. MASTERCARD, VISA, AMERICAN EXPRESS. NO SMOKING IN DINING ROOM. PARTIALLY WHEELCHAIR ACCESSIBLE. RESERVATIONS ACCEPTED. MODERATE.

Half Moon Bay is a picturesque town on Highway 1, about an hour south of the city. The mild microclimate makes it a good area for growing peas, pumpkins, and a variety of leafy green vegetables. Its short main street of wooden buildings and irrepressible patches of flowers looks like small town America; indeed, the biggest event of the year is the Half Moon Bay Pumpkin Festival.

The San Benito House sits at the foot of Main Street, the most imposing building in town. A quaint Victorian inn with a perpetually busy, smoke-filled saloon in front, and a contrastingly genteel parlor-like dining room in the back, it is the place where you would naturally stop on a trip down the coast. Now, on Thursday through Sunday nights and for brunch on Sunday, it has become a destination in its own right.

The dining room looks out onto a deck and garden through French doors. Freshly picked flowers and sprigs of herbs from the restaurant's gardens decorate the tables which are covered with flower printed tablecloths. Wrought iron chandeliers and candles provide flickering light. Oil paintings of the local landscape, and farm-house tables and cupboards arranged with flowers, dishes, and cooking implements look natural in this rustic room.

The cooking matches the homey setting. When you sit down, a basket of warm, freshly baked, country breads are brought to the table, exceptional for their crunchy crusts, and soft, yeasty, aromatic interiors.

One evening's prix fixe dinner began with a salad of paper-thin slices of raw fennel, parmesan, kumquats, and sprigs of watercress in a lemon and olive oil dressing, simultaneously refreshing and stimulating to the palate. The next course brought a bowl of rich risotto, Italian rice cooked with wild and domestic mushrooms, smoked prosciutto, and a lot of thyme.

Each night diners are offered a choice of three main courses. This has included a pair of perfectly sauteed quail with crisp skin and pink, juicy meat in a nest of chard with scalloped potatoes and two bunches of tiny, fresh Zante currants marinated in brandy. A barely sweet wine sauce on the bottom of the plate melded the flavors together. A tender, cured pork chop comes smothered in grilled red onions accompanied with spinach and polenta. A smart tarragon-caper butter melted under the onions onto the pork.

A well-chosen, reasonably priced, small California wine list features aromatic, dry white rieslings made by neighboring Obester winery. Another welcome feature of the list is the selection of half bottles, especially convenient for those who like both a white and red wine with dinner, but face a twisty drive over the coastal hills to get home.

Desserts are a highpoint of the meal. A delicate, crisp-topped bread pudding with apricot and currant-studded custard vies with a hazelnut shortcake of unseasonably sweet strawberries and softly whipped cream for sheer pleasure. An ice cream terrine with a fudgey chocolate center is wonderful too.

Sunday brunch offers the same kind of straightforward appeal that comes from use of honest ingredients. Irresistible eggs Benedict get a purely classical preparation. One Sunday, a crisp tortilla was spread with pureed red beans, poached eggs, and melted mozzarella, the whole topped with a spicy ranchero sauce. Another choice brought a whole trout baked in parchment, carefully seasoned with lemon zest. Breads and muffins, warm from the oven, are worth a trip alone.

All too often quaint country inns serve a lot of frozen or processed foods on some pretty stodgy menus. The San Benito House has renewed my faith in the genre. It has the advantage of having its own garden but it is close enough to the city to get fresh ingredients that aren't raised locally. No compromises are made here.

PATRICIA UNTERMAN

SASIPIM'S THAI RESTAURANT ★★½

16 MAIN STREET, TIBURON. 435-3834. OPEN 11:30 A.M. TO 10:30 P.M. DAILY, FRIDAY AND SATURDAY UNTIL 11 P.M. BEER, WINE. 100% NONSMOKING. FULLY WHEEL-CHAIR ACCESSIBLE. RESERVATIONS RECOMMENDED. INEXPENSIVE.

Many Thai restaurants in the Bay Area are run by people who may be good home cooks, but who lack professional training. Their talents as chefs are often redeemed by the exotic and enticing flavors of Thai cuisine.

Sasipim's in Tiburon is different because the professionalism in the kitchen is evident. The chef, Amporn Saysaray, studied cooking in

■ TENDER SPINACH LEAVES ARE ARRANGED ON A PLAT-
TER AROUND SMALL BOWLS OF TOASTED COCONUT, PEA-
NUTS, LIME PULP, DICED GINGER, DRIED SHRIMP, DICED
PEPPERS, AND A SAUCE TO MOISTEN IT. YOU FILL THE
LEAVES WITH THE VARIOUS MIXTURES TO CREATE A
MAGICAL BLEND.

Thailand and has been at the restaurant since shortly after it opened in February 1989. The 85-seat restaurant is owned by Joe Kaharick, the former vice president of a development firm, and his wife, Sasipim Nuanual, who owns an engineering firm.

The chef's talent shows in butterfly garnishes crafted from daikon radishes, flower-cut red onions, and thin threads of raw carrots that add color, flavor, and texture to most dishes. At Sasipim's, you pay a bit more for some items, but the results are worth it.

Stuffed chicken wings, for example, have a perfect texture because of uniformly minced chicken flecked with herbs and woven with glistening threads of clear noodles and equally delicate threads of carrots. *Gaeng Keow Wahn*, a green curry with chicken, is presented with turned potatoes, rather than the uneven chunks you often find. The flavor is more refined, too. Although the chef starts with the same packaged curry base used at many restaurants, he embellishes it with fresh ingredients, creating a clean-tasting sauce redolent of coconut milk and basil.

Whole fried catfish is presented on a plate garnished with a nest of thread-like cut carrots, a purple onion flower, and lettuce. It is served with two sauces: a standard spicy chile sauce and a creamy coconut-curry sauce.

Every dish is worth recommending. One of the best is *Miang Khum*, an appetizer of tender spinach leaves arranged on a platter around small bowls of toasted coconut, peanuts, lime pulp, diced ginger, dried shrimp, diced peppers, and a sauce to moisten it. You fill the leaves with the various mixtures to create a magical blend.

I usually avoid desserts at Asian restaurants, but I'd come back just for the coconut ice cream. It had the intense essence found in a sorbet. Sweet sticky rice, topped with a tangy yogurt-style sauce and mango slices, is delicious. Although the tapioca in coconut milk pudding may at first seem a little bland and slippery, the dessert soon becomes addictive.

The 30-item wine list at Sasipim's has been chosen with care, including California pinot noirs, French rhones, and other reds that are excellent with the intensely flavored food.

Sasipim's is one of the best Thai restaurants in the Bay Area.

MICHAEL BAUER

SINGAPORE MALAYSIAN RESTAURANT ★★

836 CLEMENT STREET, SAN FRANCISCO. 750-9518. OPEN FROM 11:30 A.M. TO 10 P.M. DAILY. BEER, WINE. MASTERCARD, VISA. 50% NONSMOKING. PARTIALLY WHEELCHAIR ACCESSIBLE. RESERVATIONS ACCEPTED. INEXPENSIVE.

Malaysia is a melting-pot society whose cuisine has dishes originating in Indonesia, China, Thailand, and many other places. I don't know whether it's this lack of distinctiveness, or the small number of Malaysians in the Bay Area, but the few times I've heard about a Malaysian restaurant in these parts, they had disappeared by the time I got there to try them.

But now I've found a Malaysian restaurant still in business—actually flourishing—and it's a total delight. It's called Singapore Malaysian, run by a Malaysian family of Chinese origin. The owner, Siong Tan, employs his brother, sister, and brother-in-law, and he and his brother-in-law do the cooking. The menu sounds heavily Chinese, but the food actually tastes nothing like Chinese. Many of the dishes incorporate the fish paste and shrimp paste that are staples of Malaysia; the spices come from Malaysia, and the restaurant mixes the curry powder itself, to produce authentically Malaysian curries.

Prices here are remarkably low. You also get a lot more than typical Clement Street slap-it-on-the-table service. The waiters are friendly and helpful, and they're happy to bring out dishes one at a time.

Before I get into the food, a little word of warning. Fish paste and shrimp paste are a fermented product, just like the fish sauce in Vietnamese cooking, and not every Western palate exactly embraces the stuff. There are enough dishes without it at Singapore Malaysian to make several fine meals. But if you avoid things like the sauteed green beans because of the fish paste, you're going to be missing some spectacular dishes. This dish has sweet, tender al dente stringbeans in a sauce that includes lemongrass, chilies and onions, and it's one of the most wonderful vegetable dishes I can ever remember eating.

Among the small list of appetizers, two stand out. The satay mixes beef, pork and chicken, with the flavorful meat marinated in lemongrass and coconut milk, grilled, and served with a peanut dipping sauce that includes lemongrass, turmeric, onions and garlic. What's called "Chinese spring rolls" aren't very Chinese at all. The ingredients—egg, shrimp, bean sprouts, jicama, and carrots—are cooked first, then assembled in a thin rice-paper wrapper. If you want an appetizer that's very Malaysian and very unique, try the *rojah*, a cold salad of apple, pineapple, cucumber chunks and bean sprouts, tossed with a dressing that includes shrimp paste.

The centerpiece of Malaysian food is the curries, flavorful and aromatic, but not nearly as hot as Thai or Indian curries. Chicken curry presents a peasant-like stew of chunks of chicken on the bone and potatoes in a rich sauce that tastes of coconut milk. There's also a whole pompano pan-fried in curry powder, turmeric and onions; this is one of the rare pompanos I've had in an Asian restaurant that didn't taste frozen and fishy. Noodles are a staple of Malaysian food, and the two noodle dishes I tried here were excellent. *Chow u mee* is a complete change of pace from other dishes that are spicy or taste of fish paste; these are thin pan-fried noodles tossed with shrimp, bok choy, fish balls, and pork slices, and coated with a mild but flavorful sauce based on sharply reduced chicken broth. *Chow kway teo* by contrast is a huge platter of broad rice noodles with bean sprouts, prawns and clams, in a fiery sauce of chilies and garlic.

STAN SESSER

690 ★★★

690 VAN NESS, SAN FRANCISCO. 255-6900. OPEN FOR LUNCH MONDAY THROUGH FRIDAY 11:30 A.M. TO 2 P.M.; DINNER MONDAY THROUGH FRIDAY 5.30 TO 10:30 P.M., UNTIL 11 P.M. SATURDAY; SUNDAY BRUNCH 11 A.M. TO 2:30 P.M. AND DINNER 5 TO 9 P.M. FULL BAR. VISA, MASTERCARD, AMERICAN EXPRESS. 70% NONSMOKING. FULLY WHEELCHAIR ACCESSIBLE. RESERVATIONS SUGGESTED. EXPENSIVE.

In the two years since opening, 690 has evolved into a whimsical, fun restaurant—a tropical oasis planted in what was once a carburetor repair shop. The soaring industrial ceiling with sky lights and open beams is softened by lots of plants and colorful hand-carved wooden fauna from Bali. The aqua, pink, and yellow accents help to carry out the tropical motif.

The restaurant has become so popular, in fact, that the majority of the bar area has been converted to table service. This section is defined by a loosely hanging canvas oil painting wrapping around three sides, featuring scantily clad bodies frisking in the ocean.

The main dining area, on the other side of the double-sided bar, is defined by large canvas umbrellas hanging over cloth-covered tables. A mezzanine is perched over this area, affording a panoramic view of the open kitchen and bustling activity below.

It's a toss up as to whether the food or the crowd is livelier. Patrons seem to feel at home in anything—Spandex biking pants with leather jackets or button down shirts and tweed sport coats. There's always a boisterous crowd at the bar and always something to watch. However, noise can be deafening, even with the newly installed carpet in the dining area.

The food comprises a smorgasbord of exciting flavors from the tropics, as conceived by Jeremiah Tower and the chef, David Robins. The one dish not to miss is the barbecued baby back pork ribs, that come out of the kitchen succulent and blanketed in an acidic-sweet sauce redolent of ginger. Taking the barbecue theme to playful heights, he pairs the ribs with a potato salad accented with preserved lemons and fresh rosemary.

Fried calamari is placed on a crisp lentil cake and drizzled with an electric-yellow saffron sauce. Lamb is marinated with cardamom and punched up with red curry and couscous. Oysters are deep-fried and served with sprightly tomatillo salsa and rich smoky chile mayonnaise.

The playful blends extend to the main course fish dishes, too. Red snapper gets a cross-cultural boost with a pumpkin seed sauce and mint eggplant relish, or it may be served on a bed of spicy black beans and a light-fruit salsa. Salmon may be encrusted in an intense Sichuan peppercorn crust, or poached and served with a spicy-sweet papaya salsa.

Desserts are limited to about three a night. The signature item is a tropical trifle consisting of a rich blend of cake, fluffy mascarpone cheese and fresh fruit.

Early on there were some real problems with service, but most have been corrected. It's still not up to the caliber of Stars, but if you take a laid-back tropical attitude—easy to do in such surroundings— you'll be able to escape the everyday traumas of big-city living.

MICHAEL BAUER

SOL Y LUNA ★★½

475 SACRAMENTO STREET, SAN FRANCISCO. 296-8696. OPEN MONDAY THROUGH THURSDAY FROM 11:30 A.M. TO 11 P.M., UNTIL MIDNIGHT FRIDAY, 5 P.M. TO MID-NIGHT SATURDAY. FULL BAR. MASTERCARD, VISA, AMERICAN EXPRESS. 50% NONSMOKING. FULLY WHEELCHAIR ACCESSIBLE. RESERVATIONS RECOM-MENDED. MODERATE.

One expects old wood, tile, and hanging Serrano hams at a tapas bar, but at Sol y Luna, the chic new tapas restaurant in the Financial District, you get leather, metal, stone, and plaster. From the moment you push open the glass and chrome doors and walk into a starkly modern, abstractly designed room, you realize that both the surroundings and the vaguely Spanish food have been radically rethought.

I find the revisionism at Sol y Luna to be exciting, especially when it comes to the food. Chef Amaryll Schwertner, whose eccentric and experimental cooking surfaced at other well-regarded restaurants, has developed a stunning repertoire of dishes for Sol y Luna. Though these creations resemble nothing one ever tastes in Seville or Madrid, they do start off with Spanish ingredients like seafood, salt cod, olives, sherry vinegar, saffron, and rice. Schwertner adds winter squashes, goat cheese, yams, local oysters, mangos, chiles, and tomatillos from the Americas, so the menu becomes a panorama of Spanish and Latin

American flavors, tied together with stunning presentations on specially chosen pottery.

The lunch menu is the most traditional in format with soups, salads, and main courses. At night, the kitchen specializes in small, exotic compositions from an intriguing menu of tapas only. On Friday and Saturday nights, the tapas menu is augmented with main courses, though it is the tapas that are the most original and successful.

One evening superb *morcillas*, velvet textured blood sausages seasoned with sweet spices, shared a tapas plate with fruit-laced chicken sausage, garlicky chorizo, and a creamy chicken liver mousse spread on toast. Whether the blood sausages appear as a lunch entree with green lentils, warm artichokes, and spinach, or as a simple tapa with a roasted tomato, they deserve to be on the menu at all times. A black plate piled high with crisp, deep-fried squid can come with an orange-scented garlic mayonnaise or a spoonful of pepper-laced, *romesco* sauce. Spanish rice croquettes deliver the surprise of pinenuts and raisins, and enjoy a sharp, shalloty, citrus dipping sauce.

Sol y Luna makes the most appealing version of salt cod I've tasted. Served in a gratin dish with garlic mashed potatoes, a light, roasted tomato sauce, and a topping of big, crunchy bread crumbs, it joins the *morcillas* as a dish to return for. Other fine tapas have been skewers of juicy, marinated chicken breast simply served with a sour cream sauce aromatic with cilantro, cumin, mint, and achiote, and a refreshing Mediterranean orange salad with slices of blood oranges and navel oranges tossed with black olives, red onion, and tangy lettuces.

At lunch, a bacon-flavored chicken broth with al dente garbanzo beans, cabbage, and sweet potatoes comes to life with a buoyant seasoning of fresh mint and threads of lime and lemon peel. A pair of quail stuffed with fresh white cheese, pinenuts, sage, and breadcrumbs are succulent served over a warm salad of pumpkins and plantains sprinkled with mint. At weekend dinner one night, the kitchen made the delicious Spanish version of pasta called *fideus*, noodles cooked in broth like Italian risotto. In typical, offbeat, Sol y Luna style, the noodles were topped with crisp nuggets of deep- fried sweetbreads. Grilled rack of lamb chops, marinated in red Spanish wine, are tender and flavorful with a ragout of flageolet beans, mushrooms, and braised leeks.

Dessert proves how creative the kitchen can be with featherlight, sweet potato and raisin stuffed *empanadas*, or turnovers, served with sparkling Meyer lemon ice cream; an elegant, thin, plate-sized cream caramel with oceans of dark caramel; and a flat bowl of intense mango, strawberry, and passion-fruit sorbets that go well with a plate of fresh cookies.

PATRICIA UNTERMAN

SPLENDIDO'S ★★

NO. 4 EMBARCADERO, PODIUM LEVEL, SAN FRANCISCO. 986-3222. OPEN FOR LUNCH MONDAY THROUGH FRIDAY 11:30 A.M. TO 2:30 P.M.; BAR MENU AFTER 2:30 P.M.; DINNER 5:30 TO 10 P.M. MONDAY THROUGH SATURDAY. FULL BAR. ALL MAJOR CREDIT CARDS. 80% NONSMOKING. FULLY WHEELCHAIR ACCESSIBLE. RESERVATIONS RECOMMENDED. EXPENSIVE.

The interior of this Pat Kuleto designed restaurant is one of the splashiest to open in the last few years. He has masterfully transformed a space in the cold concrete Embarcadero Center into a spectacular Mediterranean oasis.

The entry is marked by a domed brick ceiling, in front of a pewter bar handmade in Portugal. The rugged rock walls, set with ledges banked with candles, give off a warm glow. There's a large oven in the middle of the room and a seating counter that extends in front of brick pizza oven, grill line and dessert preparation area.

There's a lot going on and it makes for fun dining. And so does the food, stylishly produced by Christopher Majer with bold flavors and presentations. This might include quail in a rich sauce of morel mushrooms or seared tuna encrusted with black pepper and served on a mound of chive-flavored potatoes and an orange-scented sauce. Pork chops are cooked to a pinkish white and served in a sauce studded with clams, chorizo and tomatoes, presented on a bed of chard. A particularly clever dish is a Napoleon of St. Pierre with layers of spinach and tomato confit, sandwiched between thin, crisp, fried potatoes.

In a more traditional mode, braised lamb shanks are served with pappardelle noodles, flageolets, and lemon zest. Majer makes risotto with tomatoes, tuna, capers, and anchovies that add a briny flavor. You can't go wrong with the pizza with a bread-like crust.

Desserts are fine, but not as good as the appetizers or main courses. Try the tiramisu layered in a martini style glass or a Beaujolais *granite* served with zippy black-pepper flecked butter cookies.

Although the food combinations at times don't hold together firmly, the flavors are bold and the dishes are fun to eat. Combined with the interior and warm service, Splendido's offers a truly festive experience.

MICHAEL BAUER

■ THE FOOD, STYLISHLY PRODUCED BY CHRISTOPHER MAJER, MIGHT INCLUDE QUAIL IN A RICH SAUCE OF MOREL MUSHROOMS OR SEARED TUNA ENCRUSTED WITH BLACK PEPPER AND SERVED ON A MOUND OF CHIVE-FLAVORED POTATOES AND AN ORANGE-SCENTED SAUCE.

SQUARE ONE ★★★½

190 PACIFIC AT FRONT, SAN FRANCISCO. 788-1110. OPEN FOR LUNCH MONDAY THROUGH FRIDAY FROM 11:30 A.M. TO 2:30 P.M.; DINNER SERVED MONDAY THROUGH THURSDAY 5:30 TO 10 P.M., UNTIL 10:30 P.M. FRIDAY AND SATURDAY, 5 TO 9:30 P.M. SUNDAY. FULL BAR. MAJOR CREDIT CARDS. SMOKING IN THE BAR ONLY. FULLY WHEELCHAIR ACCESSIBLE. RESERVATIONS RECOMMENDED. EXPENSIVE.

This large, airy, California-Mediterranean restaurant is the continuing work in progress of multi-talented Joyce Goldstein who brings an enormous amount of creativity and energy to what has become her passion. Each day the menu changes, offering a new set of Moroccan, Spanish, Italian, and provencal French dishes, with California-inspired compositions thrown in. A sophisticated new bar has been installed, decorated with a fantastic, surrealistic wall mural, which is worth a visit in itself. All sorts of wines and champagnes by the glass, and a blackboard list of small dishes are available there. A new, private dining room, with its own separate kitchen, has been opened, and the smart, main dining room has been outfitted with comfortable booths and Persian carpets, softening what had been a slightly austere room. There's no telling what will be next. In the meantime, Square One's kitchens continue to bake the best breads in town for their customers and turn out luscious, colorful, spice-laden dishes that combine authentic, rustic, and regional international recipes with Goldstein's skillful restaurant cooking techniques.

Meals might begin with a Middle Eastern mezza, a plate of roasted eggplant and peppers, blood orange and radish salad, stuffed grape leaves and marinated olives; or something as light and refreshing as a perfectly ripe avocado, grapefruit, and endive salad. A salad of warm asparagus with a pancetta dressing and sieved egg still stands out in my memory as the best asparagus dish I've tasted. Soups are thick and rich vegetables purees, full of intense flavor.

Main courses bring generously filled plates of grilled, marinated swordfish in a tart Moroccan sauce called *charmoula*, accompanied with grilled vegetables and roasted potatoes. The restaurant always offers a tasty grilled rib eye steak or lamb chops, with delicious potato gratins. Goldstein has a special love for the regional dishes of Italy. Her deep-fried risotto balls, filled with mozzarella, are famous in San Francisco and something as familiar as a pasta with Goldstein's incomparable, featherlight meatballs and fresh tomato sauce, turns out to be one of the best versions of this dish you'll ever encounter. A richly flavored, soupy paella, served in its own clay casserole, studded with shellfish, chicken, and housemade chorizo, is a winning Square One interpretation of this Spanish rice dish, as is seafood couscous with an aromatic broth and searing hot, housemade red chile sauce served on the side.

There's something for everyone on the carefully constructed menus. For those who aren't charmed by a *feijoada*, a Brazilian casserole of black beans, sausages, and cured pork and beef, served with orange salad and kale, there is a poussin, or small chicken, roasted and stuffed, or pristine grilled salmon served with spinach. Low-fat and low cholesterol dishes are always included and marked on the menu.

Desserts are rich and a little bit homey. Fresh fruit pies with housemade ice cream, dense chocolate cakes, plates of cookies; and hot fudge sundaes with toasted nuts will satisfy every sweet tooth. Service is friendly, efficient, and personable. The wine list, put together by Goldstein's master sommelier son, is extensive and pricey, though many fine bottles are available for those who care to explore it.

When San Francisco is ranked as one of the best restaurant cities in the world, it is because we support restaurants like Square One, with exciting, original menus, impeccable ingredients, and full, professional service in every way. Everything is truly made from scratch here, and that's what makes this restaurant so special.

PATRICIA UNTERMAN

ST. ORRES ★★★

6601 HIGHWAY 1 (ONE MILE NORTH OF GUALALA, ON THE RIGHT). (707) 884-3335. OPEN FOR DINNER 6 TO 9:30 P.M. SATURDAY AT 5:15 P.M. BEER, WINE. NO CREDIT CARDS. 100% NONSMOKING. PARTIALLY WHEELCHAIR ACCESSIBLE. RESERVATIONS NECESSARY. EXPENSIVE.

Located about 100 miles from San Francisco, just across the Sonoma County border in Mendocino, St. Orres is a restaurant that can hold it's own with big-city competition.

Yet it has such an elegantly rustic and distinctive look, you know you're in the country. The naturally-weathered exterior, featuring Russian-style turrets and stained-glass windows, is nestled into a tree-shaded environment with coastal hills on one side and a panoramic view of the ocean on the other. The main building, which houses the restaurant, has eight guest rooms with shared baths. A half mile up the road are eleven cabins with private baths and a large deck area with sauna and hot tub.

The dining room is located in one of the turrets, so the ceiling soars more than three stories, with plants and windows above your head, luring you to look skyward. The tablecloths, copper accents, and professional but friendly service, however, bring the focus back to the food. It all combines to make dining a special event.

You'll be hard pressed to find a better meal than that constructed by Rosemary Campiformia. She's a brilliant self-taught chef who has been cooking there five years. She creates some of the most innovative food, combined with creative presentations. The fixed-price three-course meal changes daily and features soup, main course, and salad; appetizers and desserts are extra.

The meal may begin with a creamy, hot, wild fennel soup that's totally seductive. The salad always has a dramatic twist such as baby greens mixed with Stilton, peppered walnuts and smoked apple vinaigrette, topped with two slices of jicama cut in a five-point star.

You'll probably want to indulge in several appetizers such as flaky puff pastry filled with dices of smoked boar and a round of warm breaded goat cheese, all resting in a pool of tomato-basil sauce.

Main courses always combine myriad flavors and preparations on one plate. Quail marinated in tequila and lime is presented on two yam-and-green-onion pancakes. Arranged around the quail is a quarter of red onion, fanned flower-like with two snow peas and two yellow beans tucked between the petals and a rosette of beet puree in front. There are also three wontons filled with duck, and two baby carrots and kohlrabi crisscrossed on the plate, which act as a platform for a delicate fried quail egg with a still-runny yolk.

There are generally six main courses each night such as sweetbreads, fillet of beef, rabbit, venison, and several fish specials.

Dessert may include individual huckleberry pies, with a marvelous filling and a great crust, or a dense-textured bread pudding studded with dried cherries and complemented with a caramel sauce and nutmeg ice cream.

It all adds up to a magical blend; particularly enticing if you decide to stay at the lodge and can spend a few minutes after the meal soaking in the hot tub under a star-filled sky.

MICHAEL BAUER

STARS ★★★★

750 REDWOOD ALLEY, SAN FRANCISCO. 861-7827. OPEN MONDAY THROUGH FRIDAY FOR LUNCH 11:30 A.M. TO 2:30 P.M.; DINNER NIGHTLY FROM 5:30 TO 10:30 P.M.; SUPPER MENU 10:30-11:30. FULL BAR. MAJOR CREDIT CARDS. 25% NONSMOKING. FULLY WHEELCHAIR ACCESSIBLE. RESERVATIONS RECOMMENDED. EXPENSIVE.

Stars earns four stars from me because I rarely finish a dinner there without being dazzled. Of all the restaurants in the city, Stars is one of the most exciting. The menu always contains three or four dishes that are so original in conception and brought off with such finesse that I'm won over. Chef/owner Jeremiah Tower has an instinct for knowing what people really want to eat and giving it to them in a stylish and savory form. His menus make your mouth water when you read them. It's as if he has divined your own secret food fantasies and figured out how to fulfill them in ways you never imagined.

Beyond the menu wizardry, Stars philosophy is to provide patrons with anything and everything they could possibly want in a cafe or restaurant. In the bustling center of the restaurant at the crowded bar, amidst the tiny cocktail tables, on narrow ledges, and at counters in front of the oyster station, people drink and eat casual things like pizzas, grilled fish burgers, and brochettes. They can drink glasses of fine champagne with a grilled hot dog, or a glass of beer instead. The whole kitchen is wide open, almost a part of the dining room, and certainly a part of the decor. This integration of kitchen and dining room adds a high level of energy to the room. I'm reminded of La Coupole, the great Parisian cafe on the Boulevarde Montparnasse that serves its patrons, from all levels of society, from early in the morning into the wee hours of the night.

At raised, cordoned off dining areas, customers of Stars eat lavish, rich, full scale meals. A recent dinner brought a saffron risotto topped with diced sea scallops barely poached in a clam liquor, the whole thing garnished with fried beet chips. As weird as this dish sounds, the combination was delicious. Another starter brought a tangle of battered, deep-fried, green beans tossed with chopped, pickled mushrooms, placed over slices of prosciutto, the whole plate drizzled with aioli.

You can expect to find something deep-fried, something drizzled, and something cured on most Jeremiah dishes. I suppose it does get redundant when a rare, juicy lamb loin with a thin, crisp potato gratin, and a ragout of artichokes and chanterelles is drizzled with aioli, after a first course so drizzled. Yet, somehow it all tastes so good that you forget that you've just had it on something else. Another main course, a crisp skinned little poussin, absolutely full of flavor, with baked white beans, celery root and turnip julienne, is drizzled with thyme-scented aioli. An exquisite preparation of salmon steamed in butter, covered with creamed mushrooms, surrounded by squashes and peppers merits a lobster sauce instead.

Desserts are very handsome but almost simple in comparison to the multi-faceted main courses and appetizers. In late fall, warm steamed pumpkin pudding comes with vanilla ice cream and caramel pecan sauce, and a classic cream puff is stuffed with a custard infused with ground hazelnuts and napped in warm chocolate sauce. Lemon chess pie has a lovely, generous filling of bright lemon curd garnished with ginger-scented whipped cream.

Service is always cordial, unpretentious, and as efficient as it can be, given the constant crowds. The wine list is long, international, and overpriced.

There are bound to be disappointments here—some of the wackier dishes don't satisfy; sometimes in the heat of turning out so many meals some aren't executed well, and it's all too easy to order two courses that taste the same. By the same token, many of the dishes are so original and well-prepared that you are willing to overlook the lapses. Stars shines on so many levels that it lives up to its name.

PATRICIA UNTERMAN

STARS CAFE ★★½

555 GOLDEN GATE AVENUE, SAN FRANCISCO. 861-4344. OPEN MONDAY-THURS-DAY 8:30 A.M. TO 10 P.M FOR BREAKFAST, LUNCH AND DINNER, 8:30 A.M. TO 11 P.M. FRIDAY, 10 A.M. TO 11 P.M. SATURDAY AND SUNDAY. FULL BAR. 40% NONSMOK-ING. PARTIALLY WHEELCHAIR ACCESSIBLE. MAJOR CREDIT CARDS. NO RESER-VATIONS ACCEPTED. MODERATE.

There's a warm, inviting European quality to Stars Cafe, the tiny sister restaurant next door to the much more glitzy Stars. It's a perfect place to go before the theater or opera, and since it's open daily for breakfast, lunch, and dinner, it's a prime spot for off-hours dining.

The food is as good in quality as you'll find at Stars, and often as imaginatively prepared. I'll admit that it's one of my favorite places in town but, regrettably, over the last few months, prices have inched up. It's still a good deal. You'll find such things as lightly breaded calamari with a chunky tomatillo salsa. One dish that continues to appear is the light fry—an absolutely irresistible blend of different fish, lightly dusted and quick fried, and served with fries and a container of malt vinegar.

Choose from six or seven entrees, such as crusty grilled skirt steak with creamy mashed potatoes and spinach, served with a generous dollop of garlicky aioli. Grilled pork tenderloin comes with eggplant puree, cumin-scented polenta, and a mushroom relish. Penne pasta is topped with confit duck and mushrooms, but it has a decidedly dull edge without any salt. In fact salt seems to be in short supply on many of the dishes.

For desserts the restaurant has begun to use the Stars dessert menu (and the same prices). However Emily Luchetti's creations are delicious, alternating between refined—such as different-flavored Napoleans—to American homespun including crisps and cobblers. When they're on the menu, head for the polenta pound cake or the warm gingerbread. The cookie plate, featuring regular and chocolate shortbreads, are always good to end the meal.

The interior features a long service bar with stools and a single row of tables. There's also an upstairs mezzanine. The pastry preparation area is located at the back of the restaurant, separated by a medal rack. About a year ago the Stars Fish and Chip operation was closed and the restaurant took over that small area. All this adds up to a feel that the restaurant just happened, rather than being planned and designed, which adds a warming psychological lift to the spirits. Service is friendly and enthusiastic, but there are not-so-subtle hints to turn tables, such as bringing the check with the desserts.

Overall eating at Stars Cafe is a great experience, but the slowly escalating prices are turning the cafe from a casual drop-in spot to a destination restaurant. Why does success always breed higher prices?

MICHAEL BAUER

SUSIE KATE'S ★★★

2330 TAYLOR STREET, SAN FRANCISCO. 776-5283. OPEN TUESDAY THROUGH SATURDAY NOON TO 2 P.M.; DINNER 5 TO 10 P.M.; SUNDAY BRUNCH 10:30 A.M. TO 2:30 P.M. FULL BAR. MASTERCARD, VISA. 85% NONSMOKING. PARTIALLY WHEEL-CHAIR ACCESSIBLE. RESERVATIONS RECOMMENDED WEEKENDS. MODERATE.

Susie Kate's sets its blue and white checked tables with Mason jars of corn relish, pads of ordering checks, glasses of small sharpened pencils and terrycloth handtowel napkins—and comes off homey rather than hokey. This pine paneled cafe hidden away on a North Beach sidestreet combines gentle hospitality with delicious Southern-inspired home cooking and an immaculate dining room. The warm biscuits and cornbread, strawberry and pecan pies, collard fribble, applesauce, ham steak with cider sauce, juicy seafood and duck jambalaya, and authentic mint juleps are all special.

All the meals are reasonably priced. You can start with a green salad made with an assortment of hearty lettuces in a spicy horseradish buttermilk dressing, or a soup, such as puree of fennel, celery and green pepper that worked magic together in one evening's offering.

The small menu includes a few a la carte appetizers, such as an unexpectedly spicy curried mushroom pie with a crumbly crust, or deep-fried grit balls, both of which go well with drinks.

Main courses are original and tasty. My favorite is a thick, tender, moist ham steak cooked in cider with a whisper of garlic. Ham steak is too often dry and boring, but this kitchen made it sparkle. Thin slices of fried sweet potato and a pile of sweet corn completes the satisfying plate. Shrimp and duck jambalaya is a hot and juicy seafood stew that comes in its own metal ramekin. Shrimp, rock fish, and strips of duck, rice, lots of different peppers, celery, and okra all melt together on a deep-flavored, incendiary Louisiana broth.

Texas Meatballs with Chipotle Sauce feature moist, well-seasoned, light meatballs—but the sauce is a little too thin to pull the plate of plain rice, corn, and meatballs together. An unusual preparation called Grilled Maryland Duck turns out to be a highly marinated sliced breast, purposely winey, rare, and infused with aromatic vegetables and herbs accompanied with fried sweet potatoes and some of the best applesauce I've ever eaten.

Baking is clearly a strength here. You know that from the feathery biscuits and the savory mushroom pie, and it is confirmed with wonderful desserts. A rendition of Paul Prudhomme's strawberry pie is held together with barely set strawberry gelatin, and a pecan pie is buttery, but not too sweet. A gingerbread sundae brings a square of dense, moist gingerbread with a texture like a gingerbread brownie topped with ice cream and warm caramel sauce. Chocolate-chocolate bourbon pie pairs a rich boozy chocolate mousse with a chocolate cookie crust.

Everything, including the ginger ale, is made from scratch. Ironically, busy people these days go to restaurants for "home cooking." Happily, Susie Kate's makes them feel very much at home.

PATRICIA UNTERMAN

TADICH GRILL ★★½

240 CALIFORNIA STREET, SAN FRANCISCO. 391-2373. OPEN 11 A.M. TO 9 P.M. MONDAY THROUGH SATURDAY. FULL BAR. NO CREDIT CARDS. NO RESERVATIONS. MODERATE.

Tadich Grill, a San Francisco fish restaurant that dates back to the Gold Rush days, is a piece of the City's history. The ancient, dark wood paneling, the booths that enclose white-linen covered tables, bentwood chairs, pressed plaster ceilings, and the veteran waiters all give Tadich its splendid ambience. There's always a crowd at the door having a drink at the small bar and waiting for a table. However, if you don't want to wait for a table, you can usually get a seat immediately at the long, wooden counter that extends the length of the restaurant. The counter seats turn over quickly, and people are gracious about moving over a stool to accommodate a pair that wants to sit together.

The traditional menu and straightforward food feels like a real find these days, when most of the downtown restaurants are serving eclectic, complicated food. What a pleasure to hang your coat on a brass hook at Tadich's and dig into a seafood salad slathered with excellent Louie sauce, and a plate of fresh sand dabs, fried in butter and served with Tadich's gigantic fried potatoes. Charcoal grilled rex sole is another local specialty that Tadich does well, especially with their unique and addictive tartar sauce thickened with sieved potato. The waiters here will even quickly filet your fish for you, an old-fashioned luxury.

The best way to proceed is to ask the waiter what fish has come in fresh that day, and order it charcoal grilled or pan-fried. Salmon, petrale, rex sole, sand dabs, swordfish, Pacific oysters, and rock fish simply prepared in this way will be an authentic taste of San Francisco bay cooking. Order the generously cut, charcoal grilled salmon and swordfish rare if you want it moist in the middle. Creamed spinach or sauteed fresh spinach, thick, old-fashioned clam chowder, and poached salmon with chopped egg sauce are other Tadich favorites. Some of the fancier casserole dishes don't live up to today's standards.

The wine list is refreshingly inexpensive with good bottles from well known California houses, like Robert Mondavi and Fetzer. Desserts have an old San Francisco air about them too, with the likes of baked Rome Beauty apples with heavy cream, and rice custard pudding. I can't end a meal at Tadich's without at least splitting one of them.

The Yugoslavian families that have run this restaurant since the turn of the century, started a San Francisco grill tradition that has influenced a whole new generation of restaurants. Fresh fish grilled over mesquite charcoal was part of a successful formula a hundred years ago, brought over from the Dalmatian coast, where the Croats are still grilling fish over charcoal today.

PATRICIA UNTERMAN

| TEMASEK ★★½

1555 CLEMENT STREET (AT 17TH AVENUE), SAN FRANCISCO. 387-6556. OPEN EVERY NIGHT FOR DINNER FROM 6 TO 10:30 P.M.; BRUNCH ON SUNDAY FROM 10:30 A.M. TO 2:30 P.M. BEER AND WINE. MASTERCARD AND VISA. 100% NONSMOKING. PARTIALLY WHEELCHAIR ACCESSIBLE. RESERVATIONS RECOMMENDED. INEXPENSIVE.

Temasek distinguishes itself as modest neighborhood restaurant because it serves such fresh, colorful food. Against a stark background of white walls, white lace curtains, low white ceilings and white linen covered tables, the plates look like splashes of intense color from a lush tropical palette. Self-described as a restaurant that specializes in "natural cuisine with Asian flavors," Temasek uses the brightest colored vegetables—red cabbage, carrots, jicama, green beans, red and yellow peppers, red and yellow tomatoes—in almost every dish. With spicy Singaporean and Indonesian sauces, pungent vinaigrettes and garnishes of fried shallots and fragrant fresh herbs, this concentration on vegetables, both cooked and raw, forms a unique kind of cuisine.

Some of the dishes are startlingly good. A delicious shrimp "bisque" turns out to be a clean, lemongrass-scented broth, with whole, tender, bright pink shrimp. The broth is enriched with a little brown butter, sprinkled with deep-fried shallots and Thai basil. The flavors sing together. Another exciting creation comes as multi-colored haystacks of julienned cucumber, red cabbage, and carrots topped with marinated, ceviche-like scallops, nutty, crunchy, deep-fried shallots, and roasted peanuts. What makes this dish so extraordinary is its hot/cool, sharply balanced, lemon-ginger vinaigrette, one of the best I've ever tasted. Another terrific dressing, perfumed with mint, goes on a smoky, grilled, white Japanese eggplant, sliced, fanned, and covered with chopped mint.

Pretty salads are included when you order an entree, and they aren't just throwaways. The freshest, mid-sized, redleaf lettuce comes with the pretty shredded vegetables and a luscious pineapple juice vinaigrette. A basket of yeasty, house-baked, whole grain bread comes with a saucer of hot, garlicky, mayonnaise-like sauce instead of butter.

The special pasta one evening brought a plate of soft, fresh, linguine scattered with toasted pinenuts and a picturesque assortment of snap peas, spinach, carrots, peppers and zucchini in a delicate, creamy sauce seasoned with Vietnamese fish sauce, a successful east-west merger. Another fine vegetarian dish is a Sumatran-style vegetable stew called Jasmine, a melange of Japanese eggplant, beans, carrots, and squashes, all cut into matchsticks, surrounding a mold of rice and black beans. A similarly composed seafood stew brought together a medley of vegetables, sun-dried tomatoes, walnuts, squid, scallops, shrimp, and rock fish, all truly fresh for once, in a gently sweet, hot and sour sauce.

The kitchen also knows how to handle meat, as evidenced by a spice- infused, roasted game hen served with ginger scented rice and pretty vegetable sticks—beans, squash, peppers, and carrots. A slice of pork loin stuffed with moist sausage, in a cognac and five-spice sharpened cream sauce, tastes surprisingly good with a pile of crisp shoestring potatoes.

Ripe mango sliced into a goblet with a few ice cubes couldn't be a much better dessert after a meal here. Yet a sophisticated French pithivier, flaky pastry filled with housemade almond paste, is surprisingly good. A yam mousse is like a dense piece of crustless sweet potato pie.

One problem with Temasek is that most dishes have the same ingredients in them, making it difficult to order a whole meal without duplication. However, the food is so lively, healthy, and fresh, Temasek proves that you can never get too much of a good thing.

PATRICIA UNTERMAN

TERRA ★★★

1345 RAILROAD AVENUE, ST. HELENA. (707) 963-8931. OPEN FOR DINNER 6 TO 9:30 P.M. CLOSED TUESDAY. BEER, WINE. MASTERCARD AND VISA. RESERVATIONS REQUIRED. EXPENSIVE.

The new Terra offers an interesting, cross-cultural, culinary experience in a historic St. Helena stone building. The chef, Hiro Sone, formerly of Spago, has put together an offbeat list of dishes that includes everything from glazed, barbecued eel with Japanese cucumber salad, to crisp, deep-fried quail with chanterelles and wild rice risotto. Mr. Sone goes out of his way to create dishes around unusual ingredients, like octopus, sweetbreads, duck liver, and veal shanks, and he often uses non-traditional methods to cook them. The result, in the hands of a less serious cook, might be a disaster, but Mr. Sone has such strong technique, that his flights of fancy take off from solid ground.

On the summer menu look for a stunning and refreshing tomato and beet gazpacho, an ice-cold, red puree garnished with bread crumbs and finely diced cucumbers. Sweet and velvety duck liver goes into deep-fried wontons napped with a creamy, wild mushroom sauce. Whenever salad greens appear on a plate, they are coated in an aromatic vinaigrette. They come with scallops, barely warmed through under the broiler, or a pile of deep-fried rock shrimp coated in bread crumbs.

Main course plates don't look or taste fussy but they have six or seven different foods on them, like a tender, sliced duck breast in piquant dried cherry sauce, with sweet potato puree, a julienne of raw vegetables, cooked baby artichokes and snow peas. The rustic dishes are very appealing, like a ragout of sauteed sweetbreads with braised lentils in a sherry vinegar-spiked sauce; or a braised veal shank served with a marrow fork and the traditional accompaniment of saffron-scented risotto. For the less adventurous, there's a crusty, delicious New York steak, cut into juicy slices served with scalloped potatoes and roasted red and yellow tomatoes.

Dessert brings a superb local berry shortcake with creme fraiche; a smart tiramisu served in a small, earthenware Japanese bowl; true-flavored sorbets, and a luscious warm apple tart with vanilla ice cream.

The two dining rooms are cool and inviting, with beamed ceilings, terracotta tile floors, and modern canvases hung on the walls. A long, reasonably priced local wine list offers rare bottles not often seen as far away as San Francisco. Friendly waiters work smoothly. Terra is an unusual, personal, first culinary statement, that also happens to be professionally run.

PATRICIA UNTERMAN

THAI THAI ★★

1045 SAN PABLO AVE., ALBANY. 526-7426. OPEN 11 A.M. TO 2:30 P.M. MONDAY THROUGH FRIDAY, AND 4:30 TO 10 P.M. NIGHTLY. FULL BAR. VISA, MASTERCARD. 90% NONSMOKING. FULLY WHEELCHAIR ACCESSIBLE. RESERVATIONS RECOMMENDED ESPECIALLY ON WEEKENDS. INEXPENSIVE.

There are so many new Thai restaurants these days that only the most exceptional places find their ways into reviews. Thai Thai is one of these. The food is splendid: fresh, colorful, and scrupulously avoiding the two major pitfalls of Thai cooking, which are excessive oil and salt. And, because the space once housed a California seafood restaurant, the decor is about as attractive as California-cuisine ambiance

■ GREEN CHICKEN CURRY IS ABOUT AS GOOD AS IT GETS, A MOUTHFUL OF FLAVORS AND, WITH CARROTS AND SNOW PEAS, BEAUTIFUL BRIGHT COLORS.

gets: a big skylight, gray stucco walls, sconce lighting, and the obligatory pink neon squiggles. On each table is a yellow or red rose, and soft Thai classical music plays in the background.

The menu here isn't all that unusual, but many of the dishes are done with a delicacy that make them stand out. Two of the appetizers are on every Thai menu, but I've never seen them done better. Calamari salad, with fresh-tasting, warm pieces of squid, is roaring hot, but the chilies don't mask the flavors of lemongrass, garlic, ginger, lime juice, and fish sauce. Stuffed chicken wings, for once, offer the predominant taste of chicken meat and the pork and mushroom stuffing, rather than thick, greasy batter. There are also two *laabs*, the blend of ground meat and onions with herbs and spices that's a staple of the Lao-influenced Issan cuisine of northeast Thailand. *Laabs* are much too rarely offered around these parts, and both the chicken *laab* and pork *laab* at Thai Thai will make you wish for them more often.

Don't miss the soups. *Tom kar gai* is a rich chicken broth with chunks of chicken, fresh mushrooms, and a touch of coconut milk, unusually light and delicate for a Thai soup. Something I've never seen before on a Thai menu called *ruammit* offers a hearty bowl of greens and mixed seafood in a peppery broth.

Among the entrees, I'd begin with the spicy sausage, another staple of Issan cooking. Thai sausage is like no other; the pork is blended with so many aromatic herbs that the whole sausage smells and tastes perfumed. Thai Thai's version includes exotic kafir leaves, chopped lemongrass, ginger, galanga, shallots, garlic, pepper, and ground red chilies. Then there are the curries. Green chicken curry is about as good as it gets, a mouthful of flavors and, with carrots and snow peas, beautiful bright colors. Vegetables in a curried peanut sauce, called *pra rama pak*, feature a big variety, including red peppers, squash, spinach, cauliflower, and snow peas, in a peanut sauce that for once isn't heavy and gloppy.

Other winners include *pad scallops*, very fresh and sweet-tasting scallops sauteed with several different al dente vegetables in a sauce that doesn't betray a globule of oil. *How mok poo*, an unusual version of the Thai fish mousse, has a top layer of ground fish mixed with red curry paste and coconut milk, and a bottom layer of shredded crab. The delicious Thai Thai boneless duck demonstrates how conscientiously this restaurant rids its dishes of excess fat, while duck in red curry offers the same tender duck meat in a hearty stew of vegetables and coconut milk.

STAN SESSER

TI BACIO ★★

5301 COLLEGE AVE. (NEAR BROADWAY), OAKLAND. 428-1703. OPEN 4 TO 10 P.M. MONDAY THROUGH SATURDAY AND 10 A.M. TO 10 P.M. SUNDAY. BEER, WINE. VISA, MASTERCARD. FULLY WHEELCHAIR ACCESSIBLE. 100% NONSMOKING. RESERVATIONS RECOMMENDED. MODERATE.

If you enjoy eating at unusual restaurants, consider this: you walk into an Italian restaurant and are greeted at the door by a pile of pamphlets explaining how calves are tortured for the production of veal. There's not a single red-meat item on the menu; the standard veal dishes are made with turkey breast. Everything is cooked with an absolute minimum of salt and oil. The menu has been evaluated by a nutritionist. And no smoking is allowed.

All of the above takes place at Ti Bacio ("I kiss you"), a small, pleasant restaurant in the Rockridge district of Oakland. Most of what Ti Bacio serves is delicious, even if it manages to be healthy at the same time. I have mixed feelings about the turkey breast as a substitute for veal, but I'm totally enthusiastic about what they can do with pastas and many of their other dishes. As for vegetables—which can be so wonderful in Italy and so pitiful in Italian restaurants here unless you never tire of sauteed zucchini—Ti Bacio is sensational. It's not surprising when you discover many of the vegetables come from the owner's organic farm in Sonoma County.

The good news at Ti Bacio is that nothing tastes undersalted or bland. In fact, the flavors of the ingredients and spices come out more clearly when they're not masked by excessive grease and salt. A perfect example is the *vongole* pasta, shell-like noodles with clams. The pasta is tossed with a mixture of baby clams, garlic, tomatoes, basil, oregano, parsley, vegetable stock, and white wine. Then, steamed clams in the shell are added. Two other winners are the pasta primavera and the linguine with calamari. For the first, the spinach noodles are mixed with a host of vegetables sauteed with garlic, parmesan cheese, and olive oil. The linguine, cooked perfectly al dente, features butter-tender, fresh-tasting squid in a tomato-based sauce. Vegetarian lasagne is another interesting dish, with very fresh vegetables baked with noodles, ricotta cheese, and a mixture of pesto and marinara sauces.

But you don't have to eat pasta to walk away happy. Calamari Ti Bacio and chicken cacciatora are both first-rate. The squid is sauteed in a light but spicy tomato-herb sauce, while the huge portion of chicken comes stewed in homemade tomato sauce and bell peppers.

There are some excellent appetizers, too. A plate of cold, marinated vegetables lightly dressed with garlic, lemon, and olive oil features string beans, broccoli, yellow squash, carrots, and artichoke hearts on a big plate of green leaf lettuce. They are all lightly cooked and thankfully served at room temperature rather than out of the refrigerator.

Homemade artichoke and zucchini frittata, the Italian version of an omelet, couldn't be better; light, smooth-textured, and not too eggy.

STAN SESSER

❙ TOMMASO'S ★★

1042 KEARNY STREET, SAN FRANCISCO. 398-9696. OPEN TUESDAY THROUGH SATURDAY FROM 5 P.M. TO 11:45 P.M. SUNDAY 4 P.M. TO 9:45 P.M. BEER AND WINE. MASTERCARD AND VISA. 50% NONSMOKING. PARTIALLY WHEELCHAIR ACCESSIBLE. NO RESERVATIONS. INEXPENSIVE TO MODERATE.

It's as if time has stopped when you step down into Tommaso's poorly lit, cave-like dining room, with partitioned-off tables along the walls and a long communal table stretched down the middle. You can barely see the murals of the Naples coast from the poor light of ancient fixtures—and perhaps it's just as well. Decor is not the reason anyone goes to Tommaso's. It's the luscious smell of pizza baking in a wood burning oven that makes you endure the long waits inside the drafty, chairless front vestibule. The restaurant takes no reservations and Tommaso's is popular.

If there's one universally loved item that Tommaso's makes, it's their pizzas. Way before pizza baked in a wood burning oven was a glimmer in Alice Water's eye, Tommaso's was turning them out with perfectly crisp, sweet, chewy crusts scented with smoke, and layered with copious amounts of whole milk mozzarella, among other ingredients. The aroma of vegetarian pizza blanketed with green pepper, onions, fresh mushrooms, and olives drives me wild. The super deluxe pizza with mushrooms, peppers, ham, Tommaso's allspice scented Italian sausage, and anchovies is spectacular—without the anchovies which are too strong for this particular blend of ingredients. The pizza a la Neapolitan with just the usual generous amount of cheese and Tommaso's tasty tomato sauce is a delight. The superlative crust, so elastic, so full of character, so beautifully browned, so enticingly smoky, needs very little elaboration.

Tommaso's also puts out a massive calzone stuffed with a skillful blend of ricotta and mozzarella, prosciutto, and Tommaso's special spice mixture. All the elements seem to melt together in a happy way inside the impeccably crisp, folded over crust. Another terrific calzone is stuffed with slices of spicy Italian sausage, mushrooms, and a little tomato sauce.

Of course, Tommaso's still offers their famous starters, plates of peeled peppers, crisp whole string beans, and trees of bright green broccoli, all lightly dressed in lemon juice and olive oil. They're tasty, refreshing, and just what you want before the rich pizzas and calzones.

What surprised me about Tommaso's on my recent visits was the quality of the pastas. A daily lasagne special layered with tender fresh

257

noodles and that winning combination of ricotta, mozzarella and pleasant tomato sauce, was light and airy. Calamari are tender and sensitively fried, and a bowl of steamed clams, in an odd but not unpleasant broth seasoned with vinegar and oil, are plump and juicy.

For dessert, a custardy spumoni frozen into individual bowls, comes as a happy departure from the artificial tasting spumoni served all over North Beach.

Fifty-year-old Tommaso's is still run with real vigor. The original recipes must have been carved in stone and executed with precision, because this beloved North Beach joint really is as satisfying today as it was when I first ate there—and I won't tell you how long ago that was.

PATRICIA UNTERMAN

| TORTOLA ★★

3640 SACRAMENTO, SAN FRANCISCO. 929-8181. OPEN TUESDAY THROUGH FRIDAY 11 A.M TO 2 P.M.; DINNER 5 TO 10 P.M., SATURDAY 11:30 A.M. TO 10 P.M., SUNDAY 5 TO 10 P.M. BEER AND WINE. MASTERCARD, VISA, DISCOVER. 70% NONSMOKING. FULLY WHEELCHAIR ACCESSIBLE. RESERVATIONS RECOMMENDED. INEXPENSIVE.

Tortola is a striking, but casual, neighborhood restaurant with prices that allow families to dine out without spending a fortune. I've rarely been in more stylish surroundings where you can eat heartily for under $10.

Tortola, which originally opened on Polk Street years ago, moved to a long, narrow space in what looks like a renovated brick garage in Pacific Heights. Customers enter from an airy, skylit, tiled corridor into a high ceilinged room furnished with blond wood benches and tables, and squared off, red wood chairs. The austere lines of the restaurant are softened by rectangles of loosely mounted canvas dyed the same color as the walls. Color comes from some bright paintings and a rainbow of paper placemats on the handsome wooden tables.

Probably the best way to order is to start with an unadorned bowl of simply made guacamole, just avocado mashed with garlic and hot chiles, and a bowl of very mild, fresh tomato salsa, for which, deservedly, there is a charge. These can be scooped up with Tortola's thick, fried-to-order tortilla chips.

The use of good ingredients and healthy cooking practices is a philosophy of this restaurant. Lard, which gives beans and many other Mexican dishes an authentic flavor, has been passed over for cholesterol-free peanut and corn oil. Everything is made fresh daily and looks like it. The pretty salads glisten. The best is a whole leaf Tortola Caesar salad that gets a reasonably traditional dressing seasoned with a whisper of ground chiles. Dry jack is grated over the leaves, roasted red peppers and cubes of deep-fried polenta instead of croutons are scattered here and there.

The quesadilla of the day is one of the best dishes in the house. At one lunch, it turned out to be a griddled sandwich of whole-wheat tortillas filled with melted smoked mozzarella, red onions, and spicy andouille sausage, cut into eight, easy-to-eat wedges, garnished with salsa and sour cream. Tortola's version of chicken fajitas is exceptional. You get a big plate of marinated, tender chicken, stir-fried with strips of hot and sweet peppers, red onion, cilantro, and lime, piled on three thin, warm corn tortillas. What really makes this dish fly is Tortola's Southwestern coleslaw of crisp, finely cut cabbage, lots of onion, and chile-spiked vinaigrette. Fabulous by itself, but even better tucked into the tortillas with the fajitas.

The margaritas made with agave wine capture the best flavors of this popular drink without the alcohol content. The wine list offers some excellent wines by the glass at very reasonable prices. The soft Spanish reds go wonderfully with the food. Espresso and coffee are both well brewed and good with several of Tortola's housemade desserts. A polenta poundcake has an unusual, dense, moist, chewy texture; a flan boasts a luxuriously rich, creamy texture. Both are lovely desserts.

Tortola tries so hard to please its constituency, and is succeeding so well at it, that it doesn't need a troublemaker like me to say that the food should be hotter, grittier, and more authentic. But, with a few little adjustments, like a snappier salsa, this place could please us all.

PATRICIA UNTERMAN

THE TOWNHOUSE ★★

5862 DOYLE STREET(POWELL STREET EXIT OFF HWY 80), EMERYVILLE. 652-6151. OPEN FOR LUNCH MONDAY THROUGH FRIDAY FROM 11:30 A.M. TO 2:30 P.M.; DINNER MONDAY THROUGH SATURDAY, 5:30 TO 9:30 P.M. FULL BAR. MASTERCARD AND VISA. 75% NONSMOKING. PARTIALLY WHEELCHAIR ACCESSIBLE. RESERVATIONS RECOMMENDED. MODERATE.

The Townhouse in Emeryville is a very hip spot. Located on a sidestreet in a neighborhood of artists' studios, high tech laboratories, and warehouses, this weathered wooden building looks like something left over from the Gold Rush. However, when you walk through the jaunty, red front door, it turns into a stylishly converted space with a breezy, casual, half finished look. This is Emeryville's version of the arty, South of Market look.

A long, weathered, but inviting bar runs along one side of the large, open room. The old wooden floors have been polished. The ceiling plaster has been removed to expose beams, wooden slats, and electrical conduit. Naked lightbulbs are wrapped with wire screening. The kitchen is visible behind a large, chicken wired window. The only other windows open directly onto a brick wall. Large, sculptural oil paintings and oversized, glazed clay pots look stunning in this loft-like ambience. The solid wooden tables and chairs of all different sizes and shapes, look like they have been carefully picked out at second-hand stores. White linen and butcher paper dress them up. Jazz plays cooly in the background.

The lunch and dinner menus are almost identical—inexpensive, unfussy, a little quirky. The chef, Ellen Hope, comes to Emeryville via stints in such L.A. kitchens as Spago, Michael's, and L'Orangerie. The inspiration for her dishes comes from all over the place, yet balance out to a typical melange of Italian, Mexican, and "California" preparations.

Lunch begins with a pretty and delicious wilted spinach salad. The leaves seem to melt into a piquant sherry-shallot vinaigrette along with crisp bacon and browned mushrooms, without seeming the least bit oily. Beautiful, tissue thin slices of gravlax, raw cured salmon, come with a perfectly dressed salad of distinctive greens. A plateful of sweet, hollowed out, deep-fried, baby potatoes are filled with dill cream and three different kinds of fish eggs, all in a laudable state of freshness. Just baked, rosemary-scented white bread comes wrapped up in a napkin.

A filet of salmon, carefully grilled, comes on a bed of fresh tomatoes and cream with buttery fresh spinach on the side, and a pile of the Townhouse's characteristically limp, pale, skinny french fries. A bowl of risotto, with just the right texture, is drizzled with a deeply flavored red wine sauce and topped with a mirepoix of aromatic vegetables.

For dessert, a soft, creme bruleé has a few chopped strawberries folded into it, and a pale apple tart with tough apples on doughy puff pastry is almost redeemed by a warm caramel sauce.

A visit on a busy Saturday night made me think that this new restaurant needs time to pull itself together. The purposely unfinished look of the place seemed to cross over to some pretty tired food and vague, unprofessional service. Yet, the good lunch proves what the kitchen is capable of. My feeling is that the Townhouse will become more consistent, even under the pressures of a full house.

PATRICIA UNTERMAN

TRA VIGNE ★★

1050 CHARTER OAK AVENUE, ST. HELENA. (707)-963-4444. OPEN DAILY NOON TO 9:30 P.M. FULL BAR. MAJOR CREDIT CARDS. 90% NONSMOKING. FULLY WHEEL-CHAIR ACCESSIBLE. RESERVATIONS REQUIRED. MODERATE.

Cyndi Pawlcyn and her partners at Fog City Diner, in San Francisco, and Mustards, in Yountville, have opened a second major Napa Valley place right off Highway 29, called Tra Vigne, which translates "among vines." It is one of the most beautiful restaurants in California and a delightful place to stop on a visit. Located in a gorgeous stone house surrounded by tiled patios, Tra Vigne's designers have created a strikingly austere but romantic ambience. The restaurant is one gigantic room with a long bar along one side and an open kitchen along the other. Dan Friedlander the head designer at Limn studios is responsible for the neo-medieval look. Somehow he captured the feeling of ancient Italian villas by being completely modern. The plastered walls look like old stone, while the marble work on the bar suggests Florentine opulence.

The menu offers lots of antipasti and small portions of pasta, as well as pizzas from a wood fired oven, Italian sandwiches, and some grilled meats and fish. You make a meal by ordering lots of different things. Practically everything is colorful, tasty and fun. It's not exactly Italian food as you would get it in Italy, but the ingredients are authentic.

From the antipasti section, you won't want to miss mozzarella and prosciutto wrapped in romaine lettuce, and grilled over a fire. It's sauced in a sharp, sun-dried tomato vinaigrette, and surrounded by a wreath of arugula and baby greens. Also delicious are quartered heads of radicchio grilled until they wilt a little, sauced with a warm vinaigrette enriched with black olives and pancetta.

Another terrific first course comes from the pasta section, a warm pasta salad, really, of corkscrew noodles tossed with still crunchy radicchio, shiitakes, and a fresh tomato sauce, called Fusilli Michaelangelo. The small pizzas are nice too, like the pizza Margherita with fresh tomatoes, mozzarella and basil.

The foods cooked on the grill have their ups and downs. Successful, one afternoon, were prawns, wrapped in crispy pancetta, in a savory, roasted garlic vinaigrette. But from the same grill came sausages covered with a soapy sauce seasoned with too much rosemary. Sometimes grilled foods are cooked over fires that are too hot, and turn out unpleasantly smoky.

Desserts are delightful. Crisp chocolate cannoli shells are filled with lightened, sweetened, fresh ricotta, golden raisins, and pistachios, and a barely poached pear comes in a merlot custard with crisp, chocolate bread sticks. As one would expect from a Napa Valley restaurant, there's a good selection of local wines at reasonable prices, as well as an interesting Italian list.

Last summer, Tra Vigne opened a Cantinetta, a charming, wood-paneled Italian wine bar and market where customers can buy wines by the bottle and glass, and ice-cold draft beer at a marble bar. Cheese, delicious grilled sandwiches of pancetta, tomato, and lettuce on focaccia, pizzas, and plates of Tra Vigne chef Michael Chiarello's house-cured sausages and salami can be ordered at the food counter. People eat at marble tables in the shade of leafy plane trees in Tra Vigne's courtyard. They return to the counter to buy biscotti and espresso for dessert. The Cantinetta is such a natural stopping place for people touring the Napa Valley, that I wonder why there aren't several of them up and down Highway 29. One reason may be that the Cantinetta is supplied by the hard-working kitchen of Tra Vigne, whose food tastes even better outdoors.

PATRICIA UNTERMAN

TRADER VIC'S ★½

20 COSMO PLACE, SAN FRANCISCO. 775-6300. OPEN FROM 4:30 TO 11 P.M. SUNDAY THROUGH THURSDAY, UNTIL MIDNIGHT FRIDAY AND SATURDAY. ALL MAJOR CREDIT CARDS. 10% NONSMOKING. PARTIALLY WHEELCHAIR ACCESSIBLE. RESERVATIONS ADVISED. EXPENSIVE.

Trader Vic's, the famous Polynesian-style restaurant, is going through trying times trying to attract a younger crowd.

Last year, the Tiki Room was redecorated with lighter neutral colors and English-style brass chandeliers, giving it the feel of a civilized oasis in the middle of a jungle. The Captain's Cabin, the "A" room, has remained pretty much the same with its red upholstered chairs and somewhat dark tone.

The most significant change, however, was hiring a French chef, Alfred Schilling, to head up the kitchen. Schilling, who owned the cute Chez Chez on Union, is faced with updating the once exotic flavors from the 1950s to the 1990s.

Although there are some sacred dishes, Schilling has been allowed to reformulate some overly sweet sauces, adding heartier seasonings for a more contemporary flavor.

Schilling shines on the new dishes, applying his European sensibilities to Asian ingredients. Duck Alfred is an excellent example of a confit, prepared with Chinese spices, served on a bed of greens tossed with tamarind dressing, and served with two elongated coins of pickled carrot.

Mauna Kea Mahi Mahi with vanilla sauce sounds as if it wouldn't work, but it is fabulous. The smell is intensely vanilla, and the taste is balanced with acid for a perfumed, creamy sauce. The crusty-sauteed fish, crisscrossed with vanilla beans, created a beautiful complement. Another great dish is Jade Prawns, named for the piquant green sauce of pureed baby bok choy, wine, and ginger, served with rice and snow peas.

For the diet conscious, Schilling steams salmon or other Pacific fish with lemongrass and a soy-sesame sauce. Moist and infused with flavor, it is served on a bed of Chinese noodles with sugarsnap peas and diced tomato.

The main disappointments came with classic dishes. Peach-Blossom Duck has a tutti-frutti sauce that is sweet but pleasant, but the meat tastes warmed over and the canned peach half went a long way to wreck what the chef was trying to accomplish with fresh ingredients.

The Cosmo Salad with celery, mushrooms, and a mustard dressing is marred by sliced artichoke bottoms that taste metallic. The curry dishes always have been pleasant, though timidly seasoned, presented with half a dozen condiments on a special serving dish. The pu pu's haven't changed a bit. On the Cosmo Tidbit platter, crispy prawns tend to be dry and thickly breaded. Crab Rangoon has the classic '50s cream-cheese crab filling. Smoked spareribs and Chinese barbequed pork, done in Chinese smoke ovens, are delicious.

The twelve-item dessert menu has some fabulous selections, including a French Island Creme Brulée flecked with tropical fruit, and a Menehune Torte, a kind of cheesecake with apricot preserves, banana purée, and lemon-cream mousse. This seesaw quality illustrates how tough it is to balance innovation and tradition. Few other restaurants are so ingrained in the city's culinary fabric as Trader Vic's. Started in 1951, it was the Stars and Postrio of its day.

Service, however, is a consistent problem. The attitude of the servers and managers puts an arctic chill on what should be a tropical paradise. The people controlling reservations cling to an elitist attitude that was built over decades. If you're not known, you can be ignored. If service can be corrected, Trader Vic's could be a fun, upbeat place to go.

MICHAEL BAUER

TRE SCALINI ★★½

241 HEALDSBURG AVENUE, HEALDSBURG. (707) 433-1772. OPEN WEDNESDAY THROUGH MONDAY FROM 5 TO 9 P.M., FRIDAY AND SATURDAY UNTIL 10 P.M. BEER AND WINE. MASTERCARD AND VISA. 100% NONSMOKING. FULLY WHEEL-CHAIR ACCESSIBLE. RESERVATIONS RECOMMENDED. MODERATE

Located just off Healdsburg's main square, Tre Scalini has the sophistication of a San Francisco restaurant. A high ceilinged store-front with big, plate-glass windows, the dining room has been painted a smart shade of soft pink. Butcher paper-covered tables are set with elegant, heavy silver and thin glassware. Waiters and waitresses in black pants and white shirts are friendly and unusually competent. Though Tre Scalini attracts a country-casual crowd, all the details of this restaurant are attended to in the style of a more formal restaurant.

Each dish on the menu is followed by a concise description, making it easy to order, though not to decide. From the antipasti section, my affections go to a superb *vitello tonnato,* the best version of this dish I have ever tasted. Paper-thin, carpaccio-like, slices of tender, pink veal are napped in a lovely, light, creamy, mayonnaise sauce flavored with capers, and barely textured with tuna. The plate

■ **A PERFECT STARTER BRINGS A PLATE OF GRILLED EGG-PLANT AND ROASTED RED, GREEN, AND YELLOW PEPPERS WITH SLICED TOMATOES, ANCHOVIES AND OLIVE OIL. THOUGH EVERYTHING ON THE PLATE HAS A BIG FLAVOR, THE OVERALL EFFECT IS LIGHT AND REFINED.**

arrangement is simple and appealing, with the thin slices lifted up off the plate, tent-like, and drizzled with the sauce. Another perfect starter brings a plate of grilled eggplant and roasted red, green, and yellow peppers with sliced tomatoes, anchovies and olive oil. Though everything on the plate has a big flavor, the overall effect is light and refined.

Most of the pasta dishes use Tre Scalini's housemade egg noodles, which are cooked pleasantly al dente. The pasta dishes are light, juicy, and exceptionally fresh as evidenced by tagliarini with fresh clams in the shell, red peppers, Italian sausage, and fresh tomatoes. *Cappellini alla puttanesca* somehow balances anchovies, capers, and lots of garlic with fresh tomatoes to come out lively and refreshing. Beware of the unpitted olives in this dish. Some kids, one night, wanted just plain tomato sauce on their noodles and the kitchen rose to the occasion by delivering a plate of pasta in a bright marinara sauce made with fresh tomatoes sprinkled with grated parmesan.

The main courses are also savory without being heavy. Rack of lamb chops in a subtle soy marinade couldn't be sweeter or more succulent. Almost as good is Tre Scalini's version of chicken saltimbocca, a moist, free-range chicken breast stuffed with slices of prosciutto, sage, and mozzarella in a rich marsala sauce. I was let down by a baked salmon filet spread with chopped mushrooms and wrapped in lettuce leaves. It didn't taste fresh enough.

Tre Scalini has a varied and intelligently chosen wine list. The range includes a big, concentrated but smooth Sonoma pinot noir from nearby William Selyem, Rocchioli Vineyards, as well as appealing Italian chiantis and pinot grigios.

For dessert don't miss Tre Scalini's bisquit tortoni, a whole bowl of the most heavenly, semi freddo–style ice cream, textured with ground hazelnuts and coconut, served with a crisp biscotti on the side. Espresso is excellent.

My one thought about Tre Scalini is that the menu is a little too large for a restaurant of its size, especially when it comes to seafood. The clams, which hold up well, were fine in the pasta but more perishable items like rock shrimp and salmon could have been fresher. Otherwise, Tre Scalini has earned my complete trust and frequent Sonoma patronage.

PATRICIA UNTERMAN

TRILOGY ★★

1234 MAIN ST., ST. HELENA. (707) 963-5507. OPEN FOR LUNCH TUESDAY THROUGH FRIDAY NOON TO 2 P.M.; DINNER TUESDAY THROUGH SATURDAY 6 TO 9:30 P.M. WINE, BEER. VISA, MASTERCARD. NONSMOKING DINING ROOM. FULLY WHEELCHAIR ACCESSIBLE. RESERVATIONS HIGHLY RECOMMENDED. MODERATE.

Wine lists are often designed to enhance profits, not meals. But at Trilogy in the Napa Valley, the wine list is something special. Their collection of California wines turns out to be a virtual encyclopedia of anything you could conceivably want to drink. With about 300 wines on the list, you can choose from 22 different merlots, from four or five different vintages of some winemakers' cabernets. And most amazing of all, lots of these wines are priced at just 25% to 50% over what they'd sell for in a wine store, compared to the doubling or tripling of the retail price that's so much more common in restaurants today.

Trilogy's chef is Diane Pariseau, whom I last encountered at the Mount View Hotel in Calistoga. There, she made a menu of what sounded like boring American dishes into a really pleasurable meal. At Trilogy, Pariseau again presents what appears to be a very conventional menu, this time California cuisine instead of classic American. And again she enlivens the dishes with superb cooking, light, flavorful sauces, and beautiful presentations.

You can either choose the fixed price menu or order a la carte. But even if you select the fixed price dinner, be sure to supplement it with two appetizers that are Pariseau's signature dishes. They're so stunning they shouldn't be missed. One is a ragout of wild mushrooms, sauteed with shallots, white wine, and cream, and served with delicate crepes whose batter includes fresh corn and chives. The second is a beet soup, a thick, bright-red combination of beets, carrots, onions, and chicken stock, that captures the absolute essence of beet taste.

The fixed price menu might be reasonably priced, but it doesn't skimp on expensive ingredients. At my second dinner, you could start with a terrine of lobster and rockfish, the sort of terrine that handles the ingredients so well that the taste of very fresh seafood stands out. The pieces of seafood were bound with a combination of lobster butter, olive oil, egg yolk, and chives. Alternatively, a second choice as an appetizer was sauteed louvar, a tropical fish I've never heard of before. It turned out to be light, delicate, and fresh-tasting, with a superb red wine butter sauce and braised endive on the side.

Of the three choices for entrees on that fixed price dinner, pheasant was far and away the best. It's a bird with so little fat that it normally dries to sawdust, but Pariseau kept it deliciously juicy. The boned pheasant meat was served in a sauce that included sauteed chanterelles and reduced stock from the pheasant bones.

I've had several other good dishes at Trilogy. Steamed Manila clams not only are sparkling fresh, but benefit from pesto and sun-dried tomatoes in the broth. Local lettuces in a dressing that includes hazelnut oil and ground hazelnuts taste like they were picked five minutes before dinner. Sauteed poussin in a spicy black bean sauce, and medallions of veal in a cream sauce with oyster mushrooms are two great entrees on the a la carte menu.

STAN SESSER

TRIO CAFE ★★

1870 FILLMORE STREET, SAN FRANCISCO. 563-2248. OPEN TUESDAY THROUGH SATURDAY 8 A.M. TO 6 P.M., SUNDAYS 10 A.M. TO 4 P.M. BEER AND WINE. NO CREDIT CARDS. NO RESERVATIONS. INEXPENSIVE.

The Trio Cafe, which opened as a small and charming, stand-up coffee and sandwich bar, now offers quick and efficient table service as well. Happily, the menu at Trio has maintained its original focus. The cafe au lait and the herb and leaf teas, all served in deep, speckled bowls, are piping hot and well made. The Trio shows particular strength at baking. Their toasted, buttered scones and miniature muffins taste like they've just been pulled out of the oven. Buttery, crisp almond cinnamon cookies, and moist almond cake are delicately sweet and wonderful with tea or coffee.

The Trio puts out an eccentric but tasty Croque Monsieur, with a thick layer of thinly sliced but ice cold ham between two slices of soft French bread, topped with melted gruyere. The sandwich comes with three little shredded salads of carrot, beet, and zucchini, all separately dressed. Buttered garlic toast with thin slices of cheese and Roma tomatoes, a seemingly too simple combination, tastes awfully good when you eat them all together. Thin slices of coppa on bread dressed with vinaigrette is another fine match with the trio of salads.

What makes this little cafe so special is its ambience. Even on the gloomiest days it feels bright and airy. Against a clean-lined, white space with gray slate tile floors, faux marble tables, and counter and windows that look out onto Fillmore, the glass vases of flowers and floral upholstered banquettes stand out. There are picture books to browse through and a basket for newspapers. The sun always seems to shine on the white metal tables set outside on the sidewalk. The Trio's small expansion, that allows for tables, has only improved it.

PATRICIA UNTERMAN

■ BUTTERY, CRISP ALMOND CINNAMON COOKIES, AND MOIST ALMOND CAKE ARE DELICATELY SWEET AND WONDERFUL WITH TEA OR COFFEE.

231 ELLSWORTH ★★★

231 SOUTH ELLSWORTH STREET, SAN MATEO, 347-7231. OPEN DAILY FOR LUNCH AND DINNER MONDAY THROUGH SATURDAY UNTIL 10 P.M. BEER AND WINE. RESERVATIONS AND CREDIT CARDS ACCEPTED. EXPENSIVE.

231 Ellsworth is one of the best, high-style restaurants on the Peninsula, featuring an eclectic blend of elements. Although the art work and the sleek pink and aqua decor looks Southwest, the plates look Californian, and the food is billed as French. There is a European sensibility in the flavors and composition of the elegant food. Often the ingredients sound incongruous, but the combinations can be stunning.

Four filets of ono (a firm-fleshed Hawaiian fish) are presented on a bed of diagonally cut Chinese long beans, swimming in a potent broth of tomato and fennel. A duck breast, mounded over a fried potato pancake and a pile of sauteed cabbage and bacon, is served with a chocolate-raspberry sauce. It sounds strange, but it works.

One of the heaviest dishes, but it is light years away from being leaden, is composed of a mustard cream sauce that clings to toothsome cheese ravioli stuffed with herbs, topped with luscious pieces of prawns. There are sauteed scallops on a pool of celery root puree, ringed by a light meat sauce that is slightly reduced to intensify flavor.

One dessert for the hall of fame is a hot, gooey, chocolate timbale of cake served in a light caramel sauce with zest of lime and a scoop of whipped cream.

Prices are reasonable for such fine ambience and professional service. A particularly good deal is the fixed priced meal offered Monday through Thursday.

The wine list is well chosen to go with the elegant, light style of the food. It includes a good selection of drinkable pinot noirs, for example, and you can find an excellent bottle for less than $25.

MICHAEL BAUER

UNDICI ★★½

374 11TH STREET, SAN FRANCISCO. 431-3337. OPEN FOR LUNCH MONDAY THROUGH FRIDAY FROM 11:30 A.M. TO 2:30 P.M.; DINNER MONDAY THROUGH SATURDAY FROM 6 TO 11 P.M. FULL BAR. MASTERCARD AND VISA. 70% NON-SMOKING. FULLY WHEELCHAIR ACCESSIBLE. RESERVATIONS FOR 6 OR MORE AT LUNCH. RESERVATIONS RECOMMENDED AT DINNER. MODERATE.

Undici, a smart, south of Market, Italian cafe gets its vitality from being a little off beat. It is owned by a group that includes maitre d' Tim Dale from Eddie Jack's and chef Donna Nicoletti of The Atrium and Greens. They gave the unconventional, somewhat awkward, space a stunning face lift, and put together a small, unusual, menu to fit the limited capability of the restaurant's tiny kitchen.

The restaurant shows itself best during the day when natural light streams in to reveal the subtleties of the decor. The walls, in this high ceilinged space, are sponged to look like old Italian stone. A gargoyle fountain spits water into a plant-filled basin, and decorative wrought iron gates are mounted high up. The faux-stone floors, brass arm chairs, and silk screened banners with olive branches and heads of garlic, evoke some idealized Italian piazza.

The bar at Undici is a gem—a cozy, wood paneled, low ceilinged space between the breezy front room and a more intimate back dining area. Bowls of marinated green and black olives and herbed popcorn sit enticingly on the bar. Drinks are well-made and generous; Italian wines by the glass are drinkable, reasonably priced, but not out of the ordinary. I found myself happily waiting there on several occasions when the crowded dining room was running a bit off schedule.

The menu loosely concentrates on hitherto unexplored regions of Italy; Sicily, Sardinia, and the south. This means that some surprising flavor combinations and textures pop up in various dishes, some of which take a moment to get used to. One of the most successful is a stuffed globe artichoke served warm in a flat bowl of lemony, olive oil-laced cooking broth. A moist, soft, herby breadcrumb mixture is pushed down between the leaves. Breadcrumbs are used again in a sauce on tubular mostacioli, tossed with fennel, chopped tomato, fresh anchovies and olive oil. The effect is a little like eating noodles coated in garlicky stuffing. Undisputedly delicious is Sardinian rabbit fricassee, a smoky, pancetta-rich stew with lots of carrots, tomatoes, and a luscious, subtly sweet and sour sauce.

Roasted Chicken Vesuvio is like a chicken saute that is achieved without cooking in oil. This terrific preparation combines pieces of crisp chicken and crusty roasted potatoes moistened by the chicken's natural roasting juices. The main seasoning is a generous sprinkling of chopped Italian parsley. A seafood antipasto features a piquant calamari salad, mussels and clams in the shell with a shredded cucumber salad, all marinated in a fine, aromatic, oregano infused vinaigrette. Some coarse-textured Sicilian fennel sausages were laced with fennel seeds and smothered with roasted peppers in a hearty preparation.

The pastry department has come up with several lovely Italian desserts. Crisp cannelloni, stuffed with orange-scented ricotta, dipped in chopped pistachios on one end and shaved chocolate on the other, go perfectly with espresso, as do buttery, crumbly biscotti with pinenuts and anise seed. A delicate hazelnut semifreddo is like an airy, nut-infused ice cream. Even more fabulous is an ethereal zuccotto filled with espresso and hazelnut cream, and encased in chocolate sponge cake.

This restaurant gets very cramped when it is full and you get the feeling that the physically small kitchen is barely keeping up. The food can come out slowly. Excellent service makes up for the inconvenience. Water, wine, bread, and olive oil keep coming.

For all its rough spots, Undici gets a lot of credit for an original, non-intrusive design, and an Italian menu that actually explores some new culinary ground. The prices are very reasonable; the kitchen is dedicated to fresh ingredients and cooking to order. The whole operation has an appealing, lively style that draws people in. Happily, it is one south of Market operation that is run professionally enough to keep them coming back.

PATRICIA UNTERMAN

UNION HOTEL ★★½

401 FIRST STREET, BENICIA. (707) 746-0100. OPEN MONDAY THROUGH SATURDAY FOR LUNCH 11:30 A.M. TO 2:30 P.M.; DINNER 6 TO 10 P.M., SATURDAY 5:30 TO 10 P.M.; SUNDAY BRUNCH 9:30 A.M. TO 2:30 P.M., DINNER 5:30 TO 9:30 P.M. FULL BAR. ALL MAJOR CREDIT CARDS. 100% NONSMOKING. FULLY WHEELCHAIR ACCESSIBLE. RESERVATIONS RECOMMENDED. EXPENSIVE.

With the quaint charm of antique wooden tables and a wall of three stained-glassed windows, the Union Hotel restaurant makes you feel you've traveled back 100 years. In fact you've only driven 35 miles from the city to Benicia, a pretty little town that has become a quiet haven for artists who work in glass and ceramics. The feel of the room is country Victorian. The white-clothed tables with mix-and-match antique high back chairs look warm, inviting, and nostalgic.

The food takes a modern American turn; it's fresh and vibrant, featuring an eclectic blend of cultures. At lunch you'll find grilled eggplant with roasted peppers, a seasonal pizzetta, grilled chicken breast marinated in lime and tequila, or a pasta with spicy roast pork, chicken, and mushrooms.

However, chef Lev Dagan really shines at dinner, with a limited menu featuring several appetizers and about eight specials, each carefully matched with a wine from the small, well selected list. A good starter is the assertive, well-integrated blend of angel hair pasta, escargots, tomato, garlic, and feta cheese, or clams and two kinds of mussels in a tomato-based broth flavored with sausage and Pernod. It's so good you'll probably end up using your spoon to finish off the broth.

Entrees are reasonably priced. The standard New York steak gets a well-conceived flavor boost with a sauce of Jack Daniels and green peppercorns, which adds a smoky-spicy quality. A nightly special of leg of lamb in a sauce with coconut milk, chiles and mango didn't blend as successfully, but all the ingredients tasted good. It is easy to appreciate the creativity behind the combination. Shellfish stew gets a vibrant flavor boost from mussels, clams, sausage, and a generous splash of Pernod, which intensifies the anise-qualities of a fresh basil seasoning.

Aside from the wines, the restaurant has a impressive list of distinctive spirits including 11 single malt scotches and four others selected by the Society of Sing Malt Whiskey Connoisseurs in Scotland. There are also 15 armagnacs and cognacs and 13 ports.

For dessert the peach pie tastes fresh, with a good crust and lots of peaches, although the fruit flavor on my visit was overpowered by nutmeg. The parfait with hazelnut brittle and a mocha sauce also goes a long way to quiet a sweet tooth.

One of the most pleasing aspects of the restaurant is the service, which strikes a good balance between efficiency and casualness.

If you finish your meal and don't want to drive, a dozen charming rooms are available upstairs.

MICHAEL BAUER

VANESSI'S ★★

1177 CALIFORNIA STREET, SAN FRANCISCO. 771-2422. OPEN 11 A.M. TO 10 P.M. MONDAY THROUGH THURSDAY, UNTIL 11 P.M. ON FRIDAY, 4:30 TO 11 P.M. SATURDAY AND 4:30 TO 10 P.M. ON SUNDAY. FULL BAR. MAJOR CREDIT CARDS. 15% NONSMOKING. FULLY WHEELCHAIR ACCESSIBLE. RESERVATIONS RECOMMENDED. MODERATE-EXPENSIVE.

Vanessi's menu looks much like it did when the restaurant opened on Broadway in 1937. Descriptions of appetizers are brief: escargots, smoked salmon, steak tartar. Entrees, including chicken piccata and veal Milanese, are so classic they need little explanation. Pastas come with a choice of bolognese, Alfredo, marinara, or several other familiar sauces.

The food is not innovative, but it's generally well-prepared and tasty. And, at a time when trends dictate what we eat, it's nice to know what you're getting.

The crowd is older for the most part. But there's plenty of action in the dining room that harks back to the 1960s, and Vanessi's is an original, probably the first full-scale restaurant to feature an open kitchen and a seating counter.

And, it's still the focal point of the restaurant. The three cooks on the expansive saute line deserve a medal. Most restaurants have twice as many cooks doing half as much work.

For dessert, don't miss the hot zabaglione, a frothy, eggy, and alcoholic delight.

MICHAEL BAUER

RISTORANTE VENEZIA ★★

1902 UNIVERSITY AVENUE (AT MARTIN LUTHER KING WAY), BERKELEY. 644-3093. OPEN TUESDAY THROUGH THURSDAY 6 TO 10 P.M., FRIDAY AND SATURDAY 5:30 TO 10:30 P.M., SUNDAY 5 TO 9 P.M. BEER, WINE. VISA, MASTERCARD. 100% NONSMOKING. FULLY WHEELCHAIR ACCESSIBLE. RESERVATIONS RECOMMENDED ON WEEKENDS. MODERATE.

Ristorante Venezia (not to be confused with Caffe Venezia, a pasta place across the street under the same ownership), not only has some of the nicest Italian food in the Bay Area, but it's also great fun. Clothes hanging from wash lines serve as decoration. On occasion, you get an opera singer. Always there's a manic bustle of waiters, cooks, and a crowded room of customers, all of them seemingly having a great time.

The food is inventive, although sometimes the emphasis on trendy California cuisine can be overdone. Particularly good are the appetizers and pastas. If it's your first visit, a good place to start is with the antipasti *misti* for two, a colorful and bounteous platter that includes roasted peppers, high-quality mozzarella cheese, marinated eggplant, and toast spread with homemade pesto. The pastas are nothing less than sensational. *Spaghetti alla puttanesca* is the spaghetti dish for those of us who haven't ordered the stuff in years because anything on a restaurant menu called "spaghetti" is usually so terrible. In this case, the noodles are perfectly al dente and the sauce a magnificent blend of oil, capers, hot peppers, hunks of fresh tomato, and chunks of mildly blanched garlic.

Then there's the seafood risotto. This is risotto exactly as it's supposed to be done, with the moist rice retaining its texture and taking on the flavor of the sea. Scallops, mussels, and prawns are all tender and absolutely fresh tasting.

With the entrees, you have to be a little more picky. *Saltimbocca* is a good choice, an unusual preparation in which the veal slices, stuffed with prosciutto and fontina cheese, are rolled as tight as a sausage. Grilled pork tenderloin is also excellent, with very flavorful meat enhanced by a pear sauce that isn't the least bit heavy or sweet.

The waiters are wonderful, and it's not their fault that they're so overworked when Venezia is crowded; service at these times can deteriorate.

Ristorante Venezia is nothing if not great fun. That, plus some very good food, makes it a crowd pleaser in Berkeley.

STAN SESSER

■ **GRILLED PORK TENDERLOIN IS EXCELLENT, ENHANCED BY A PEAR SAUCE.**

VICOLO PIZZERIA ★★½

201 IVY (AT FRANKLIN). 863-2382. OPEN MONDAY-SATURDAY 11:30 A.M. TO 11:30 P.M.; SUNDAY 2 TO 10 P.M. BEER AND WINE. 30% NONSMOKING. FULLY WHEELCHAIR ACCESSIBLE. NO RESERVATIONS OR CREDIT CARDS. INEXPENSIVE TO MODERATE.

Many agree that Vicolo makes the best pizza in the city. But those are fighting words, just like proclaiming the best barbecue or chili. Everyone's idea is different.

Vicolo's version is like no other. The pizza has a rich, oily crust studded with grains of corn meal. It's thicker than most, making a firm platform for all the unusual but perfectly matched toppings.

There's one with spinach sauteed with garlic and combined with red onion, tomato, Parmesan, mozzarella and ricotta; another combines crumbled sausage with sauteed onions, green pepper, tomato, garlic and mozzarella. The salty combination of coppa and green olives, accented with oregano and provolone, tops another selection.

At Vicolo you also get great salads with fresh marinated vegetables such as fennel, carrots and green olives, with a smooth and tangy Champagne vinaigrette; or a substantial blend of broccoli, black beans, mushrooms and balsamic vinegar.

Desserts get short shrift: either *zuccotto*, a whipped cream cake, biscotti or ice cream.

Service can be a bit scattered and disorganized too, even at a self-service style establishment. The menu board above the service counter is too lengthy and hard to read, which creates a long line of hungry patrons wanting to order. When you first read the prices, you may gasp: often you pay more than $3 for a slice and $16 for a whole one. However, two pieces will satisfy most appetites. And since you can buy a slice you can try lots of different combinations.

The kitchen help act like they are cooking for friends at home. They stand and chat, pop things in their mouth and then go on cooking. It's not the best behavior for a restaurant. Pizzas are placed in a deep dish pan, and diners are given an inadequate strip of waxed butcher paper instead of a plate. That may be fine for a sidewalk operation, but leaves me cold in surroundings like Vicolo, which has a high-tech bent.

The corrugated aluminium covering outside is carried out inside with a large, mangled sculpture of corrugated siding on the wall. Industrial style glass, crisscrossed with wire, forms a partition between the entrance/ordering line and the dining room. The same glass gives a crisp look to a cathedral window overlooking the street.

The walls are pink, the linoleum floor is gray and white, and disc-style industrial lights hang from the ceiling. You know it didn't cost a lot to construct but it has a real sense of style, just like the pizza combinations.

The crowd is just as eclectic. Lots of young people come to visit their friends who work there. There are also young children who like to bounce on the black banquettes that line the wall, and intellectuals talking about the state of the world. Then you get the symphony and opera crowds in for a quick bite before the performance and a smattering of body-builder types who wander in from the gym on Hayes.

It proves one thing—every body really does love pizza.

MICHAEL BAUER

VIETNAM II ★★★

701 LARKIN AT ELLIS, SAN FRANCISCO. 885-1274. OPEN FROM 10 A.M. TO MIDNIGHT DAILY. BEER, WINE. VISA, MASTERCARD. (BE PREPARED FOR CIGARETTE SMOKE; I DON'T THINK "NONSMOKING SECTION" TRANSLATES WELL INTO VIETNAMESE.) RESERVATIONS ACCEPTED. INEXPENSIVE.

Vietnam II—don't ask me what Vietnam I is, since no one at the restaurant speaks enough English to explain the name—is a huge, brightly lit place on Larkin Street at the edge of the Tenderloin. A cavernous restaurant with no atmosphere and only a few occupied tables is not where I'd normally look for a good meal. The restaurant is freezing cold; you'll want to bundle up for dinner. Everything you order comes together even if you ask for things one at a time, so only order a few dishes at once. Very little English is spoken and even when the restaurant isn't crowded, it's hard to get a waiter's attention to take your order and bring you the check.

But the problems definitely don't extend to the food, which is some of the best Asian cooking I've ever tasted. The menu includes a mind-boggling 171 dishes, including such exotic items as eel, goat, and turtle. To make things hopelessly confusing, about half are Vietnamese and the other half Chinese, but they're mixed together on the menu under the type of meat or seafood, so it's not always clear which nationality's food you're eating.

I tried to order mainly what I recognized as Vietnamese, but when I veered over to the Chinese food, I discovered it didn't really matter—almost everything in this place is delicious. What Vietnam II does with fowl is sensational, whether you're eating Vietnamese roasted squab or Chinese crunchy duck. And the seafood is great, much of it coming from fish tanks in the window.

To get you started, three traditional Vietnamese appetizers are terrific. The spring rolls, with noodles, shrimp, and vegetables wrapped in rice paper and steamed, are a much better choice than the deep-fried imperial rolls. The Vietnam II salad is an enticing blend of shredded jellyfish, carrots, cucumbers, thin slices of pork, shrimp, and grated peanuts, all tossed in a light vinegary dressing. Best of all are the

273

shrimp rolls, a dish I've never seen before in this country. Ground shrimp meat is laced onto pieces of sugar cane and grilled, and along with it comes a heap of mint leaves, lettuce, carrots, cilantro, noodles, and rice-paper pancakes to wrap it all together.

Now it's bird time, since you can do nothing better at Vietnam II than fill up on the various fowl dishes. The traditional five-spice chicken has never been done better, a huge portion of juicy, flavorful barbecued chicken pieces. A similar and equally good dish but with different spices is grilled lemongrass chicken. After the chicken, it's essential to move on to the pigeon, quail, and duck. When I tasted the Vietnamese roasted squab, served head and all and as succulent as could be, I was deterred from ordering seconds only by the long list of things to come. Barbecued five-spice quail is equally good, and if you're adventurous you'll find yourself chewing on the head and bones. Finally, probably from the Chinese side of the kitchen, is crunchy duck, an absolutely crisp, greaseless, deep-fried half a duck.

There's one thing, however, that competes with these bird dishes for best-on-the-menu, and that's definitely Chinese. I'm talking about the baked salt-and-pepper crab. It starts out as a whole Dungeness crab from the fish tanks and ends up as dry-roasted pieces of perfectly cooked crab absolutely infused with salt, pepper, garlic, and green onions.

I have a vision of Vietnam II tonight that makes me smile. I see every table filled with people huddled in down jackets and heavy sweaters, trying to flag down waiters who can't provide good service even when the restaurant is empty. Then I see faces light up as the food finally comes, realizing that all the hassle has been worth it.

STAN SESSER

VINOTECA JACKSON FILLMORE ★★

586 BUSH STREET, SAN FRANCISCO. 983-6200. OPEN FOR LUNCH MONDAY THROUGH FRIDAY FROM 11:30 A.M. TO 2:30 P.M.; DINNER MONDAY THROUGH THURSDAY 5:30 TO 10:30 P.M., FRIDAY TO 11 P.M., SATURDAY 4:30 TO 11 P.M., SUNDAY 4:30 TO 10 P.M. CAFE/BAR OPEN MONDAY THROUGH FRIDAY 11:30 A.M. TO 1 A.M. FULL BAR. ALL MAJOR CREDIT CARDS. SMOKING IN CAFE/BAR ONLY. FULLY WHEELCHAIR ACCESSIBLE. RESERVATIONS RECOMMENDED. MODERATE.

Vinoteca Jackson Fillmore is a rare new restaurant that has been able to capture an old-style ambience. In the space once occupied by The Palm, next door to the Hotel Juliana, the spacious rooms evoke the feeling of Italy.

The restaurant looks as if it evolved naturally rather than at the hands of a designer. The wood floors, the brightly painted blue tin ceiling and contrasting gold walls add a comfortable and unassuming note. Red, black, and blue-checked cloths seem a bit clichéd, but the feeling certainly isn't. The focal point of the main dining room is a massive sideboard with the shelves lined with wine and produce and the marble top loaded with delicious antipasti.

Owner Jack Krietzman has put together a weekly changing menu that won't seem much different to those who are used to his creations at Jackson Fillmore, which is one of the top small Italian restaurants in the city. He also owns Jackson Beach in the Cannery and La Fiammetta on Octavia.

Although there are many creative touches, the food has a warm, gutsy appeal. For starters, small artichokes are quartered, fried, and sprinkled with herbs and cheese. Most pastas are excellent, particularly the spaghetti with plump red beans and sausage in a tomato sauce. Bow tie pasta with salmon and fresh tomato had a great sauce, though the pasta needed salt, which was also a problem of the penne with veal, sausage, and mascarpone cheese on another visit.

I could become addicted to the plump, juicy rabbit with sausage, all mixed with roasted potatoes, garlic, and perfect, small, whole button mushrooms and loads of fresh rosemary. Vinoteca does best on the hearty meat courses. Many are simply grilled.

Desserts are also winners. Four small profiteroles with delicately rich pastry cream are alternately topped with a chocolate sauce and a buttery-tasting caramel. Even if you don't love chocolate, it's easy to appreciate the chocolate torte. It's filled with two layers of chocolate zabaglione, and the top is dusted with shavings of white chocolate and the sides are encrusted in nuts. Don't miss the wonderful, cold Meyer lemon zabaglione with strawberries, or the Italian crumble cake with a zabaglione sauce.

Although the name Vinoteca would seem to indicate an emphasis on wine, the list is surprisingly short, featuring 60 wines. More than 80 percent are Italian. There are 10 wines by the glass.

MICHAEL BAUER

VIVANDE ★★★

2125 FILLMORE STREET, SAN FRANCISCO. 346-4430. OPEN DAILY FOR LUNCH FROM 11:30 A.M. TO 4 P.M. BEER, WINE. MAJOR CREDIT CARDS. 100% NONSMOKING. PARTIALLY WHEELCHAIR ACCESSIBLE. MODERATE.

Vivande is the fantasy of chef, teacher, and cookbook writer Carlo Middione. Every day, he and his staff prepare a wide range of beautiful Italian take-out dishes in a spectacular open kitchen. They include fresh noodles, roasted chickens, savory Italian tortas, *caponata* and other antipasti like roasted onions in balsamic vinegar, crusty walnut breads, biscotti, and fabulous Italian desserts. In my estimation, Middione is the best Italian pastry maker in the city.

While some customers buy food to go, as well as cookbooks, extra virgin olive oil, and imported pasta at the counter, another group sits at tiny cafe tables covered with butcher paper, to lunch on the displayed items plus a small menu of hot dishes which are made to order. Middione's creamy pasta carbonara, rich and light at the same time; his barely sauced but exquisite fettucine with vegetables, olive oil, and butter, his impeccable deep-fried oyster sandwich; a perky spinach salad and deep-fried *arrancini*, or risotto balls filled with mozzarella are always appealing.

Middione is a Sicilian so he brings particular passion to dishes like pasta a la Norma with creamy slices of eggplant, housemade fennel sausages sauteed with roasted potatoes, peppers and mushrooms, and rustic dishes like lentils and white beans braised with *coteghino*, a coarse-grained Italian sausage. Soft, fruity Italian reds, served in thick tumblers, go wonderfully with this fare.

Save room for dessert because Vivande prepares some fabulous ones. The single layer, unfrosted chocolate cakes look deceptively simple but they melt in your mouth in an extraordinary way. Luscious, custardy, *zuppa inglese* and tiramisu take on new definition here. Puckery lemon tarts and crisp meringue cakes filled with apricot whipped cream are a dream. To finish off, espresso is good and strong without being bitter.

Eating here is so much fun because you really are in the middle of a shiny working kitchen, with chickens turning over a real Italian upright rotisserie, the pasta machine cranking away, and doughs being rolled out in a glassed-in pastry kitchen. If you sit at the counters and observe carefully, you will get a cooking lesson thrown in for the price of your lunch. At Vivande, customers are surrounded by beautiful foodstuffs and all the cooking utensils related to cooking them. Just walking by the store makes me hungry.

Patricia Unterman

WOLFDALE'S ★★★

640 NORTH LAKE BLVD., TAHOE CITY. (916) 583-5700. OPEN FOR DINNER WEDNESDAY THROUGH MONDAY FROM 6 TO 10 P.M. FULL BAR. MASTERCARD, VISA. 75% NONSMOKING. FULLY WHEELCHAIR ACCESSIBLE. RESERVATIONS HIGHLY RECOMMENDED. EXPENSIVE.

It seems California cuisine restaurants these days must spend a lot of time looking over each other's shoulders. When one introduces a new dish or concept, you quickly see the same thing on menus all over the place. Wolfdale's, by contrast, really fits the slogan on its front sign: "Cuisine unique." In the relative gastronomic isolation of Lake Tahoe, chef Douglas Dale draws on his years in Japan and on his own strong sense of aesthetics, to create a light and beautiful cuisine, but one that follows none of the usual rules for trendiness.

Everything about Wolfdale's is a joy: the unpretentious but very comfortable dining room; the excellent, friendly service unaccompanied by even a hint of the condescension so often found in resort areas, and above all, the food. Dale's kitchen staff has gotten so skilled that even a meal when he's not there will be perfect.

Dale's cooking can be described as California cuisine with a Japanese accent, but that doesn't really do it justice. The food is not only delicious and innovative, but as much attention is paid to presentation, textures, and colors as is to taste. Even the plates and bowls—some of which Dale made himself when he studied pottery-making in Japan—are visually exciting.

The small menu, which changes frequently, sounds simple, but there's a great complexity to most of the dishes. Much of the menu features fish, and at Wolfdale's you needn't fear ordering seafood so far from the ocean. When Dale does frying in tempura batter, as one night with soft-shelled crab, it emerges unmatched by any Japanese restaurant.

Meats and poultry are equally good. Two boneless quail come stuffed with couscous, homemade sausage, and goat cheese; they are marinated in juniper berries and white wine, and served with a version of red pepper beurre blanc. An appetizer of duck sausage, made in Wolfdale's kitchen and scented with fennel, parmesan cheese, red wine, cracked pepper, and shallots, couldn't be more meaty and delicate.

Wolfdale's has always had irresistible homemade ice cream that somehow manages to capture the absolute essence of the fresh fruit or whatever else is being used. The pastries don't take a back seat, either.

From the home-baked bread flavored with fresh herbs that starts your meal, to the espresso that finishes it, Wolfdale's is virtually faultless. In San Francisco, a restaurant like this would stand out above its competition. For Tahoe, where there is little culinary tradition, and where good fresh ingredients are harder to come by, Wolfdale's is nothing less than miraculous.

STAN SESSER

WU KONG ★★★

ONE RINCON CENTER, 101 SPEAR STREET, SAN FRANCISCO. 957-9300. LUNCH 11 A.M. TO 2:30 P.M., DINNER 5:30 TO 9:30 P.M. EVERY DAY. FULL BAR. VISA AND MASTERCARD. RESERVATIONS ACCEPTED. MODERATE.

Wu Kong, a Shanghai restaurant that comes to San Francisco via Hong Kong, brings a whole new set of dazzling, regional dishes to Chinese dining in the Bay Area. The ingredients Wu Kong uses are impeccable and the breadth and depth of its kitchen impressive.

Wu Kong is located in the atrium of Rincon Center, a hollow-centered building with a series of shops and eating places rimming a dramatic common space dominated by a 90-foot-high "rain column." The fully enclosed restaurant has a handsome bar and entryway, and a brightly lit dining room filled with white, linen-covered tables and black lacquer chairs with blue floral upholstered seats. A cadre of uniformed waiters and captains work the many, large, round tables efficiently.

Wu Kong's intriguing starters let you know right off how highly skilled the kitchen is. One of the most beloved dishes at Wu Kong is Vegetable Goose, a Taoist monk's dish of layers of fried bean curd wrapped around a savory mushroom stuffing. Sliced, it actually looks like a breast of crispy goose and the flavors are superior to most goose I've eaten. Drunken squab, sliced, marinated in Shaoxing rice wine, and served cold, is refreshing, boozy, and velvet textured. A salad of jelly fish, which usually reminds me of rubber bands, has a completely different texture here. It is crisp/tender, seasoned with a tasty sesame and soy marinade, and scented with lacy sprigs of Chinese parsley. Crunchy-all-the-way-through, deep-fried eel, in a subtle sweet and sour sauce is simply one of the best dishes I've ever had in any restaurant.

The special, miniature Shanghai dumplings made at Wu Kong are the restaurant's signature dish. They include fragile, steamed baby dumplings stuffed with delicate ground pork and clear broth; and steamed vegetable dumplings filled with bright Chinese greens and fruity winter melon.

Deep-frying at Wu Kong defines the technique. Yellowfish fritters, speckled with threads of seaweed, melt in your mouth. All the deep-fried dim sum dishes served on the weekends come from the kitchen piping hot and greaseless.

Seafood dishes are a highpoint here. The natural sweetness of the meat in tiny, stir-fried blue crabs with fresh soy beans is worth all the trouble it takes to get at it. The shrimp in spicy, bright red Chili Sauce Shrimp, are so firm they're almost crisp, a stunning contrast to the copious, oil rich sauce. The same crisp-cooked shrimp are also wonderful with creamy braised cabbage and shredded bamboo shoots. Something as simple as a plate of baby fava beans, so young they can be eaten with their skins, are unexpectedly delicious.

Cantonese style dim sum dishes served on the weekends like shrimp dumplings, cilantro flecked fish balls, savory ducks' feet with black bean sauce, fragrant steamed pork ribs, crunchy deep fried pancakes of bean curd stuffed with mushrooms, and pillowy barbecued pork buns are all light, clean and honestly flavored. Then, there are some smashing Shanghai specialties like onion cakes, which are little balls of deep-fried, flaky pastry, much like French puff pastry, dotted with sesame seeds and filled with green onions. Thank goodness they are available daily from the small dim sum appetizer of the day card. And it is at Wu Kong that I was served the best bowl of chicken noodle soup I've ever had in a restaurant. The broth was pure essence of chicken. The little cubes of chicken breast were miraculously tender, the noodles and vegetables toothsome.

Wu Kong also specializes in Shanghai desserts and they are a revelation. My favorites are deep-fried poufs of eggwhite with a little red bean paste at the center. They practically levitate off the plate. Others are deep fried bean curd pancakes stuffed with red bean paste, and a pan-fried Seven Treasures Rice dotted with raisins and dried fruit. Warm steamed sponge cake served at tea lunch, and firm but tender red bean gelatin are surprisingly refreshing.

PATRICIA UNTERMAN

YANK SING ★★★

427 BATTERY, SAN FRANCISCO. 362-1640. OPEN MONDAY THROUGH FRIDAY 11 A.M. TO 3 P.M., SATURDAY 10 A.M. TO 4 P.M. FULL BAR. MASTERCARD AND VISA. RESERVATIONS ACCEPTED. INEXPENSIVE.

Post-revolution Chinese tea lunchers used to have to travel to Hong Kong for the ultimate dim sum, but many aficionados now consider tea lunch a San Francisco experience. We have dim sum parlors of every dimension here, from the gigantic multi-floor dining halls of Ocean City and Canton Tea House to the medium-sized and more refined operations of Yank Sing and Harbor Village, to tiny tea parlors like Tung Fong. And they all seem to be packed. Dim sum is taking this city by storm.

On weekends you have to steel yourself for a mob scene, but, of course, that's when the variety and freshness of the dim sum is at its highest. Slightly off-hours and weekdays are the best, but you should find a group of at least three or four to go with you in order to sample a respectable number of different tid bits.

One of the best dim sum houses in the city is Yank Sing. The restaurant is so modern and well-appointed that you feel like you're in a typically upscale Financial District eatery, until the carts laden with exotic Chinese delicacies come around. The dim sum here is beautifully made with the brightest tasting shrimp and crab, tender noodles and the cleanest deep-frying.

The kitchen shows particular strength and invention in everyone's favorite part of the dim sum repertoire, the dumplings. The translucent, shrimp-stuffed *har gow*, boast the freshest and sweetest of shrimp. Liberal use of black mushrooms add a wild, meaty flavor to rice noodle-wrapped dumplings, such as an addictive vegetarian dumpling seasoned with pickled turnip or a chicken stuffed dumpling with bamboo shoots. The pork filled *sui mai* are colorfully decorated with carrots and peas. There are perhaps eight different variations of wrappers and stuffing served each day, all excellent.

Other dim sum to look for are succulent, foil wrapped chicken in a sweetly caramelized sauce; heavenly deep-fried crab balls; rich, crisp shrimp toasts; spicy chicken feet, first deep-fried then braised in a Hunan-style sauce, that are delicious; a magically crunchy, lacy, taro ball filled with a tasty pork stuffing; a lotus leaf wrapped around sticky, sweet rice, stuffed with pork; and deep-fried noodle dumplings stuffed with shrimp.

Yank Sing also prepares dishes from heated carts, and if you want something as familiar as won ton soup, theirs is excellent. The won ton are stuffed with smoky barbecued pork and the chicken broth has good flavor. A bowl of tiny, tender fish balls in a lively brown gravy also comes from the cart.

Currently the ever innovative kitchen is turning out individual Peking duck sandwiches, which gives you two little, soft, white buns with slices of burnished duck skin and scallions swabbed with black bean sauce inside; deep-fried water chestnuts, bacon and scallions on a toothpick; and stunning little plates of fiery, strongly flavored Chinese eggplant, a northern Chinese dish not usually found in Cantonese dim sum service. You can expect some new, delicious dim sum everytime you go.

For dessert, try to nab a saucer of flaky-crusted egg custard tarts when they're still warm. Yank Sing does them better than any other dim sum house and they are worth a visit alone.

PATRICIA UNTERMAN

YAYA ★★

397 1/2 EIGHTH ST. AT HARRISON, SAN FRANCISCO. 255-0909. OPEN FOR LUNCH 11:30 A.M. TO 2 P.M. MONDAY THROUGH FRIDAY; DINNER 5:30 TO 9 P.M. MONDAY THROUGH THURSDAY, AND 5:30 TO 10 P.M. FRIDAY AND SATURDAY. BEER, WINE. VISA, MASTERCARD. 30% NONSMOKING. FULLY WHEELCHAIR ACCESSIBLE. RESERVATIONS ACCEPTED. MODERATE.

The words *California cuisine* these days throw up a warning flag, an indication that trendiness is going to count more than food. Would the Middle Eastern-California cuisine advertised by Yaya's turn out to be some dumb things like adding kiwi slices to the shishkebab skewer? Or would it deal with a fundamental problem: the tendency of Middle Eastern restaurants to turn out food that's too heavy and too greasy, and to either ignore vegetables or cook them to mush?

I'm happy to report that Yaya's is taking the latter approach, and turning out some wonderful food that's totally unique. The presentations are magnificent, everything is sparkling fresh, vegetables are used in abundance, and the sophisticated sauces don't have a speck of

■ **EACH MEAT (YOU CAN CHOOSE FROM PORK, BEEF, LAMB, VEAL, CHICKEN, OR DUCK) GETS ITS OWN SPECIAL MARINADE AND ITS OWN SPECIAL SAUCE. THEN IT'S SERVED SURROUNDED BY ALL SORTS OF PERFECTLY COOKED COLORFUL VEGETABLES.**

grease. The flavors, the spices of Middle Eastern food remain, but the heaviness is gone.

Yaya's is the creation of Iraqi-born Yahya Salih, who formerly cooked at that hotbed of food innovation, the Hilton Hotel. Salih bought a truck-stop restaurant at 8th and Harrison and converted it into a cute and airy room that's delightfully out of place in its grimy neighborhood. The gray carpet, light pink walls, fresh flowers on every table, and a brightly tiled, open kitchen create an atmosphere that makes you forget that the prices are so reasonable.

The centerpiece of Yaya's menu is the kabobs, done Iraqi-style. This means the meat is marinated, ground three times (the finer the grind, the better it holds together), skewered, and grilled. Kabobs can be pretty boring stuff, but not here. Each meat (you can choose from pork, beef, lamb, veal, chicken, or duck) gets its own special marinade and its own special sauce. Then it's served surrounded by all sorts of perfectly cooked colorful vegetables. On the side is a platter of bulgar wheat made with mushrooms, almonds, and pine nuts.

Both the marinades and sauces combine Middle Eastern and California cuisine ingredients, and they work beautifully. There's sage and mint for the lamb marinade, cardamom for the duck, orange and lemon zest in the pork, and thyme and sweet basil for the veal. Many of the sauces start with homemade vegetable stock, wine, garlic, and cream, but they're then individualized through other ingredients. The duck gets *tahini*, the pork gets sun-dried limes from the Mideast, the lamb gets green peppercorns, and the veal gets shiitake mushrooms.

The appetizers aren't to be ignored either. Grilled Japanese eggplant, with a slightly smoky taste and a perfect texture, comes with a remarkable sauce that includes garlic, cream, and pomegranate juice. Slices of smoked salmon top the traditional Mideastern cucumber salad, and the yogurt in the dressing is actually imported from the Mideast. Fresh-tasting *seviche* rests on a bed of extraordinary *tabouli*.

Yaya's clearly is much more than an attempt to create something trendy. When you look at the room, at how the food is presented, at the clever combinations of sauces and marinades, you realize that a tremendous amount of thought has gone into this restaurant. It's not only good; it's totally unique.

STAN SESSER

YUET LEE ★★

3601 26TH STREET (NEAR VALENCIA), SAN FRANCISCO. 550-8998. OPEN MONDAY
THROUGH THURSDAY 11 A.M. TO 10 P.M., FRIDAY AND SATURDAY 11 A.M. TO 11 P.M.,
SUNDAY 4 TO 10 P.M. BEER AND WINE. MASTERCARD, VISA. 25% NONSMOKING.
FULLY WHEELCHAIR ACCESSIBLE. RESERVATIONS ACCEPTED FOR PARTIES OF
FIVE OR MORE. INEXPENSIVE TO MODERATE.

Yuet Lee, a Hong Kong style noodle and seafood house on
Broadway and Stockton, started out not much bigger than an Asian
food stand. The miniscule kitchen, really a galley lined with fero-
ciously hot woks, was barely partitioned off from a narrow dining area.
The room was fashioned out of worn vinyl, linoleum and plastic, but
tanks of fish, crabs and lobster belied the subsistence appearance of the
place. You could get a stew in a clay pot, or a bowl of noodles, but the
freshest delicacies from the sea were available as well, always wonderfully prepared.

The place became so popular that it expanded by annexing a small
space next door. At first, you didn't even notice that Yuet Lee was
bigger because the new part had exactly the same vintage look as the
original space. There were a few more plastic tables set with metal
napkin holders and somehow a coat of Yuet Lee's signature and
remarkable shade of green paint was extended seamlessly into the new
section. But the food was often not quite as good as it had been in
smaller quarters.

Then, Yuet Lee opened a second store way across town on the
edge of the Mission. The interior, brand new and sparkling clean, has
a completely separate kitchen, large fish tanks and two sets of bathrooms, but you know immediately that this could only be Yuet Lee.
That singular lime green color has been lavished on the exterior of the
whole building this time, and all the same materials have been used.
Red speckled linoleum tile floors, plastic tables in a fake wood veneer,
acoustic tile ceilings, arched insets in tall windows covered with
Venetian blinds and a glowing green line painted around the circum-
ference of the room are present and accounted for, under the glow of
fluorescent light.

What's exciting is that the food is better than at the original Yuet
Lee, though the location isn't nearly as much fun. Dishes are prepared
more carefully and consistently, and look more attractive. Also, ordering is easier. A pink sheet of specials will steer you to the restaurant's
best dishes. Two of them, pepper and salt roasted fresh squid, and
pepper and salt roasted shrimp, are Yuet Lee's signature dishes. The
squid, crunchy and spicy outside, are contrastingly tender and rich
beneath their thin crust. The same balance of flavors and textures
works on the shrimp.

Spicy black bean sauce, minced pork, fresh chiles, scallions, and loads of fresh Chinese parsley work magic on crab. Fresh, large, briny, clean tasting clams release their liquor into a similar black bean sauce, giving it a different dimension.

The restaurant keeps catfish in tanks, but also produces spectacularly fresh flounder and rock fish from the kitchen. The flounder steamed with ginger and scallions, soy sauce, and stock, garnished with bright green Chinese parsley, is just about the best fish dish you could hope for. The meat of the flounder stays firm but delicate, and ever so moist. Steaming with aromatics brings out all its finest qualities.

Vegetables are either sauteed with a little garlic and practically no sauce or steamed with oyster sauce. Chinese broccoli, *ong choy* or Chinese watercress, and asparagus always look intensely green and fresh. Noodle dishes, prepared Hong Kong style on super hot woks, are also a specialty here. They get a delicious smoky flavor from this method of cooking.

I see the cooking at Yuet Lee as an extension of the way I like to eat Western food. High standards of freshness for both fish and vegetables, quick cooking with skillful technique and tasty, simple sauces make the food at this restaurant appealing.

PATRICIA UNTERMAN

ZOLA'S ★★★½

395 HAYES STREET AT GOUGH, SAN FRANCISCO. 864-4824. OPENS AT 5:30 P.M. TUESDAY THROUGH SATURDAY AND AT 5 P.M. ON SUNDAY. FULL BAR. MAJOR CREDIT CARDS. 100% NONSMOKING. FULLY WHEELCHAIR ACCESSIBLE. RESERVATIONS RECOMMENDED. EXPENSIVE.

The new Zola's, after it moved from the Polk Street neighborhood to a location near Davies Hall, has done what I thought was impossible; it has combined three-star French food, stunning decor, and caring service with prices that you'd pay at any ordinary California-cuisine restaurant.

Even if you never intend to eat at Zola's, look through the window at the corner of Hayes and Gough to see how pretty a restaurant can be. There's not a fern, not a painting, no neon, no brass tubing. Instead, it's all stark simplicity—deeply textured paint of a pinkish-yellow hue on gently curved walls, with high-tech Italian glass lighting fixtures on the ceiling and sculptured metal fixtures throwing indirect light against the walls. Fabric banquettes, two massive flower arrangements, and a carpet that picks up the colors from the walls soften the room.

Over the years, the cooking at Zola's has become more idiosyncratic, basically French but with trendy California influences. Making Zola's more like everyone else isn't necessarily a positive move, but in this case the two chefs, Rachel Gardner and co-owner Catherine

Pantsios, have clearly grown on the job. Almost everything is wonderful, and some of the dishes positively memorable.

It's the usual story of the best ingredients, and simple but skillful preparations that bring out the natural flavors. So many restaurants adhere to this philosophy today that such a description sounds like a broken record. But wait until you see how successful Pantsios and Gardner have been in pulling it off.

Among appetizers on the frequently changing menu, a tomato and basil tart brings slices of flavorful red and yellow tomatoes in a crusty, paper-thin tart shell, accompanied by marinated goat cheese on a bed of arugula. Roasted garlic soup, thick and aromatic but not heavy, combines pureed garlic and onions with a rich, homemade chicken stock. A grilled quail salad might be a cliché today, but no one has done it this beautifully: The juicy quail is glazed with chestnut honey, and served with mesclun and figs in a dressing of reduced game stock, hazelnut oil, and vinegar.

These were just warmups for sensational entrees. Pantsios and Gardner are at their best with dishes that are assertively spiced, and nothing illustrates that more than the Moroccan rack of lamb with chickpea puree on a bed of spinach. In a very clever combination of two cuisines, they do a classic rack of lamb, but season the meat with the spices of a Moroccan lamb tangine. Big, fresh-tasting, pan-fried Gulf Coast prawns come with a tomato-based sauce that included pulverized toasted almonds. A roasted breast and confit leg of duck has tender, fat-free meat with crispy skin, remarkable especially for the confit, which is cooked in its own fat. The sauce includes duck stock, tomatoes, and olives, and alongside are crispy paper-thin potato slices that have been tossed in clarified butter, stacked into a cake shape, and browned in the oven.

Some of the desserts are memorable. The essence of fresh cherries pervades bing cherry chocolate chip ice cream with a warm cherry sauce. Chocolate almond cake with ginger cream combines rich chocolate with the taste of fresh ginger. A fresh nectarine and blueberry crisp is made even better by an unusual mint-basil ice cream.

If all this isn't enough, Larry Bain has put together what should be a model for a restaurant wine list. More than merely selecting good wines, he's tried also to make them affordable. So there are a number of good California and French selections, plus some older wines with markups so low that in some cases they beat the prices at a wine store.

STAN SESSER

ZUNI CAFE AND GRILL ★★★½

1658 MARKET STREET, SAN FRANCISCO. 552-2522. OPEN TUESDAY THROUGH SATURDAY 7:30 A.M. TO MIDNIGHT, SUNDAY 7:30 A.M. TO 11 P.M. FULL BAR. MASTERCARD, VISA, AMERICAN EXPRESS. 30% NONSMOKING. FULLY WHEEL-CHAIR ACCESSIBLE. RESERVATIONS RECOMMENDED FOR LUNCH AND DINNER. MODERATE.

There are some restaurants that encourage you to linger. It doesn't much matter exactly what's on the menu or how efficient the service is or what time of day it is, because the place always feels so good. The Zuni Cafe is one of those places. With a long, copper bar, French-style oyster stand, an aromatic wood burning oven in the middle of the dining room, and early morning 'till midnight hours, you can practically live there, much the way Parisians live in their neighborhood cafes.

There's something for everyone at Zuni, no matter when you walk through the door—espresso, oysters, cocktails, snacks, sandwiches, full meals, sidewalk seating on nice days, even Berkeley's incomparable Acme bread for sale, all under the creative direction of one of the best and most interesting chefs in town, Judy Rodgers. She has built the eating experience at Zuni into something that combines the best traditions of French, Italian, and California cooking.

Zuni has the largest selection of oysters in town, served in the traditional French manner on a metal platter of shaved ice set on a wire stand. Underneath goes a plate of chewy Acme rye bread and butter. You buy the oysters by the piece, along with plump East Coast clams, fresh cracked Dungeness crab, and whatever else happens to be good that day, which makes for some fantastic seafood platters.

At dinner there might be two perfectly grilled quail on a bed of bitter wilted greens with toasts spread with buttery squab liver, or a fine, simple lamb stew with sweet carrots and turnips. Zuni is famous for an extraordinary *fritto misto* of crunchy deep-fried seafood, fennel, and lemon slices, and an addictive antipasto of shaved parmesan, anchovies, and celery, sprinkled with extra virgin olive oil and lemon. Another favorite antipasto of mine brings together shredded raw artichokes tossed with slivers of parmesan cheese and pine nuts and tissue-thin slices of coppa and salami.

At lunch there might be thick, garlicky lamb sandwiches moistened by baked onions, or a wonderful warm spinach salad with handfuls of diced, peppery bacon, hard boiled eggs, and delicious croutons. Crisp, thin crusted pizzas emerge from the wood-fired oven irresistibly smoky as does Zuni's gorgeous signature dish, a whole roast chicken for two served with Tuscan bread salad. The free-range chicken, stuck with cloves of garlic, acquires the most heavenly flavor and juicy texture from the oven.

A different ice cream is made each day, like a superior vanilla laced with chunks of chocolate-covered almonds. The cannoli are so fresh and crisp, a mafia don would be seduced. Wine prices are not cheap, but there are always interesting bottles and glasses selected by knowledgeable and adventurous sommelier Sylvie Darr.

The truth is that Zuni is possessed of a marvelous spirit. It's one of those eccentric, very personal establishments that runs on ideological energy rather than businesslike procedure. Just the look of the place, with its many odd-shaped rooms, expanses of window, unmatched chairs, romantic flower arrangements, a revolving exhibit of paintings and photos, asymmetrical tables, and garret-like stairs, reveals a unique nature. The tall, handsome, rather formal, but unfinished wooden doors that let you into the place are emblematic. Zuni has soul, style, and substance, yet there's something winsomely unfinished about it. It doesn't take itself too seriously.

PATRICIA UNTERMAN

GEOGRAPHIC INDEX

INDEX BY TYPE OF CUISINE

INDEX BY STARS